THE ANALYTIC FR

'Escaping the sterile debates over the "scientific" status of his work, this collection demonstrates the fertility of Freud's thought in several key topics in the philosophy of mind and moral philosophy'.

John Cottingham, University of Reading

This is a timely and stimulating collection of essays on the importance of Freudian thought for analytic philosophy, investigating its impact on mind, ethics, sexuality, religion and epistemology.

Marking a clear departure from the long-standing debate over whether Freudian thought is scientific or not, *The Analytic Freud* expands the framework of philosophical inquiry, demonstrating how fertile and mutually enriching the relationship between philosophy and psychoanalysis can be.

The chapters are divided into four clear sections, addressing the implications of Freud for the philosophy of mind, ethics, sexuality and civilization. The contributors discuss the problems psychoanalysis poses for contemporary philosophy as well as what philosophy can learn from Freud's legacy and undeniable influence. For instance, *The Analytic Freud* discusses the problems presented by psychoanalytic theories of the mind for the philosophy of language; the issues which current theories of mind and meaning raise for psychoanalytic accounts of emotion, metaphor, the will and self-deception; the question whether psychoanalytic theory is essential in understanding sexuality, love, humour as well as the tensions which arise out of personal relationships.

The Analytic Freud is a critical and thorough examination of Freudian and post-Freudian theory, adding a welcome and significant dimension to the debate between psychoanalysis and contemporary philosophy.

Michael P. Levine is Professor of Philosophy at the University of Western Australia. He is the author of *Hume and the Problem of Miracles* and *Pantheism: A Non-Theistic Conception of Deity*.

THE ANALYTIC FREUD

Philosophy and psychoanalysis

Edited by
Michael P. Levine

London and New York

First published 2000
by Routledge
11 New Fetter Lane, London EC4P 4EE

Simultaneously published in the USA and Canada
by Routledge
29 West 35th Street, New York, NY 10001

Routledge is an imprint of the Taylor & Francis Group

Typeset in Times by
Keystroke, Jacaranda Lodge, Wolverhampton
Printed and bound in Great Britain by
Biddles Ltd, Guildford and King's Lynn

British Library Cataloguing in Publication Data
A catalogue record for this book is available from the British Library

Library of Congress Cataloging in Publication Data
The analytic Freud : philosophy and psychoanalysis / edited by Michael
Levine.
p.   cm.
Includes bibliographical references and index.
ISBN 0–415–18039–2 (hb : alk. paper). — ISBN 0–415–18040–6 (pbk.
: alk. paper)
1. Freud, Sigmund, 1856–1939.   2. Psychoanalysis and philosophy.
I. Levine, Michael P. (Michael Philip)
BF109.F74A84 1999
150.19′52—dc21   99–24182
CIP

ISBN 0–415–18039–2 (hbk)
ISBN 0–415–18040–6 (pbk)

When there are so many we shall have to mourn,
When grief has been made so public, and exposed
   To the critique of a whole epoch
   The frailty of our conscience and anguish,

Of whom shall we speak? For every day they die
Among us, those who were doing us some good,
   And knew it was never enough but
   Hoped to improve a little by living.

      W. H. Auden, *In Memory of Sigmund Freud,*
              d. September 1939

CONTENTS

CONTENTS

CONTRIBUTORS

José Brunner is Senior Lecturer at the Buchmann Faculty of Law and the Cohn Institute of the History and Philosophy of Science and Ideas, Tel Aviv University. He is the author of numerous publications on the history and politics of psychoanalysis and contemporary political theory. His *Freud and the Politics of Psychoanalysis* was published by Blackwell in 1995.

Marcia Cavell is Visiting Associate Professor in the Department of Philosophy at the University of California, Berkeley. She was formerly a Research Candidate at the Columbia Psychoanalytic Institute for Training and Research in New York City, and is now a Candidate in Training at the San Francisco Psychoanalytic Institute. She is the author of *The Psychoanalytic Mind: From Freud to Philosophy* (Harvard 1993), and of numerous articles on psychoanalysis and the philosophy of mind.

Grant Gillett is Professor of Medical Ethics at the University of Otago and a practising neurosurgeon. He is a founding editor of the journal *Philosophy, Psychiatry and Psychology* and author of *Representation, Meaning and Thought* (Oxford University Press); *Reasonable Care* (Bristol University Press); and recently *The Mind and its Discontents* (Oxford University Press). He is co-author of *The Discursive Mind* (Sage) and *Medical Ethics* (Oxford University Press).

Elizabeth Hegeman is a Professor of Anthropology at John Jay College, CUNY, and a practising psychoanalyst. Her writings focus on trauma, memory and dissociation, and cross-cultural issues in psychoanalysis.

Jim Hopkins is Reader in Philosophy at King's College, London, and an Editor of *Mind*. His publications on psychoanalysis include work in *Philosophical Essays on Freud* (Cambridge University Press), co-edited with Richard Wollheim, *and Psychoanalysis, Mind, and Art: Perspectives on Richard Wollheim* (Blackwell) co-edited with Anthony Savile.

Marguerite La Caze is Lecturer in Philosophy at the University of Tasmania. She has published in the areas of aesthetics and feminist philosophy and also has interests in ethics, philosophical psychology and history of philosophy.

Michael P. Levine is Professor of Philosophy and Head of Department at the University of Western Australia. He is the author of *Hume and the Problem of Miracles* (Kluwer 1989) and *Pantheism* (Routledge 1994). He has published in the areas of philosophical psychology, ethics, metaphysics and the history of philosophy.

Graeme Marshall is Reader and Associate Professor in Philosophy at the University of Melbourne with a long-standing interest in Wittgenstein and in the philosophy of mind with a special concern for problems associated with the will. He has been Visiting Associate of the Chicago Institute for Psychoanalysis and several times Visiting Professor at King's College, London.

Tamas Pataki is Honorary Senior Fellow in the Department of Philosophy, University of Melbourne. He has taught in universities in Australia and Hungary and has published articles on the philosophy of mind, psychoanalysis and moral philosophy.

Jennifer Radden was educated in Australia and the United Kingdom and is Professor of Philosophy at the University of Massachusetts, Boston Campus, in the US. She has a long-standing interest in issues concerning mental disorder and is currently President of the Association for the Advancement of Philosophy and Psychiatry. Her most recent published work is *Divided Minds and Successive Selves: Ethical Issues in Disorders of Identity and Personality* (MIT Press, 1996), and a collection of readings on melancholy, melancholia and depression of which she is editor is to be published by Oxford University Press in 1999.

Paul Redding is Associate Professor in the School of Philosophy at the University of Sydney. He has a long-standing interest in the German idealists, and especially in their approaches to subjectivity and their influences on later conceptions of the mind. He is the author of *Hegel's Hermeneutics* (1996) and *The Logic of Affect* (1999), both published by Cornell University Press.

Amélie Oksenberg Rorty is the Director of the Program in the History of Ideas at Brandeis University. She has edited *Explaining Emotions: The Identities of Persons*, and (with Brian MacLaughlin) *Perspectives on Self-Deception* (University of California Press). Her most recently edited book is *Philosophers on Education: Historical Perspectives* (Routledge 1998). She has published widely in the philosophy of mind and in the history of ethics.

Nancy Sherman is Professor of Philosophy at Georgetown University and a research candidate at the Washington Institute for Psychoanalysis. Sherman was an Associate Professor of Philosophy at Yale; a Visiting Professor at the University of Maryland and Johns Hopkins; and was the inaugural holder of the Distinguished Chair in Ethics at the United States Naval Academy. She is the author of *Making a Necessity of Virtue* (Cambridge University Press, 1997), and *The Fabric of Character* (Oxford University Press, 1989), both of which focus on the role of emotions in virtue. She is the author of numerous articles on moral philosophy and moral psychology.

David Snelling has taught at various colleges in the University of London and at the University of Kent, including teaching philosophy of psychoanalysis at Birkbeck College, London, and for the MSc in psychoanalytic studies at University College, London. He is currently Lecturer at Birkbeck College.

Michael Stocker is the Guttag Professor of Ethics and Political Philosophy, Syracuse University. His writings focus on ethics and moral psychology, with a strong interest in Aristotle.

Edmond Wright holds degrees in English and philosophy, and a doctorate in philosophy. He was a one-time Fellow at the Swedish Collegium for the Advanced Study for the Social Sciences, Uppsala. He has edited *The Ironic Discourse (Poetics Today,* 4, 1983*); New Representationalisms: Essays in the Philosophy of Perception* (Avebury, 1993); and is co-editor of *The Žižek Reader* (Blackwell, 1999). He has published over forty articles on language, perception and the philosophy of science in *Mind, Philosophy, Philosophy and Phenomenological Research, Philosophy of Science, Synthese* and other journals. He has also published two volumes of poetry.

ACKNOWLEDGEMENTS

My thanks to the contributors – many of whom also acted as referees. My thanks also to Marie-Louise Carroll; Judith Chapman; Damian Cox; Guy Douglas; Jim Hopkins; Amy Barrett-Lennard; Helen McLaughin Jones; Carol Mack; John O'Neill; Wendy Pedersen; Ted Roberts; Amélie Oksenberg Rorty; Elizabeth Wright; The University of Western Australia; and the Australian Research Council.

INTRODUCTION: HOW RIGHT DOES PSYCHOANALYSIS HAVE TO BE?

Michael P. Levine

> In every age, there must be truths people can't fight – whether or not they want to, whether or not they will go on being truths in the future. We live in the truth of what Freud discovered. Whether or not we like it. However we've modified it. We aren't really free to suppose – to imagine – he could possibly have been wrong about human nature. In particulars, surely – but not in the large plan.
>
> A. S. Byatt (1990: 254)[1]

In *An Autobiographical Study* Freud (1925d: 59) said that his avoidance of philosophy was 'greatly facilitated by constitutional incapacity'. Yet despite his disclaimer Freud was as much a philosopher as he was a psychologist. Indeed according to many (experimental) psychologists he was, if anything (worthwhile), far more the former than the latter. Of course this is usually meant deprecatingly. Nevertheless, even if Freud was not first and foremost a philosopher, it would be interesting, maybe even momentous, if it turned out that the philosophical implications of psychoanalytic theory were perhaps more significant than the merely psychological – albeit crucial to the latter as well. The essays in this volume take that possibility seriously.

Far from intimating closure or regarding his work as final, Freud frequently reiterates that psychoanalysis has a bright future regarding 'further discoveries' about the individual, civilization, and their connections. Surprisingly, however, there has been relatively little written *by analytic philosophers*, on the philosophical implications of Freudian and post-Freudian theory. Only within the past twenty years or so have more than handful of analytic philosophers turned their attention to Freud – and even then not in great numbers. Instead of focusing on a critique of psychoanalytic theory with an eye towards undermining it in some major way, the essays in this volume seek to critically and speculatively elaborate upon it. This volume shifts the direction of debate away from the recent scholarly and public criticism that has been levelled at Freud and anything psychoanalytic. It moves

1

away from the man and his (arguably) relatively inconsequential claims to science, to a positive and substantive discussion of psychoanalytic insight in relation to a broad range of contemporary philosophical issues.

There are two principal schools of thought about Freud in contemporary analytic philosophy. There are those who think he has conclusively been shown to be wrong – if not an outright charlatan and cheat. On the other hand, psychoanalytic theory is seen as a source from which to develop approaches to the philosophy of mind, language, theory of meaning, and ethics that are consonant with, and expand upon the work of what some regard as the best and most influential analytic philosophy of our time. Some even see an integration of psychoanalytic theory with philosophy as necessary to both. Many in the second school have spent their time primarily with the somewhat negative task of defending Freudian theory and psychoanalysis generally as an insightful and useful extension of common-sense psychology. However, if psychoanalytic theory is fundamentally correct, then studies of its wider philosophical implications – studies prevented in various ways by arguably irrelevant criticism – are worthwhile and overdue.

Psychoanalysis refers (i) to a theory of the structure and workings of the mind, and (ii) to the psychotherapeutic method – both originally based on Freud's theoretical and practical (clinical) work. The connection between (i) and (ii) has long been a source of dispute.[2] Just about everyone's account of the relation between psychoanalytic theory and practice maintains that they mutually inform one another. But what more can be said about it? While it is unclear what would constitute the overall failure of psychoanalytic theory, it does seem that its failure, however established, would seriously undermine the rationale for psychoanalytic practice. We have a clearer idea of what would constitute, in particular cases and perhaps even generally, the failure of psychoanalytic practice. But it is far less clear, Freud's so-called 'Tally Argument' notwithstanding (see below), that the demise of psychoanalytic practice, its failure, would likewise undermine psychoanalytic theory to the same degree.

Different views as to the nature of the connection between theory and practice take one to the source of both (a) the most common lay critique of psychoanalytic practice – 'it doesn't work' (and, incidentally, 'it is expensive'), as well as to (b) its more sophisticated cousin – the claim that the 'Tally Argument' in support of the truth of psychoanalysis fails (i.e., because psychoanalysis does not, or cannot be shown to, work in practice, it evidentially fails as an adequate theory of the structure and workings of the mind as well). Both (a) and (b) are facile ways of avoiding the more complex question of 'how right does psychoanalysis have to be in order to be right?' The lay critique is perhaps understandable, but its scholarly cousin is not.

Though Freud may have himself confused or conflated questions of the truth of psychoanalytic theory with the efficacy of psychoanalytic practice, it is a mistake to do so. The difficulties and failures associated with the latter are contingently and tangentially related to the former in a variety of ways – some complex, and others straightforward.

Until recently most, but by no means all, of the specifically philosophical work in connection with Freud has been concerned with whether or not Freud's work was scientific.[3] The specific concern has been whether it was testable – verifiable or falsifiable – in accordance with accepted scientific procedure. Grünbaum (1984; 1993); Erwin (1996; 1993); Macmillan (1997);[4] Cioffi (1988; 1985); and others (cf. Robinson 1993) have been far less concerned with the wide-ranging philosophical implications of Freud and psychoanalytic theory generally than with the nature and methods of science. (It seems to go largely unnoticed that much of the recent criticism is a reiteration, in substance and tone, of criticisms Freud faced throughout his career.) But arguably the scientific status of psychoanalysis has always been a problem for philosophy of science rather than having any intrinsic connection to psychoanalysis. What constitutes a scientific theory (cf. Lear 1990: 216ff)? What are appropriate scientific inductivist canons? (cf. Hopkins 1988: 50)?[5]

Grünbaum's (1984) account of what he calls Freud's 'Tally Argument' shows that Freud was himself responsible for focusing so much attention on the scientific status of his theories. Freud (1917, XVI: 452; quoted from Grünbaum 1988: 14–15) says: 'After all, his [the patient's] conflicts will only be successfully solved and his resistances overcome if the anticipatory ideas [i.e. psychoanalytic interpretations] he is given tally with what is real in him. Whatever in the doctor's conjectures is inaccurate drops out in the course of analysis . . . it has to be withdrawn and replaced by something more correct.' Grünbaum (1988: 14) interprets this 'as a conjunction of the following two causally necessary conditions. 1) Only the psychoanalytic method of interpretation and treatment can yield or mediate for the patient the correct insight into the unconscious causes of his neuroses. 2) The patient's correct insight into the conflictual cause of his condition and into the unconscious dynamics of his character is in turn causally necessary for the durable cure of his neuroses'. He refers to the conjunction of these claims as Necessary Condition Thesis, and notes (1988: 14) that Freud 'asserts it with respect to the "psychoneuroses" [those caused by repressed infantile experiences] as distinct from the so-called actual neuroses [those caused by aetiological factors in an "adult's current life situation"]'. Such claims appear subject to inductive assessment in accordance with scientific (inductivist) canons, and Freud's apparent adherence to the Necessary Condition Thesis suggests that he agrees.[6]

No doubt Freud believed his theories to be scientific and testable to a degree. However, it should not be overlooked that whether or not Freud had sound and/or ulterior motives in claiming psychoanalysis to be a science, it was probably a good thing for psychoanalysis that he did since it is possible, even likely, that psychoanalysis would not have received the attention it did, had it not associated itself early on with the aura and mystique of science in a scientistic age. At any rate, even a cursory reading of Freud – perhaps especially a cursory reading – suggests that his theories were clearly not based wholly on clinical data and 'evidence' but also, and in my view more so, on his observations of everyday life. He understood only too well mitigating factors and the difficulty of achieving a psychoanalytic cure. Textual evidence notwithstanding, he never strictly adhered to the Necessary Condition Thesis. Freud carried his couch around with him. In psychoanalysis, like anything else – too selective a reading – too close a reading, can at times be as misleading and confusing as their counterparts if what one is trying to do is to understand.

As far as possible, the essays in this volume seek to put issues relating to the scientific status of psychoanalysis to one side and to explore the philosophical implications of psychoanalytic thought for contemporary philosophical issues. (That is what the contributors were asked to do.) Philosophers have recently begun, in earnest, to examine the breadth and impact of the philosophical dimension of Freud's work. This volume assumes that psychoanalytic theory is a useful and profound extension of common-sense psychology with wide-ranging philosophical import that has been, as Richard Wollheim (1993: 91) has said, only lately and barely touched upon.[7]

Part I (Mind) focuses on psychoanalytic theory in relation to the nature and function of the mind as philosophically conceived, and to issues in contemporary philosophy of mind and language. What problems do current theories of mind, meaning, language and consciousness present for psychoanalytic accounts of mental functioning; intentionality and the Will; wish-fulfilment; emotions; explanation; dreams; subjectivity; and the temporality of mind? Conversely, but no less signifi-cantly, what challenges does psychoanalytic theory pose for important philosophical theses in these areas? Part II (Ethics) examines ways that psychoanalytic theory and practice have impacted on moral philosophy with discussions of moral authenticity; emotions and agency; and akrasia and regression. A psychoanalytic understanding of human nature must have ramifications for moral philosophy. The essays in Part III (Sexuality) range over implications of psychoanalysis for understanding emotion; mourning and melancholia; love and emotion; issues relating to the erotic; and a range of everyday problems that arise in connection with oneself and personal relationships. Part IV (Civilization) includes essays on sublimation, love and creativity; jurisprudence and the rule of law; and 'the joke'. As is to be expected, at times there is significant overlap between parts.

Editors have wish lists and among essay topics I would have liked to include – a few of which I solicited to no avail – are the following:[8] Freud's epistemology; psychoanalysis and 'bringing up baby' – an essay that addresses the common misconception that Freud or psychoanalysis 'blames it all on the mother'; uses and abuses of Freudian readings of literature (art or films) – with reference to particular works; marriage (and divorce); Freud on the imagination; on the fragility of the ego; psychoanalysis, clothing and fashion; Freud on racism and the narcissism of minor differences; Freud's use of metaphor (Hopkins's essay addresses this in relation to the concept of mind); Humean and Freudian principles of association; The Great Genealogists: Nietzsche, Marx, Darwin, Freud; psycho-history: is there any other kind?; politics (all kinds of essays); utopias; neuroscience, cognitive science, psychoanalysis and dreams.[9] It begins to look like the more interesting volume(s) has yet to be produced – and this is the way it should look.[10]

In revolutionizing the most cherished conception we have – that of ourselves and how we relate to others – Freud was also undermining the foundations of a great deal of moral theory.[11] Philosophers with disparate views on the nature of ethics nevertheless agree that moral theory, along with social and political philosophy, must be connected to a theory of human nature. Psychoanalysis is the twentieth century's most significant account of what it is to be human. But as recent feminist thought in particular has shown, even where Freud himself is regarded as demonstrably mistaken, the implications of psychoanalytic theory extend beyond Freud to fundamental questions of morality, sexuality and problems of living. If it is basically right and insightful, then arguably there are few aspects of philosophy to which psychoanalytic theory is irrelevant. The relation, however, is mutual, and philosophy can be shown to be relevant, even necessary, to psychoanalytic theory as well.

For anyone who feels daunted by the prospect of picking up a volume that discusses the philosophical implications of psychoanalysis, let me assure them that it is possible to profitably discuss philosophy and psychoanalysis without memorizing the complete *Standard Edition* of Freud's works, supplemented by the works of Melanie Klein and others. Aspects of psychoanalysis's technical apparatus are frequently no more or less dispensable to particular discussions than whatever philosophical technicalities may be brought to bear. It varies from case to case, and from essay to essay. Puzzling over some of the alleged philosophical implications of psychoanalysis can provide an especially interesting introduction to some central issues in psychoanalysis – just as psychoanalytic theory can at times raise key philosophical issues in a particularly useful, pressing and even disturbing way.

Notes

1 It is Maud who says this in the novel.
2 Lear (1990: 16) says: 'Psychoanalytic theorizing cannot properly be conceived as detached from psychoanalytic practice.' But I cannot glean just what he takes the relationship to be.
3 Some of the most widely known (and best) philosophical discussion of Freud has been by non-professional philosophers such as Rieff (1959), Gay (1988) and other sociologists, historians, political and literary theorists, psychologists, novelists, essayists, etc.
4 See Macmillan (1997) for an extensive bibliography.
5 Hopkins (1988: 50) says: 'Schematically, Grünbaum and many he criticizes as "hermeneuts" agree that causal claims generally cannot be supported other than in accord with scientific (e.g. inductivist) canons, and that much psychoanalytic evidence about motives is non-canonical. One party sees that psychoanalytic accounts of motive have non-canonical support and so ignores the causal role of motives, while the other keeps causality in clear view but ignores non-canonical support. Neither draws the obvious conclusion from the fact of non-canonical evidence for the causal role of motives, namely that the canons leave evidence on certain causes – motives – out of the account. This, I think, is because neither attends to the way common-sense understanding uses and displays causal information.'
6 Grünbaum's account of 'actual neuroses' versus psychoneuroses may not be accurate. Actual neuroses result in symptoms that lack the meaning or sense which the symptoms

of pychoneuroses have. Children can have actual neuroses too. See Hopkins (1988) for a detailed and wide-ranging discussion of Grünbaum on the Tally Argument.

7   Wollheim (1993: 91) says: 'Virtually all those who are not either ignorant of Freud or totally sceptical of his findings believe that he altered, radically altered, our conception of the mind. He effected a change in what we think we are like, and it was a big change. Astonishingly enough, it is philosophers who have been of all people the slowest to recognise this fact. They have been slowest to recognize that this fact has anything to do with them'. Cf. Hopkins (1982; 1988).

8   Some of these were suggested by Amélie Rorty and other contributors.

9   Owen Flanagan (1995) gives an account of dreams and dreaming he claims is the one supported by contemporary scientific research on dreaming. What is unclear in his article is the extent to which his account is compatible or incompatible – supports or undermines – a Freudian view of the meaning, function and content of dreams. Is Flanagan's account an anti-Freudian view; or is Freud's analysis of dreams supported by Flanagan's interpretation of scientific research on dreams? It seems to me that they are by and large compatible. On Flanagan's account *some* dreams might be meaningless, but this leaves Freud's account largely intact. What is baffling is that Flanagan did not address directly the issue of compatibility. The title of his essay invites (demands) such a discussion.

10 Readers will want to see other recent collections of essays on Freud and psychoanalysis including Shamdasani and Münchow (1994); O'Neill (1996); and Hopkins and Savile (1992) on Wollheim.

11 See Scheffler (1992) for an excellent introduction to some of the far-reaching implications that psychoanalytic theory has for moral philosophy. Psychoanalysis utterly changes the face of contemporary moral philosophy in ways that Scheffler touches upon. See Pataki (1996) for what can well serve as an additional introduction to this book.

References

Byatt, A.S. (1990) *Possession*, London: Vintage.

Cioffi, Frank (1988) 'Exegetical Myth-Making in Grünbaum's Indictment of Popper and Exoneration of Freud', in P. Clark and C. Wright (eds), *Mind, Psychoanalysis and Science*, pp. 61–87, Oxford: Blackwell.

—— (1985) 'Psychoanalysis, Pseudo-Science and Testability', in G. Currie and A. Musgrave, (eds), *Popper and the Human Sciences*, pp. 13–44, Dordrecht: Nijhoff.

Erwin, Edward (1996) *A Final Accounting: Philosophical and Empirical Issues in Freudian Psychology*, Cambridge, MA: MIT Press.

—— (1993) *Philosophers on Freudianism: An Examination of Replies to Grünbaum's 'Foundations'*, in J. Earman, A.I. Janis, G.J. Massey and N. Rescher (eds), *Philosophical Problems of the Internal and External Worlds: Essays in the Philosophy of Adolf Grünbaum*, pp. 409–60, Pittsburgh: University of Pittsburgh Press.

Flanagan, Owen (1995) 'Deconstructing Dreams: The Spandrels of Sleep', *Journal of Philosophy*, XCII, pp. 5–27.

Freud, Sigmund (1953–74) *The Standard Edition of the Complete Psychological Works of Sigmund Freud*, J. Strachey, trans. and ed., London: Hogarth Press.

—— 1925d [1924] *An Autobiographical Study*.

Gay, Peter (1988) *Freud: A Life for Our Time*, London: Papermac.

Grünbaum, Adolf (1993) *Validation in the Clinical Theory of Psychoanalysis: A Study in the Philosophy of Psychoanalysis*. Madison, CT: International Universities Press.

—— (1988) 'Précis of *The Foundations of Psychoanalysis*', in Peter Clark and Crispin Wright (eds), *Mind, Psychoanalysis and Science*, pp. 3–32, Oxford: Blackwell.

—— (1984) *The Foundations of Psychoanalysis*, Berkeley: University of California Press.

Hopkins, Jim and Savile, Anthony (1992) *Psychoanalysis, Mind and Art: Perspectives on the Philosophy of Richard Wollheim*, Oxford: Blackwell.

—— (1988) 'Epistemology and Depth Psychology: Critical Notes on *The Foundations of Psychoanalysis*', in Peter Clark and Crispin Wright (eds), *Mind, Psychoanalysis and Science*, pp. 33–60, Oxford: Blackwell.

—— (1982) 'Introduction: Philosophy and Psychoanalysis', Introduction to Richard Wollheim and Jim Hopkins (eds), *Philosophical Essays on Freud*, pp. vii–xlv, Cambridge: Cambridge University Press.

Lear, Jonathan (1990) *Love and its Place in Nature: A Philosophical Interpretation of Freudian Psychoanalysis*, New York: Noonday Press.

Macmillan, Malcolm (1997 [1991]) *Freud Evaluated*, Cambridge, MA: MIT Press.

O'Neill, John (1996) *Freud and the Passions*, University Park, Pennsylvania: Pennsylvania State University Press.

Pataki, Tamas (1996) 'Psychology, Psychiatry, Philosophy', *Quadrant* April, pp. 52–63.

Rieff, Philip (1959) *Freud: The Mind of the Moralist*, Chicago: University of Chicago Press.

Robinson, C.L. (1993) *Freud and His Critics*, Berkeley: University of California Press.

Scheffler, Samuel (1992) 'Psychoanalysis and Moral Motivation', in Jim Hopkins and Anthony Savile (eds), *Psychoanalysis, Mind and Art: Perspectives on the Philosophy of Richard Wollheim*, pp. 87–109, Oxford: Blackwell.

Shamdasani, S and Münchow, M. (eds) (1994) *Speculations After Freud*, London: Routledge.

Wollheim, Richard (1993) *The Mind and its Depths*, Cambridge, MA: Harvard University Press.

Part I

MIND

1

PSYCHOANALYSIS, METAPHOR AND THE CONCEPT OF MIND

Jim Hopkins

Freud's work has made it possible for us to extend thinking involving such concepts as desire, belief and phantasy, and in a way which there is good reason to take as at least partly sound.[1] In what follows I consider how this same work also extends thinking involving symbolism and metaphor, and how in this psychoanalysis is consilient with recent work on conceptual metaphor.[2] The main example concerns the way we think about the mind. I argue that we can see such thinking as an important part of our concept of mind, and try, following Wittgenstein, to show how it provides an approach to the mind–body problem.

1 Symbolic mapping in psychoanalysis

The development of the psychoanalytic view of the mind went hand in hand with the idea that much everyday mental life can be seen as informed by something like metaphor or symbolism. To see this let us take it that we begin with an understanding of intentional action as prompted (caused) by desire: we assume that successful action on a desire that P (e.g. that I get a drink) should bring it about that P (that I get a drink), so that the desire is satisfied; and this in turn should bring it about that the agent experiences or otherwise comes to believe that P (that I have got a drink), so that the desire is *pacified*, that is, ceases to govern action. We thus tacitly assume that the operation of desire is partly regulated by experience or belief, that is, by a form of representation of the situation in which desire is satisfied.

Freud's work indicates that the regulation of desire by representation extends far beyond the case of intentional action. His discussions of dreams and symptoms, for example, enable us to see them as forms of representation which serve to regulate desires (or wishes) in the *absence* of any real satisfying situation. We can readily see this in the simple case in which someone thirsty dreams he is drinking, for here we have a desire that P (that I get a drink) which is temporarily pacified by an experience- or belief-like representation that P (I dream that I get a drink), without actual recourse to water.

In *The Interpretation of Dreams* Freud showed that the same pattern was to be found in more complex cases as well. Thus (1900: 106ff) his apparently non-wishful dream that his patient Irma was suffering from a toxic injection given by his colleague Otto could be seen as representing the satisfaction of, and thereby pacifying, a desire not to be responsible for Irma's continued suffering, which had been roused by a comment from Otto the day before, which Freud had taken as critical. In representing Otto as giving toxic injections, moreover, Freud seems also to have been pacifying a connected wish which originated years before: a wish not to have been responsible for the death of a patient by a toxic drug which he had administered, and that of a friend who had died as a result of injections of cocaine, which drug Freud had recommended to him.[3] The pacification of a contemporary and potentially conscious desire concerning Irma went together with that of deeper and presumably more painful desires originating from the past.

Although the point is often missed, Freud's analysis of this dream can also be seen to support a distinct claim about representation in his waking life. In understanding the dream as representing the fulfilment of Freud's wish not to be responsible for the deaths of his injection-killed friend and patient, we take the figure of Irma in the manifest content of the dream to *stand for*, and so in this sense to *symbolize*, these other figures. But then it is also plausible to hold that these same relations – relations of one figure standing for others – also serve to explain aspects of Freud's waking motives and actions. For seeing that Irma stood in Freud's mind for these significant figures from the past apparently enables us to understand not only why he dreamt about her as he did (e.g. in terms of toxic injections) but also why in his waking life he reacted so strongly to Otto's comment about her, and with an attempt to justify his treatment of her (by writing up her case history) which preceded the fantastic elaboration of the same theme in his dream. Freud's analysis, that is, also suggests that the waking significance which Irma held for Freud before the dream was partly derived from that of the past figures and situations for which, as consideration of the dream showed, she stood in his mind.

The same applies to Freud's analyses of other dreams in which one person stands for another. So we can regard Freud's first extensions of common-sense psychology as providing tacit support for an idea about the significance we attach to persons and situations in daily life: present significant figures and situations partly inherit their meaning from past ones, to which they are unconsciously mapped. The role which such across-time and across-situation mapping could play was made clearer in further work. Thus consider the female patient discussed in the *Introductory Lectures* (1915: 261–3). Her obsessional symptoms included a compulsion to run repeatedly into a neighbouring room, take up a particular position beside a table, and ring for the maid, who after this – the obsessional action completed – had to be fobbed off with some pointless errand.

This patient, who was unhappily separated from her husband, related her symptom to her wedding night, in which her husband had run repeatedly but unsuccessfully into her room to try to have intercourse, and, to avoid feeling ashamed before the maids, had faked a bloodstain on the sheets, but in the wrong place. This showed a series of links between the particulars of the symptom and the wedding night, which was completed when the patient took Freud to the table in front of which she stood, and explained that she took up her position in front of it in such a way that the maid could not fail to see a stain which was a prominent feature of the cloth. Thus in her symptomatic activity she was representing her wedding night, and pacifying her wish that things had been different then by showing the maid the stain which (stood for the earlier stain which) would have made clear that her marriage had been consummated.

2 Symbolic representational pacification

In this example there are both mappings between present and past persons, and also the less direct and so more recognizably symbolic instances of a table standing for a bed, a tablecloth for a sheet, and a stain from eating for a stain from sexual activity. These relations made it possible for a present intentional action (ringing for a maid and standing in a certain way) to provide representational pacification for desires relating to a situation long past. Such relations can also be seen in the transference, in which the analysand unconsciously maps past objects and situations on to the person and situation of the analyst, so that present activities again acquire a significance as pacifying desires or wishes originating in the past which can easily be discerned.

Freud also held that such symbolic relations were also naturally established over the course of a person's life. As early as 1895 he hypothesized a process of symbolic 'substitution':

> When an old maid keeps a dog or an old bachelor collects snuffboxes, the former is finding a substitute for her need for a companion and the latter for his need for – a multitude of conquests . . . this normally operating mechanism of substitution is abused in obsessional ideas . . .
>
> (1895: 209)

Freud distinguished the mere setting up of a symbolic substitute for a past object of desire from the deeper process of transformation which he called sublimation, by which early sexual and aggressive motives obtained new and more acceptable objects. But post-Freudian work (see for example Segal 1957, 1978) indicates that these processes are best seen as intertwined. In consequence many analysts now regard symbol formation as central to psychological development, and hence also to therapeutic success.

Something of the life-pervading role of symbolism hypothesized on this way of thinking can be illustrated by the example of a relatively successful teacher and writer, who was surprised when one of his pupils – who had made a special effort to be taught by him, and was trying hard to master his ideas – offered to suck his penis. This offer was neither expected nor welcome, but that night the teacher dreamt that *a lamb had come to suck milk from his finger* . . . On waking he realized that the lamb represented the pupil who had come to imbibe his ideas, and the milk-giving finger the penis his pupil had wanted to suck. So the dream could be seen as representing the fulfilment, in a form more acceptable because symbolic, of a sexual wish which had arisen on the day before.

The symbolism, however, went deeper, for the dream also represented him in the position of a mother nursing a child. His finger/penis was fulfilling the role of a feeding breast, and his writing and teaching represented as the production of milk as well as semen. The dream thus also expressed early desires for a combination of male and female roles which was incoherent and impossible to actually attain, and which did not govern the dreamer's mature waking life. But owing to the symbolic meaning which he attached to his work, these desires could nonetheless still be pacified through it. For in writing or teaching the dreamer could with some justice see himself in reality – to use metaphors which are more familiar and indirect – as potent, seminal and providing others with food for thought.

Freud's work on symbolism and substitution thus made it possible to reconceive desire in terms of an underlying continuity-in-difference which provides both a radically holistic perspective on the role of motive in the causation of action and a naturalistic description of the unconscious generation of present meaning from past experience.[4] On this account the desires of childhood and infancy are so unrealistic as commonly to be frustrated, but are nonetheless not psychologically lost. Rather they are constantly rearticulated by mapping to new objects and situations, so as to direct action towards their symbolic representational pacification during the rest of life. New goals therefore acquire significance as representatives of the unremembered objects of our first and most visceral passions; and the depth of satisfaction we feel in present accomplishments flows from the unacknowledged pacification of unknown desires from the distant past.

3 Symbolic mapping in conceptual metaphor

According to the ideas we have been considering our thought and action about a present situation is likely to be at least partly derived from motives related to past situations to which the present is unconsciously mapped. This bears comparison with some claims recently advanced by George Lakoff, Mark Johnston, Mark Turner and a number of others (see Lakoff 1993). These writers argue that metaphor should not be seen merely as a linguistic device, but rather as a form of thinking which is widespread, systematic and fundamental. Their claim is that we very often think about objects, properties, or relations in one domain (called the *target domain*) by systematically mapping these on to objects and properties in another domain (called the *source domain*). The correspondence relation between these domains constitutes a potentially large and organized *conceptual metaphor*, by means of which we think, or conceive, the one domain in terms of the other.

Where the source domain is A and the target B, so that in mapping the domains we think of B in terms of A, we can speak of the *B as A* metaphor. Thus we seem to make use of a metaphor of *relationship as journey*. In this we use concepts of objects, properties and relations from the domain of *travel* or *journeys* in order to conceptualize objects, properties and relations in the domain of *cooperative personal relationships*, such as *love*. In doing this we systematically take *persons* in such relations to correspond to *travellers*, their particular *relationship* to the *vehicle* in which they are travelling, and their *goals* in the relationship to their *destinations* in travelling. Thus we may speak of such a relationship as *going along well*, *slowing down*, *going nowhere*, *getting stuck*, *at a crossroads*, *at a dead end*, and so on.

In this metaphor, as in many others, the source domain in terms of which we think is intuitively more concrete than the target domain which we think about. Also we relate the domains tacitly, in the sense that we may be unaware both of using such correspondence relations, and of their richness and systematicity. Thus we may tacitly represent a relationship by one or another sort of vehicle, as seems appropriate to the rest of our thought. The relationship may be *taking off* (airplane); *on the rocks* (boat); *off the rails* (train); *in the slow lane* (car); and so on. A relationship which is *taking off*, say, will be one in which things are *moving fast*, and also getting better or more exciting, as in accord with such related metaphoric mappings as those of *increase as upward motion* (*rising* excitement, *rising* prices, *rising* in one's career, etc.) and *better as higher* (*high* status, *high* profile, *high* achiever, etc.) Thus it may be connected with the participants in the relationship feeling *high on love*, and so forth.

Further, as our understanding of familiar words enables us to form and understand new sentences, so our understanding of familiar correspondence relations enables us to form and understand new instances of metaphor. Thus, to take another of Lakoff's examples, in hearing a song lyric like 'We're driving in the fast lane on the freeway of love', we are immediately able to understand the metaphor in terms of the relationship-as-journey mapping, and others associated with it. The vehicle (relationship) is going fast, and this again is connected with excitement (fast cars, fast women); this speed, moreover, is compared to fast driving, which may be reckless or dangerous, and so lead to a crash in which someone will be hurt; the idea that the road is a freeway links with the idea of sexual freedom, free love, and so on. Such understanding ordinarily remains tacit, but in making it explicit we realize that it is already latent in our original response.

We also reason in terms of such mappings. We take it, for example, that if a relationship is *stuck*, those involved have reason to try to do something about this. They may try to *start over* or to *get the relationship started again*, or to *get going* or *going forward*, once more. *Towards this end* they may, for example, try to *get over* the problem, or to find their *way out* of the difficulty. Alternatively they may decide that the relationship has *broken down*, or perhaps been *wrecked* by the actions of one or both of them, in which case they will *get out* and *go their separate ways*.

Once we start to delineate such a metaphor, we can usually find additional examples, in which the hypothesized mapping serves to explain further responses we are aware of. Thus consider the phrase 'spaceship earth'. Why do these words evoke the idea that human beings have a significant cooperative relationship in virtue of being inhabitants of a common planet? This is explicable on the hypothesis that the phrase constitutes an instance of the correspondence between relationship and vehicle in the metaphorical structure we have been discussing. The metaphor, as we might say using another from the same family, reminds us that we are *all in the same boat*, and so should *pull together*. Again, one might ask why the song which begins 'Trains, and boats, and planes, all bound for Paris, New York, and Rome . . . ' should be so evocative of solitude and loneliness. Here also there seems a plausible answer, in terms of the same metaphor: these vehicles which the singer is not in, going on journeys which the singer is not taking, represent relationships in which the singer, sadly, has no part. Such individual instances may not be particularly convincing one by one, but each mapping of the kind we are taking seems to generate a class of examples which is open and readily extensible, and which thus has considerable cumulative weight.

Students of conceptual metaphor have tried to show in detail how tacit mappings of this kind permeate our thinking about a great range of topics, including time and space, objects, events and properties, logical and semantic categories, and the pursuit of human goals. They have also stressed how the ultimate source domain for many of these mappings is the human body (see particularly Johnston 1987). This work thus bears out William James's claim that

> My own body and what ministers to its needs are thus the primitive object, instinctively determined, of my egoistic interests. Other objects may become interesting derivatively through association with any of these things, either as means or as habitual concomitants; and so in a thousand ways the primitive sphere of the egoistic emotions may enlarge and change its boundaries.
>
> (1890, 1: 324)

4 Pschyoanalytic findings about symbolic mapping complement those of conceptual metaphor, and link them with concrete thinking

The psychoanalytic hypotheses about symbolism sketched in section 1 complement these claims. Psychoanalysis is mainly concerned with the relations between past and present phantasies and desires, but takes these to be mediated by mappings which can be regarded as cognitive and metaphorical. Thus in the symptom of the tablecloth lady above, we find not only a cross-time mapping as between past and present, but also a cross-domain mapping as between eating and sexual activity (the mapped roles of bed and table, sheet and tablecloth, and the origins of the stains). The same domains, again, are mapped in the teacher's dream above, in which nutritive represents sexual sucking. Indeed an extensive metaphorical connection between eating and sexual activity seems part of the representational practice of every culture.

In representing many domains, according to psychoanalysis, we map them to relations to or among persons (object relations), and our representations of present object relations partly map them to past ones. The ultimate source for these mappings are therefore object relations in childhood and infancy, which begin with those involving emotionally significant parts of the body and their functions. Both disciplines thus see conscious thought as underlain and informed by a system of mappings linking distinct objects and domains, a principle source of which is the human body.[5]

Psychoanalysts and students of conceptual metaphor also conceive faulty symbolic/metaphoric thinking in ways which are closely related. Such thinking, as we have seen, maps objects, events and properties across times and domains; and the sources of such mappings are often more concrete or basic, or more closely related to the human body, than the targets. It is therefore a requirement for such thinking that the source and target domains be both appropriately connected to, and appropriately differentiated from, one another. If sources are not appropriately connected with their targets they cannot be used to represent them; and if they are connected but not differentiated from their targets the one may be confused with the other. In both cases – that in which the source of a would-be metaphor is not linked with a target, and that in which a source is confused with a target – the metaphor is likely to be understood in terms of its source, and hence too concretely.

According to psychoanalytic theory as well as much psychological and psychiatric observation, such failures of source–target relations are shown in a number of psychological disturbances characterized by concrete thinking. For example Segal (1957) describes a concert violinist, who during a schizophrenc breakdown refused to play his violin. When asked why, he replied: 'Do you expect me to masturbate in public?' This can be understood in terms of two hypotheses: (i) that the significance of the man's violin playing was partly determined by a symbolic/ metaphoric connection with earlier activity involving his own body, and (ii) that he had ceased to differentiate the source and target domains of this mapping. To take a different example, a ten-year-old autistic girl showed catastrophic anxiety when a nurse, about to do a blood test, said: 'Give me your hand; it won't hurt.' She calmed down immediately when another person said 'stretch out your index finger'.[6] She had apparently understood the nurse as requesting her to give her hand *away*, so that she would not have it afterwards. This too seems a case of concrete thinking, but one which may not require to be understood in terms of a collapse of source and target domains. Rather it may be that the girl simply understood 'give' in terms of the domain of the giving of objects from one person to another, and had not effected any further mapping.

Lakoff represents the maintenance of correct source/target relations in terms of what he calls the Invariance Principle. This principle, as he says,

> explains why you can give someone a kick, even if that person doesn't
> have it afterward, and why you can give someone information, even if you

don't lose it. This is a consequence of the fact that inherent target domain structure automatically limits what can be mapped.

(1993: 215–16)

To think that someone given a kick would possess that kick afterwards would be to fail properly to distinguish the source domain of physical objects transfered from one person to another in givings, from the target domain of kickings of one person by another. As in the examples above, this failure might arise either from confusion between source and target, or from an initial failure to use the source to map the target. Lakoff's invariance principle thus also marks the natural avoidance of concrete thinking which is characteristic of normal symbolic/metaphorical thought.

5 Metaphoric representation and the concept of mind: the metaphor of the mind–body container

If metaphorical thinking is as important a part of our cognitive repertoire as analysts and students of conceptual metaphor claim, then we should be able to understand significant aspects our concepts in terms of it. I think that this holds for aspects of the concept of mind which have been particularly important for both philosophy and psychology, namely those which generate the problem of other minds and the problem of consciousness. We can begin to consider this by reviewing a family of metaphoric/symbolic mappings which represent *the mind as a container*, where the container in question might also be taken as the body. We can call this the metaphor of *the mind–body container*.

Some examples are particularly simple and direct, as when we say that a stupid or forgetful person – one who cannot *keep things in mind* – has a *hole in his head*. Others involve a variety of further comparisons. One familiar instance, for example, involves comparing the mind to the inhabitant of a *house*. There is a joke in which we knock on the forehead of an inattentive or *vacant* person, asking if anyone is *at home*. (There is also a children's game along the same lines, which even very little children instantly understand and enjoy.) Again, when a person's mind is not present, in one way or another, we may say that *the lights are on* (the eyes are open) *but there is no one at home*. Likewise we speak of the *house* of reason; of the mind as *housed* in the body; of the eyes as *windows* of the soul, the senses the *doors* of perception, *portals* of the mind, and so forth.

Metaphors from this family appear in very many contexts, as when we say that someone who has failed to keep something concealed has *spilled the beans*, i.e. let them spill out of his mind–body container, and in a way that makes them difficult or impossible to replace. They are, however, particularly common in our conceptualization of emotion and feeling (Kovecses 1990). Thus we speak of people as *full* of feelings of all kinds, which may *bubble up, well up*, or *overflow*, unless they are kept *contained*. We take it that if a person's feelings are *bottled up* then he or she should perhaps seek to *express* them, or *let them out* in one way or another, say, by *channelling* them into to an activity like art or exercise, *venting* them by

18

talking to an acquaintance, or even *taking them out* on the cat, or something of the kind. Otherwise the *pressure of feeling* may be damaging or dangerous.

A number of the variants of this metaphor are highly detailed and systematic. Thus, for example, we seem to conceive certain emotions as *fluids* in the mind–body container. We think of anger, for example, as a *hot* fluid: the feelings of someone who is angry may *seethe* or *simmer* and so are *agitated*. A person who is *hot under the collar* in this way may be *fuming* as the anger *rises*, or *wells up* in him; and so he may have to *simmer down*, or *cool down*, so as not to *boil over*. If he can't do this, and doesn't somehow manage to *let off steam* he may be at risk of *bursting with anger*, or *exploding with rage*. The spectrum of feeling between calmness and uncontrollable anger is thus represented relatively strictly in terms of the temperature of the emotion-liquid, which may be cool (no anger), agitated or hot (some degree of anger), or boiling (great anger).[7] By contrast a source of fear may make one get *cold feet* or make one's *blood run cold*, so that, in the extreme case, *cold fear* or *icy terror* may render one *frozen to the spot* and so unable to move. Here the opposition in the nature of the feelings is marked by one in the properties of the metaphorical fluids to which we map them.

Where we take the mind–body container as enclosing feelings, we also take it that emotionally significant events may affect the container itself. This happens when we become frozen to the spot, for in this case the coldness of the contents of the mind–body container are represented as affecting (immobilizing) the bodily container. The container can be put at risk from within, from the kind of *eruption* in which someone *blows his top*, *flips his lid*, or *blows his stack*. The container can also suffer damage which originates outside, as when a person is *crushed*, *shattered*, or *broken*. Particularly serious is the kind of episode in which a person *cracks up* in such a way that the mind–body container is entirely *fragmented*. Such involuntary fragmentation is quite different from the small and precisely controlled exchange, in which *we give another a piece of our mind*. In this case we are relieved of our aggression, which is metaphorically passed on to the other, who has now to cope with it. This is different from the case in which a person *goes to pieces* so completely as to *lose his mind*.

Our taking the mind–body as a container has a further aspect, which is that we liken good things to those we would like to *take into* the container, particularly by eating, and bad things to those which should be put or kept *out*, and by processes which include excretion. Thus, in general, we regard good things as *sweet*: life is sweet, youth is sweet, peace is sweet, and so, according to our way of speaking, are hope, freedom, victory, revenge, nothings whispered in the ear, people's faces, a moment's relief, dreams, babies (whom one could sometimes just *gobble up*, because they are so sweet and delightful), children (particularly little girls, who as we know are made of *sugar* and *spice*), young animals, melodies both heard and unheard, and an endless variety of other things.

The idea of having good things in the container also applies to other persons in the environment. Those whom we love, for example, we *keep in mind*, *keep in our memories*, and *keep in our heart*; and this – strikingly – goes with a capacity actually to feel the other as a represented and valued presence somehow inside us, as if they had in some sense actually been internalized. Hence also the characterization of things which are good or desirable as things we would like to eat is especially striking in the case of love and lust. Terms of endearment include numerous variations on *honey, sugar, sweetness* and the like; she or he may be *the cream in my coffee, the sugar in my tea,* my *sweetie-pie* and so on. There are also variants of these expressions which extend to coarser *appetites,* such as that for *cheesecake* or *beefcake* or *meat*; and one can want to meet a *dish* or a *hunk,* or take an interest in very many other bodily things compared to food. This is another aspect of the metaphorical comparison between nutrition and sexuality, which also appears fleetingly in the symptom of the tablecloth lady and the dream of the successful teacher above.

As indicated, we often represent communication of thought and feeling in terms of actual or attempted *transfer* of things from container to container. The eyes can be used to transfer the temperature of emotion, for example, as when they *set one alight* (*afire, aflame,* etc.), or when one is *frozen* by an *icy look* or a *cold stare.* Again, opinions and sentiments are *put into* words – which can therefore be *full of meaning,* not, say, *hollow* or *empty* – and thus *given* to others (*passed* to them, *exchanged* with them, etc.) who may or may not *receive,* or *take them in.* This kind of transfer of thought or feeling can also affect the mind–body container towards which it is directed: just as another's words may *convey* or *carry* things from their container to ours, so their words or deeds may *strike* us, and they may *penetrate, pierce, perforate, cut, sting, lacerate, lash,* or otherwise attack or injure the mind–body container. One may be *stabbed* by a sharp look, as by sharp words, even if the person is not *looking daggers* at one; and looks and words may also be *acid, poisonous,* or *full of venom.* Also the mind can be entered, or threatened with entry, in other ways which are connected with bodily entry, as when someone *gets under our skin, gets up our nose,* or again *bugs us* like some insect intruding on the body.

Since we represent what is in the mind–body container as having great power to affect it, the question of what we *take in* from what others attempt to *put across* is highly significant. We seem to regard various forms of truth as providing *food for thought,* and hence *intellectual nourishment,* and various forms of falsehood in an opposite way. Just as we systematically relate anger or fear to metaphorical internal fluids, so we systematically relate the badness of various kinds of misrepresentation to the unpleasantness or toxicity of the materials in terms of which we represent them. Thus we may hold that bad ideas or opinions are *tosh, trash, rubbish, garbage,* or even *horse manure* or *bullshit,* and we characterize their sources in related ways. If someone's utterances or opinions are *without substance* we may say that they are *just gassing.* If someone regularly engages in bragging or other relatively harmless and *self-inflating* misrepresentation we may say that they are *full of hot air.* We may call someone who is fluent at minor misrepresentation a *piss-artist*; and someone prone to more serious or pernicious misrepresentation will be said to be *full of piss,* or, if the falsehood is still more *noxious, full of shit.*

20

Likewise we may say that opinions which we characterize in this way *stink*, and regard them as *distasteful, repellent, repulsive, disgusting* or *nauseating*. Hence we hope that no one (or at least no one who is not some kind of *sucker*) will be inclined to *swallow* them. But people may *imbibe* such falsehoods in childhood, or be *fed* them through propaganda, in which case their minds may be *infected* or *poisoned*, without their being able to do anything about it. *Contaminating, corrupting,* or *polluting* others with ideas of this kind is decidedly not giving them the proper *intellectual sustenance*. Hence if people *air* such *unsanitary* views, or try to force such *filth* or *junk* into others' minds, or *down their throats*, they are at risk of being told to *shove it*, that is, to put these things back into the inner space of their own mind–body containers, and by a route which reflects their nature.

This sample of our thought and talk can be taken to indicate that we have a metaphorical representation of the mind as a container, which we can represent in diagram form (Figure 1).

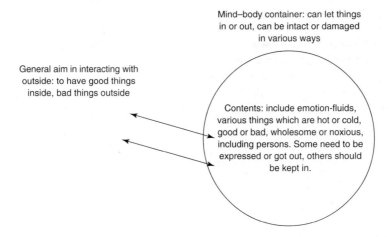

Figure 1 The metaphor of the mind as a container

6 This metaphor is extensively used in unconscious representation of the mind

This too is continuous with what we find in psychoanalysis. Thus consider the following from Kohut's (1977: 105) account of what he calls 'indescribable states of self-dissolution'.

Here are some examples taken at random from my psychoanalytic practice: a negligible crack in the plaster in one room might indicate the presence of a serious structural defect of the patient's house; a tiny skin infection of the patient or of someone he experiences as an extension of himself is the first sign of a dangerous septicaemia; or, in dreams, the frightening infestation of the living quarters with spreading vermin; or the ominous discovery of algae in the swimming pool. Much as these fears might occupy the patient's mind, however, leading to states of endless brooding, worry, or panic, these fears do not constitute the core of the disturbance, but have been generated as a result of the patient's attempt to give a circumscribed content to a deeper unnameable dread experienced when a person feels that his self is becoming seriously enfeebled or is disintegrating. The ability of the analyst to conceive of psychic conditions that cannot be described in terms of verbalizable meaning allows him to consider an important band in the spectrum of possibilities as he scrutinizes the analysand's anxiety – the fragmentation of and the estrangement from his body and mind in space, the breakup of his sense of continuity in time.

Although Kohut takes these examples 'at random', it is clear that they have something in common. The representations by which these patients register their dread that something is going seriously wrong with their selves are all versions of the metaphoric representation of the mind–body container described above. In each case – the plaster cracking in the house, the living quarters invaded with vermin, the infected skin, the fluid-filled pool infested with algae – the mind–body container and/or its contents are represented as threatened. So the states which Kohut regards as indescribable are nonetheless naturally expressed through what we have seen as a systematic metaphor, as instances in which the house of reason, or the fluids of emotion and feeling, are in one way or another endangered.

This kind of metaphorical/symbolic representation of the self, moreover, is familiar from many other psychoanalytic sources. It has a clear role, for example, in the dream of Irma's injection. Freud remarks that the toxic solution which the dream represents Otto as having injected into Irma is in fact a chemical which he took to be involved in the sexual process, and that this was related to his having thought that Irma's problems were the result of her widowhood, and might be relieved by the accompaniments of marriage. (As he says in his letter in Abraham [1965], discussing the 'sexual megalomania' which he took to underlay the dream, 'There would be one simple therapy for widowhood, of course. All sorts of intimate things, naturally.') Thus the dream is constructed around a mapping as between the intellectual *sexual solution* which Freud was offering Irma, and the physical and toxic *sexual solution*, which Otto was portrayed as injecting into her mind–body container (using his own dirty syringe).

7 This representation has also been assigned an important theoretical role

Owing to its clinical frequency, this representation of the mind also plays an important role in psychoanalytic theory. Freud described the mind as it appears in this kind of portrayal in terms of an 'internal world', which he took to be related to 'the most basic instinctual impulses' of taking in and putting out (1940: 205).[8] This he described in terms of a 'bodily ego', which was 'ultimately derived from bodily sensations, chiefly those springing from the surface of the body' and so 'a mental projection of the surface of the body' (1923: 26, authorized footnote). We may take this together with Freud's account of some aspects of early mental life, in which he says that our attitudes of acceptance and rejection as applied to thoughts are originally related to taking things into and out of the body.

> Expressed in the language of the oldest – the oral – instinctual impulses, the judgement is 'I should like to eat this', or 'I should like to spit it out'; and, put more generally: 'I should like to take this into myself and to keep that out'. That is to say: 'It shall be inside me' or 'It shall be outside me'. As I have shown elsewhere, the original pleasure-ego wants to introject into itself everything that is good and to eject from itself everything that is bad.
>
> (1925: 26)

If we remember that this is said to be at the root of attitudes towards thoughts themselves, and take the space into which good is introjected and from which bad expelled to be that established as inner by 'a projection of the surface of the body', we arrive at a representation of the mind which accords with the metaphoric picture as diagrammed in Figure 1 very closely.

This representation has also figured extensively in post-Freudian thinking. Melanie Klein (1975) found such an internal world to be shown in a multiplicity of ways in the representational activities of little children, where it was related to the inside of the mother's body as well as the children's own; and Wilfred Bion (1967; 1977) made the role of containment for this world explicit in his discussions of container and contained.[9]

8 Multi-domain mapping

Although students of conceptual metaphor characteristically speak of cross-domain mapping, psychoanalytic instances often show mappings involving serveral domains at once. This is so, for example, in the dream of the successful teacher. For the dream showed not only a clear representation of sexual by nutritive sucking, but also a phantasy – upon which the student also seems to have been acting – that the teacher's knowledge could be internalized in this concrete way. Hence it also involved an instance of the mind–body container, and a particular form of concrete thinking about knowledge, the possibility of which is foreshadowed also in the metaphors (imbibing ideas, food for thought, etc.) noted above. (The same holds for the intellectual/sexual solution as represented in the dream of Irma's Injection.)

This kind of multi-domain mapping frequently figures in phantasies of internalization, in which good things or persons are represented as taken into the self. This is particularly notable, for example, in representations involving the automobile. People very often represent themselves in terms of their cars, or their cars as extensions of themselves. (This seems to be one cause of road rage.) But cars are also vehicles, and so travelling in them is also used to represent relationships to others. This, as well as the role of concrete thinking about the mind, is illustrated by the case of the 'mechanical boy' discussed by Bettleheim (1959; 1967).

This little boy, diagnosed as autistic, was fascinated by machines of various kinds, and identified himself with them. He converted his bed, for example, into a complex car-machine that would 'run him' or 'live him': this included a carburettor which enabled him to breathe, a motor that ran his body, a 'speaker' that enabled him to talk or hear, and so forth. In this he gave the clearest possible indications of the way he took this car as representing, and extending, his self; and this was also the topic of many of his drawings and other communications. But the symbolism was shown to have a further significance in an interview with the boy several years later. As he then said:

> I can remember being interested in mechanical and electrical things almost as far back as I can remember . . . I made a car . . . that's one of the main things I made out of the bed . . . it was something in which a person was enclosed . . . when I started coming closer to people . . . I'd have fantasies about a car or anything that moved on wheels that was enclosed and I'd have a fantasy that I was in it myself . . . I'd always picture that somebody else was in it with me . . . one person was Barbara, and it was right after I'd been here a year and a half that I had put up a device on my bed to make it [the bed] look like a car. I told her to get on the bed while I pretended to drive the car . . . on other occasions I pretended to drive home, you know, to where my family was. And mostly, I think, it was a way of thinking of the time when I would be living with my family and would trust people enough to want them.
>
> (1967: 334)

Here we see a double use of the metaphors we have considered. The car was an enclosed space which by which the little boy represented his self, and into which he wanted to bring those he might trust and relate to, as in accord with the metaphor of *the mind as container*; but as a vehicle it also provided an instance of the metaphor with which we began, that of *relationship as journey*. In this case, however, the metaphor was used concretely: wanting to ensure and extend the functioning of his self, and also to form relationships, the boy actually constructed an enclosed space which was also a vehicle, as if thereby constructing a relating self. As he later realized, however, this was not a way of bringing such things about, but rather 'a way of thinking' – a form of thinking in terms of metaphor or symbolism – of relationships which he might yet form. His improvement went with a recognition of the symbolic nature of what he had previously confused with the real.

It is now widely recognized that many individuals diagnosed as autistic have difficulty in employing the common-sense concept of mind. Most work in this field (Baron-Cohen et al. 1993; Baron-Cohen 1995) has concentrated on the understanding of propositional attitudes like belief. It seems, however, that there may also be significant difficulty in employing the conception of the mind as a container, which is a focus in psychoanalytic treatments of autism.[10] Workers in this field often quote the example of an observant autistic youth who said: 'People talk to each other with their eyes . . . What is it that they are saying?' (Frith 1993). The discussion above indicates the extent to which we articulate the language of the eyes via the metaphor of the mind as a container. Lack of the capacity to use this metaphor seems an important aspect of failure to conceptualize the mind.

9 Metaphoric representation and the mind–body problem: the problem of other minds and the problem of consciousness

The use of the metaphor of the mind as a container is thus integral to our way of thinking about the mind, and also liable to go wrong in certain ways. Let us now consider the role of this metaphor in philosophy.

Philosophical thinking about the mind has been dominated by two related problems: the problem of consciousness, and the problem of other minds. We can think of these problems as arising as follows: the experiences which present the world to us seem to be *internal* to the mind, whereas the world which they present seems *external* to it. Thus when I feel pain or see a tree, the experience of pain, or the visual impression of the tree (and the visual field of which it is a part) are *internal* to me, and hence presented in *introspection*, whereas the tree itself, by contrast, is part of the *external* world. These internal experiences, moreover, seem to have a *phenomenal* character, which we cannot envisage being possessed by any external *physical* thing. This character seems *subjective*, in the sense that what it *is*, is wholly and fully presented in how it *seems* in introspection; whereas an external physical thing like a tree is *objective*, in the sense that there is a potentially rich distinction between how it seems in perception and how it is in itself. Finally, the internal experience seems *private*, in the sense that it can be introspected or apprehended only by one person, the person to whose mind it is internal, whereas a physical thing is *public*, in the sense that it can be perceived and hence known about by more than one person.

Taking the case of visual perception, we can present these contrasts in the form of a diagram (Figure 2).

The oppositions diagrammed here seem conceptual or logical. It seems a part of our way of thinking about these matters that no one thing could be both internal to the mind in the way experiences are, and also external to it in the way physical things are; and likewise that the same thing could not be both introspectible and externally perceiveable, phenomenal and physical, subjective and objective, or private and public. Hence this picture gives rise to dualism, the view that mental phenomena are not physical phenomena, and hence that human experience does not, as we have every scientific reason to believe, go on in the brain or nervous system. Also, and connectedly, it gives rise to the problem of consciousness, and that of other minds.

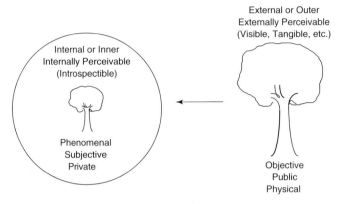

Figure 2 The dualistic image of the mind

The problem of consciousness is that of understanding how events in the brain could realize, or otherwise produce, the distinctive properties apparently manifested in experience. This problem is not solved by accepting that mental events do in fact occur in the brain, for the difficulty is precisely that of understanding *how* this can be so – how events which occur in the brain, and hence are physical, public and objective, can be phenomenal, subjective and private, as experiences seem to be. Hence it is also not solved by holding that mental events can have *aspects* or *properties* which are phenomenal, subjective, or private, since this again is a version of what requires to be explained. Nor finally is it solved by supposing that we have distinctive first-person *ways of thinking* or *modes of presentation* of the neural events which realize our experience, although this certainly seems to be so. For the question remains, as to how and why these modes of presentation should render neural events phenomenal, subjective and private, or make them seem so despite their physical nature. To many, therefore, this problem suggests the need for a new approach, or even a new science. Thus in a recent collection of articles (Metzinger 1995), the situation is described as follows:

> To be able to speak seriously about a *science of consciousness*, a number of fundamental questions would have to be answered. It is interesting to note that with the emergence of consciousness private worlds – spaces of inner experiences – are opened up. These spaces, however, are *individual* spaces: ego-centres of experience that suddenly appear in a centerless universe. Each such centre of consciousness constitutes its own perspective on the world. This perspective is what philosophers sometimes like to call the 'first-person perspective'. A phenomenal world of its own is tied to each of these perspectives. These individual worlds of experience also possess a historical dimension: almost always a psychological biography emerges together with them – what we call our 'inner life'. This

too can be seen as the history of the genesis of a world, or a *phenomenal cosmology*: within each of us a cosmos of consciousness unfolds temporarily, a *subjective* universe develops. The first part of the problem is to understand how a variety of subjective universes can constantly form and disappear in our objective universe.

(Metzinger 1995: 6)

The problem of other minds is also a direct consequence of this picture, for according to it an other's experiences are internal and private, and hence inaccessible to me and not part of the external world in which I locate that other. This being so, it seems I can know nothing about the other's experiences, and indeed can have no reason to assume that an other has experience. For if all that the other does – all the ways the other's body moves, for example – can be taken to flow from events in his brain that are distinct from experiences, why should I postulate anything further? And even if I identify the other's experiences with events in his brain, still I seem to have no access to the phenomenal character of those experiences, and hence might well still wonder how far they are comparable to mine.

10 Wittgenstein's claim that these problems are due to metaphor

As is familiar, Wittgenstein (1954) held that philosophical problems arise, among other ways, from metaphors or comparisons between the way we use words in different regions of language, and applied this with particular effect to the problems of mind. These, he said, arose from a 'picture' of the mind:

> 425. In numberless cases we exert ourselves to find a picture and once it is found the application as it were comes about of itself. In this case we already have a picture which forces itself upon us at every turn – but does not help us out of the difficulty, which only begins here . . .
> 427. 'While I was speaking to him I did not know what was going on in his head'. In saying this one is not thinking of brain-processes, but of thought-processes. The picture should be taken seriously. We should really like to see into his head. And yet we only mean what elsewhere we should mean by saying we should like to know what he is thinking. I want to say: we have this vivid picture – and that use, apparently contradicting the picture, which expresses the psychical.

This picture, as Wittgenstein describes it, emerges as the dualistic picture of the mind described above. In it the mind is conceived as an *enclosed space*, distinct from the space inside the body, whose contents are in themselves psychological and phenomenal rather than physical ('one is not thinking of brain-processes, but of thought-processes'), and detected by a process analogous to sight (introspection).

Wittgenstein observed that the privacy which this picture gave to phenomenal properties would render them incapable of description in a public language, and so incommunicable. He took this as a clear *reductio* of the view, which he put as follows:

> 293. If I say of myself that it is only from my own case that I know what the word 'pain' means – must I not say the same of other people too? And how can I generalize the one case so irresponsibly?
>
> Now someone tells me that he knows what pain is only from his own case! – Suppose everyone had a box with something in it: we call it a 'beetle'. No one can look into anyone else's box, and everyone says he knows what a beetle is only by looking at his beetle. – Here it would be quite possible for everyone to have something different in his box. One might even imagine such a thing constantly changing. – But suppose the word 'beetle' had a use in these people's language? – If so it would not be used as the name of a thing. The thing in the box has no place in the language-game at all; not even as a *something*: For the box might even be empty. – No, one can 'divide through' by the thing in the box; it cancels out, whatever it is.
>
> That is to say: if we construe the grammar of the expression of sensation on the model of 'object and designation' the object drops out of consideration as irrelevant.

Here the argument clearly turns on an instance of the container metaphor, that is, the box which represents the mind. So, as we can say, Wittgenstein took the dualistic image of the mind, which we have portrayed in Figure 2 above, as a particular instance of the metaphor of the mind as a container, which we have portrayed in Figure 1. The problem of other minds is thus partly constituted by the imposition of this metaphor.

Wittgenstein seems to have taken the same metaphor to give rise to the problem of consciousness; but in this case he does not seem to have been able to make the connection fully explicit. For example he writes:

> 296. 'Yes, but there is *something* there all the same accompanying my cry of pain. And it is on account of that that I utter it. And this something is what is important – and frightful'. – Only whom are we informing of this? And on what occasion?
> 297. Of course, if water boils in a pot, steam comes out of the pot and also pictured steam comes out of the pictured pot. But what if one insisted on saying that there must also be something boiling in the picture of the pot?

We can describe Wittgenstein's thinking here as follows. Things happen in our bodies which cause the verbal and other behaviour through which we express pain, as things happen in a boiling pot which cause the expression of steam. (The box in the previous metaphor is replaced by the pot in this.) In order to understand these internal events we form a representation (picture) of them in terms of the mind–body container (the picture of the pot). But in using this picture, we perforce represent the internal events as occurring, not in the physical space of the body where they actually occur, but rather as in a space of a distinct kind. We are misled by our form of representation, in such a way that we think of the internal events with which we are concerned as occurring not in the pot (the body), but in the picture of the pot (the metaphorical space internal to the mind–body container).

11 The metaphor of containment and the notion of a virtual inner space

Wittgenstein's thinking here is very compressed, but we have reason to consider it worth exploring. We have stressed in previous sections how metaphorical/symbolic thinking is an important part of our conceptual repertoire, and how representations of the mind as a container pervade both our conscious and unconscious thinking. Wittgenstein's analysis of these problems thus represents them as springing from a preconscious mode of thought to which we have access through other disciplines, and which we have other grounds for considering as significant.

We can make his claim clearer via the notion of a *virtual space*. A virtual space is one which is not real, but an artefact of our modes of representation. We create a virtual space if we treat a space which is in fact only represented or imagined as if it were real. Thus we can think of the space shown in a mirror, not as that of the actual room, including ourselves, which is reflected in it, but as an alternative space which we might enter by passing through the looking-glass. In this case the space through the looking-glass is a virtual space – a space we can consider in detail, think of ourselves as entering and having adventures in, etc., but a space which nonetheless is not real. We can treat the space presented by a cinema or television screen, or that shown in a video game, in the same way; and if the representation of space with which we are dealing is part of a sufficiently comprehensive and compelling illusion, we may characterize it as a *virtual reality*. Taking a virtual space as a real space, in turn, is an error in representation comparable to concrete thinking. In this case the source for a representation is linked, not with the real or imaginary domain which it should represent, but with an alternative imaginary domain, taken as real.

This is the notion involved in Wittgenstein's metaphor. Someone who insisted that there had to be something boiling in a picture of a pot would be taking a represented space, represented as having something boiling in it (the picture of the boiling pot) as a real space with someone boiling in it, and so would be creating a virtual space in the sense above. (The space in the pictured pot would be like the space behind the looking-glass, taken as real.) So the idea which we are to consider is that the distinct inner space in which we are inclined to insist that conscious events go on is in fact a virtual space, and therefore an artefact of our representation of the mind as a container. Thus take the 'phenomenal cosmology' introduced by

29

Metzinger above, with its range of 'individual spaces', which constitute 'subjective universes', which appear with birth and disappear with death. The view under consideration is that this picture is not literally true. It is not actually the case that the physical space in the vicinity of persons or other conscious creatures is like a Swiss cheese, filled with other spaces of a mysteriously different kind containing experiences. Rather on this account the spaces Metzinger is talking about – and those depicted in the figures we have drawn above – are *virtual* spaces, things that we are inclined to take as real spaces because of the way we represent them in spatial terms.

12 Virtual inner space and the representation of real inner events

Wittgenstein's comparison has a second aspect, which is that the metaphor of the mind as a container actually serves as a representation of events in the body. (The picture of the boiling pot, although it does not actually contain anything boiling, does nonetheless represent the boiling in the pot.) We can see this clearly in the connected case of thinking of anger as a hot fluid inside us, or representing emotion in terms of internal fluids generally. This way of thinking serves as a representation of things that go on in us when we experience emotion, and hence it serves as a representation of physical processes which are otherwise unknown to us, but which are in fact contained within the body. In speaking of levels of temperature of an imaginary emotion-fluid, for example, we seem to be indexing levels of behaviour-governing neurophysiological processes, particularly those which are occurring in the autonomic nervous system. Since this system produces and monitors emotion-related changes in the guts, for example, it seems that we are mapping its activity in feeling that our guts have run cold, or turned to water, or whatever. How such mappings work in detail we have yet to discover, but it seems reasonable to suppose that they underpin the metaphor.

As a first approximation, therefore, we can see the metaphor of the mind as a container as representing something inner by something inner: we can take the representation of the mind as an *inner space* as a primitive natural way of representing the working of the nervous system in the space *inside the body*. This seems to apply to the metaphoric picture generally, for the business of getting good (for us) things into the body and keeping bad (for us) things out of it is one of the basic things we think the brain and nervous system are designed to do, and this holds for animals of all kinds. This mode of representation, however, seems designed to work in the absence of explicit knowledge about its representational function. Hence the question whether we are dealing with a representation of the real space inside our bodies, or an alternative virtual space, will depend upon how we construe the representation in question.

13   Virtual inner space and the apparently non-physical features of consciousness

This approach enables us to use the account of metaphoric representation discussed above to explain the features of mind which we regard as problematic. Recall that in thinking of the mind as a container, it is essential that we not do so in too concrete a manner. For example if we think of anger as a hot fluid inside us, and so actually feel the anger in this way, we still do not think that if someone's anger *wells up*, *boils over*, or *spills out*, this anger will subsequently be found spattered on the carpet. To use the metaphor thus would clearly be to think of anger and its locus in too concrete a way, and most people automatically do not do so. Rather we subtly and systematically *de-concretize* and so *de-physicalize* both the space occupied by the anger-as-fluid and the metaphoric fluid itself.

This means that we tacitly treat the anger-space as a *non-physical space*, not to be confused with the actual internal space with which, nonetheless, it may phenomenologically overlap; and likewise we treat the anger-fluid as a *non-physical fluid*, not to be confused with physical things actually inside us. To say this, however, is to say that the anger-fluid and the anger-space are virtual entities, which we represent as differing from the real ones on which they are modelled. Still we can see that this representational de-physicalization actually involves nothing which is really non-physical. Rather it flows from the tacit imposition of the requirement of avoiding concrete thinking (something like the invariance principle) upon a mapping which has both physical sources (physical fluids and containers) and physical targets (changes inside the body involved in emotion). Since nothing which is both real and non-physical actually comes into question, we can say that the apparent non-physicality of the anger-space and fluid are a sort of cognitive illusion, engendered by this spatial mode of representing the inner. So it seems that the same process might likewise account for the apparent non-physicality of the inner space and contents involved in our everyday conception of the mind.

If this approach is correct, then it may be possible to see the features of experience which constitute the problem of consciousness as virtual properties, that is, as appearances engendered by our way of representing the neural events which realize experience. This would be a substantive account of the way our modes of presentation generate the problem of consciousness. On this account the problematic distinction between the inner and the outer would be a result of our representing experience as occurring in one or another kind of inner field or space – visual space, auditory space, the space in which we feel pain, etc. – where these were 'spaces' modelled on space as it appears to us in perception. (This is the role of the container metaphor.) This means, in effect, that we do not directly represent experiences as in the bodily space in which they actually are, but rather use an image derived from the perception of space outside the body, which is therefore liable to be understood as that of a distinct virtual space.

We can perhaps start to see this in the dualistic image of visual experience, as portrayed in Figure 2. In this case we seem to be representing neural events in the visual system by a straightforward mapping from outer to inner – a metaphoric internalization of the space and process of visual perception itself. It is as if in this way of thinking of experience the ordinary space in which we see things had simply been transposed inside (and hence stripped of its physical substance and made the object of a further special sense) so as to become the non-physical, quasi-spatial visual field, which we think of as somehow internal. So long as we think of the mapping in question as just a mode of representation of what is inside the body, it presents no difficulty; but if we construe it in terms of an alternative virtual space, we perforce feel that the entities and properties displayed in that space are not those of concrete physical things, and hence regard them as phenomenal. Again, if we represent something as phenomenal just insofar as we represent it as perceived within a virtual internal space, then there will be no more to phenomenal objects than is manifested in the space in which they appear, so that what is phenomenal will also be subjective. So this approach may also go some way towards explaining why we feel that the *esse* of phenomenal properties is their *percipi*, and why these properties seem, puzzlingly, both distinct and yet not distinct from our apprehension of them. And finally, since these virtual properties are represented as perceived within the space representing a single mind, they also seem private.

These remarks are of course only indications of an approach, and to be taken seriously the account hinted at here would require to be developed in greater detail.[11] Still they suggest that the kind of metaphorical or symbolic mapping studied in psychoanalysis or as conceptual metaphor may structure our thinking about the mind in the way Wittgenstein seems to have envisaged. In this respect the role of metaphoric/symbolic mapping may be deeper than the disciplines which explore it have so far hazarded.

Notes

1 For a recent discussion of this extension see Hopkins (1999a), the account of interpretation in which is related to Wittgenstein and Davidson in (1999b). A connected sketch of Freudian theory appears in (1999c). I am grateful to the British Academy for leave which facilitated the writing of these as well as the present article and (forthcoming) cited below.

2 For a recent discussion of symbolism see Petoćz (1999).

3 The account of this dream sketched here is discussed in Hopkins (1991) and argued more fully in Hopkins (1999a).

4 Freud also expressed this conception in regarding desires as underlain by drives which acquire new aims and objects; so we are considering a place at which a reconceived notion of desire starts to merge with the more explicitly theoretical notion of drive.

5 These are not the only points of connection, for analysts often interpret in accord with conceptual metaphors which are not directly bodily: Freud, for example, gives the instance of death as departure, discussed in Lakoff and Turner (1989), in his short chapter on symbolism in the *Introductory Lectures*, as well as emphazing the representation of the human body by a house, an instance of the container metaphor discussed below.

6 This example is from Frith (1989), as discussed in Goldman (1995).

7 It is worth noting that we also think of love and lust in a way connected with that which we apply to anger, for we speak of both in terms of heat and flame. Something may

kindle love, lust, or anger, and one may *smoulder, burn*, be *inflamed, on fire*, or *consumed* by them, and so on. (The notion of being *consumed* here is derived here from the conception of fire as a devourer, and so is doubly metaphorical.) We speak of the *flame* of love, and this as *burning brightly*, or dying, or now just glowing embers, or having gone out, or of love having turned to ashes, and so on. Someone whom one has previously loved is an *old flame*, and someone who continues in love which is not returned is *carrying a torch* for the other, that is, both *keeping the flame alight*, and openly displaying it. Here as elsewhere everyday expressions carry metaphorical meanings which are surprisingly detailed and exact.

8 The bodily ego is also discussed philsophically in Wollheim (1993), particularly in 'The Bodily Ego' and 'Psychology, Materialism, and Sexuality'.

9 The relevant claims by Bion are given a clear exposition and related to the work of Klein in Ch. 4 of Segal (1991). Kumin (1996) attempts to synthesize work by Kohut and Bion, including that on containment, with attachment theory.

10 For a discussion which bears out these points see Ch. 3 of Segal (1991). The treatment of the autistic child discussed on pp. 35ff illustrates how psychoanalytic therapy serves at a very basic level to facilitate the establishment of a representation of inner space, which apparently makes thinking of oneself as having a mind possible.

11 It is carried further in Hopkins (forthcoming), and also in 'Mind as Metaphor: A Physicalistic approach to the Problem of Consciousness', at the website of the Department of Philosophy, King's College, London, as follows:
(http: //www.kcl.ac.uk/kis/schools/hums/philosophy/staff/jimh.html).

References

Abraham, H.C. and Freud, E.L. (eds) (1965) *A Psycho-analytic Dialogue: The Letters of Sigmund Freud and Karl Abraham, 1907–1926*, London: Hogarth Press.

Baron-Cohen, S. (1995) *Mindblindness: An Essay on Autism and Theory of Mind*, Cambridge, MA, and London: MIT Press.

Baron-Cohen, S., Tager-Flusberg, D., Cohen, D. J., (1993) *Understanding Other Minds: The Perspective from Autism*, Oxford: Oxford University Press.

Bettleheim, B. (1959) 'Joey, a Mechanical Boy', *Scientific American*, March. Reprinted in R. C. Atkinson (ed.) *Contemporary Psychology*, San Francisco: Freeman, 1971.

—— (1967) *The Empty Fortress: Infantile Autism and the Birth of the Self*, New York: Collier Macmillian, Free Press.

Bion, W. (1967) 'A Theory of Thinking', in *Second Thoughts*, London: Heinemann.

—— (1977) *Seven Servants*, New York: Jason Aronson.

Freud, S. (1895) 'Draft H – Paranoia', *The Standard Edition of the Complete Works of Sigmund Freud*, ed. A. Strachey and A. Tyson, 24 vols, London: Hogarth Press, 1953–73, *S.E.* 1.

—— (1900) *The Interpretation of Dreams*, *S.E.* 4–5.

—— (1915) *Introductory Lectures on Psycho-Analysis*, *S.E.* 15.

—— (1923) *The Ego and the Id.*, *S.E.* 19.

—— (1925) 'On Negation', *S.E.* 19.

—— (1940) *An Outline of Psychoanalysis*, *S.E.* 23.

Frith, U. (1989) *Autism: Explaining the Enigma*, Oxford: Blackwell.

—— (1993) 'Autism', *Scientific American*, June.

Goldman, A. (1995) 'In Defense of the Simulation Theory', in M. Davis and T. Stone (eds), *Folk Psychology*, Oxford: Blackwell.

Hopkins, J. (1991) 'The Interpretation of Dreams', in J. Neu (ed.), *The Cambridge Companion to Freud*, Cambridge: Cambridge University Press.

—— (1999a) 'Patterns of Interpretation: Speech, Action, and Dream', forthcoming in L. Marcus (ed.), *Cultural Documents: The Interpretation of Dreams*, Manchester: Manchester University Press.

—— (1999b) 'Wittgenstein, Davidson, and Radical Interpretion', in F. Hahn, (ed.), *The Library of Living Philosophers: Donald Davidson* Carbondale: University of Southern Illinois Press.

—— (1999c) 'Freud and the Science of Mind', in G. Howie, (ed.), *The Edinburgh Encylopaedia of Continental Philosophy*, Edinburgh: Edinburgh University Press.

—— (forthcoming) 'Evolution, Consciousness, and the Internality of the Mind', in P. Carruthers (ed.), *Evolving the Mind*, Cambridge: Cambridge University Press.

James, W. (1890) *The Principles of Psychology*, New York.

Johnston, M. (1987) *The Body in the Mind: The Bodily Basis of Meaning, Reason and Imagination*. Chicago: University of Chicago Press.

Johnston, M. and Lakoff, G. (1980) *Metaphors We Live By*, Chicago: University of Chicago Press.

Klein, G. (1976) *Psychoanalytic Theory*, Chicago: International Universities Press.

Klein, M. (1975), *The Psycho-Analysis of Children*, London: Hogarth Press.

Kohut, H. (1977) *The Restoration of the Self*, Chicago: University of Chicago Press.

Kumin, I. (1996) *Pre-Object Relatedness*, New York: Guilford Press.

Kovecses, Z. (1990) *Emotion Concepts*, New York: Springer Verlag.

Lakoff, G. (1993) 'The Contemporary Theory of Metaphor', in A. Ortony (ed.), *Metaphor and Thought*, second edition, Cambridge: Cambridge University Press.

Lakoff, G. and Johnston, M. (1980) *Metaphors We Live By* Chicago: University of Chicago Press.

Lakoff, G. and Turner, M. (1989) *More Than Cool Reason: A Field Guide to Poetic Metaphor* Chicago: University of Chicago Press.

Metzinger, T. (1995) 'The Problem of Consciousness' in T. Metzinger (ed.), *Conscious Experience*, Paderborn: Schoningh/Imprint Academic.

Petoćz, A. (1999) *Freud, Psychoanalysis, and Symbolism*, Cambridge: Cambridge University Press.

Segal, H. (1950) 'Some Aspects of the Analysis of a Schizophrenic', *International Journal of Psycho-Analysis*, 38: 268–9. Reprinted in Segal (1981).

—— (1957) 'Notes on Symbol Formation', *International Journal of Psycho-Analysis*, 38: 391–7. Reprinted in Segal (1981).

—— (1978) 'On symbolism' *International Journal of Psycho-Analysis*, 59: 315–19. Reprinted in Segal (1997).

—— (1981) *The Work of Hanna Segal*, New York: Jason Aronson.

—— (1991) *Dream, Phantasy and Art*, London: Tavistock/Routledge.

—— (1997) *Psychoanalysis, Literature and War*, London and New York: Routledge.

Turner, M. (1987) *Death Is the Mother of Beauty: Mind, Metaphor, Criticism*, Chicago: University of Chicago Press, 1987.

—— (1991) *Reading Minds: The Study of English in the Age of Cognitive Science* Princeton: Princeton University Press.

Turner, M. and Lakoff, G. (1989) *More Than Cool Reason: A Field Guide to Poetic Metaphor*, Chicago: University of Chicago Press.

Wittgenstein, L. (1954) *Philosophical Investigations*, ed. and trans G.E.M. Anscombe, Oxford: Blackwell.

Wollheim, R. (1993) *The Mind and its Depths* Cambridge, MA: Harvard University Press.

2

HOW FAR DOWN DOES THE WILL GO?

Graeme Marshall

1 The problems Freud poses for philosophy

It is commonly believed, even by philosophers, that philosophy has never recovered from Freud. The strictures of philosophers of science aside, one reason is that the clinical data encountered by Freud and those who followed him appear to demand a theory of mental functioning that makes it both intentional and involuntary. It is mediated by belief and desire and so is rational enough to be intentional but it often appears to be not under our conscious control and so it seems involuntary. Contradictions lurk. This has long been recognized by many, Freud himself included. He says that philosophers 'could not conceive of such an absurdity as the "unconscious mental"', and adds that 'this idiosyncrasy of the philosophers could only be disregarded with a shrug'.[1]

But it is not so easy for philosophers to shrug off what looks like a tension in Freud's thought between his regarding the wish both as the unit of causal force and the unit of meaning.[2] Causes are not meaning-related to their effects: prolonged lack of rain does not mean the financial ruin it may cause, though it does mean drought. And there is the related apparent conflict between Freud's mechanistic and anthropological accounts of psychological phenomena, his metapsychology and his clinical theory. 'The clinical theory is concerned with actions rather than with bodily motions, with reasons and not mere causes, with intentionally characterised states rather than with the object-less states of physical science, with "experience-near" rather than "experience-distant" concepts, with empathetic understanding rather than ordinary explanation.'[3] These conflicts do nothing to dispel worries about theoretical incoherence.

A second reason for analytic philosophy's hesitations over Freud derives from Action Theory. If an intentional action necessarily occurs under a description, and if agents can come to see that the description they thought they were acting under is different from the description they now realize they were acting under, then it would appear that the intentionality of the original actions is impugned. For example, a student fails her degree because she thinks the work is too hard and she is not up to it. She comes to see that the very contrary is true and that really she did not want her certain success to alienate her mother. She gave up but not under the description she thought she was acting under. Or, in other examples, one may succeed in destroying others under the description of helping them but come to see what one's real intentions were all along. Such self-deception appears to require a theory that accommodates unconscious intentionality which again seems impossible. If actions are identified by the descriptions under which they are done, then different descriptions mean different actions. How can one's particular conceivings be causally effective for desired ends if they use the wrong concepts?

These problems have not been ignored but they have not often been allowed to modify the philosophical theories of mind, intentionality and action which have created them.[4] I want here to deal with the problems by locating them in those theories. I propose to make use of the distinction between acting which is never involuntary, and acting intentionally, a distinction which has its roots in our practical understanding of our own activity which itself has significant consequences for accepted theorizing about it. My argument is that there have occurred some serious conflations, particularly of the voluntary and the intentional. When acting is properly understood problems about unconscious intentionality do not arise. There is and must be acting which is not goal-directed and not totally desire-driven. So it is not to be construed on the model of intentional action which is goal-directed and desire-driven. The illusion of tension in Freud's thought is due to our past and present action-theoretic understanding of being active which is seriously deficient.

It is characteristic of the most creative minds to put such stress on certain of our ordinary concepts that they break apart into significant distinctions. Shakespeare is pre-eminent here – for example, in forcing the split between conscience and consciousness. Freud is another in forcing the split between being active and acting intentionally. The difference is that in his case there were already distinct concepts to use, though neither he nor any one else[5] seemed to realize it, despite his awareness of the ambiguity in the concept of the unconscious. Kant had given us those concepts, crucially of spontaneity and autonomy.[6] Freud was quite right to say that 'consciousness is the surface of the mental apparatus'.[7] He could also have made it plain that it is where, inter alia, the instinctual shows itself through the spontaneity of awareness and perception. He came close to saying this in his short piece on the Mystic Writing-Pad[8] where the traces of perceptions remain on the waxen block. My thought is that in his later work the dominance of desire gives way to the pre-eminence of concepts of perception and consequently makes central its kind of characteristic mental activity which is neither involuntary nor intentional.

Freud had always seen the significance of perception and did not change his mind about it. The system Pcpt.–Cs. – perception–consciousness – was early in place and remained theoretically intact. He said: 'We may regard this system, which is there [in *The Interpretation of Dreams*] called the Pcpt., as coinciding with the system Cs., on whose activity becoming conscious usually depends',[9] adding: 'The ego is especially under the influence of perception . . . perception may be said to have the same significance for the ego as instincts have for the id.'[10] Since it is not the instincts themselves but rather their mental representatives which are significant for the id, on this analogy it is the real perceptions, not just sensory irradiations, that are significant for the ego. Of course, 'the Cs. must have at its disposal a motor innervation which determines whether the perception can be made to disappear or whether it proves resistant'[11] but this is to be expected; perceptions, desires, interests and the rest are not merely atomistically related. What at any one time is perceptually salient occurs in the context of active desire and interest, and desire is kindled and interest quickened by what is noticed and realized. This is true of repression as well which Freud came to think of as a more immediate act under the pleasure principle.[12]

We shall return to Freud but we need to go by way of the surrounding hills.

2 Mental activity and Action Theory

Let us consider mental activity. First, there is much mental activity which is unquestionably activity but which is strikingly different from the overt physical activity which has been the concern of Action Theory. Clear examples are phenomena of attention such as recognizing, noticing, realizing and perceiving; making decisions, some acts of thinking; beginning and ending, affirming and denying, accepting and rejecting, assenting and dissenting. One feature these all share is that the acts in question have no course: they take no time but occur at a time; they are punctiform.

Often these acts are associated with more protracted activities such as looking, listening, savouring, touching and sniffing; other attentional activities such as paying attention and concentrating; tryings – trying to remember or solve a problem or make up one's mind; trains of thought, following an argument, reading silently, doing mental arithmetic, and so on. Mental activity of this kind can be brought within the scope of conventional Action Theory: it is intentional, it can be said to be caused by beliefs and desires and it is either successful or not depending on whether the results aimed for actually occur or not.

It would appear, however, that much of our punctiform mental activity cannot easily or perhaps at all be accommodated within Action Theory. It is neither intentional nor unintentional: one neither intentionally nor unintentionally notices, realizes or recognizes anything, or takes something as salient or comes to a decision. There is no description under which one perceives anything though there is when one has perceived it. One's intellectual discoveries are not caused as intentional actions are by one's beliefs and desires – if they were they would not be discoveries – for all that they may be just what one was hoping for and impossible for a creature which lacks beliefs and desires. And there is nothing further to notice when one notices or realizes or recognizes something; each is complete, though not necessarily right, in itself.

Second, the absence of features which are characteristic of the overt actions of

Action Theory may be taken to prove that the mental acts in question are not unquestionably acts at all but mere mental events. But that would be question-beggingly wrong. It is a mistake, commonly made, to think of one's activity in general and one's mental activity in particular as consisting of the occurrence of actions. That reduces activity ultimately to the occurrence of events, events of a particular kind to be sure, of the kind that is characteristically caused by beliefs and desires, but events nonetheless. Actions remain a subset of events. Our activity, however, is more than this. If it were not, it would be simply observable, as is any other causal relation between events, by both agents and spectators alike. In the case of agents, that is absurd, since to observe an act requires that the events constitutive of it exist to be observed. We should have to have acted already in order to know that we have.

Activity, as distinct from ordinary natural causality, has been misconceived and then dismissed by all those philosophers who seem in the end seduced by scientific monism. The early Freud was amongst them. This misunderstanding of activity is amazing. We know that we act and we know it, as has been said for centuries, without observation, research or conjecture.[13] We know that we act through non-representational awareness of it. That is what Hintikka called maker's knowledge. We move our bodies even if the rest is up to nature. But where is there room in current theory for our knowing we are moving our bodies? Davidson says[14] that bodily movements constitute an action only if there is a description of them under which the agent brought them about intentionally. That seems to make room for our activity. But he goes on to make our activity vanish into the mentalistic description of the relevant physical events which are their real causes. As Thomas Nagel says, 'action isn't anything else alone or in combination with a physical movement: not a sensation, not a feeling, not a belief, not an intention or desire. If we restrict our palette to such things plus physical events, agency will be omitted from our picture of the world'.[15]

The actions of Action Theory can be represented as ordered pairs of acts and intended results. The occurrence or otherwise of the results is known on the basis of observation. So it is not by its results that we know that we are being active. That applies to bodily movements as much as to other events. So it is our present activity. That can only be our present mental activity.

Third, it seems to follow that we should agree that there is after all something in William James's view that effort of attention is the essential phenomenon of will.[16] And it seems that we should further agree with Landry's patient who was asked to raise his arm when he had no sensory feedback at all from it. It did not in fact rise but the patient said he did what he normally did to raise it.[17]

But these look like objections. If the truth of an action claim depends partly on the occurrence of the events constitutive of the action in question, and those events do not occur, as in the case of Landry's patient, and the possibility is in any case, then James or the patient or we cannot know that something is an act of ours merely because we know we are mentally active in familiar ways, merely because we know we are makers.

That is true when we are talking of the occurrence of acts or actions but not when we are talking of being active: the truth conditions for activity claims and action claims are different. I can see no satisfactory alternative to saying that it can be true that we are acting while false that an action has occurred. Indeed it would seem that for any intended result, we could fail to achieve it, though if that happened every time we should seriously wonder about our own agency.

The argument has been that there is mental activity and without it actions would not be actions. It cannot be reduced to what can only be observed so it is not wholly constituted by the occurrence of actions, or of mental events, let alone the physical events action theorists have so often had final recourse to.

3 Primitive mental acts: Kant on spontaneity

Our primary mental activity is what Kant called the spontaneity of the mind and it is entirely voluntary, of our own accord, in accordance with our will, but not premeditated. Discussion of Kant's treatment of the will is usually confined to what he has to say about autonomy but this is a serious shortcoming and Susan Hurley, amongst others, is to be commended for objecting to this.[18] It should include spontaneity as well. Spontaneity is Kant's term for our synthesizing the sensory manifold. Kant thinks it is a mistake to hold that the senses themselves combine impressions. We only get what we take. Our spontaneous activity is a condition for the intelligibility of our passivity and for our even having a sensory manifold at all. Perception involves the active faculty of synthesis.[19] The manifold must be 'run through and held together', representations must be 'connected' and if 'representations produced one another in any order, just as they happened to come together, this would not lead to any determinate connection of them but only to accidental collocations'; we should never find order and regularity in appearances 'had we not ourselves, or the nature of our mind, originally set them there'.

Note what he does not say. He does not say that impressions are first given and only then run through and held together or synthesized. Bennett makes this point and says of Kemp Smith's translation of B136 in the *Critique of Pure Reason* that the 'vital word "first" which commits Kant so explicitly to the view that transcendental synthesis is an act which predates what it produces, has no warrant in the German'.[20] And it does not. Spontaneity and receptivity together are constitutive of intelligible experience. One might say, adapting Kant's own famous remark,[21] that spontaneity without receptivity is empty and receptivity without spontaneity is blind.

Spontaneity and autonomy must not be confused. Regrettably, Hurley ends by confusing them. She regards spontaneous acts as intentional which she then understands in Davidsonian terms and so wrongly accuses Kant of the myth of the Giving.[22] She wrongly assumes that there is a description under which we act spontaneously. This is the source of all error about this subject. It ignores, besides, the distinct ways of identifying spontaneous and intentional acts. Our voluntary autonomous or intentional acts are standardly identified through their causes in our beliefs and desires as Davidson and the tradition agree; but voluntary spontaneous acts are identified by their contemporaneous effects in synthesis.

Autonomy concerns self-determination, hence rational causality and freedom from determination by past events. Spontaneity and autonomy are clearly related though distinct. Spontaneity is necessary for both perception and overt action and so is an element in both, though is not exhaustive of them. Sensory receptivity needs to be added in perception and desire or interest in action. So spontaneity is a necessary condition for perception while autonomy is not, and it is one of the necessary conditions for action as well: as Kant says action requires that one collect oneself. Both spontaneity and autonomy depend on our possession and use of reason but the use is different. Our autonomy rests on our ability to do what we have come to think we ought to do, as we conceive it in a moral or any other practical sense, and there are no oughts in nature. Hence the connection between being autonomous and non-natural, rational causality which involves practical reasoning. Spontaneity also involves the use of reason but not construed as practical reasoning. It is rather reason as the unconditioned condition for the use of the concepts of the understanding. Spontaneity transcends anything with which sensibility can provide it. It does not spring from our having reasons or reasoning. It is presupposed by reasoning.

4 Kant illuminated by Wittgenstein on 'seeing-as'

Kant might seem forbiddingly obscure but Wittgenstein makes the same concerns plainer and more familiar in his discussion of perception in general and seeing-as in particular. He thought that if one could resolve philosophical problems about perception one could solve problems of action as well. His insight was that perception itself is active.[23] There are the usual experiences of seeing and otherwise sensing, suggestive of our passively receiving impressions of the world, but there are also experiences of sensing-as, seeing-as: one can see two faces as alike, Jastrow's duck–rabbit drawing as a duck or as a rabbit, a triangle as hanging from its apex or sitting on its base, a curved line as convex or concave, a gesture as threatening, a smile as false, an object as beautiful, and just about anything as something else again.[24] Indeed, characteristically perceiving is perceiving-as. This can be described as aspectual perception.

The issue Wittgenstein returns to most persistently in his consideration of perceiving an aspect is whether it is seeing or interpreting, though 'interpreting' may be too misleading a term to capture what is so intrinsic to the experience.[25] His fundamental thought seems to be that the use of the words that give the interpretation is the primary expression of the experience. It is not an indirect expression which it would be if it were an interpretation as ordinarily understood. If it were only an indirect expression – in Wittgenstein's example 'the colour of blood' is an indirect description of a colour – it should be possible to describe the experience directly, but this is not possible. 'The description using the terms of the interpretation is essential to the description of the experience of seeing in accordance with that interpretation.'[26] Wittgenstein says that the inclination to use the verbal expression is a characteristic utterance (*Äußerung*) of the experience. It is our response to the experience and shows how it speaks to us and through us. That is, we are not entirely passive in perception. In ways that cannot be crystalized out, we are active in interpretation of and response to what we perceive.

Wittgenstein adds that what we perceive in perceiving an object under a certain aspect is not a property of it. It is rather an internal relation between it and other objects. In his example it is like realizing that something one is listening to is a variation on a theme.[27] The variation is internally related to the theme and we can be described as hearing the relations between them.

Internal relations abound. An internal relation is partly constitutive of its terms – they would not exist unless they were related in the way they are. In one pertinent strand of his 'Transcendental Deduction' in the *Critique of Pure Reason* Kant argues that all our experience is in time but we would not understand any particular experience unless each item in that experience satisfied the conditions under which we could identify it as the same as or different from any other item. Mere temporal difference is not enough without presupposing something nontemporal to give us a fix on the temporal item in question. So the intelligibility of our experience requires at least that each item brings its nontemporal differences and similarities with it. That is, it comes as internally related to something else. Wittgenstein could have said that these internal relations are what are shown when we perceive something.

What this comes to, most minimally, is that all perception involves recognition. Perception comes in a package in which there is no first item of knowledge. We do not arbitrarily synthesize the manifold and our basic mental activity does not occur in a vacuum. More needs to be said on this, but the point now is that if we generalize that conclusion to all thought we have Kant's conception of the spontaneity of the mind. The only mental events there are, are those which are partly constituted by our recognition of them and their realized internal relations to other mental acts and events.

Why not generalize the perception result? There could be difficulties with sensations – of pain, heat, smoothness, and the like. Does sensing-as make sense? I should say so, because pain may be nothing more than painful sensations of, for instance, heat, that is heat taken as painful. What of a sensation of heat itself? There is a general argument relevant here. As Wittgenstein said, we learnt the concept pain (and heat and smoothness, etc.) when we learnt the language. Having that language we do not know what our sensations would be without it. We would not know what it would be to have sensations that we do not take as sensations of heat, pain, smoothness and so on. That is not to say that biological responses to sensations unmediated by concepts do not occur. There are startle responses, for example, some cases of shock, twitches and spasms, which do not seem to be mediated by concepts. They can be caused by anything and do not even require that we be awake in some cases; we can be startled awake.

42

Forgetting, except where it is pathological and voluntary, might seem to be a problem since that is absence rather than presence of mind. But just as death is not an event in life, so non-pathological forgetting is not an event in the life of the mind. Here we reach the usable limits of the concept of consciousness, as we shall see in the next section when we begin our descent to Freud.

5 'The will goes all the way down' explained

If at its most minimal all perception and thought involves recognition, the question is whether recognition involves the will. Only if it does, can it be said that the will goes all the way down and that Freud's conflicts vanish. Now recognition like the other basic phenomena of attention such as noticing and realizing, is at first sight not voluntary: it happens or it doesn't. Yet it remains the clearest instance of mental activity. If we could not do anything with what we recognize, we would have recognized nothing. Recognition is being in a position to do more. What we recognize is, as it were, where we have been and where we can further go. The flash or dawning of recognition is getting the internal relations, making the connections, to some degree placing the object recognized. When the will is paralysed through impossible obscurity or ignorance, we recognize nothing.

The claim that the will goes all the way down requires further explanation, however. First, we cannot dispense with the threefold distinction between spontaneity, intentionality and the voluntary. The voluntary embraces both spontaneity and intentionality. Intentionality is shown, inter alia, in premeditated actions caused partly by agents' conception of them which includes how they think they are related to their other beliefs and desires. This is not true of spontaneity which is shown principally in punctiform acts of synthesis and recognition. The present object of my spontaneous attention is, say, the tree I recognize outside my window. My present intentional activity is the visual exploration of the patterns of sunlight on the leaves: that is the description under which I am now sensorially engaged with this part of the world. My voluntary powers are exercised in both spontaneous and intentional ways because I am, like us all, alert to similarities and differences and mostly in control of my attention. Without the concept of the voluntary we could not speak of acting. Without the concept of spontaneity we could not speak of noticing, realizing, or recognizing anything. Without the concept of the intentional we could not speak of plans, purposes, or policies. We need all three concepts.

Second, something is an object of spontaneous attention only if it is a possible object of intentional attention, or: one can think x only if it is possible to think about x. This is what Kant meant when he said 'it must be possible for the "I think" to accompany all my representations; for otherwise something would be represented in me which could not be thought at all, and that is equivalent to saying that the representation would be impossible, or at least would be nothing to me.'[28] Wittgenstein lends support, as we have seen, to my acceptance of Kant's argument. The alternative is the absurdity that there would be some information we would have that would tell us nothing, including the fact that it was information.

Third, to say that the will goes all the way down is to say that all objects of spontaneous attention are open to a range of intentional acts describable as thinking about them either individually or in relation. This applies to all contents of consciousness, including so-called unconscious contents. Nothing could be a content of consciousness without being an object of at least possible attention and nothing could be an object of attention without being an actual content of consciousness.

So, fourth, contents of consciousness are such that a certain possibility is partly constitutive of the actual existence of the phenomena in question. This might be taken to mean that the possibility is already actualized, or that Proust's thought, for example, 'Let me not think of her!' already involves his actually thinking about her. Well, it may, but not as a matter of logic. We need not always know how to think about things further. All we need is the point that the objects of our attention are such that they can always be thought about further and it is that thought which is always part of our thinking them or thinking about them.

This constitutive possibility is not simply that p entails possibly p, for that is not puzzling at all. Nor is it a matter of a teleological characterization of a developing thing: for example, this is an acorn only if it is a possible future oak tree. While it is true that an acorn is now a possible future oak tree, whether or not something is a content of consciousness does not at all seem to depend upon its actually undergoing some further process of change, only that it can be the possible object of further conscious thought. The contention here is more like the claim that an action is rational insofar as it can be changed by adducing some logically relevant considerations. This is so because it is already determined by other such considerations taken so far to be good enough. Critical reflection on a piece of reasoning is just more, though doubtless different, reasoning.

It is important to observe here that it does not follow that in thinking x and thinking about x we must be aware of what we are doing. We might be so absorbed that we are not even aware that we are doing it – reading a particularly exciting book for example. Consciousness as a category of acts, states and events may include phenomenal awareness of them and must at least be such that some phenomenal awareness of them is possible – the basic insight of positivism – otherwise they would actually be nothing to us. An act, process, or object is a content of consciousness if and only if the subject in question thinks it, whether he or she is aware of it or not. Awareness is perhaps well-enough determined by the old test for intentionality of being able, when interrupted in an activity, to answer the question 'What are you doing?' without observation, research, or conjecture; especially if, after the reply, the rejoinder 'Yes, but what are you really doing?' can be met with a further answer.

It does, however, seem to follow that one and the same act can be voluntary insofar as it is spontaneous but involuntary insofar as its object resists any intentional attempts to replace it. For example, you may find that you cannot get a certain tune out of your head. You recognize all too clearly the tune in question but something resists the desire to remove it. So it might be said that your continued attention to it is involuntary even though its being an object of attention at all entails the possibility of further intentional attention.[29] But there is no inconsistency here. The will is often partially frustrated as it is when, for example, we cannot remember a name, try though we might. No voluntary act guarantees its result. The point is important, however, for showing how ingrained is the identification of the voluntary and the intentional, and the involuntary and the non-intentional, with spontaneity nowhere.

What this comes to is that we can say that the will goes all the way down provided that we confine ourselves to what is thought and hence what can be thought about. We are active in spontaneously thinking and in thinking about something. Both are within the compass of the will. The whole of our mental life depends upon it. We dream our dreams, invent our fantasies, repress what is too hot to handle, recognize danger when we see it, regress, and mount our defences. Kant would not have disagreed with Freud here. Their radical move, like Wittgenstein's later, was to push activity beyond the dichotomy with passivity. It embraces passivity.

6 Freud vindicated if Action Theory is modified

This both makes good sense of Freud and shows how his work can properly modify philosophical theory. His data require a person's spontaneous acknowledgement of them and the real constitutive possibility of intentional work for their existence. It is because the possibility of thinking about x is recognized and so often feared or wished for that a phenomenon has the force it has. But this requires a philosophical Action Theory which accommodates voluntary but not intentional punctiform mental activity in general, and spontaneity in particular.

It is essential in this context to remember that thinking x and thinking about x can be either primary processes or secondary processes; either, that is, thinking which is largely governed by similarity, or the more developed sort that involves progressively sophisticated differentiation as well. Freud's linking of the unconscious with the primary process thought of the id is entirely consistent with this construal. That it is thought, not the mode of thought, is what counts. Repression may be initially the consequence of primitive strategic secondary process thought, in which case it is briefly intentional, or it may be a more immediate – spontaneous – act under the pleasure principle as I think Freud came to believe. Primary-process thought is the usual way of dealing with material when repressed and explains its continued unconscious causal efficacy in condensation, projection, sublimation, foreclosure, and denial: similarity is what counts. Such causal efficacy, however, requires spontaneous recognitional activity. Repression, that is, is more like Wittgensteinian perception-as against a background of desire than an intentional strategy. Something similar, I believe, can be argued in connection with so-called self-deception.

The internal relations recognition brings resist reduction to talk of energy cathexes; to that extent Freud's metapsychology is hopeless and he was right to reject the Project ('Project for a Scientific Psychology' [1895]). There can be nothing unconscious which cannot possibly not be so. On this turns, incidentally, the objective viability of clinical evidence in psychoanalytic work as properly scientific – hypotheses do not remain untestable. Unconscious motivation must be in principle dynamically recoverable though it may never in fact in the course of a life be so recovered.

Morris Eagle[30] reminds us that 'rendering a mental content unconscious is only one possible means (albeit the most frequently employed means) of rejecting and disowning an unacceptable mental content'. In the present context, however, what we should focus upon is our spontaneity in the acts of rejecting and disowning the impersonal and the alien. This fits well with our taking owning as already central to our ordinary practices concerning responsibility for affects and responses. Accepting responsibility is being prepared to own them and refusing to do so is actually disowning them. But what is owned and disowned is at least recognized; taking something to be impersonal or alien would be inexplicable otherwise. Our spontaneity is where we begin and end.

A paradox may loom here since each of us is a case of what Davidson calls the paradox of irrationality in general: 'if we explain it too well, we turn it into a concealed form of rationality; while if we assign incoherence too glibly, we merely compromise our ability to diagnose irrationality by withdrawing the background of rationality needed to justify any diagnosis at all'.[31] Unconscious phenomena and functioning may be possibly conscious and such that we can become aware of them, but we must be on our conceptual guard against failing to accommodate our actual unawareness of much of the unconscious and the necessity of working through the phenomena. What needs to be insisted upon is that if anyone were to use the concept of the unconscious without the implications about thinking here discussed they would have to show how talk of unconscious contents necessary for psychoanalytic theory and practice makes sense.

The argument, then, is that Freud's tensions vanish when we see that unconscious functioning like conscious functioning need not be directly intentional but is at least spontaneous and so voluntary. The will goes all the way down and intentionality does not, though the possibility of it does. Freud's defences are not goal-directed strategies so much as spontaneous responses to recognized objects with threatening and possibly alien internal relations – under the pleasure principle. There is no need for the dubious concept of unconscious intentionality because its work is better done by the concept of possibly unconscious spontaneous thought as here described. There is still the need for 'motor innervation' but it is recognition which triggers it. No question arises about the differing descriptions under which that triggering and its consequences occur since there are none.[32]

So Freud is restored to us, not isolated as before we worried about unconscious intentionality, not in a box as when that conceptualization mastered us, but in a spontaneous chorus.[33]

Notes

1 *An Autobiographical Study*, 1925, *S.E.*, 20, p. 31.
2 See, for example, Yankelovich and Barrett (1971).
3 Michael Moore, 'Mind, Brain, and Unconscious', in Clarke and Wright (eds) (1988).
4 These matters were under discussion in the 1940s and 50s by philosophers such as Stephen Toulmin, Antony Flew, Richard Peters, Gilbert Ryle and Alastair MacIntyre. The emerging view seemed to be that much of Freud could be accommodated if only the right distinctions were made. However, the suspicion of central conceptual confusion remained, sufficient not for dismissing him outright but for putting him with some nagging doubts largely aside. See, for example, Margaret MacDonald (1954), ch. 6.
5 Hegel at least is an exception but he subjected them to too much theory. See, for example, Charles Taylor (1985), *Philosophical Papers*, vol. I, ch. 3.
6 See section 3.
7 *The Ego and the Id*, 1923, *S.E.*. 19, p. 19.
8 1925, *S.E.* 19, p. 227.
9 'The Metapsychology of Dreams', 1917, *S.E.* 14, p. 232.
10 *The Ego and the Id S.E.* 19, p. 40.
11 'The Metapsychology of Dreams', p. 233.
12 See, for example, *Inhibitions, Symptoms and Anxiety*, 1926, *S.E.* 20, pp. 163–8.
13 Aquinas writes that 'our intellect knows itself not by its own essence but by means of its activity' and adds that for this kind of knowledge the very presence of mind is sufficient (*Summa Theologiae*, Ia, q87, a1; quoted in Haldane, Clarke and Wright (1988), p. 137.
14 *Essays On Actions and Events* (1980).
15 *View from Nowhere*,p. 111.
16 *Psychology: Briefer Course* (1962), p. 446.
17 The case is discussed for example by Jennifer Hornsby (1980), pp. 40ff.
18 Hurley (1994).
19 *Critique of Pure Reason*, especially B130–40.
20 Bennett (1966), p. 112.
21 *Critique of Pure Reason*, A51/B75.
22 Hurley (1994) p. 160.
23 A.C. Jackson, personal communication. See also his notes in *Wittgenstein's Lectures on Philosophical Psychology 1946–47*, ed. P.T. Geach (1988).
24 See Wittgenstein, *Philosophical Investigations*, (1953), pt II, sect. xi.
25 See Budd (1989), pp. 90–1.
26 Ibid., p. 93.
27 Wittgenstein (1953), p. 213.
28 *Critique of Pure Reason*, B131–2.
29 I am indebted to Behan McCullugh and John Campbell at the La Trobe seminar for this point.
30 'Psychoanalysis and the Personal', in Clarke and Wright (1988), p. 94.
31 'Paradoxes of Irrationality', in Wollheim and Hopkins (1982), p. 303.
32 I am particularly indebted to Paolo Baracchi, Paul Fahey, Tamas Pataki, Yasmin Mahdi and Adrian L'Armand for discussion of these matters.
33 With apologies to John Wisdom in the concluding sentence of his memorable 'Philosophy, Anxiety and Novelty', in *Philosophy and Psychoanalysis* (1953).

References

Ameriks, Karl (1982) *Kant's Theory of Mind*, Oxford: Clarendon Press.

Bennett, Jonathan (1966) *Kant's Analytic*, Cambridge: Cambridge University Press.

Budd, Malcolm (1989) *Wittgenstein's Philosophy of Psychology*, London: Routledge.

Clarke, Peter and Wright, Crispin (eds) (1988) *Mind, Psychoanalysis and Science*, Oxford: Blackwell.

Davidson, Donald (1980) *Essays on Actions and Events*, New York: Oxford University Press, 1980.

Freud, Sigmund (1953–73) *The Standard Edition of the Complete Psychological Works*, ed. and trans. James Strachey, 24 vols, London: Hogarth Press.

Gardner, Sebastian (1993) *Irrationality and the Philosophy of Psychoanalysis*, New York: Cambridge University Press.

Geach, P.T. (ed.) (1988) *Wittgenstein's Lectures on Philosophical Psychology 1946–47*, Brighton: Harvester Wheatsheaf.

Hornsby, Jennifer (1980) *Actions*, London: Routledge and Kegan Paul.

Hurley, Susan (1994) 'Kant on Spontaneity and the Myth of the Giving', *Proceedings of the Aristotlelian Society*, vol 94, pt 2.

James, William (1962) *Psychology: Briefer Course*, New York: Collier.

Kant, Immanuel (1963) *Critique of Pure Reason*, trans. Norman Kemp Smith, London: Macmillan.

Kohut, Heinz (1977) *The Restoration of the Self*, New York: International Universities Press.

MacDonald, Margaret (ed.) (1954) *Philosophy and Analysis*, Oxford: Blackwell.

MacIntyre, A.C. (1958) *The Unconscious*, London: Routledge and Kegan Paul.

Nagel, Thomas (1986) *View from Nowhere*, Oxford: Oxford University Press.

O'Shaughnessy, Brian (1980) *The Will*, 2 vols, Cambridge: Cambridge University Press.

Pippin, Robert (1987) 'Kant on the Spontaneity of Mind', *Canadian Journal of Philosophy*, 17, 2, June.

Rieff, Philip (1961) *Freud: The Mind of the Moralist*, New York: Anchor Books.

Taylor, Charles (1985) *Philosophical Papers*, 2 vols, Cambridge: Cambridge University Press.

Wisdom, John (1953) *Philosophy and Psychoanalysis*, Oxford: Blackwell.

Wittgenstein, Ludwig (1953) *Philosophical Investigations*, trans. by G.E.M. Anscombe, Oxford: Blackwell.

Wollheim, Richard and Hopkins, James (eds) (1982) *Philosophical Essays on Freud* Cambridge: Cambridge University Press.

Wollheim, Richard (1991) *Freud*, 2nd edition, London: Fontana.

Yankelovich, Daniel and Barrett, William (1971) *Ego and Instinct*, New York: Vintage Books.

3

FREUDIAN WISH-FULFILMENT AND SUB-INTENTIONAL EXPLANATION

Tamas Pataki

1

Some desires are impossible, and some very difficult, to satisfy. When the owner of some such desire realizes either circumstance, then the desire may be relinquished altogether or replaced by a wish. William James said: 'If with the desire there goes a sense that attainment is not possible, we simply *wish*, but if we believe the end is in our power we *will*' (James 1950 [1890], II: 486). Thus, one cannot knowingly desire to undo the past, but wishing that one had been born into wealth or gone to a better school is not uncommon. Although the concept of wishing overlaps those of wanting and desiring (and yearning and longing), wishing, by and large, does not prompt to action in the way that most of the other orectic dispositions do; rather, in its *conceptually distinctive* uses the wish-locution presupposes an acknowledgement that action is impossible, or close to being so: it indicates a velleity which is a mere expression of preference. 'How I wish I could have been there' or, even, 'I do wish I could go', do not place me in causal relation to action but instead tell, indirectly, of my preferences.

The distinction between wish and desire is not sharp, and the German *Wunsch* has a stronger affiliation with action than our 'wish' does,[1] but it is worth keeping in sight for it points to an important feature of Freud's perspective. Freud frequently notices the difficulty we have of relinquishing desires and routes to satisfactions once enjoyed.[2] Repressed wishes, in particular, remain, Titan-like, 'ever on the alert and, so to say, immortal' waiting for opportunity to convulse their limbs (Freud 1900a: 553; 1937) The declension of desire into wishing does not end the tyranny of ineluctable desire. We are creatures of such intense strife and striving that even confrontation with impossibility will not still us. There are a number of important ways, which Freud explores under the concepts of *wish-fulfilment* and *substitutive satisfaction*, in which the mind provides an uneasy accommodation to this tyranny. In Freud's view, dreams, neurotic symptoms, daydreams, phantasy of various kinds, magical thinking, some kinds of joke, much art, parapraxes like slips of the tongue or bungled actions, hallucinations, delusions and illusions like religion are the results of processes which operate to satisfy or allay desire with the various modes of wish-fulfilment. When the usual route to satisfaction is unavailable to desire because, for example, one is immobilized in sleep or yearning for the impossible, wish-fulfilment may be available in default. If prevented from directly transforming the world to fit our desires, then sometimes we can bring about transformations in ourselves – symptoms, self-deceptions, consoling phantasies – which, in one way or another, substitute for the real objects of those desires and provide, in Freud's significant phrase, substitutive satisfactions. So, in dreams the blind see; in phantasy we merge with longed-for but unattainable objects; in hysterical symptoms achieve perverse sexual gratifications; and in religion retrieve the security once provided by seemingly omnipotent parents. From one useful metapsychological perspective (Hartmann 1958 [1939]) wish-fulfilment can be considered a form of adaptation: one in which, roughly speaking, autoplastic action (changing one's self) substitutes for alloplastic action (changing one's environment).[3]

Now how are we to understand these singular modes of satisfying wish or desire? Apart from Freud, psychoanalysts have not, by and large, given much *critical* attention to wish-fulfilment, generally regarding it as transparent, or at least as transparent enough for clinical work.[4] But recently there has been a good deal of penetrating study by philosophers. Most of this study has focused on the paradigms of dreaming and infantile hallucinatory satisfaction, less so on symptom formation, and hardly at all on their Freudian congeners listed above. Unsurprisingly, these accounts provide models of wish-fulfilment based on Intentional (the capital 'I' will mark that sense of 'intention' we owe to Brentano, and the idiom characterized as 'common-sense' or 'folk-psychology') but non-rational causation: on wishful imagining, expressive or, in a wide sense, sub-intentional action (Wollheim 1979, 1984, 1991 [1971]; Hopkins 1982, 1988, 1995; Grünbaum 1984; Moore 1984; Eagle 1984; Johnston 1988; Lear 1990; Gardner 1993; Cavell 1993;). Here I use 'sub-intentional action' in a broader way than is used in O'Shaughnessy's (1980) original formulation, to compass all those acts, including mental acts, which are caused by wish or desire without facilitation by instrumental beliefs or anything else. On this use 'sub-intentional' refers to action which has teleology but is caused non-rationally i.e. is not performed for a reason, standardly understood as a belief–desire pair. It is to be distinguished from the kind of expressive behaviour which has an archaeology, as when I clench my fists in (out of) anguish, and from the processes Wollheim (1984: 59ff) designates 'mental activity', which arise from the conjunction of desire and what he calls (unfelicitously) 'instinct', and from other forms of Intentionally but non-rationally caused action which do not involve desire and cannot be conceived as expressive. However, for ease of exposition I will generally refer to all these types as being *broadly* sub-intentional.

Now, although not even the authors listed above would assent to all its proposed features, a *broadly sub-intentional approach* to the clinical domain of psychoanalysis and related or overlapping phenomena like self-deception and akrasia can be characterized as follows: (i) most of these phenomena require for their explanation an Intentional theory which goes beyond the resources of ordinary or common-sense psychology; (ii) the deepest such theory we have is psychoanalytic; (iii) psychoanalytic theory, at least in significant part, extends the patterns of explanation found in common-sense psychology; (iv) psychoanalytic theory's claim to explanatory rectitude depends, at least in significant part, on the validity of that extension; and (v) the pattern of explanation typical of, or predominant in, psychoanalysis is broadly that of sub-intentional causation. (These points have been most cogently argued by Wollheim and Hopkins.)

With propositions (i) to (iv) this essay has no quarrel. However, the *scope* of sub-intentional activity, it will be argued here, is far more modest than that represented in (v) and (it will also be argued) the attempt to press many paradigmatic kinds of so-called psychoanalytic phenomena into the mould of sub-intentional explanation has resulted in significant error and misunderstanding. The Will, as sub-intentional operation of desire, expression, spontaneity, does indeed go deep; but the Will as practical reason, as unconscious deliberation and intention, or as something very like them, also goes deep, in ways that sub-intentionalists have been disposed to deny. In particular, by failing to recognize the unconscious intentionality or strategy involved in certain kinds of wish-fulfilling processes, sub-intentionalists have neglected important aspects of the self's activity, especially those adaptive, self-solicitous strategies in which the self in caring, or in hatred, takes itself as its own object. This latter theme casts a shadow over much that follows, but my principal aims here are less constructive than critical. I want to show that a number of recent, important sub-intentional accounts of wish-fulfilment are inadequate to the clinical phenomena which are the touchstones of adequacy. And since I believe that Freud's views have been more or less distorted in the service of these particular philosophical accounts, a second, complementary aim will be to clarify these views, and to use them in pursuit of the first, controversial end.

2

Here is the passage from which much of the philosophical discussion proceeds.

> A hungry baby screams or kicks helplessly . . . A change can only come about if in some way or other (in the case of the baby, through outside help) an 'experience of satisfaction' can be achieved which puts an end to the internal stimulus. An essential component of this experience of satisfaction is a particular perception (that of nourishment, in our example) the mnemic image of which remains associated thence forward with the memory trace of the excitation produced by the need. As a result of the link that has thus been established, next time this need arises a psychical impulse will at once emerge which will seek to re-cathect the

mnemic image of the perception and to re-evoke the perception itself, that is to say, to re-establish the situation of the original satisfaction. An impulse of this kind is what we call a wish; the re-appearance of the perception is the fulfilment of the wish; and the shortest path to the fulfilment of the wish is a path leading direct from the excitation produced by the need to a complete cathexis of the perception. Nothing prevents us from assuming that there was a primitive state of the psychical apparatus in which this path was actually traversed, that is, in which wishing ended in hallucinating. Thus, the aim of the first psychical activity was to produce a 'perceptual identity' – a repetition of the perception which was linked with the satisfaction of the need.

(Freud 1900a: 565–6)

How does wishing end in hallucinating? Only *one* part of the story is provided here: when a wishful impulse's immediate access to mobility or to consciousness is blocked, as it is in the helpless hungry infant and the sleeper, a topographical regression to the perceptual system of the psychic apparatus ensues, and a re-activation of a memory of satisfaction as a hallucinatory experience provides a wish-fulfilling 'perceptual identity' with the original satisfaction.[5] But, as Freud elsewhere emphasises, hallucination cannot consist merely in the regressive reactivation of memories or sensory images: hallucination 'brings belief in reality with it' (1917d: 230). Dreams, for example, which are hallucinatory and which (at least in Freud's early writings) share the basic structure of infantile hallucinatory wish-fulfilment, are not just thoughts or sensory images, 'their ideational content being transformed from thoughts into sensory images, *to which belief is attached* and which appear to be experienced' (Freud 1900a: 535; 50; my italics).

If the secret of hallucination is nothing else than that of regression, every regression of sufficient intensity would produce hallucination with belief in its reality. But we are quite familiar with situations in which a process of regressive reflection brings to consciousness very clear mnemic images, though we do not on that account for a single moment take them for real perceptions. Again, we could well imagine the dream-work penetrating to mnemic images of this kind, making conscious to us what was previously unconscious, and holding up to us a wishful phantasy which rouses our longing, but which we should not regard as a real fulfilment of the wish.

(Freud 1917d: 231)

It is *belief* which converts the wishful phantasy which pictures fulfilment into the 'real fulfilment of the wish'. And how does belief do that? Here Freud harks back to an old tradition: when an idea isn't contradicted, it's accepted (1900a: 50–2, 535; 1917d).[6] When nothing in the mind 'contradicts' or contrasts with a particular idea or perception, because all incompatible ideas or perceptions have been excluded or decathected, 'reality testing' is inoperative, and the idea or perception is 'believed'. This is the condition of the neonate, Freud supposes, and of the dreamer.

> The state of sleep does not wish to know anything of the external world; it takes no interest in reality ... Hence it withdraws cathexis from the system Cs. as well as the other systems, the Pcs. and the Ucs., in so far as the cathexis in them obey the wish to sleep. With the system Cs. thus uncathected, the possibility of reality testing is abandoned; and the excitations which independently of the state of sleep, have entered on the path of regression will find the path clear as far as the system Cs. where they will count as undisputed reality.
>
> (Freud 1917d: 234)

Freud's metapsychological description can be recast cogently without the quasi-mechanistic underpinning. The process could be viewed like this. It is a truth about desire that it tends to express itself in action or in the generation of mental states and dispositions. We are familiar with the way in which it stimulates imagination and generates phenomenal content. As Freud put it: 'every desire takes before long the form of picturing its own fulfilment' (1916–17: 372). This statement is too strong, but it is not far from the truth, and in the infant mind with its lack of Intentional differentiation, its intermittent incapacity to distinguish perceptions from internally generated experiences like dream or phantasy and (what may in part underlie the latter condition) its propensity to be engrossed (Wollheim 1979: 53), it may be very close to the truth. When the wish has brought about the representation of the conditions which would satisfy it, the first step towards perceptual identity is achieved. When, in addition, there is a poverty of engagement with the external world and with sections of the internal world, as in neonatal states, sleep or psychosis (Freud 1924b, 1924e), or when the sheer intensity of an idea captures the mind as in engrossment of various sorts, the process of achieving perceptual identity is completed. In these conditions wishful representations brook no contradiction and succeed in presenting themselves as the irrecusable 'evidence' on which critical occurrent beliefs are based: the infant acquires a belief to the effect (roughly, in oratio obliqua) that what was wished has come to pass.[7] That there are mental states in which a heightened degree of engrossment in events, internal and external, succeeds in excluding not only the contingently incompatible like disturbing noises but also incompatible beliefs, and that these states can generate transient, wish-fulfilling beliefs, even such as are otherwise known to be counterfactual, are undeniable facts about us. (Consider the easily accessible experience that we can enjoy a sexual phantasy or compensatory daydream of which we, ourselves, are the authors. Engrossment in the phantasy deprives us of the occurrent knowledge of our authorship. It is an ephemeral deprivation but it is enough.) So, as a consequence of the infant's acquired belief that the conditions it has wished for have come to pass, the wish is, albeit temporarily, extinguished and wish-fulfilment is attained.

That last sentence is too swift. What, precisely, are the connections between a wish, the belief which extinguishes it and the terminus of Freudian wish-fulfilment? Let's start with our ordinary conception of what it is for a wish to be fulfilled. Suppose I wish that I were in Spain and one evening dream or hallucinate that I am in Spain; will my wish have been fulfilled in any ordinary sense? No, a person's desire that p is not fulfilled or satisfied, in the ordinary understanding of these terms, unless it becomes the case that p. For the holiday wish to be fulfilled it is necessary that I get to Spain, that it be a fact that I am in Spain. Necessary, but not sufficient: for as well as being in Spain I must know or believe that I am in Spain: if I do not believe that I am in Spain even when I am, I will continue wishing: my wish will not have been extinguished. Here then are three marks of the ordinary, full-blooded conception of what it is for a wish to be fulfilled. First, the wished-for state of affairs (or action) must obtain or come to pass. Second, the agent must – giving 'belief' broad compass – come to believe that the desired state of affairs obtains. Third, for an agent's wish (i.e. wishing) that p to be fulfilled it must be extinguished, he must cease to wish that p.

There is a further condition which can be introduced by means of a fanciful but possible case. I wish to be in Spain and have acquired the delusional belief that I am, though in fact I am not. One night, while asleep, I am whisked off to Spain. I awake, still dominated by my delusional belief and I have, let's suppose, no more evidence for believing that I am in Spain than I had before. All three prescribed conditions appear to hold: I believe (delusionally) that I am in Spain; I am in Spain; my wish to be in Spain is temporarily extinguished. Yet this case is not an instance of ordinary wish-fulfilment. Why? The reason seems to be that it is a necessary condition of a wish being fulfilled in the ordinary way that its extinction be a causal consequence of the relevant disposition of states of affairs in the world. But in the present case, although the relevant state of affairs aimed at by the wish (my being in Spain) does obtain, no use is made of that state of affairs in the wish's satisfaction. The existence of the state of affairs is causally inert in relation to my belief and to the satisfaction of my wish. Hence condition (iv), in the following summary of our progress to date.

For any wish that p, it is fulfilled only if:

  (i)   the wish is extinguished: the agent ceases to wish that p;
 (ii)   the agent comes to believe that p;
(iii) it is a fact that p: the wished-for state of affairs or action occurs;
(iv) the wish is extinguished because of the occurrence or institution of p.

We are now in a better position to appreciate the relations between wishing, belief and fulfilment in the Freudian conception of wish-fulfilment. It is distinctive of those phenomena identified by Freud as wish-fulfilling – dreams, daydreams, hallucinations and so on – that whilst conditions (i) and (ii) are necessary, conditions (iii) and (iv) are not. Characteristically in Freudian wish-fulfilment (henceforth 'wish-fulfilment' will refer only to the Freudian variety), either the wished for states of affairs do not exist or come to pass or, if they do, they have no causal role in the extinction of the wish. The causal role must, therefore, rest entirely with (ii).[8] The beliefs generated by the dream, the hallucination etc. are insensitive to the way things are in the world and at least temporarily extinguish the wishes which actuate them. The relevant states of affairs *may*, of course, exist and be known to exist, but it is not *necessary* that they should exist and, typically, it is their painful absence that mobilizes the wish-fulfilment in the first place.

Another important singularity of wish-fulfilment must be noticed here. Suppose that I am deceived into believing that I won a lottery, give notice to my employer, fly out to Spain. Here, my wish to win the lottery and other wishes will have been extinguished on my acquiring wish-fulfilling beliefs, yet this is not wish-fulfilment. Why not? It is not because in all, or perhaps nearly all, cases of wish-fulfilment described by Freud the agent *initiates* the fulfilment of the wish or a process which entails the fulfilment.[9] Contrast the lottery example with some typical cases of wish-fulfilment, compensatory daydreams or masturbation phantasies. These activities are transparently tendentious. It is not just that these phantasies are manufactured intentionally and then have wish-fulfilling consequences fortuitously (though this, too, can occur); solace, excitement or gratification of specific wishes is intended, albeit the intention may be unconscious. However, even in those cases where no intention operates it is clear that the agent, or some orectic disposition of the agent, initiates the wish-fulfilment. Wish-fulfilment cannot be something that *entirely* befalls an agent.

So a further condition recognizing agency must be added to (i) and (ii). Since there may be degrees of intentional involvement it will be useful to mark the limits, from the maximally intentional cases like the compensatory daydream to the simplest sub-intentional cases like hallucinatory satisfaction. This can be done by distinguishing two forms of the condition which replace conditions (iii) and (iv) above. The weaker form (iiia) is that the agent initiates – in a sense that does not entail but does not exclude intention – the wish-fulfilling process. The stronger form (iiib), identifies the maximal cases: in maximal cases of wish-fulfilment, where a wish that p of an agent A is fulfilled, the process that fulfils the wish can be truly described as intentional under some such descriptions as 'A fulfilling the wish that p' or 'A gratifying (consoling) A'. Wanting to satisfy the wish or the agent's wanting to gratify or console herself enter into the reasons for performing the sequence of actions which in part constitute the wish-fulfilment. Between these limits there is generous conceptual space to accommodate a variety of wish-fulfilling processes. For example, in one important hybrid a stage of the process is performed intentionally but wish-fulfilment follows only adventitiously: wish-fulfilment *befalls* the process initiated by the agent. Some types of daydreaming may be of this kind: I begin by reviewing the nicer aspects of the holidays and end up 'losing myself' in sweet reverie. Such cases are neither non-intentional nor maximal; hence the second arm of the qualification in (iiia). Here, representations of wished for states of affairs – wishful phantasy – are generated intentionally, though not yet for the purpose of achieving wish-fulfilment. And this suggests that there may be types where wishful representations *are* used for this purpose, by a mind capable of intentionally providing for itself substitutive satisfactions. This important species of wish-fulfilment will be revisited below.

Now, it must be emphasized that *the mere occurrence of the representation of the state of affairs that would fulfil the wish does not suffice for wish-fulfilment*. In wish-fulfilment a wish is not merely represented as fulfilled, it is, at least temporarily, extinguished. This is a necessity of Freudian theory even though, as has long been observed, for example by Shope (1967), Freud himself was not always careful to distinguish between the representation of a wish fulfilled and the fulfilment of a wish. In fact the situation with Freud's practice is somewhat worse. If we distinguish between, at least, (i) a wish (ii) a representation of a wish (iii) the object or action or state of affairs whose occurrence would fulfil the wish (iv) a representation of such an object, action or state of affairs (v) a representation of a wish being fulfilled and (vi) the fulfilment of the wish, the process (or, what is different, the end state) of the wish being fulfilled as this occurs (a) when the wish finds its true objects and (b) when the wish is fulfilled by some counterfeit, as in a dream or phantasy; then we will find failure consistently to distinguish between (i) and (ii), (iv) and (v), but most significantly between (v) and (vi) and between (vi)(a) and (vi)(b). When he is *most* careful Freud does remark the difference between the latter pair i.e. wish-fulfilment when the wished for state of affairs doesn't (necessarily) occur and ordinary wish-fulfilment or satisfaction, when it does. He notes of hallucinatory wish-fulfilment, for example, that 'satisfaction does not follow; the need persists' (Freud 1900a: 566; 1917d: 231). This is an important distinction, marked by Wollheim (1979) as between satisfaction and gratification, and by Hopkins (1994, 1995) as between satisfaction, in which the wished for item obtains, and pacification, in which the wish is caused to cease to operate temporarily, with or without satisfaction. However, it does not follow, as these and other commentators have thought, that because wish-fulfilment falls short of satisfaction, *all* there is to wish-fulfilment, in Freud's view, is the production of the representation of a wish fulfilled i.e. (v) or, perhaps, (iv). Hopkins was wrong, in an earlier paper (1988: 40), to impute to Freud the reasoning that: 'Since the dream represents the wish as fulfilled, the dream can be regarded as wish-fulfilment'. Freud, rightly, did not think representation sufficient. Wish-fulfilment involves *less* than satisfaction but *more* than the mere representation of satisfaction: it involves, as well, (adopting now Hopkins's later term) pacification, a cessation of wishing. That the wishful representation alone cannot constitute wish-fulfilment is evident from the fact, noted by Freud (1917d: 231), that a particular representation may at one time, and not at another, fulfil the wish it represents as fulfilled. Just as there is a difference between entertaining a thought and believing it, so there is between experiencing an imaginal representation and taking it 'for real'.

It *is* true that Freud sometimes emphasises only the representation: of the famous Irma dream he says that 'its content was the fulfilment of a wish and its motive was a wish' (1900a: 119); and he speaks of a 'delusion having as content the fulfilment of the wish' (1917d: 226). But more frequently something stronger is advanced. Freud writes of a child's dream that it 'produces a direct undisguised fulfilment of a wish' (1916–17: 128); of phantasies that 'every single phantasy is the fulfilment of a wish, a correction of unsatisfying reality' (1908e: 146); and of symptoms: 'that they too are to be regarded as fulfilments of unconscious wishes' (1900a: 568–69). Freud occasionally glossed the distinction in question because he was less interested in the falling short of satisfaction, than in the occurrence of pacification: both ordinary wish-fulfilment and (Freudian) wish-fulfilment produce pacification. That is why, importantly, Freud asserts of the wish-fulfilling neurosis that it is substitutive satisfaction, which is not just the representation of satisfaction, but something of the order of satisfaction.[10] And, of course, the distinction between wishful representation and representation which succeeds to wish-fulfilment is significant in clinical work. Freud noted, for example, that dreams, though representationally intact, can fail to be wish-fulfilling when, as in some anxiety dreams, anxiety disrupts the dream and sleep is abandoned. Again, it is essential to distinguish between a delusional thought and a delusional belief with identical content. Freud considers the event of persecutory or other irrational ideas entering consciousness 'without finding acceptance or belief' there (1922b: 228). The person who has a *wishful phantasy* or thought of killing his father, consciously or unconsciously, who represents to himself this wish fulfilled, may feel guilt at having evil thoughts. But this is a very different phenomenon from the fully-fledged *wish-fulfilling phantasy* or delusion, conscious or unconscious, that he has killed his father. The latter is likely to have a sequel of depression and remorse.

The significance of pacification in wish-fulfilment emerges clearly from the adaptational perspective: there is no advantage to the incapacitated organism in merely expressing or representing wishes as fulfilled: the organism which cannot act alloplastically still demands an end to the painful stimulus of ineluctable wish or desire and tries to pacify it, in default of realistic action.

3

I want now to use this fragment of Freudian exegesis to expose deficiencies in some of the recent sub-intentionalist reconstructions of psychoanalytic phenomena. In Sebastian Gardner's major attempt (Gardner 1993) to provide an essentially sub-intentional metapsychology for psychoanalysis infantile hallucination and dreaming are presented as the paradigms of wish-fulfilment (1993: 120); whether they are intended to exhaust it is a question considered below. It is important for Gardner's project to distinguish propositional attitudes, intentional action and rational (reason-giving) explanation, on the one hand, from 'psychoanalytic states', 'activity' and non-rational modes of explanation, on the other. First, psychoanalytic states like wishes and phantasies are pre-propositional and 'are not to be thought of as sub-classes of non-psychoanalytic states – they are not species of beliefs and desires, or combinations of such – for their associated way of mental processing differs fundamentally from that of the propositional attitudes' (1993: 116). Gardner enforces this segregation largely because his understanding of propositional attitudes and psychoanalytic states exclusively connects the former to language, truth and holistic constraints, and the latter, as they must given their affiliation with infancy, to the pre-linguistic (1993: 154–5). Second, psychoanalysis forces us to recognize that there are two types of agency or exercises of the will: action and activity. Activity is 'due to desire's *giving expression to its intrinsic tendency to cause the realisation of its conditions of satisfaction*' (1993: 118); it is short of desire joining belief to cause intentional action but more than brute sub-rational association, which is best explained at the sub-personal level. This is crucial: 'The fundamental idea on which a psychoanalytic extension of ordinary psychology hinges is that of a connection of content, driven by the operation of desire freed from rational constraints' (1993: 229; 88–9). And third, *most* of the domain of psychoanalysis can only be explained as activities or the effects of activity: psychoanalytic explanation is not modelled on the practical syllogism but is essentially sub-intentional (186–9). Gardner is driven to this conclusion chiefly because of his anxiety that unconscious rational explanation entails unconscious intentional action and strategy, which in turn threatens an intolerable sub-systemic or 'Second Mind' personology; something, Gardner believes, he has thoroughly discredited (1993: 76–7, 114).

The large claim that psychoanalysis deals mainly with the sub-intentional expressions of will is, I am persuaded, mistaken, even for the varieties of wish-fulfilment. But sub-intentional causation, construed now as a direct relation between pre-propositional wish and the representation of its fulfilment, certainly seems to fit the bill for primitive processes like infantile hallucinatory wish-fulfilment. On Gardner's reconstruction, the wish directly causes a representation of its object; this representation, a sensory or imaginative experience, then brings about a 'subjective event', an 'experiential registration of satisfaction'; this experience then 'puts the feeling of need in abeyance, and terminates the subject's action disposition to fulfil the goal set by its motivational state' (1993: 125). Wish-fulfilment and rational satisfaction are both held to involve an experiential registration of satisfaction; but the latter is more complex: there, the registration of satisfaction is preceded and in part caused by the belief that the relevant action has been performed; and it is followed by the belief that the desire prompting the action is satisfied. However, belief can play no fundamental role in a (putatively) pre-propositional process like wish-fulfilment.[11] How, then, does a representation of the wish's object, the 'wish-fulfilling representation', cause the registration of satisfaction and the consequent pacification, the cessation of the wish? Gardner's answer is that 'a sensory experience takes over the causal role' of the beliefs operative in rational satisfaction: the 'simplest assumption' is that 'in wish-fulfilment, the experiential registration [of satisfaction] is the direct effect of a sensory experience [i.e. the wish-fulfilling representation], and that, once it has been produced, the cessation of trying and temporary abeyance of the action-disposition follow . . .' (1993: 125).

Against the backdrop of Freud's exploration of hallucinatory satisfaction and dream formation we can discern two conclusive objections to this spare reconstruction. The first observes that the putative event of the experiential registration of satisfaction crucial to this account, whilst it *may* occur in some infantile hallucinatory satisfaction, is *absent* in the dream and related wish-fulfilling products, except perhaps in unusual cases. This reconstruction therefore leaves wish-fulfilment, at least in the dream and many of its kin, unexplained, a serious matter in this line of things. Gardner has overlooked, what Freud's later metapsychological investigations make explicit, that the fundamental work of pacification in wish-fulfilment is performed by the *identity of perception* and *belief*. On reflection it becomes evident that the *experience of satisfaction* noted by Freud in the key passage (quoted p. 51–2 above), on which Gardner has erected his entire account, is only a contingent consequence of belief attaching itself to a suitable perception in the special case Freud is there examining, the hungry baby's situation. That an experience of satisfaction cannot be essential, even in hallucinatory wish-fulfilment, becomes especially evident when one recalls its clinically significant *negative* forms e.g. the denial or hallucinating away of persecutory objects (Klein 1975 [1952]: 64–5): for in such instances the experience of satisfaction can have no representational content whatsoever if the denial is to succeed; but an experience of satisfaction without such content is, for all perhaps but the most primitive cases, inconceivable. As regards dreams, to my knowledge Freud nowhere states that they involve an experiential registration of satisfaction, though some, of course, may be pleasant. And he is rightly untroubled with this particular hiatus in phenomenology because he takes (successful) dreams to be experiences to 'which we attach complete belief' (1900a: 50; 535), and belief to suffice for pacification. Gardner's account, unlike Freud's, is fatally restricted, for in endeavouring to make do without belief, it leans upon a phenomenology largely fictitious.[12]

The second objection questions the alleged causal connection between the 'wish-fulfilling representation' (better: the representation of the wish-fulfilment or of what would fulfil the wish) and the putative registration of satisfaction. As we saw above (Freud cited 1917d: 231), Freud distinguished between wishful phantasy i.e. the representation of the wish fulfilled, and *real* wish-fulfilment involving pacification. Between these two there is a gap. It cannot be spanned by just *insisting* on a brute causal connection between them. The passage from the production of a wishful representation to the alleged experience of satisfaction requires explanation: merely having a wishful phantasy does not have the pacific consequences that 'believing it to be real' has. But having prescribed an austere pre-propositional framework for psychoanalysis, Gardner is unable to provide the materials which could account for this contingency, and for then spanning the gap which exercised Freud very considerably.

The resistance shown by many philosophers to attributing a capacity for propositional attitudes to pre-linguistic creatures (Cavell 1993) spills over naturally to the unconscious (Gardner 1993).[13] They express concerns about the specification of conceptual or, indeed, *any* mental content in the absence of language, about mental holism and about the threat of unconscious strategy and the implied diremption of the self. The prevailing analyses of those heterogeneous attitudes and dispositions which Russell pre-emptively fixed as 'propositional attitudes', and in particular the (essentialist) analyses of *belief*, seem to me misconceived, and the concerns I noted largely misplaced. But even if they are not, we have seen reason to think that the deployment of *something like* the distinction between entertaining a proposition and believing it or, to borrow F. P. Ramsey's metaphor, between (what purports to be) a map and a map by which we steer, is indispensable if we are to arrive at an understanding of pacification in wish-fulfilment. In recent articles (1994; 1995), in the course of illuminating discussion of many aspects of psychoanalytic theory, James Hopkins has produced an account of wish-fulfilment which seems to satisfy this requirement without apparent commitment to the tie between pacification and belief in particular, and to unconscious propositional attitudes in general. Wish-fulfilment or wish-fulfilling phantasy is, he writes, 'a form of wishful thinking or imagining, in which a wish or desire causes an imaginative representation of its fulfilment, which is experience- or belief-like' (1995: 461). In it 'we take desire to cause satisfaction-like experience and quasi-belief directly and so to yield pacification without satisfaction' (1995: 471). Belief is then included as a limiting case of experience- or belief-like representation or b-rep, for short. Condensed into a formula: 'A's desire that P -[causes] → A's b-rep that P -[causes] → A's desire that P is pacified' (1995: 472).

I think that this strategy, in which representational items like dreams and symptoms[14] function as b-reps, as intrinsically pacifying entities, cannot succeed. It may be possible to provide just enough of the argument to indicate why this is so. B-reps are radically heterogeneous. The class includes fully-fledged beliefs, quasi-beliefs, imaginative representations and experiences. Take these items in turn. It will be plain that I have no quarrel with the notion that fully-fledged beliefs can pacify desire. But this species of b-rep won't do in a story of wish-fulfilment in which b-reps are directly caused by desires: producing fully-fledged belief is, as is generally agreed, something that desire cannot directly do. That's why (proceeding now to the second item) concepts of attenuated belief like *quasi-belief* were invented. Quasi-beliefs are supposed to have the convenient properties of being pacific, of bearing no conceptual ties to relevant evidence and of being potentially the direct effects of desires. The view that desire can sub-intentionally create such wish-fulfilling, non-probative quasi-beliefs was developed in detail by Mark Johnston (1988), in a way that has significant affinities with Hopkins's own earlier views (Hopkins 1982: xxiiff; cf. 1995: 462). Now, the conceptual credentials of a *kind of empirical belief* unsecured in relevant evidence, and therefore potentially in conflict with evidence accepted as such by its owner, are very dubious (Price 1975 [1954]; Collins 1979); empirical belief and evidence appear to be (see note 7) internally related. But Johnston knows the objection and takes a heroic measure to disarm it.

[W]e can deal summarily with . . . [the] . . . objection that such purely motivated belief that p does not really deserve the name of 'belief' because it is neither grounded in what one takes to be evidence for p nor reliably connected to the state of affairs that p. Granted, its claims to the title of belief that p do not lie there but in its being a disposition to the occurrent thought that p, in its action-guiding potential, and its potential to allay anxiety that not-p. Call it 'quasi-belief' if you must, but recognise its similarity on the output side to the best grounded beliefs.

(1988: 73)

I have no conclusive argument against quasi-belief, as understood by Johnston and Hopkins. But even if there are instances of it, there is strong reason to think that they play no, or almost no, role in wish-fulfilment. Consider this typical case:

you will find if you get to talk with the exhibitionist, that his purpose in displaying his genitals is not to seduce a woman into making love with him but rather to shock her. If she is upset – is embarrassed, becomes angry, runs away – and especially if she calls the police, he has, he feels, absolute proof that his genitals are important. When you learn that he is likely to exhibit himself following a humiliation earlier in the day, you will be alert to the hostile components he experiences in his excitement. For him, this sexual act serves as a kind of rape – a forced intrusion (at least that is the way he fantasises it) into the woman's sensibilities and delicacy. If he cannot believe that he has harmed her, the act has failed for him . . . His idea – his fantasy – of what is going on includes, then, the following features. He has done something hostile to a woman; he has been the active force, not the passive victim as he was earlier in the day when someone humiliated him. He has converted this trauma to a triumph, capped by his success in becoming sexually excited . . . He seems to be running great risks: he may be caught and arrested, his family and job put in jeopardy. But the true danger that perversion is to protect him from – that he is insignificant, unmanly – is not out there on the street but within him and therefore inescapable. It is so fundamental a threat that he is willing to run the lesser risk, that of being caught.

(Stoller 1979: xii)

This man is reeking, in Johnston's phrase, anxious desire. Why doesn't anxious desire just install the wish-fulfilling quasi-beliefs in his mind and save him from the perils of this masquerade? It is especially in these 'hot' instances that one would have expected anxious desire to be most active in disposing its subjects to wish-fulfilling quasi-beliefs. It is indeed remarkable that these putative quasi-beliefs, supposed to be generated by an abundance of sub-intentional mechanisms or tropisms, should not be generated precisely in those desperate pathological conditions that cry out for their subvention. It seems that *instead* of wish-fulfilling quasi-beliefs we find dreams, symptoms, delusions and so on. These are items which we know have a role in the cycle of wish-fulfilment, but which the sub-vention of quasi-beliefs would render superfluous: for then the quasi-beliefs would suffice for wish-fulfilment. But since there is no dearth of pathology, that suggests, at the least, that the role of quasi-beliefs in wish-fulfilment must be very limited indeed. Quasi-belief cannot take us far, if any distance at all. What demands explanation is how the pathological and related products themselves function in the cycle of wish-fulfilment.

So we turn, finally, to these b-reps, the imaginative representations and experiences like dreams and symptoms. They are phenomenologically nothing like beliefs or quasi-beliefs. The similarity which qualifies imaginal or experience-like things as b-reps must therefore be a similarity in causal powers, such as the capacity to pacify wishes or terminate action. But then the summons remains, as it did on Gardner's account, to explain just how such representations can have these convenient, intrinsic belief-like powers: otherwise the conspicuous gap between wishful representation and wish-fulfilment simply remains unbridged. We are driven to conclude, therefore, that the conception of a *b-rep* does not advance our understanding of wish-fulfilment. It does not because the b-reps which are imaginal or experience-like cannot by themselves deliver pacification, and the b-reps which are belief-like leave unilluminated what most needs to be illuminated, the role of dream, symptom and their congeners in the cycle of wish-fulfilment.

These revisionist attempts to explain the mechanics of primitive wish-fulfilment are neither faithful to Freud's much richer account (though presented as Freudian exegeses or elaborations) nor successful. Unfortunately, when it comes to the more complex cases of wish-fulfilment, those in which, prima facie at least, intention is manifest, the same austere, sub-intentional machinery gets pressed into service. Consider the tablecloth lady. Several times a day Freud's patient would rush to a particular table with a stained tablecloth, stand beside it, ring for the maid, ensure that the maid saw the stain, and then send her away. This behaviour was inexplicable until she recalled some events of her wedding night. Her husband had been impotent and ran many times from his room to hers, without success. In the end, in an attempt to conceal his impotence and shame from the hotel staff, he stained the nuptial bedsheet with red ink. The recollection made the lady's performance-symptom intelligible. It could now be seen as a kind of pantomimic undoing or correction of the wedding night, in which she was identified with her husband and the maid with a confirming witness: he was *not* impotent, he had no need to be ashamed: 'It represented this wish, in the manner of a dream, as fulfilled in the present day action; it served the purpose of making her husband superior to his past mishap' (1916–17: 263).

Hopkins has argued influentially (1982: xxivff) that although it is natural to assume that behaviour like the tablecloth lady's can be explained on the pattern of intentional action, it is impossible to do so. The overriding difficulty is the apparent failure to identify a credible instrumental belief that will couple with her animating unconscious wish to (let's say) vindicate her husband, and confer intentionality on their issue. Without such an instrumental belief there can be, on the standard account, no intentional action. The solution, according to Hopkins, is to see that wish-fulfilment is achieved, not on the pattern of practical reason, but through the non-intentional activity of imagination producing representations of gratified desire (1982: xxv; Cavell 1993: ch. 9).

> Wish-fulfilment may seem most like action where it is effected by bodily or intentional activity . . . Someone may indeed imagine himself to be performing one kind of action [vindicating husband] by actually performing another [showing maid spot]; his imagining, that is, may consist partly in his doing something which symbolises, resembles, or otherwise represents (to him) what he imagines doing. That imagining may govern someone's intentional actions in this way, however, does not show that the imagining itself is intentional. Characteristically, it seems, the action will be intentional but the imagining not. This is because imaginative activity seems not to be governed by belief and desire in the way intentional action is.
>
> (1982: xxv; I have replaced Hopkins's examples with ours)

There seem to be at least two ways of understanding this passage as it applies to our example. In the first, the lady's performance, under the description of calling the maid etc., is intentional and, given the various symbolic correspondences between components of the performance and the relevant events of the wedding night, she comes unconsciously to imagine, perhaps to believe, that her husband has been vindicated. On this interpretation the imagining and the consequent fulfilment of her wish supervene on the intentional performance. But now notice that the example involves an indirect or symbolic fulfilment of an unconscious wish. How is that achieved?

To sharpen this question it may help to first define indirect or symbolic wish-fulfilment by briefly contrasting it with two other vicissitudes of wish or instinct with which it is sometimes confused. Freud was aware that wishes could be relinquished and replaced by others in such a way as to satisfy their subject without providing wish-fulfilment. He refers on occasion to the *plasticity of instinct*: 'the sexual instinctual impulses in particular are extraordinarily *plastic*, if I may so express it. One of them can take the place of another, one of them can take over another's intensity; if the satisfaction of one of them is frustrated by reality, the satisfaction of another can afford complete compensation' (1916–17: 344). Sometimes in life a desire for a Drumstick (a kind of ice-cream) has to be relinquished and you make do with a Cornetto (very much like a Drumstick). Were this an instance of wish-fulfilment, then the original desire for the Drumstick would have to be pacified. But that need not happen for *you* to be satisfied, and is not entailed in the plasticity Freud describes. Nor is symbolic wish-fulfilment the same as *sublimation*. In an early formulation Freud describes sublimation of libido as consisting 'in the sexual trend abandoning its aim of obtaining a component or reproductive pleasure and taking on another which is related genetically to the abandoned one but is itself no longer sexual and must be described as social' (1916–17: 345). In this process the originary wish is neither relinquished nor fulfilled but transformed. In successful sublimation the resulting wishes do not retain the significance of the older ones: the new activity is not a *symbol* for the older one, the meaning connection is broken altogether and the originary wishes are not being pacified.[15]

In contrast to these two vicissitudes, the originary wish in symbolic wish-fulfilment is neither relinquished nor transformed, but fulfilled in the manner of Freudian wish-fulfilment, which entails being pacified. So the question now is, how can the maid-fetching performance, conceived 'in the manner of a dream' as symbolic or disguised imaginative representation, fulfil in this way the lady's unconscious originary wish that her husband be vindicated? On the view that the symptom is wish-fulfilling merely by virtue of it being a wishful representation (Hopkins 1982: xxi) the answer is straightforward, for the notion of wishful representation easily accommodates disguised or symbolic representation. But that view of wish-fulfilment has been shown to be mistaken, for representation alone, as we've repeatedly noted, does not suffice for pacification and, therefore, for wish-fulfilment. In the present example, what is required is not just a symbolic representation of the lady's originary wish fulfilled, but a pacification of that wish. Insisting that the performance is belief-like, a b-rep, won't rescue this account, for all the reasons already marshalled against the utility of b-reps, but also because if there is to be pacification of the originary wish, if *that* wish is to be caused to cease to operate temporarily, then the performance-as-belief-like-representation must somehow be understood as the state of affairs which is the satisfying condition of the wish. It must be for the lady *as if her husband had been vindicated* (Wollheim 1979: 51ff), a complex mental state that would seem to involve at least an unconscious belief that he *had* been vindicated (or was potent or whatever). Without supplementation by some such notion of unconscious understanding it is quite mysterious how the performance symptom could acquire its pacific powers.[16] I think that *with* the supplement (which may be implied in the passage under consideration) we do arrive at a form of wish-fulfilment: the lady does something: it is seen or understood unconsciously as a wished for state of affairs: which pacifies an unconscious wish. But even so the account remains deficient, for the wish-fulfilment is adventitious: the lady does something which happens in the circumstances to pacify an unconscious wish. What we do not yet have is an understanding of why she did what she did. And clearly, both Hopkins and Freud believe that the wish-fulfilment in a case like this is more than adventitious in the described sense.

So we abandon this account and turn to the second, stronger, reading of Hopkins's passage. Hopkins in fact says more than that wish-fulfilling imagination supervenes on the performance, he says that the imagining *governs* the performance; and the kind of imagining appropriate here is the natural (sub-intentional) expression of desire (1982: xxiv–xxv). The performance – the symptom – is conceived as a product of desire expressing itself sub-intentionally in plastic imagination. This step does create a sought link between the lady's unconscious wish and her action, but it also encounters an insurmountable difficulty. Although an action-event may be intentional under some descriptions and not others, it cannot be intentional under a description and *also* be caused sub-intentionally. This much seems clear about intentional action: it is action performed for and from a reason, standardly understood as a belief–desire pair. Sub-intentional action – O'Shaughnessy's (1980) examples were idle, unawares tongue-moving and shifting one's body weight – is caused by desire, understood in a broad sense, acting *alone*. Sub-intentional causation brutely precludes intentionality: for if a putative example of a sub-intentional action-event were redescribable as intentional, and therefore as having a reason among its causal conditions, it would not be sub-intentional. So if the performance *is* the imagining, and if the imagining is sub-intentional, the product of 'an exercise of will of a kind prior to that in intentional action' (1982: xxiv), then the performance cannot be intentional. But the performance seems to be intentional and, as the passage makes clear, Hopkins thinks that it is.

The sub-intentional way appears to lead to paradox. But there are still a few unexplored turns in it. Gardner's approach to the more complex cases is instructive but also, ultimately, unsuccessful. There is the suggestion in Gardner's text that where psychoanalytic explanation needs to invoke phantasy, especially when phantasy imposes itself on intentional action, as in the phenomena he designates 'acting out' (such as the performance of the tablecloth lady), wish-fulfilment is superseded (1993: 140, 172). Of course, jettisoning the supposition of wish-fulfilment would disburden any such account of the obligation to explain the refractory feature of pacification and, indeed, of representation. But elsewhere Gardner refers to acting out as a wish-fulfilling expression of desire (1993: 171), and my criticism here will assume that it is.

Gardner proposes the following analysis of the lady's complaint:

> The analysis . . . has several components, which are not assembled to form a practical syllogism or strategy. There is, first, a phantastic modification motivated by a wish, of the woman's painful nuptial memory; second, a relation of unconscious seeing-as between the maid and a phantasised witness of her identification with her husband's sexual potency; and, third, an intention directed towards a real person, the woman's present maid, to get her into the room.
>
> (1993: 170)

What is the causal connection between the wishful phantasy and the performance? If the performance were the immediate sub-intentional, plastic expression of the phantasy then, as we have seen, there could be no description under which the performance is intentional. However that is not what occurs on this account. Instead, the phantasy is conceived to generate an intervening intention to call the maid, on which the lady acts. But now how do pre-propositional phantasies generate intentions? Gardner says that pre-propositional phantasies have 'content whose description requires concepts which the subject need not possess, or exercise, in order to have those contents' (1993: 155). He likens them to pictorial representations (1993: 161) and 'the relation between phantastic and propo-sitional thought to that between images and discursive descriptions'. This is plausible and illuminating. We can perhaps 'read off' beliefs from pictures and 'come away' with desires. But the matter seems more complicated with intentions because an intention, it can be argued plausibly, involves a kind of plan, even if only the minimal plan articulated in an instrumental belief; and it is quite unclear how a pre-propositional representation which, although potentially generative of desire, can determine the way in which desire is to be satisfied; which is precisely what is involved in intention. Here, it would seem, is intention without reason: the lady, on this account, has no reason for calling the maid, conscious or un-conscious, yet acts intentionally. To my mind this is a difficulty for the account, at least a point of obscurity. It would not, however, be perceived as such by Gardner, for he is prepared to sever the link between intentionality and acting for a reason, and rejects the conception of intentional action as necessarily instrumental (1993: 170, 186). He argues explicitly that intention engendered by phantasy need not be supported by reasons, and finds warrant for this claim in our understanding of ordinary expressive behaviour. He says that expressive behaviour like throwing crockery in anger or raising one's hands in despair is intentional but non-instrumental action.

This seems to me mistaken. The examples of expressive behaviour Gardner considers are either enthymematically intentional or not intentional at all, but – expressive. If I clench my fists in anguish, raise them in despair, smile at your joke or smash the crockery, and I do so expressively, then intention is precisely what these actions do *not* manifest. They have an archaeology which precludes a telos. That is not to deny, of course, that the same movements can also be performed intentionally – but then they are not expressive, in the indicated sense. The category of the expressive indicated here consists of those actions which achieve their particular revelatory force and poignancy *precisely because they bypass reason and are contraposed to the intentional*. They expose a nakedness which intention clothes over. So, for example, to describe someone as being convulsed with despair or with laughter, to state that this behaviour is genuinely expressive of states of mind, but to then add that the subjects acted intentionally, is to undermine the distinct expressive force and illumination of the original descriptions. But even if this characterization of the expressive is rejected and I conceded cases of expressive, non-rational, intentional behaviour, its proponents would have to concede a point also: that the (putative) intentionality manifest in such expressive cases is *radically unlike* the intentionality manifest in the complex performance of the tablecloth lady. All that then transpires is that the hiatus which previously existed between unconscious phantasy and intention opens up between these very different forms of intentional behaviour. That is hardly progress. The tension is palpable: if psychoanalytic explanation strays too far from ordinary psychology then it cannot claim its protection.

Perhaps, though, the process can be conceived like this: first the phantasy, transformed by the prism of the seeing-as relations, generates a desire to call the maid which generates a second-order desire to satisfy that desire and an instrumental belief about how to do that. This gives us a conscious reason and therefore a reading which satisfies the intuition about the intentionality of the performance, while bypassing the problematic relation between phantasy and intention. But in solving one problem it gives rise to another. For it now becomes mysterious how the performance can be – and this is the salient fact about it – compulsive. Between *conscious* desire and action there must always be a space for withholding or modifying action, and this flexibility seems to be lacking in the lady's case. Could it be that the lady's desire to call the maid is just *too strong* for her to resist? Perhaps, but then we need an explanation of this circumstance: why is this lady so regularly defeated by her desire to call the maid? Now, Gardner has developed an explanation of compulsion in another context: phantasy, he contends, can dominate desire, and desire action, in such a way as to provide for compulsion, when desire is 'misrepresented as issuing from a bodily need, and thereby takes over the psychological force of such a need' (1993: 165). Regressive reinstinctualization of this sort certainly occurs; but the trouble with applying this process to the lady's case is that there is no clinical warrant whatsoever for supposing that anything like it occurs here. And since no other explanation of the compulsion is in sight, it seems that Gardner's account is unable to explain the most significant features of the symptom. Our interim conclusion therefore is that the non-strategic, sub-intentional explanations assayed so far fail to illuminate the Intentional structure of a large and significant class of wish-fulfilling symptoms, of which the tablecloth lady is typical.[17]

Can a conception of sub-intentional activity richer than imagination or phantasy, or a different, deeper conception of wish-fulfilment, rescue this philosophical approach? Richard Wollheim (1991 [1971]: xxixff; 1993: 99ff) has catalogued a number of ways in which Freud has deepened and elaborated the standard explanatory schema for action. Two of these extended schema may be relevant for our case. Under the first, the lady's performance is an instance of 'displaced action': a desire and belief jointly rationalize some action e.g. vindicating husband, but that action is not what the person does; instead another action, e.g. calling the maid, reached by a chain of association, is performed. Wollheim leaves it open whether the latter is an action *tout court*, i.e. is intentional. And he seems to hold that (to adapt his example to ours) the tablecloth lady would not actually think of herself as vindicating her husband (1991 [1971]: 90). But if this is so, then for the reasons already considered (pp. 63–4), it is very difficult to see how the displaced action, in the woman's case the performance, could pacify her originary wish and be wish-fulfilling, though this is a characteristic which Wollheim would wish to preserve. It is difficult to see how the unconscious originary wish could be fulfilled if she does not think of her action as providing conditions satisfying her wish. However this may not be crucial, for Wollheim has an account of wish-fulfilment which appears to circumvent the difficulty. According to it, when the mind is operating under the aegis of a belief in omnipotence or, better, an 'archaic theory of mind', then the representation of a wish (or its object) is mistaken for its object, and the wish is gratified. The notion of displaced action in isolation is vulnerable to the animadversion of the related views already examined, but it may fare better when considered against this novel backdrop.

The second construal also depends on this backdrop. Much that Wollheim says – about the links between expression, acting out and wish-fulfilment – suggests that he would classify the tablecloth lady's performance as an example of expressive action. Expression, as Wollheim conceives it, is the result of desire operating without facilitation by belief or instinct (see p. 50 above). It is a mode of sub-intentional agency, a kind of eruption of desire 'indicative of what moves the person'. It is responsible for producing dreams, some parapraxes and neurotic symptoms, and acting out (1991 [1971]: xxxv). Expression, on this scheme, covers a broad range of behaviour, not all of it wish-fulfilling. Its capacity to produce wish-fulfilment is not intrinsic to it but depends, as may displaced action, on the special condition of the mind operating under the archaic theory, the remarkable circumstance to which we now turn.

In a creative paper Wollheim (1979) recalls a second strand in Freud's thinking about the power of wishes. This strand subtends from Freud's account of 'the omnipotence of thought' (Freud 1909d; 1912–13). It is not entirely clear whether Wollheim conceives of the omnipotence of thought as supplementing or as undergirding wish-fulfilment (1979: 54–5). The latter reading, on which wish-fulfilment is explained by the omnipotence of thought or, rather, Wollheim's elaboration of it as the 'corporeal' (1979) or 'archaic theory of mind' (1984), is vulnerable to criticism in ways that the first is not. Here I consider only the reading on which the omnipotence of thought is taken as more basic than, as explanatory of, wish-fulfilment.

Freud had observed that certain patients imputed to their thoughts and wishes exaggerated powers and efficacy. If the Rat Man 'thought of someone, he would be sure to meet that person immediately afterwards . . . if he suddenly asked after the health of an acquaintance . . . he would hear that he had just died . . . If, without any really serious intention, he swore at some stranger, he might be sure that the man would die soon afterwards' (Freud 1912–13: 86–7). Freud linked this disposition to the magical thinking of children and 'primitive man', and gave it a name: 'the principle of the omnipotence of thought' (1912–13: 85). The person governed by this principle is best understood, Wollheim suggests, as subscribing to a primitive theory or as holding a belief: if I think (imagine, wish, believe) that p, then p. In a mind so affected imagination does not function as imagination; instead 'the person believes that what he imagines is also real' (Wollheim 1979:

56). Wollheim states that the holding of such a belief or theory can explain wish-fulfilment as a systematic phenomenon. At least part of what this means is, I think, that in a mind operating under the impress of the omnipotent belief the passage from 'I wish (imagine) that p' to '(I believe) that p' is systematically facilitated: wishing that p becomes inseparable from believing that p. But then, 'how does the person come by such a useful belief?' (1979: 56). Wollheim, like Freud, links the provenance of the belief to narcissism.[18]

> The infant or primitive man – or, we must add, regressive man – is led by the theory he embraces to think of his thoughts as some part of his body or, again, of his thinking as a particular piece of bodily functioning, and this conceptualisation provides us with the explanation of such a person's belief in the omnipotence of thoughts. For as he comes to attach, in accordance with developmental norms, an exaggerated efficacy to this part of the body or to that particular piece of bodily functioning, so he will correspondingly overvalue the psychic phenomena he has equated with them. So, for instance, in *Totem and Taboo* Freud says that primitive man sexualises his thoughts, by which I take him to mean that for primitive man not only is thinking an object of sexual attention, it is also a form of sexual activity: and if he assigns unreal powers to his thoughts, it is because be has already assigned similar powers to his sexual activity.
>
> (Wollheim 1979: 57)

There are difficulties with this, whether as a reconstruction of Freud's thinking about the omnipotence of thought or as an independent, genetic account of it. The two issues can be considered together. Wollheim's explanation turns on a transition from the idealization of bodily, sexual activity, which he says is a developmental given, through to the equation of this idealized activity with thought, to the resulting idealization of thought. Now, Freud certainly recognized that thought can be 'equated' with physical and sexual processes; that it can become sexualized or idealized; and consequently assigned unreal powers. It's much less certain, however, whether in his view the sexualization or over-valuation of thought is always or even typically effected through its equation with bodily, sexual activity. By the sexualization of thought Freud meant that it is hypercathected with libido; alternatively, that it acquires the significance of bodily, sexual activity. Neither outcome (or the one outcome described differently) presupposes that sexualization is arrived at through the identification of thought with sexual activity, though clearly such an identification may be *one* path to sexualization. Indeed, it seems a precarious advance to try to explain the sexualization and consequent omnipotence of thought in this way. For if there is a problem about the omnipotence of thought, there is a larger problem about the omnipotence of bodily, sexual activity. Whence the exaggerated efficacy assigned by the infant or primitive man to this activity, which is the first step in

Wollheim's explanation, but left by him unexplained? It is no explanation of this idealization to baldly assert that it is in accord with developmental norms, for precisely that development is part of what we wish to understand. Freud is able to explain it, but only because he held something like the reverse of Wollheim's assumption that narcissistic investment in bodily activity precedes such investment in psychic processes. Expounding magic performance and play as 'motor hallucination', he wrote:

> If children and primitive men find play and imitative representation enough for them . . . [it] is the easily understandable result of the paramount virtue they ascribe to their wishes, of the will that is associated with these wishes and of the methods by which these wishes operate. As time goes on, the psychological accent shifts from the *motives* for the magical act on to the *measures* by which it is carried out . . . It thus comes to appear as though it is the magical act itself which, owing to its similarity with the desired result, alone determines the occurrence of that result.
>
> (1912–1913: 84)

It is largely because child and primitive man *wish* that their play and magical gestures be powerful that they come to believe that they are; and this explanation spreads to other idealized sexual or bodily activities. In other words, for Freud the omnipotence of bodily or sexual activity supervenes on the omnipotence of thought (or, rather, of wishes: 1909d: 235, n. 1), not the other way round. But now the question re-emerges: how does child, primitive and regressed man arrive at the 'immense belief in the power of his wishes' (1912–13: 83)? Contrary to Wollheim, I think that Freud provides no detailed answer to this question. But the most natural supposition, that the belief emerges from the *experience of omnipotence*, was articulated by Sándor Ferenczi (1956 [1913]: 219) at the very time Freud was writing *Totem and Taboo*, in a way which is consistent with the few hints provided by Freud (Freud 1911b: 219). Ferenczi delineated overlapping developmental stages, each with its own confirming experiences. He recognizes a period of pre-natal omnipotence when all the organism's needs are met unconditionally; a period of magical hallucinatory omnipotence which is supported by close nursing; a period of magic gestures when the infant controls the nurse, first with uncoordinated and later with intentional gestures; a period of magic thoughts and words to which the nurse responds; and others. On this account the experiences from pre-natal plenitude (which is, of course, controversial) and hallucinatory wish-fulfilment, to the later interactions between infant and responsive environment, engender and confirm the belief in the omnipotence of wish, gesture, bodily activity and, eventually, language. Almost from the first, however, subsists the wish, and each later development in omnipotence – or, rather, the illusion of it – both supervenes on and confirms its power. If this is correct,[19] then the idealization of thought through its identification with idealized

70

bodily activity, as described by Wollheim, is only a late-coming, subsidiary process. It therefore cannot explain the omnipotence of thought and underpin wish-fulfilment. First, because wish-fulfilment precedes omnipotent thinking developmentally; and, second, because omnipotent thinking could not get purchase on a mind which had not had a consolidated experience of wish-fulfilment. It appears that Wollheim's reconstruction of the principle of the omnipotence of thought as the operation of an archaic theory of mind is neither a sustainable exegesis of Freud's thinking nor a viable, independent account of the genesis of wish-fulfilment. Indeed, it is striking that Freud nowhere explicitly states that the omnipotence of thought leads to wish-fulfilment, and it would be remarkable if so potent a connection could have entirely escaped him. For Freud, the omnipotence of thought has, in the main, quite different effects: generating, not pacifying wish-fulfilment in the way of the dream or hallucination, but fears and expectations concerning the eventuality of *real* fulfilment, as a glance at the Rat Man's anxieties will confirm. When the Rat Man thinks, wishes, that someone will die it is not for him as if that person *has* died; rather he fears that the person *will* die.

It follows that if the archaic theory of mind can explain neither the genesis nor efficacy of wish-fulfilment then it cannot provide the conditions in combination with which the sub-intentional processes of displaced action and expression can be revived as adequate explanations for the test cases of wish-fulfilling processes.

4

In the preceding sections we have questioned both the fidelity of some recent interpretations of Freud's views on wish-fulfilment and the explanatory success of the sub-intentional models which animate them. The interpretations have not been faithful and the models have not fared well. It has not been denied that sub-intentional processes have a place in the explanation of some psychoanalytic phenomena, even in wish-fulfilling phenomena. Instances of what are known as defence mechanisms, infantile hallucinatory wish-fulfilment and perhaps some hysterical symptoms are patently sub-intentional or expressive processes. However, we have seen reason to think that the reach of such processes goes not much further. And if that is true, then it would seem to follow by default that the Will, as unconscious deliberation and intention, asserts a radical dominance over the life of the mind. This intentionalist alternative will be touched on in the final section. But first it may be useful to invoke Freud's authority and to review some of the evidence for *his* intentionalism, his progressive recognition of ever more mental phenomena as intentionally engendered.

In the course of reflecting, in *An Autobiographical Study*, on his earliest views about unconscious aetiology, Freud wrote that he was, from the beginning, 'inclined to suspect the existence of an interplay of forces and the *operation of intentions and purposes such as are to be observed in normal life*' (Freud 1925d: 23; my italics). There are many similar passages (e.g. 1916–17: 248, 299; 1909a:

231) but, by and large, these have not persuaded philosophers, who tend either to deny that Freud meant what he said, or that he could have meant by such declarations what we would mean. There is some justification for the caution: Freud often blurs distinctions we would not, and he believed, after all, that some non-Intentional metapsychology, an 'organic foundation' (1916–17: 389), would eventually supersede the psychology of psychoanalysis. Still, the evidence for Freud's intentionalism in relation to many kinds of wish-fulfilling processes is overwhelming. Consider what he says about daydream and masturbation phantasies. Freud presents these as exemplary wish-fulfilling items, though they are only remotely related to the model of sub-intentional hallucination. Mostly they are crafted products (Freud 1912f; Stoller 1979) intentionally manufactured for the purpose of gaining satisfaction or consolation. Freud says that 'every single phantasy is the fulfilment of a wish' (1908e: 146; also 1908a: 159, 164; 1909a) and that phantasizing 'begins already in children's play, and later, continued as daydreaming, abandons dependence on real objects' (1911b: 39). This assimilation of phantasy and daydream to play suggests the intentional provenance of the former because play is clearly instrumental to things like fun. Freud also links daydream and phantasy to artistic activity which involves a covert but intentional means of wish-fulfilment (1908e; see note 2).

Freud's later account of hallucination (1924b; 1924e) assimilates it to phantasy and emphasizes the ego's intentional role in its construction. The dream too is described 'as a piece of phantasy working on behalf of the maintenance of sleep' (1923b: 151), and it is an important feature of the later account of dreams that they are *produced by the ego* as a response to disturbing demands: 'The ego succeeds in doing this by what appears to be an act of compliance: it meets the demand with what is in the circumstances a harmless fulfilment of a wish and so gets rid of it' (1940a: 170). This late, undeveloped intentionalism in dream theory remained unreconciled with the earlier reflex arc model of dream formation, though it may be noted that even in the earlier model there were suggestions of intentional process. The censorship and secondary revision were conceived along intentional lines; that is why, for example, condensation is *not* included as an effect of the censorship: it is instead, says Freud, 'traceable rather to some mechanical or economic factor' (1916–17: 173). Freud also noticed that dreams could be shaped in response to events in therapy; in particular, disconfirming dreams were produced by patients to frustrate therapeutic developments, and an avalanche of dreams, or their drying up altogether, could be used for the purpose of resistance (1911e). The analysand's dreams participate in the analytic dialogue. In later editions of the *Interpretation of Dreams* Freud included striking examples of intentional control over the shape of the dream (1900a: 570ff):

> there are some people who are quite clearly aware during the night that they are asleep and dreaming and who thus seem to possess the faculty of consciously directing their dreams. If, for instance, a dreamer of this kind is dissatisfied with the turn taken by the dream, he can break it off

without waking up and start it again in another direction – just as a popular dramatist may under pressure give his play a happier ending.

(1900a: 571–2)

According to the dream researcher Harry T. Hunt (1989) dreams of this type, so-called 'lucid dreams', are very common. He also says: 'the very existence of lucid dreams . . . seems to show just that expansion of awareness, increased self-reflectiveness and directed volition that is supposedly impossible in dreaming' (1989: 71) The intentionality manifested in this sort of dreaming suggests a very close affinity with daydream and phantasy, and it seems from a reading of the additions to the later editions of the dream-book that Freud came to see it as a model for most, if not all, dreaming.[20]

Finally[21] consider Freud's careful remarks on the evocation of hysterical symptoms. He recognizes precipitation by economic and associative factors, but adds that they can also be evoked

(3) in the service of the primary purpose – as an expression of the 'flight into illness', when reality becomes distressing or frightening – that is, as a consolation; (4) in the service of the secondary purposes, with which the illness allies itself, as soon as, by producing an attack, the patient can achieve an aim that is useful to him. In the last case the attack is directed at particular individuals, and can be put off till they are present, and it gives an impression of being consciously simulated.

(Freud 1909a: 231–2)

The description of neurosis as a consoling flight into illness is certainly suggestive of intentional strategy, and Freud could hardly have made it plainer that this was his view of the secondary purpose. It is true that the secondary purpose is *pre-conscious* and does not *form* the symptom (Gardner 1993: 192), but this does not alter its unconscious strategic character. The secondary purpose is descriptively unconscious, subject to the potent censorship between the Pcs. and the Cs. sub-systems (1915e: 196), perhaps permanently inaccessible to the patient, probably running counter to the patient's conscious intentions *and* an intentional cause of the precipitation of the symptom. Freud also came to see more complex enactments, the acting out of transference and the character disorders as wish-fulfilling, and it is very difficult indeed to render these along sub-intentionalist lines (Pataki 1996).

This rough sketch has glossed over several subtleties, for example the alleged sortal distinction between conscious and dynamically unconscious phantasies, on to which some commentators have fastened. Even so, it is plain that, at least after the structural innovations of *The Ego and the Id*, Freud was an intentionalist about much of the psychoanalytic domain, and that he was an intentionalist about some forms of wish-fulfilment even before then.

5

But intentionalism about wish-fulfilment, as about self-deception and other forms of irrationality, is not easy. Although we have focused in this essay on the failure of sub-intentionalist accounts, from that failure intentionalism is only one of several possible conclusions: the futility of the psychoanalytic project is another. It is no simple matter to establish a robustly intentionalist case: the conceptions of intentional wish-fulfilling processes necessary to the elucidation of much psychoanalytic material entail problematic forms of mental diremption and activity which require detailed treatment. However, all that can be done usefully in the space that remains is to locate intentional wish-fulfilment in a broader context which cogently recommends it.

We are subjects of ineluctable desires, some of which are unsatisfiable or close to being so. When the self can satisfy desire, it usually tries to do so; when it cannot it sometimes attempts wish-fulfilment; and if that fails it may surrender or resort to some of the more drastic measures discussed in psychiatric manuals. Wish-fulfilment involves various techniques and processes which, by deft use of imagination, illusion and so on – these things understood in their deeper psychoanalytic dimensions – provide substitutive satisfactions for ineluctable desire. The simplest forms of wish-fulfilment, of which infantile hallucinatory satisfaction is the paradigm, involve sub-intentional or expressive mechanism operating in primitive mental conditions. However, there are also more complex, reflexive processes in which imaginal representations are used intentionally by the self for the purpose of fulfilling its own wishes. Some types of daydream are examples of this, as are, less obviously, many forms of wish-fulfilling symptom and action. In fact it proves illuminating to view the reflexive, intentional forms of wish-fulfilment as members of a class of self-caring or self-solicitous activities. In the class may also be included, amongst others, self-gratification, self-consolation, self-appeasement and, in some of their forms, self-abasement and self-deception. These are all modes or instruments, albeit sometimes perverted or distorted, of caring and being concerned for oneself. They may enter into various auxiliary or superordinate relations with each other. For example, the fulfilment of wishes is sometimes in the strategic service of superordinate motives: we may want to satisfy a wish of ours without further motive, but sometimes we may want to console or pacify ourselves and this may involve the satisfaction of other wishes; but equally it may involve the elimination of painful affect or anxiety. Self-abasement can be an instrument of self-appeasement, and self-deception is *often* in the strategic service of some superordinate mode of self-solicitude, like self-consolation (Pataki 1997). In self-solicitude the self takes itself as an object to be cared for and, importantly, caring for the self involves a concern to satisfy its desires or wishes, including its unconscious desires or wishes, especially those which attach to the self's significant objects.[22]

This perspective is, once again, Freudian. In language which generally has been discounted as metaphorical, but seems to me prescient and inspired even more than elsewhere by the phenomenology of the clinic, Freud writes of the dependent relations of the ego:

> It is not only a helper to the id; it is also a submissive slave who courts his master's love. Whenever possible it tries to remain on good terms with the id; it clothes the id's Ucs. commands with its Pcs. rationalisations; it pretends that the id is showing obedience to the admonitions of reality, even when in fact it is remaining obstinate and unyielding; it disguises the id's conflicts with reality . . .
>
> (1923b: 56)

Similar remarks are made about the relationship of super-ego to ego: 'To the ego . . . living means the same as being loved – being loved by the super-ego . . . The super-ego fulfils the same function of protecting and saving that was fulfilled in earlier days by the father' (1923b: 58); and 'if the super-ego does try to comfort the ego by humour and to protect it from suffering, this does not conflict with its derivation from the parental function' (1928c: 166). Freud came to realize, though only near the end of his life, that some of these self-solicitous relations are 'decisively influenced by the identification with the nursing mother' (Hartmann, Kris and Loewenstein 1964: 39). If we bear in mind that for Freud 'an individual [is] a psychical id, unknown and unconscious, upon whose surface rests the ego' (1923b: 25) and that the super-ego is a *grade* in the ego, then the relations in question must be seen as reflexive relations of self to self-as-object. These dynamic, reflexive relations are not well-understood. The healthy internalization of maternal functions had been recognized by the pioneers (e.g. Spitz 1965: 179; Winnicott 1965: 48) though remain, so far as I know, inadequately investigated. Considerably more is known about the pathological developments in which the infant, who feels abandoned or despised, identifies with its frustrating or hated objects, or in some other way turns prematurely upon itself, and takes itself as an object.[23] It is possibly because the self-solicitous relations, including the intentional forms of wish-fulfilment, are so frequently dominated by this latter development that they often take the form of self-deceit, symptom, delusion and pernicious illusion.

Acknowledgements

I wish to thank Marcia Cavell, Raimond Gaita and, especially, Michael Levine for helpful criticism and suggestions on an earlier version of this essay.

Notes

1 Freud's translators rendered *Wunsch* into Spanish as *deseo*; into French as *désir*; and into Italian as *desiderio* though, as I understand it, alternatives closer to 'wish' are available in each language. In consonance with Freud's use I will mostly use 'wish' and 'desire' interchangeably. Gardner (1993: 120), argues that the 'psychoanalytic

wish' uncovered by Freud is a novel kind of mental creature, different from, though related to, the ordinary kind, and is 'necessarily engaged in the process of wish-fulfilment' (1993: 126). Other philosophers have said that Freud distinguished amongst kinds of wishes, or should have, or that he distinguished sharply between wishes and desires. Lear (1990: 75–6) says 'a wish is a motivating force, but, unlike desire, its products are not actions. Freud implicitly recognizes that a wish differs from a desire. For he characterizes a wish by its role within the archaic functioning of the infantile mind'. And Hopkins, who does not usually put much weight on this distinction (1982: xix ff.; 1995), wonders (in 1988: 44–5) whether, in consequence of the irrationality and detachment from reality of the wishes fulfilled in dreams, Freud should not have 'introduced a special theoretical term – perhaps something like "night-time motive derivative" – instead of the common-sense term "wish"'. Wollheim (1984: 85, 90ff) also recognizes a quasi-technical notion of wish that finds its significance in the context of the archaic operation of mind. Gardner, moreover, claims that 'Freud did not envisage wish-fulfilment as a mode of satisfaction available to propositional desires' (1993: 123); but desires can exploit wish-fulfilment by regressing to a state of instinctual demand and giving rise to a wish susceptible to wish-fulfilment. Now Freud does, of course, distinguish amongst wishes in terms of content and topographical location, but it is a mistake to think that he recognized a distinction between ordinary and psychoanalytic wishes or between pre-propositional wishes (or some hybrid: Gardner 1993: 124) and propositional desires, the latter not subject to the vicissitude of wish-fulfilment. It seems clear from the texts that wish-fulfilment befalls conscious and preconscious desire as well as the unconscious infantile wishes which decisively motivate dream and hallucinatory gratification, without undergoing the regression Gardner envisages. The significant distinction for Freud is not between the orectic kinds, wish and desire, but between the kinds of process, primary or secondary, which can take wishes and desires as their materials. First, Freud frequently uses 'wish' in a general way to cover for all the orectic states that set our minds turning, as when he writes, Hume-like, that 'nothing but a wish can set our mental apparatus working' (Freud 1900a: 567). Second, dreams frequently have 'a succession of meanings or wish-fulfilments may be superimposed on one another, the bottom one being a fulfilment of a wish dating from earliest childhood' (Freud 1900a: 269); although Freud believed that there had to be at least one infantile unconscious wish, which alone was strong enough to instigate the dream (1900a: 553), *other* wishes or desires inhering in the day residues are also fulfilled (1900a: 550–72). Third, Freud conceived of daydream, art, religion, ritual and the transference as also fulfilling wishes or desires. 'Only in art does it still happen that a man who is consumed by desires performs something resembling the accomplishment of those desires and that what he does in play produces emotional effects – thanks to artistic illusion – just as though it were something real' (Freud 1912–13: 90). What are those desires? Pre-eminently, they are 'desires to win honour, power, wealth and the love of women' (1916–17: 376). Similarly, religious ideas are 'illusions, fulfilments of the oldest, strongest and most urgent wishes of mankind' (1927c: 30).

2 Freud speaks often and justly of the 'tenacity' of libido. 'We after all know that it is a characteristic feature of the libido that it struggles against submitting to the reality of the universe – to Ananke' (Freud 1916–17: 430) is a high metaphysical expression of this truth. On a less exalted plane, the necessity of 'binding' desire becomes the essential motive in the construction of culture:

> the principal function of the mental mechanism is to relieve the individual from the tensions created in him by his needs . . . But the satisfaction of . . . part of these needs . . . is regularly frustrated by reality. This leads to the further task of finding some other means of dealing with the unsatisfied

impulses. The whole course of the history of civilization is no more than an account of the various methods adopted by mankind for 'binding' their unsatisfied wishes. Myths, religion and morality find their place in this scheme as attempts to seek a compensation for the lack of satisfaction of human wishes. [T]he neuroses themselves have turned out to be attempts to find *individual* solutions for the problems of compensating for unsatisfied wishes, while the institutions seek to provide *social* solutions for these same problems. [T]he exercising of an art [is] once again an activity intended to allay ungratified wishes – in the first place in the creative artist himself and subsequently in his audience or spectators.

(1913j: 186–7)

3 This viewpoint is adumbrated by Freud (1916–17: 366; 1924b: 185). From the (meta-psychological) economic point of view wish-fulfilment is, of course, in the service of the pleasure principle as a means of discharging psychic excitation (Freud 1900a: ch. 7). The economic conceptions have been thoroughly criticized in the past few decades and it is sufficient merely to notice them here.

4 Freud's conception of wish-fulfilment is entirely singular though he sometimes claimed the Ancients and later authorities (Freud 1900a: 96ff) as forerunners, and some commentators have accepted this at face value. E.R. Dodds (1951: 19), for example, observes that the notion that some dreams were meaningful and wish-ful-filling was common among the Ancients. There are indeed ancient records of dreams interpreted along wish-fulfilling lines. The interpretation of Alexander the Great's dream of the Satyr is discussed by Freud (1900a: 131), and Penelope's dream, interpreted as wishful by the disguised Odysseus himself, is discussed by Hunt (1989: 88). The dreams, sought with votive offerings in the temples of Asclepius and elswhere, in which a god or hero tells the dreamer how to resolve his perplexity, have an obviously wishful tincture since, naturally, the divine presences had the dreamer's interests at heart. However it would be more accurate to say that all these dreams were prognostic and conceived of as self-fulfilling, suggesting satisfying courses of action which could be implemented *when the dreamers were awake*, rather than as wish-fulfilling in the Freudian sense.

Another reason for the neglect I note is the long preoccupation in psychoanalysis, as in other contemporaneous schools of psychology, with drive theory. Revival of interest in the wish and wish-fulfilment, as presenting an alternative model of motivation to the classical drive theory, is quite recent (Gill and Holzman 1976; Schafer 1976; Sandler 1976). It remains problematic how wish and wish-fulfilment on the one hand, and instinct and instinctual drive discharge on the other, are to be related; though perhaps there is a reconciliation which would show these two models really to be aspects of one. A reasonable supposition is that Freud came to conceive of the wish as the psy-chical representative of instinct. This accords well with his later definition of the 'instinctual representative' as 'an idea (*Vorstellung*) or group of ideas which is cathected with a definite quota of psychical energy (libido or interest) coming from an instinct' (Freud 1915e: 152). Joseph Sandler is an important exception amongst the analysts who has not neglected wish-fulfilment (Sandler and Nagera 1963; Sandler 1976; Sandler and Sandler 1978; Sandler 1989).

5 For the details of the relevant processes: Freud 1900a: 575 ff; 1917d: 234ff. Jonathan Lear (1990: 78ff) criticizes Freud for arguing, improbably, that the first aim of the wish in this psychical activity is an hallucination of satisfaction. That this is Freud's view is not entirely clear because he says that the aim is *perceptual identity*, which leaves it open whether a hallucination or a perception of real satisfaction is involved. In any case, infantile hallucinatory satisfaction can be viewed – as I do above – as default action, as a kind of defence or adaptation, when the achievement of perceptual identity

through externally orientated action has failed. The occurrence of hallucinatory satisfaction in the infant is moot. Holt (1989: 268), for example, states that 'without stable objects, in an amorphous world of swirling flux, it is hard to imagine that anything we could call ideation goes on'. He adds that others reject 'the possibility of early infantile hallucination on the additional grounds that it implies the capacity to conceive or represent an absent object without some kind of action on it' (1989: 271) Some of this criticism flows from Piagetian sources and takes a dimmer view of infants' capacities than that being revealed by contemporary research (e.g. Kumin 1996). Some of it worries about pre-linguistic conceptual content (Cavell 1993), and some hinges on predicating hallucinatory satisfaction on the possibility of volitional representation. But a conception of hallucinatory wish-fulfilment which involves non-volitional sensory presentation would seem to be immune to these worries. Of course, the Freudian model has application beyond the neonate, in dream and psychotic hallucination.

6 William James cites Spinoza as the source. James asks us to consider a new-born mind presented with an imaginary visual impression of a candle:

> What possible sense (for that mind) would a suspicion have that the candle was not real? What would doubt or disbelief imply? When we, the onlooking psychologists, say the candle is unreal, we mean something quite definite, viz., that there is a world known to us which is real, and to which we perceive the candle does not belong . . . By the hypothesis, however, the mind which sees the candle can spin no such considerations as these about it, for of other facts actual or possible, it has no inkling whatever. The candle is its all, its absolute. Its entire faculty of attention is absorbed by it.
>
> (James 1950 [1890], II: 288)

He goes on (1950 [1890], II: 294): 'The world of dreams is our real world whilst we are sleeping because our attention then lapses from the sensible world. Conversely when we are awake the attention usually lapses from the dream world and that becomes unreal.'

7 I use 'evidence' idiosyncratically to mean the features of experience from which we *do* draw conclusions, not only those from which we canonically ought. Thus hallucinations would not ordinarily be accounted sound evidence for conclusions about their objects, but it is a fact that people undergoing hallucinations will draw conclusions from them. I hold that the relation between evidence and belief is internal: consequently change in belief can be wrought only through an adjustment to the agent's evidence. Such evidence includes conscious and unconscious phantasy, symptoms and enactments and the tendentious selections of data, and so on. The rationale for the manufacture of such evidence becomes much clearer in the context of self-solicitude which I expound in section 5 and is discussed in Pataki 1996.

8 It seems to me that this causal relation between belief and extinction is not amongst the necessary conditions for our *ordinary* understanding of wish-fulfilment (deviant causal chains can be concocted), whereas the conceptual connection with belief (ii), seems evident in both ordinary and Freudian wish-fulfilment. This is apparently denied by Gardner (1993: 125) who writes that 'it is not apriori that belief is a condition for the cessation of [desire]'. If Gardner means here 'conceptual condition' then 'I wish that p, though I believe that p' is in good logical order, which is doubtful. If he means 'causal condition' that *may* be true of *ordinary* wish-fulfilment, but false of Freudian wish-fulfilment. It is clear that Freud thought that belief was causally necessary to wish-fulfilment.

9 The unconscious wish-fulfilment achieved through art or religious worship and ritual may be exceptions to this condition, though even here it seems likely that wish-

fulfilment occurs only as a consequence of the initiation of a projective and introjective engagement with the work of art or the structure of religious belief and practice, in which unconscious wishes find or generate representations of their fulfilment and achieve pacification.

10 For example: 'symptoms serve for the patient's sexual satisfaction; they are a substitute for satisfaction of this kind, which the patients are without in their lives. . . . This symptom was fundamentally a wish-fulfilment, just like a dream – and moreover what is not always true of a dream, an erotic wish-fulfilment' (1916–17: 299). And: 'The symptoms of a neurosis are, it might be said, without exception either a substitutive satisfaction of some sexual urge or measures to prevent such a satisfaction; and as a rule they are compromises between the two' (1940a: 186).

11 Gardner recognizes a role for belief in wish-fulfilment *after* 'the first incursion of the Reality Principle' (1993: 128). It's not clear how he coordinates that event with the advent of language and propositionality. In any case, the supplemented account retains the kernel of the primordial process, and it is the inadequacy of the primordial account that I am trying to expose.

12 It may be helpful here to record a typical dream. Tanya, aged six, dreams in considerable distress that her little dog has been stolen. Interpretation: For Tanya the dog represented a wished-for penis. Since only what she owns can be stolen from her, the dream assures her that she *does* have a penis. Here there is no experiential registration of satisfaction, on the contrary, but there is an obvious wish-fulfilling belief.

13 Freud had no such concerns: 'All the categories which we employ to describe conscious mental acts, such as ideas, purposes, resolutions and so on, can be applied to them [unconscious mental acts]. Indeed, we are obliged to say of some of these latent states that the only respect in which they differ from conscious ones is precisely in the absence of consciousness' (1915e: 168). See also Freud 1912g; Moore 1984: 252–61. The extent to which the id can be thought of as a subject of propositional attitudes depends very much on how one understands both the id and propositional attitudes. On the other hand, the situation with the descriptively unconscious ego is unambiguous: every kind of mental act is open to it, from primary-process thought to intentional strategy. It should be remembered that not all of the unconscious ego, on Freud's scheme, is preconscious (1923b: 7).

14 Hysterical acts are 'mimetic or hallucinatory representations of phantasies' (Freud 1913j: 173; see 1908a; 1909d).

15 These vicissitudinal questions are still moot. Here I largely follow Hartmann 1964. Contrast Gardner (1993: 132) where plasticity is regarded as an aspect of the symbol formation which enables wish-fulfilment to ramify and sublimation is understood, in the Kleinian manner, in my view erroneously, as retaining symbolic significance.

16 The psychoanalyst Joseph Sandler writes:

> the symptom is not only a disguised 'surface expression' of the unconscious fantasy, but also a source of the perceptual information providing a concealed and symbolic identity of perception in relation to the unconscious wish it satisfies . . . the perceived manifest actualization is unconsciously understood and unconsciously translated back into its latent meaning. In terms of the topographical model this 'decoding' and understanding would take place in the Pcs. system, while in the structural model it can be attributed to the unconscious ego. Essential to the process is the need for consciousness to be protected from the knowledge of what is going on.
>
> (Sandler 1976: 40)

It seems to me unlikely that any poorer conception of unconscious understanding, for example the unconscious seeing-as explicated by Gardner (1993: 165ff), can do all the work unconscious pacification requires, let alone accommodate the mass of observations for which even popular psychology has advanced the notions of the subliminal or sub-conscious.

17 The criticisms levelled at Hopkins's formula and Gardner's development of it apply only in such cases – enactments, acting-out, pathological life-styles – where behaviour is plausibly construed as intentional. It may be a solution to the paradox of the tablecloth lady to deny that the performance is intentional. After all, the woman is a compulsive and cannot withhold or modify her behaviour. Alternatively, to preserve the intuition of intentional involvement it may be necessary to 'extend' the notion of intention in much the same way as Wollheim, Hopkins and Gardner have urged the extension of other concepts of ordinary psychology to accommodate the insights of psychoanalysis. I have taken the latter course in Pataki 1996 where I discuss similar cases and suggest that, briefly and not quite accurately, the compulsion *may* be explained as an unconscious, intentional act, governed by practical syllogisms.

18 'Primitive men and neurotics, as we have seen, attach a high valuation – in our eyes an over-valuation – to psychical acts. This attitude may plausibly be brought into relation with narcissism and regarded as an essential component of it. It may be said that in primitive men the process of thinking is still to a great extent sexualized. This is the origin of their belief in the omnipotence of thoughts . . .' (Freud 1912–13: 89).

19 Winnicott (1965) and many other analysts have emphasized the important role that an appropriate experience of omnipotence plays in healthy development. This, of course, is not the whole of narcissism or even of the sense of omnipotence, which in its malignant forms is often a defensive or compensatory development, but it is an important part of it.

20 That dreams are intended communications has been argued by many authors in the Freudian and Jungian traditions, recently by Charles Rycroft (1979), and is part of the religious beliefs of many traditional peoples. What psychological grounds could there be for such a view? Rycroft quotes Calvin Hall as saying that 'the dream is a letter to oneself'. Well, why send letters to oneself? If the dream is wish-fulfilling then we can see why one might be interested in self-communion: it is a form of self-consolation. The dream may be likened to an answer to the child's request 'Tell me a story', and may be influenced by that story-telling institution which consoles the child for the impending loss of his objects in sleep. The dream keeps the child – and the adult – in touch with his objects, including his self, and tries to paint them into gratifying scenarios. Weiss, Sampson and the Mount Zion group (1986) have emphasized the intentionalism in Freud's later work, and have argued, on the basis of careful clinical observation and testing, that people exercise unconscious control over their repressions, have unconscious beliefs, formulate unconscious plans and tests, make unconscious decisions and assessments of current reality and put their unconscious plans into effect, governed by the overriding consideration of safety. About dreams they say:

> the dreamer exerts control over his unconscious mental life. He regulates the production of dreams in accordance with the criteria of safety and danger . . . The ego produces dreams in an attempt to deal adaptively with its problems, including those that arise from the demands on it of the instincts, of conscience, and of current reality. It produces dreams as part of its task of self-preservation.
>
> (Weiss and Sampson 1986: 117)

Recent neuro-physiological and neuro-anatomical findings have become favourable to an intentionalist understanding of dreams, or at least of some dreams. The earlier findings which linked dreaming to REM sleep, primitive brain-stem structures and neural determination have given way to a recognition of dreaming in non-REM sleep and the predominance of higher forebrain structures. The neuro-anatomist Mark Solms concludes: 'The body of clinico-anatomical evidence strongly supports the view that forebrain structures are essential for dreaming whereas brain-stem structures are not' (Solms 1996: 54).

21 An aspect of Freud's intentionalism which has been much discussed within psycho-analysis is the change in his view of anxiety, from its early conception as automatic transformation of libido to that of signal anxiety. He says of the capacity to use signal anxiety that it 'constitutes a first great step forward in the provision made by the infant for its self-preservation, and at the same time represents a transition from the automatic and involuntary fresh appearance of anxiety to the intentional reproduction of anxiety as a signal of danger' (Freud 1926d: 52). The theme of the intentional use of anxiety to signal oneself as an internalization of the use of anxiety to signal the mother, and therefore as an aspect of self-concern, is developed in Kumin 1996.

22 Some people lack this concern or possess it to a diminished degree. It is possibly of significant relevance that autistic children cannot phantasize or play imaginatively (Tustin 1992) and that some severely schizoid patients cannot dream (Hunt 1989: 51). Other patients who have failed to internalize adequately maternal caring functions may be unable to regulate or even identify their own impulses (Kumin 1996).

23 I am eliding several distinct, complex processes. Winnicott's (1965) views on the false self's protection and solicitude for the true self are well known. A number of Kleinian analysts (Bion 1984 [1967]; Rosenfeld 1987; Steiner 1982) as well as some strongly influenced by Klein (Kernberg 1966, 1975; Ogden 1993 [1986]) and others (e.g. Bollas 1987) have written about these pathological reflexive attitudes to the self in the context of narcissistic and schizoid object relations. It seems to me that these self-reflexive relations cannot be adequately understood as relations in phantasy (Gardner 1993) or in terms of metaphorical motives (Hopkins 1982, 1995). In post-Kleinian work on structural relations, it may be said, the master is not Klein but Fairbairn.

References

Bion, W. R. (1984 [1967]) *Second Thoughts*, London: Karnac.

Bollas, C. (1987) *The Shadow of the Object*, New York: Columbia University Press.

Cavell, M. (1993) *The Psychoanalytic Mind*, Cambridge MA: Harvard University Press.

Collins, A. W. (1979) 'Could our beliefs be representations in our brains?', *The Journal of Philosophy*, LXXVI: 225–243.

Dodds, E. R. (1951) *The Greeks and the Irrational*, Berkeley: University of California Press.

Eagle, M. (1984) *Recent Developments in Psychoanalysis*, Cambridge MA: Harvard University Press.

Fairbairn, W. R. D. (1976 [1952]) *Psychoanalytic Studies of the Personality*, London: Routledge and Kegan Paul.

Ferenczi, S. (1956 [1913]) 'Stages in the development of a sense of reality', in *Sex in Psychoanalysis*, New York: Dover.

Freud, S. (1900a) *The Interpretation of Dreams, Standard Edition* IV, V.

—— (1905d) *Three Essays on the Theory of Sexuality*, VII.

—— (1908a) 'Hysterical phantasies and their relation to bisexuality', IX.

—— (1908e) 'Creative writers and daydreaming', IX.

—— (1909a) 'Some general remarks on hysterical attacks', IX.

—— (1909d) 'Notes upon a case of obsessional neurosis', X.

—— (1911b) 'Formulations on the two principles of mental functioning', XII.

—— (1911e) 'The handling of dream interpretation in psychoanalysis', XII.

—— (1912f) 'Contributions to a discussion on masturbation', XII

—— (1912g) 'A note on the unconscious', XII.

—— (1912–13) *Totem and Taboo*, XIII.

—— (1913j) 'The claims of psychoanalysis to scientific interest', XIII.

—— (1915c) 'Instincts and their vicissitudes', XIV.

—— (1915e) 'The unconscious', XIV.

—— (1916–17) *Introductory Lectures on Psychoanalysis*, XV–XVI.

—— (1917d) 'A metapsychological supplement to the theory of dreams', XIV.

—— (1922b) 'Neurotic mechanisms in jealousy, paranoia and homosexuality', XVIII.

(1923b) *The Ego and the Id*, XIX.

(1923c) 'Remarks on the theory and practice of dream interpretation', XIX

(1924b) 'Neurosis and psychosis', XIX.

(1924e) 'The loss of reality in neurosis and psychosis', XIX.

(1925d) *An Autobiographical Study*, XX.

(1925i) 'Some additional notes on dream interpretation', XIX.

(1926d) *Inhibitions, Symptoms and Anxiety*, XX.

(1927c) *The Future of an Illusion*, XXI.

(1928c) 'On humour', XXI.

(1933a) *New Introductory Lectures on Psychoanalysis*, XXII.

(1937c) 'Analysis terminable and interminable', XXIII.

(1940a) *An Outline of Psychoanalysis*, XXIII.

Gardner, S. (1993) *Irrationality and the Philosophy of Psychoanalysis*, Cambridge: Cambridge University Press.

Gill, M. and Holzman, P. (eds) (1976) *Psychology versus Metapsychology*, New York: International Universities Press.

Grünbaum, A. (1984) *The Foundations of Psychoanalysis*, Berkeley: University of California Press.

Hartmann, H. (1958 [1939]) *Ego Psychology and the Problem of Adaptation*, New York: International Universities Press.

—— (1964) *Essays in Ego Psychology*, New York: International Universities Press.

Hartmann, H., Kris, E. and Loewenstein, R. (eds) (1964) *Papers on Psychoanalytic Psychology*, New York: International Universities Press.

Holt, R. R. (1989) *Freud Reappraised*, New York: Guildford Press.

Hopkins, J. (1982) 'Introduction: philosophy and psychoanalysis', in R. Wollheim and J. Hopkins (eds), *Philosophical Essays on Freud*, Cambridge: Cambridge University Press.

—— (1988) 'Epistemology and depth psychology', in P. Clark and C. Wright (eds), *Mind, Psychoanalysis and Science*, Oxford: Blackwell.

—— (1991) 'The interpretation of dreams', in J. Neu (ed.), *The Cambridge Companion to Freud*, Cambridge: Cambridge University Press.

—— (1994) 'The unconscious' in S. Guttenplan (ed.), *A Companion to Philosophy of Mind*, Oxford: Blackwell.

—— (1995) 'Irrationality, interpretation and division', in C. and G. McDonald (eds), *Philosophy of Psychology*, Oxford: Blackwell.

Hunt, H. T. (1989) *The Multiplicity of the Dream*, New Haven: Yale University Press.

James, W. (1950 [1890]) *The Principles of Psychology*, New York: Dover.

Johnston, M. (1988) 'Self-deception and the nature of mind', in A. Rorty and B. P. McLaughlin (eds), *Perspectives on Self-Deception*, California: University of California Press.

Kernberg, O. F. (1966) 'Structural derivatives and object-relationships', *International Journal of Psycho-Analysis*, 47.

—— (1975) *Borderline Conditions and Pathological Narcissism*, New York: Jason Aronson.

Klein, M. (1975 [1952]) 'The emotional life of the infant', in *Envy and Gratitude*, London: Hogarth Press.

Kumin, I. (1996) *Pre-Object Relatedness*, New York: Guildford Press.

Lear, J. (1990) *Love and its Place in Nature*, New York: Farrar, Strauss, Giroux.

Marshall, G. This volume.

Moore, M. (1984) *Law and Psychiatry*, Cambridge: Cambridge University Press.

Ogden, T. H. (1993 [1986]) *The Matrix of the Mind*, Northvale, NJ: Jason Aronson.

O'Shaughnessy, B. (1980) *The Will: A Dual Aspect Theory*, Cambridge: Cambridge University Press.

Pataki, T. (1996) 'Intention in wish-fulfilment', *Australasian Journal of Philosophy*, 74(1).

—— (1997) 'Self-deception and wish-fulfilment', *Philosophia* 25(1–4).

Price, H. H. (1954) 'Belief and will' in R. Dearden, P. Hirst and R. Peters (eds), *Reason*, London: Routledge and Kegan Paul.

Rosenfeld, H. (1987) *Impasse and Interpretation*, London: Tavistock.

Rycroft, C. (1979) *The Innocence of Dreams*, London: Pantheon Books.

Sandler, J. (1976) 'Dreams, unconscious fantasies and "'identity of perception'"', in *International Review of Psycho-Analysis* 3(1).

—— (ed.) (1989) *Dimensions of Psychoanalysis*, London: Karnac.

Sandler, J. and Nagera, H. (1963) 'Aspects of the metapsychology of fantasy', *Psychoanalytic Study of the Child*, 18.

Sandler, J. and Sandler, A. M. (1978) 'The development of object-relationships and affects', *International Journal of Psycho-Analysis* 59(2).

Schafer, R. (1976) *A New Language for Psychoanalysis*, New Haven: Yale University Press.

Shope, R. (1967) 'The psychoanalytic theories of wish-fulfilment and meaning', *Inquiry* 10.

Solms, M. (1996) 'Neurological implications of dreaming: implications for psychoanalysis', *Psychoanalytic Quarterly* 54(2).

Spitz, R. (1965) *The First Year of Life*, New York: International Universities Press.

Steiner, J. (1982) 'Perverse relationships between parts of the self', *International Journal of Psycho-Analysis* 63(3).

Stoller, R. J. (1979) *Sexual Excitement*, New York: Simon and Schuster.

Tustin, F. (1992) *Autistic States in Children*, London: Tavistock/Routledge.

Weiss, J. and Sampson, H. (1986) *The Psychoanalytic Process*, New York: International Universities Press.

Winnicott, D. W. (1965) *The Maturational Process and the Facilitating Environment*, London: Hogarth Press.

Wollheim, R. (1979) 'Wish-fulfilment', in R. Harrison (ed.), *Rational Action: Studies in Philosophy and Social Science*, Cambridge: Cambridge University Press.

—— (1984) *The Thread of Life*, Cambridge: Cambridge University Press.
—— (1991 [1971]) *Freud*, London: Fontana.
—— (1993) *The Mind and its Depths*, Cambridge MA: Harvard University Press.
Wollheim, R. and Hopkins, J. (eds) (1982) *Freud: A Collection of Critical Essays*, second edition, New York: Anchor.

4

KEEPING TIME

Freud on the temporality of mind[1]

Marcia Cavell

Man learns the concept of the past by remembering.

Ludwig Wittgenstein

It is time to rescue the phenomenon of memory from being regarded merely as a psychological faculty and to see it as an essential element of the finite historical being of a person.

Hans-Georg Gadamer

Philosophers interested in memory have worried primarily about whether it can yield knowledge of one's past, and if so, how. These are epistemological questions. But as Locke made clear in arguing that the identity of a person over time reaches only so far back as his memory, such questions have implications for our thinking about the unity of the mind as well.

Freud's exploration of the interrelationships between mind, memory and personal identity are among his most interesting and original contributions to philosophical psychology, marking him, along with Proust and Heidegger, one of the three great psychologists of the twentieth century. From some growing concerns about the reliability of memory, Freud was led to the view that, as I would put it, temporality is constitutive of the mind, and furthermore, that the mind can be split along fault-lines that are temporal in character. He calls the process through which these splits may be healed, *remembering, repeating and working through*.[2]

Remembering is a psychological act, sometimes a difficult act. As an act it is not only *about* time; it takes place *in* time. These are features that the concept of memory does not make explicit. Though he often writes of memory, it is remembering that Freud singularly illumines.

Freud and Breuer took their early ideas about memory, and remembering as catharsis, from Janet, who viewed memory as the central organizing apparatus of the mind. Janet's work with hysterics had led him to think that memory can follow two different routes: it can function automatically, in a way that is shared by human beings and by other animals, and it can function in a narrative way peculiar to us, integrating new experience into existing mental schema. While familiar experiences can be woven without much conscious attention into an intelligible narrative, an experience that is not merely unfamiliar but also frightening and bizarre may make a tremendous psychic impact at the same time as it defies intelligibility.[3] (The experiences of Holocaust survivors, for whom scenes of the past may persevere as a kind of ahistorical hallucination, are examples of the traumatic sort of memory (Laub 1993)). Such unintegrated experiences may later surface as isolated recollections, split off from the person's sense of her own history; or they may surface as repetitive, behavioural enactments. In the course of treatment, what had been a traumatic memory becomes a narrative memory, a story now told, with all the appropriate feeling, to another person.

Janet writes:

> It is only for convenience that we speak of it as a 'traumatic memory'. The subject is often incapable of making the necessary narrative which we call memory regarding the event; and yet he remains confronted by a difficult situation in which he has not been able to play a satisfactory part, one to which his adaptation had been imperfect, so that he continues to make efforts at adaptation.
>
> (Janet 1919/25: 663)

In *Studies on Hysteria*, Freud and Breuer give voice to Janet's idea in the famous slogan, '*Hysterics suffer mainly from reminiscences*' (Freud 1893–5: 7). Though even in that work, Freud is more and more persuaded that the splitting off of psychical groups may be a product of what he calls 'defence', or intrapsychic conflict. Freud agrees with Janet that trauma disrupts memory; but in contrast to Janet's more mechanistic idea, Freud is suggesting that there is an active avoidance of remembering.

Then in a paper entitled 'The Aetiology of Hysteria', Freud writes: '*[The] symptoms of hysteria . . . are determined by certain experiences of the patient's which have operated in a traumatic fashion and which are being reproduced in his psychical life in the form of mnemic symbols*' (Freud 1896: 192, 193). It was in this paper that Freud presented to a scandalized audience the seduction theory, that 'at the bottom of every case of hysteria there are one or more occurrences of premature sexual experience, occurrences which belong to the earliest period of childhood' (1896: 203). Had he heeded Janet's admonition that 'traumatic memory' is not truly remembering, Freud might have clarified his thesis by adding that the hysteric's reminiscences are not memories as we ordinarily think of them, that what she suffers from is really a peculiar failure of remembering. Nor is that failure either a true forgetting or a motivated 'forgetting', as in what Freud will later call the parapraxes. Hysterical reminiscence is a state in between remembering and forgetting, in between knowing and never having known.

Freud soon changed his mind about the veracity of the hysteric's memory. Whereas earlier he had taken the patient's account of seduction at face value, concluding that it is memories of real events in the public world that get repressed, he came to think instead that 'psychic reality', the patient's fantasies about what happened, is the crucial issue. He wrote to Fliess: 'the psychical structures which, in hysteria, are affected by repression are not in reality memories . . . but impulses' (Freud 1897: 247). Sex keeps its importance in Freud's new view; but the traumatic seductions may have happened only in the patient's mind in the form of conflicted, wish-fulfilling phantasies.

Some critics have scolded Freud for letting the real seducers off the hook (Masson 1984). Other critics have scolded him for finding seductions where they don't exist (Crews 1995). I myself think that Freud, and psychoanalytic theory after him, took an unfortunate turn just at this juncture in minimizing the importance of the external world, *reality*, in *psychic* reality. Freud's basic point, however, is that reality does not come already interpreted, that the person's own idiosyncratic interpretation must figure in any *psychological* explanation of her thought and behaviour. And this is right.

Philosophy of mind owes Freud a debt for tracing out the complex relationships between world and thought, showing us the various ways in which thought is shaped by conflict, anxiety and desire. He himself remarked, moreover, that the exchange between phantasy[4] and veridical memory may go in either direction. In the *Introductory Lectures on Psycho-Analysis*, he says that '[P]hantasies of being seduced are of particular interest, because so often they are not phantasies but real memories' (Freud 1916–17 [1915–17]: 370).

Philosophical theorists of memory have long been concerned with whether remembering always takes the form of having a mental image. This isn't a question Freud considers explicitly. But there's an interesting suggestion of an answer in the following passage from 'The Aetiology of Hysteria':

> As we know from Breuer, hysterical symptoms can be resolved if, starting from them, we are able to find the path back to the memory of a traumatic experience. If the memory which we have uncovered does not answer our expectations, it may be that we ought to pursue the same path a little further; perhaps behind the first traumatic scene there may be concealed the memory of a second . . . so that the scene that was first discovered has only the significance of a connecting link in the chain of associations . . . it always has more than two links; and the traumatic scenes do not form a simple row, like a string of pearls, but ramify and are interconnected like genealogical trees, so that in any new experience two or more earlier ones come into operation as memories.
>
> (Freud 1896: 95, 96)

The suggestion is that remembering invokes a vast network of affectively coloured beliefs and desires, and that this network forms part of the content of what we call 'a memory'. Freud is beginning to tell us more about what a narrative remembering is, and how the transition from trauma to narrative can be made. Remembering is an activity of linking; so forgetting, or not knowing, is often a matter of un-linking, or not putting two and two together. He writes: '[F]orgetting impressions, scenes or experiences nearly always reduces itself to shutting them off . . . In the many different forms of obsessional neurosis in particular, forgetting is mostly restricted to dissolving thought-connections, failing to draw the right conclusions and isolating memories' (Freud 1914: 148). To explain these acts of dissolution and isolation, Freud was eventually moved to introduce the concepts of resistance, repression and the dynamic unconscious, the concepts that begin to shape what we know as the specifically 'Freudian' view of remembering.[5]

Freud's reflections on remembering deepened next with the idea of 'screen memory', a vivid but apparently trivial childhood memory behind which other important experiences are hidden, and which has been inflected by experiences (and unconscious phantasies) subsequent to the event that memory reports:

> The recognition of this fact [that the falsified memory is the one of which we first become aware] must diminish the distinction we have drawn between screen memories and other memories derived from our childhood. It may indeed be questioned whether we have any memories at all *from* our childhood: memories *relating* to our childhood may be all we possess. Our childhood memories show us the earliest years not as they were but as they appeared at the later periods when the memories were aroused. In these periods of arousal, the childhood memories did not, as people are accustomed to say, *emerge*; they were *formed* at that time. And a number of motives, with no concern for historical accuracy, had a part in forming them, as well as in the selection of the memories themselves.
>
> (Freud 1899: 322)

The concept of a screen memory (*Deckerinnerung*) implicitly contains that of *Nachträglichkeit*, or deferred action, the idea (later posited in the Wolf Man case) that the mind interprets the past in terms of the present, or in terms of events that happened later than the event itself. This is how Freud came to understand many childhood traumas: because of meanings with which the child has later invested it, an event may become disturbing only after the fact. For example, observing parental intercourse at the age of a year and a half might not cause the child anxiety at the time; but if he later comes to believe that women have been castrated, the wish to take his mother's place with his father may carry with it the fearful idea of castration (Freud 1918 [1914]). We tend to think of memory as memorializing an event as it happened then, forgetting both that it is the event as understood which is remembered, and that between then and now, the mind has given further directions for how to interpret its own past.

The concept of a screen memory has more than this to tell us, however. Since all interpretation, on Freud's view, is governed by considerations of pleasure and pain, as well as by other things, so too is memory. Memories are layered, and the layering is constrained not only by their temporal but also by their dynamic, or defensive, relations to each other. This that I do remember, painful though it may be, is less painful than that which I have 'forgotten', and will not remember – will not to remember. (The way of putting it suggests that the defensive activity is fully intentional. As I say later in talking about neurotic repetition, I do not think this is the case.) One memory can screen or hide another from view. Some memories are orphans that have been closeted, or disinherited, by other members of the psychological family. Psychoanalytic therapy works by locating these orphans, getting to know and name them, and in the process, changing the family.

Comparing these ideas of Freud's with a passage from Proust's *Remembrance of Things Past* may help bring out what Freud had in mind.

> Real life, life at last laid bare and illuminated – the only life in consequence which can be said to be really lived – is literature, and life thus defined is in a sense immanent in ordinary men no less than in the artist. But most men do not see it because they do not seek to shed light upon it. And therefore their past is like a photographic dark-room encumbered with innumerable negatives which remain useless because the intellect has not developed them.
>
> (Proust 1981: 931)

Developing a photographic negative makes apparent, by reversing the tonal values of light and dark, the latent image inscribed on the film. Presumably this image is already present. But Freud has put the notion of such an image in question. Nor does he think of developing a memory as primarily a matter of using one's intellect. In fact, Proust's photographic image does an injustice to his own novel, in which remembering is both a finding and a making (as it is in the psychoanalytic process). This is the remembering that his novel itself instances.

In 'Remembering, Repeating and Working Through', Freud remarks on the simple form that remembering took in hypnotic treatment: '[T]he patient put himself back in to an earlier situation, which he seemed never to confuse with the present one, and gave an account of the mental processes belonging to it' (Freud 1914: 148). In therapy as Freud comes to practise it, however, the patient does seem to make this confusion between past and present, much as Janet's traumatized patients also did. The patient repeats past traumas, 'finding' herself again and again in a self-destructive relationship with a man, or sabotaging herself at work, or enacting sexual rituals in which she is the master or the slave, or both.

But Freud has broadened Janet's notion of psychic trauma to include any interpersonal situation, often habitual, that evokes intense and unresolved intra-psychic conflict, conflict such that, below the threshold of conscious awareness, the very same activity represents on the one hand the gratification of a wish, need, or desire, and, on the other, the doing of something in some way dangerous, forbidden, reprehensible. And Freud has given up hypnosis (at which he apparently never was very good) for what his patient Anna O. dubbed 'the talking cure', because the phenomenon of resistance has led him to a more complex picture of the mind than the one with which Janet was working. He now sees that even the 'normal' mind harbours psychological constellations that reflect different periods of the person's development and different ways of dealing with intrapsychic conflict; that these constellations are typically split apart, not integrated with each other; and that the result is a kind of confusion between past and present which it is the task of therapy to resolve. The concepts of remembering, repeating and working-through are meant to bring all this to light. Freud writes:

> the patient does not *remember* anything of what he has forgotten and repressed, but *acts* it out. He reproduces it not as a memory but as an action; he *repeats* it, without of course knowing that he is repeating it. For instance, the patient does not say that he remembers that he used to be defiant and critical towards his parents' authority; instead, he behaves in that way to the doctor. He does not remember how he came to a helpless and hopeless deadlock in his infantile researches; but he produces a mass of confusing dreams and associations, complains that he cannot succeed in anything and asserts that he is fated never to carry through what he undertakes. He does not remember having been intensely ashamed of certain sexual activities and afraid of their being found out; but he makes it clear that he is ashamed of the treatment on which he is now embarked and tries to keep it secret from everybody. And so on . . . As long as the patient is in the treatment he cannot escape from this compulsion to repeat; and in the end we understand that this is his way of remembering.
>
> (Freud 1914: 150)

In *Beyond the Pleasure Principle*, Freud explicitly takes up the repetition compulsion (Freud 1920). He famously describes the game of his one-and-a-half-year-old grandson, who repetitively throws a little spool away from him with a cry that sounds like 'fort' ('gone'), then reels it back to him with a joyful 'da' ('here'). Freud suggests several motives for the game, all of which turn on anxiety: the child is rehearsing the anxiety caused by his mother's occasional departures, and attempting to master it by taking an active role; or he is symbolically making his mother come back; or he is vengefully throwing her away as he feels thrown away. (The child who plays doctor after a painful visit in which he was himself the patient is a homely example of what Freud has in mind.)

The pleasure principle is a complex concept in Freud's mature theory. It includes the tendencies to seek pleasure and to avoid pain, and in doing so to take reality into account. It alludes to a finely tuned system of self-regulation that manages pain, pleasure, the perception of reality and the avoidance, through an experience of anxiety, of anything perceived as constituting danger. So far, then, we are within the domain of the pleasure principle. But anxiety is tricky. In a later work, Freud writes:

> Either the generation of anxiety – the repetition of the old traumatic experience – is limited to a signal, in which case the remainder of the

reaction can adapt itself to the new situation and proceed to flight or defence; or the old situation can retain the upper hand and the total reaction may consist in no more than a generation of anxiety, in which case the affective state becomes paralysing . . .

(Freud 1933 [1932]: 82)

That is, anxiety may fail in its function as signal, reproducing the trauma instead. In that case the person is compelled to repeat and re-experience aspects of the trauma in order to assimilate it in a way that allows for memory, repression, adaptation, defence, perception of reality, thought and, in general, the resumption of the pleasure principle.[6]

Freud speculates in *Beyond the Pleasure Principle* that the repetition compulsion may be a bit of evidence for the existence of an instinct he calls 'the death instinct' that is basically regressive, that seeks to disorganize and return the organism to a more primitive state of functioning, indeed in theory, to a state of non-life. One can disregard this speculation, however, as most psychoanalysts have, and yet hold on to the idea that the effects of trauma can be paralysing, regressive and disorganizing.

In *Inhibitions, Symptoms, and Anxiety*, Freud says that the earliest anxieties all have to do with separation from the mother, and that these are the anxieties that are apt to echo through later development (Freud 1926: particularly 151). Studies in attachment behaviour and in mother–infant interaction confirm that there is a close connection between the infant's disposition to anxiety and his mother's responses to him (Bowlby 1969; Bowlby 1973; Ainsworth et al. 1978; Bowlby 1980). They suggest that adult styles of relating to others are modelled on these earliest infant–parent interactions (Stern 1995); that affects are aroused primarily in infant–parent interactions and are shaped by those interactions; and that these early affective reactions are a form of early mentation, knowledge of earliest object-relational patterns that are bound up in the growing child's continuity of experiences of itself and other. 'Though such affective knowledge is beyond the adult's recollective ability, its influence on personality organization may be profound' (Wilson and Malatesta 1989: 296).[7] Psychoanalytic therapy, then, is not just incidentally but essentially interpersonal, the field on which repetitions can be observed, understood and, one hopes, to some extent unlearned.

Virtually all contemporary explanations for the repetition compulsion are premised on the idea that something in the present reminds the patient of a past trauma, and that the anxieties it provoked are easily aroused again and again (Parkin 1981; Broughton 1993; Wilson and Malatesta 1989). The patient need not *consciously* perceive the present situation as resembling the past, and indeed it may be superficially very different from the one it (unconsciously) recalls. He also is not conscious of the ways in which he still feels like the anxious child he once was. But the similarity to an old threat is there, and because it is, the old emergency behaviour goes into action.

Here is an account of a repetitive scenario from the current psychoanalytic literature:

you will find if you get to talk to an exhibitionist, that his purpose in displaying his genitals is not to seduce a woman into making love with him but rather to shock her. If she is upset – is embarrassed, becomes angry, runs away – and especially if she calls the police, he has, he feels, absolute proof that his genitals are important. When you learn that he is likely to exhibit himself following a humiliation earlier in the day, you will be alert to the hostile components he experiences in his excitement. For him, this sexual act serves as a kind of rape – a forced intrusion (at least that is the way he fantasizes it) into the woman's sensibilities and delicacy. If he cannot believe that he has harmed her, the act has failed for him . . . His idea – his fantasy – of what is going on includes, then, the following features. He has done something hostile to a woman; he has been the active force, not the passive victim as he was earlier in the day when someone humiliated him. He has converted this trauma to a triumph, capped by his success in becoming sexually excited . . . He seems to be running great risks: he may be caught and arrested, his family and job put in jeopardy. But the true danger that perversion is to protect him from – that he is insignificant, unmanly – is not out there on the street but within him and therefore inescapable. It is so fundamental that he is willing to run the lesser risk, that of being caught.

(Stoller 1979: xii)

What is going on here? Presumably, something like this: the patient is a man who experienced repetitive humiliation as a child around issues that, in his mind, had to do with his male-ness and his sense of self, and that carried with them the threat of some sort of punishment. Presumably also he learned to handle this humiliation by imagining (fantasizing), or doing, something that he could construe both as turning the tables on the other, and proving, in the eyes of both the other and of himself, his masculine competence. The aggressive exhibitionism that he now acts out is itself sexually exciting, addictively so; but since the excitement occurs in the context of an old, unconscious, intrapsychic conflict, it circles into the same anxieties which the behaviour is meant to allay.

Just this combination of features characterizes the acting-out of intrapsychic conflict. It gratifies some needs, but in ways that imperil others. In addition, the patient often chooses as partners in his scenario, persons with whom the old, unsatisfying relationship can be most easily recreated. For example, in the past he experienced humiliation at the hands of an intrusive, belittling, mother or father, and it is to similarly humiliating love objects that he is now drawn. Then, too, he may be genuinely provocative; so rather than teaching the patient that things do not have to be as they once were, this new relationship confirms his assumptions and his worst fears. As Wilhelm Reich says of the masochist, 'the more he tries to get out of his suffering the more he becomes entangled in it' (Reich 1949: 226).

Where does 'the trying' figure in such a pattern? What part of it is intentional? I am going to assume that though the child's first attempts to salvage himself from a traumatic situation are purposive, they are not necessarily fully intentional. They do not fit the model of practical reasoning. The child presumably solves the problem in the best way at his disposal; then through repetition, his attempts acquire over time an automatic, routinized quality, which removes them yet further from the realm of thoughtful deliberation.

And what does the 'repeater' believe about past and present? That he can obliterate the past? Change it? Extract reparation or acknowledgement from those figures *then* by whom he feels wronged? He often acts as if he believed this, and so (unconsciously) some people do. But it need not be the case. Neurotic strategies tend to preserve the conflicts of the past much as they were, and so keep that part of oneself which is an anxious child from developing. In fact, though of course not by design, the repeater congeals the psychic past, catches, like a moth in amber, his childhood self. The neurotic's 'confusing' past with present is perhaps better understood, then, as a kind of multiplicity within what we call 'the self'.

Neurotic repetition outside the psychoanalytic situation tends to hold the neurotic structures in place; inside, it is the path to change. Transference and repetition are closely allied. Transference is the act of interpreting a present relationship as if it were a repetition of an old one in just those ways that created intrapsychic conflict. Presumably this is how the patient generally construes his world, so that we have so far said nothing to single out his relationship with his analyst. The differences enter with the fact that the analyst, one hopes, is alert to what is going on, and will not accept the role her patient assigns her. She is then perhaps uniquely in a position to bring what was unconscious, either because it was repressed or because it had never been formulated, into consciousness. She can begin to discover with her patient what those old anxieties were and to help him see that they were understandable given his situation then; but that he is now generating miseries for himself that are not called for by the present.

Consider the following clinical vignette. A man in his thirties begins an analysis because of problems at work. Repeatedly he fails to complete projects on time, or somehow fails at them. In analysis, it becomes apparent that every time something happens that he experiences as proof of his competence, or as the analyst's gratifying him, he worries about the analytic relationship. Has he harmed the analyst? Is she all right? Is she feeling demeaned? Together she and the patient begin to link the present to childhood experiences of helplessness in relation to a disabled father, and to a phantasy of omnipotence that came to the patient's aid. But power can work for good and for ill, and a child who imagines himself as very powerful is a child who can believe he is responsible for his father's death.

Repeatedly, analyst and patient work over the past. Repeatedly, the analyst does not fall apart as the patient has feared will happen when he is successful. Present neurotic anxiety begins to become comprehensible as it is linked to the past. Anxiety past, but not over, begins to lessen as it is located in the childhood situation that bred it. The real analytic present constantly reproves one's early, persistent, assumptions about the world.

The process Freud calls working through is not just a matter of integrating one's discrepant beliefs. It has a temporal meaning. It involves linking psychic past and psychic present so that one transcends the *psychic* past, informing it with what one has learned in the meantime. It is what makes remembering possible and defeats repeating. The patient starts out reliving his old infantile experiences and patterns of relating, while the analyst begins to note these patterns and interpret them, showing the patient that his infantile experiences were a part of his way then of actively maintaining relationships to the ones he loved.

'Making the unconscious conscious' is to some extent a process of articulating experience that may never have had a verbal form, and allowing it now to be accepted at a new level of psychological organization. It is a letting go of the past in an act that resembles mourning, opening the mind to new experiences in the present. *That* particular loved object is gone. *That* particular wrong turn was irrevocably taken. The man, say, who now regrets having abandoned an athletic career thirty years ago cannot make that very turn again. But he may come to one that is very similar. Let's suppose he was motivated by unconscious anxieties that such a career choice would put his relationship with his father in jeopardy. (A full psychological description of this case would of course have to explain why he had these anxieties.) We can put the general form of his unconscious question, the one he earlier answered in the negative, like this: 'Can I do something with my life that I love doing, something at which I may excel, without damaging the persons I love?' This general question might arise for him now in relation to a present activity and a present love object, and be answered, if he is not repeating in the neurotic sense, in a different way.

In *Three Essays on the Theory of Sexuality*, Freud wrote: 'The finding of an object is in fact a refinding of it' (Freud 1905: 222). Given what Freud probably had in mind at that time, we correctly understand him to be saying that all love is regressive, backward-looking, so doomed to disappointment. Freud's famous remark takes on a different meaning, however, in the context of his later work on remembering, repeating and working through. Every situation, every object, is a repetition in something like the sense that the old philosophic problem of The-One-and-the-Many formalizes. On the one hand, the particular can be recognized only if it is assimilated to a familiar pattern; on the other, this assimilation tends to blunt appreciation of its particularity. Freud implicitly translates the problem this way: How can one use the past in such a way that it helps one to notice, rather than obscure, what is peculiar about this object in the present? This is the question I have been attempting to answer on Freud's behalf with the concepts of remembering, repeating and working through. Another similar answer that makes the affective dimension of remembering more apparent is: through mourning. It is mourning that acknowledges what it is one has lost and that one has lost it, and that it is possible for old desires to be shaped by the present.[8]

Freud turned his attention to mourning for the first time in *Mourning and Melancholia*, in which he regards these two conditions as different ways of dealing with loss (Freud 1917 [1915]). A mourner is a person who has lost someone (in reality or in phantasy, perhaps a real person, but seen under the description of a certain phantasy) he values greatly, and who knows he has. The knowing is affective, and it takes time, for it requires discovering that in all the familiar places where the lost object once was, it is no longer. Mourning is the backward face of hope, acknowledging, through loss, the unrepeatability of time itself.

The melancholic behaves much like the mourner, with the difference that whereas in mourning the world has become poor and empty, as Freud says, in melancholia one experiences the poverty in oneself. Both the melancholic and the mourner have suffered a loss; but the love of the first was highly ambivalent, and he denies the loss. He will not or cannot make the mourner's affective moves. Instead he makes a ghost of the lost object, preserving it in phantasy by repetitively acting out its return (one thinks of Miss Havisham in *Great Expectations*), or by transferring its significance, its very significance, on to someone else; or he takes the lost object inside himself, again in phantasy, with the result that now his anger against the object is turned against himself.[9] While the one who has mourned is free to find a new and genuinely gratifying love, the melancholic is condemned to a form of passive repetition.[10]

Mourning and Melancholia served Freud as a kind of overture to *The Ego and the Id*, in which identification as a defence against loss is presented as one of the building blocks of the super-ego. I won't rehearse that argument here, but only remark that in my view Freud's analysis fits the pathological super-ego more closely, and that a 'healthy' moral conscience emerges not from melancholia but mourning. It is mourning that instructs one in the separateness of other persons, in the agency of the self, and in the finality of death.

Freud became increasingly sceptical about the possibility of an accurate reconstruction of the patient's psychic life (Freud 1937). Many psychoanalysts now share that scepticism. Some are even sceptical that we can make any useful generalizations about childhood development. But Freud's real insight about the temporal character of mental life is untouched. Loewald puts it this way: 'the whole orientation of psychoanalysis as a genetic approach to mental life, as an attempt to understand mental disease in terms of the history of mental development and to cure it by promoting a resumption of this history – using the faculty of remembering as the main tool – points to the importance of time as being somehow the inner fibre of what we call the psychical' (Loewald 1980: 52). Remembering is an activity that links past and present; it is the activity through which all the pieces acquire their significance. Past, present and future take their meaning only within this linking (Loewald 1980: 142). At best, the activity is constant, reworking the psychic past, making the present available as similar yet different. At worst, linking gets stuck in neurotic repetition, with the result that some of one's own feelings and behaviour, out of harmony as they are with many of one's present perceptions and abilities, are unintelligible even to oneself.

I want now to make explicit some interrelations I have been suggesting between memory and the unity of the self. The phenomena of irrationality have led a number of philosophers to think of the mind as divided. Tradition has generally followed Plato in drawing the lines between a part of the soul that is rational through and through, and another part (or two) that, like appetite, is inherently less rational. Davidson proposes instead that rationality more or less holds within each part of a divided mind, and that irrationality is a function of the way in which one part may be relatively unintegrated with the rest (Davidson 1982). But in both Plato and Davidson, the parts of the soul or mind are coeval in character. Time is simply not seen as an essential factor.

Freud too was puzzled from the beginning by irrationality. Freud too came to think that explaining irrationality requires us to see the mind as divided. But he differs from philosophical tradition in holding that some parts of the divided, irrational mind are on a different temporal footing.[11] This, I believe, is one of his most important philosophic ideas. In typical cases of 'Freudian' irrationality, mental structures early begin to be formed around anxiety involving one's connections to others. Perceptions, emotions, beliefs, that are closely related to these anxieties will be part of the structures. Imagine now that the anxiety situation is chronic – for example, a depressed mother who is unable to attend to the child's needs, or a threatening, ever-present father – and that the phantasies with which the child defends itself are ones on which he comes to rely. Then habits of mis-perception begin to harden. Through time, these structures gather yet more closely related beliefs, desires and mental attitudes into their nexus; they take on character, dividing old wishes and beliefs from newer ones with which they are in conflict. Increasingly there is a split between the past, as embedded and rewritten in phantasy, and the present (Cavell 1993: ch. 10). Metaphorically, these split-off structures are one's earlier selves.

Freud calls the refusal or the inability to keep time, neurosis. Heidegger calls it inauthenticity. One regards the past inauthentically if one thinks of oneself as one's own creator, and the past as in some way under one's present control. One regards the present inauthentically if one ignores the ways which the choices one makes now are the result of one's past choices; or thinks of these choices as out of one's hands entirely, not 'choices' at all; or fails to see that neither one's self nor the world is simply a given of experience but is to some extent the result of one's own activity. And one regards the future inauthentically if one awaits it passively. One is inauthentic so long as one denies the contingent, finite nature of human life, the fact that we did not create ourselves, the imminence of death and the singularity of one's own existence.

What I have just said of Heidegger could as well be said of Freud. Both call attention to the ways we attempt to deny both our dependence and our agency, attempt to erase the past and head off the future. Yet their hopes and visions are fundamentally different. Freud is after minimizing human misery, while happiness is no part of Heidegger's concern. Freud thinks the mind is structured, as well as hobbled, by the child's early love relations, and that love relearned in the psychoanalytic transference is one route to whatever cure there is. Heidegger holds up to us the hero's life in which love plays no essential part.

In *Le Temps retrouvé*, Marcel returns to Paris after a long absence. He is a man who has learned about time, in part, through belatedly mourning his beloved grandmother. He is at a party at the Guermantes whom he has known since childhood, waiting in the library for a concert in the drawing room to end. He is reflecting on all the *moments bienheureux* of which we have been reading, the magical moments, like the eating of the madeleine, which unfold the past into the present, the present into the past, in a way that has seemed to him to allow for a transcendence of time. He is thinking that in the novel he will write – the novel that we the readers are about to conclude, but only after a stunning dénouement – he will attempt to capture these out-of-time moments. Then he enters the drawing room and is astonished to find aged strangers whom he only gradually identifies as long-familiar friends. He now sees that the subject for his novel will not be the timeless past, but time itself, time which he will attempt to make visible, to exteriorize. He sees that the remembering which now interests him is the other side of the present as it is lived in the face of death.

Proust writes:

> it would be impossible to depict our relationship with anyone whom we have even known slightly without passing in review, one after another, the most different settings of our life. Each individual therefore – and I was myself one of these individuals – was a measure of duration for me . . . And surely the awareness of all these different planes within which, since in the last hour, at this party, I had recaptured it, Time seemed to dispose the different elements of my life, had, by making me reflect that in a book which tried to tell the story of a life it would be necessary to use not the two-dimensional psychology which we normally use but a quite different sort of three-dimensional psychology, added a new beauty to those resurrections of the past which my memory had effected while I was following my thoughts alone in the library, since memory by itself, when it introduces the past, unmodified into the present . . . suppresses the mighty dimension of Time which is the dimension in which life is lived.
>
> (Proust 1981: 1087)

In writing of the new, three-dimensional psychology he will have to develop to tell the story of a life, Proust is grappling, I think, with a problem that those psychoanalysts who speak of the therapeutic process as the telling of a new, more coherent, more serviceable story have glossed. Stories recount events that by definition have occurred in time; but time read and time lived are categorically different. We can reread a passage we have already read, picking up details we had carelessly missed; we can skip to the end of the novel to see how the story comes out. But we cannot literally relive the past, or fore-read the future. The narrativists are right that how our story goes forward depends in part on how we tell it; but this telling must acknowledge the difference between lived time and time told.

That we only seldom live our lives in full recognition of this difference is a vision that Proust, Heidegger and Freud, share in common. Again Proust:

> I thought more modestly of my book and it would be inaccurate even to say that I thought of those who would read it as 'my' readers. For it seemed to me that they would not be 'my' readers but readers of their own selves . . . It would be my book, but with its help I would furnish them with the means of reading what lay inside themselves.
>
> (Proust 1981: 1089)

The novel ends with the extraordinary 'three-dimensional' image of a human life as like a man on stilts, which grow higher and higher with the days and years, until he falls.

The concepts of remembering, repetition, working through, transference and mourning, together define a conceptual map that Freud continually refines. The patient must come to know not so much that this or that event did or did not happen precisely as he thinks it did, but that it *happened*, that it was an historical event in which he had a hand, though it was preceded by events that in various ways prepared for it. Scepticism about the possibility of historical knowledge, indeed any kind of knowledge, has come from many quarters in this century. I am claiming that the psychoanalytic narrative does indeed yield knowledge, as 'narrate' itself (Latin: *gnarus* – knowing) suggests, a knowledge about time that is gained partly through a certain kind of remembering and that changes one's relationships to both internal and external reality.

'Keep': keep back, retain, detain, hold, hold back, preserve, conserve, tie up, inhibit. But also: keep up with, husband, care for, look after, watch over, mind. The roots of 'mind' and 'memory' are etymologically related. At its best, psychoanalytic therapy is a process in which some of the splits between psychic past and psychic present are healed. The hope is that in this way one can take better care of time, acknowledging the past as *past*, the present as the moment of self-determination, and the future as what one can neither control nor foresee.

Notes

1 I want to thank Drs Adrienne Applegarth, Joseph Caston, Charles Fisher and Professor Tamas Pataki, for their very helpful remarks about an earlier draft of this essay.
2 These splits are not the same as the structural divisions between id, ego, and super-ego that Freud draws in *The Ego and the Id*.
3 Current research confirms Janet's idea that there are two sorts of memory, one propositional and narrative in character, the other not. They are sometimes called declarative versus procedural memory (the latter containing knowledge of how to do things that does not require propositional thought), sometimes explicit versus implicit memory (Kihlstrom 1987).
4 I use the 'ph' spelling in order to differentiate Freud's concept of an unarticulated, unconscious sort of scenario, the function of which is to negotiate a compromise in intrapsychic conflict, from the idea of fantasy as simply an act of the imagination.

5 Freud may have lost something in turning away from Janet's idea of dissociation. Psychoanalytic theory may need the ideas of both dissociation and repression (Van Der Kolk and Van Der Hart 1991; Goldberg 1995; Bromberg 1996).
6 My thinking about what is 'beyond' the pleasure principle is greatly indebted to conversations with Dr Charles Fisher. Freud develops the distinction between anxiety as a signal and anxiety as a reaction to trauma in *Inhibitions, Symptoms and Anxiety* (1926 [1925]).
7 The implication of these studies for the concept of repression is not clear. Is everything that is dynamically unconscious repressed? Or are there early, often painful sorts of memory that are not rememberable in a propositional form because they never had that form to begin with?
8 See Hans Loewald for a discussion of repetition, transference and working through as an integration of past and present (Loewald 1980).
9 What Freud called melancholia we would now call depression. While many psychoanalysts and psychiatrists follow Freud in thinking that repressed aggression plays a primary role in depression, many do not (Bowlby 1963; Sandler 1965).)
10 Some psychoanalysts think that at times, acting out may be the necessary prelude to remembering (Broughton 1993.).
11 Freud alludes to psychological 'splitting' in many places. Its earliest appearance is in *Studies on Hysteria* where he speaks, for example, of a 'split in the content of consciousness', or of the 'psychical group' that forms an 'incompatible idea' (Freud 1893–95: 167). At this stage Freud had not yet developed the structural model that sees the mind as constituted by id, ego and super-ego, so he could only describe splitting in terms of what is conscious or unconscious. The structural model makes it possible for him to locate the splits within the ego. The question of which ideas, and so on, are conscious and which are unconscious has now to be considered in terms of intrapsychic conflict: What is the mind keeping at bay? From which of its own systems (for example, the super-ego)? And why? Psychological splitting is the subject of a late, very influential, posthumously published paper: 'The Splitting of the Ego in the Process of Defence' (Freud 1940 [1938]). When I speak of mental structure I do not have Freud's structural model in mind, but more Freud's later idea of 'splitting'.

References

Ainsworth, M.D.S., Blehard, M.C., Waters, E. and Wall, S. (1978) *Patterns of Attachment*, Hillsdale, NJ: Erlbaum.
Bowlby, J. (1963) 'Pathological Mourning and Childhood Mourning', *Journal of the American Psychoanalytic Association*, 11: 500–41.
—— (1969) *Attachment and Loss: Vol. I. Attachment*, New York: Basic Books.
—— (1973) *Attachment and Loss: Vol. 2. Separation: Anxiety and Anger*, New York: Basic Books.
—— (1980) *Attachment and Loss: Vol. 3. Loss: Sadness and Depression*, New York: Basic Books.
Bromberg, P. M. (1996) 'Hysteria, Dissociation, and Cure, Emmy von N Revisited', *Psychoanalytic Dialogues*, 6(1): 55–71.
Broughton, R. E. (1993) 'Useful Aspects of Acting Out: Repetition, Enactment, Actualization', *Journal of the American Psychoanalytic Association*, 41: 443–72.
Cavell, M. (1993) *The Psychoanalytic Mind: From Freud to Philosophy*, Cambridge, MA: Harvard University Press.
Crews, F. (1995) *The Memory Wars: Freud's Legacy in Dispute*, New York: New York Review.

Davidson, D. (1982) 'Paradoxes of Irrationality', in R. Wollheim and J. Hopkins (eds) *Philosophical Essays on Freud*, New York and Cambridge: Cambridge University Press.

Freud, S. (1893–5) *Studies on Hysteria*, *S.E.* 2.

—— (1896) 'The Aetiology of Hysteria', *S.E.* 3.

—— (1897) Letter no. 61, *S.E.* I.

—— (1899) 'Screen Memories', *S.E.* 3.

—— (1905) *Three Essays on the Theory of Sexuality*, *S.E.* 7.

—— (1914) 'Remembering, Repeating, and Working Through', *S.E.* 12.

—— (1916–1917 [1915–1917]) *Introductory Lectures on Psycho-Analysis*, *S.E.* 6.

—— (1917 [1915]) *Mourning and Melancholia*, *S.E.* 14.

—— (1918 [1914]) 'From the History of an Infantile Neurosis', *S.E.* 17.

—— (1920) *Beyond the Pleasure Principle*, *S.E.* 18.

—— (1926 [1925]) *Inhibitions, Symptoms and Anxiety*, *S.E.* 20.

—— (1933 [1932]) *New Introductory Lectures on Psycho-Analysis*, *S.E.* 22.

—— (1937) 'Constructions in Analysis', *S.E.* 23.

—— (1940 [1938]) 'Splitting of the Ego in the Process of Defence', *S.E.* 23.

Goldberg, P. (1995) '"Successful" Dissociation, Pseudovitality, and Inauthentic Use of the Senses', *Psychoanalytic Dialogues*, 5(3): 493–510.

Janet, P. (1919/25) *Les Méditations psychologiques*, 3 vols. Paris: Félix Alcan.

Kihlstrom, J. F. (1987) 'The Cognitive Unconscious', *Science*, 237: 1445–52.

Laub, D.A.N. (1993) 'Knowing and Not Knowing Massive Psychic Trauma: Forms of Traumatic Memory', *International Journal of Psycho-Analysis*, 74: 287–302.

Loewald, H. (1980) *Papers on Psychoanalysis*, New Haven and London: Yale University Press.

Masson, J. (1984) *The Assault on Truth*, New York: Farrar, Straus and Giroux.

Parkin, A. (1981) 'Repetition, Mourning, and Working Through', *International Journal of Psycho-Analysis*, 62: 271–282.

Proust, M. (1981) *Remembrance of Things Past*, vol. III, New York and London: Random House and Chatto and Windus.

Reich, W. (1949) *Character Analysis*, New York: Farrar, Straus and Giroux.

Sandler, J. (1965) 'Notes on Childhood Depression', *International Journal of Psycho-Analysis*, 46: 88–96.

Stern, D. (1995) *The Motherhood Constellation*, New York: Basic Books.

Stoller, R. J. (1979) *Sexual Excitement*, New York: Simon and Schuster.

Van Der Kolk, B. A., and Van Der Hart, Onno (1991) 'The Intrusive Past', *American Imago*, 48(4): 425–454.

Wilson, A. and Malatesta, C. (1989) 'Affect and Compulsion to Repeat: Repetition Compulsion Revisited', *Psychoanalysis and Contemporary Thought*, 12: 265–312.

5

SUBJECT, OBJECT, WORLD

Some reflections on the Kleinian origins of the mind

David Snelling

After decades of philosophical preoccupation with the scientific status of psycho-analysis, we have seen in recent years the emergence of a new approach to the topic, from within the philosophy of mind. This new perspective may be labelled *the common-sense psychology extension view*.[1]

The concern of both approaches to psychoanalysis – that of philosophy of science and the common-sense extension view – is epistemological: with the justification of psychoanalytic knowledge-claims. What I attempt in this essay is somewhat different: to look at some specific consequences of the common-sense psychology extension view, under three heads. In the first section I set out an aspect of the hitherto largely unexplored differences between versions of the extension view. This will foreground a topic which seems to me to be central to the philosophical task of getting to grips with psychoanalysis: that of arriving at an understanding of the claims about the mind made in Kleinian theory. At stake here is the continued acceptability of Freud's picture of the unconscious mental processes – the primary processes – as a distinct form of mental activity, and the further idea, typical of Kleinian theory, that mental life begins before linguistic thought – indeed, begins at birth. This will require us to ask what is essential to mental life, and whether such an essence includes linguistic abilities and is subsequent upon induction into a linguistic community.

The theme of the second section, emerging naturally from that of the first, will be how these perhaps surprising Kleinian claims can widen philosophical thinking about the mind. As Jonathan Lear has said: 'philosophy has . . . equated mind with secondary-process mind' (Lear 1990: 191). Psychoanalysis should provide an antidote to such tendencies.

In the brief third part my concern with these ideas is to give the merest hint (all that space will allow) as to how they might lead us to think more widely about the general philosophical consequences – epistemological consequences, to be sure, but also metaphysical consequences – of the psychoanalytic understanding of mind.

1

Recently Marcia Cavell has given us a vigorous defence of psychoanalysis (Cavell 1993) in terms which both align it with a powerful position in contemporary philosophy, and strike at the heart of Freud's conception of the mind and of the nature of his own work.

The philosophical position is that of Donald Davidson. Those of Davidson's views which are pertinent to psychoanalysis can be seen to converge towards it from several directions. A common thread can be plucked out which unites those views: *mental holism* (Davidson 1970: 217). Crudely, we can say that possession of mental states depends for Davidson on whether those states can be ascribed 'third personally' (Cavell 1993: 21), by an external observer, in acts of *interpretation* (Davidson 1963: 9–10). The rationale guiding the interpreter is that of making the utterances and behaviour of the interpretee maximally intelligible by ascribing, as far as possible, *rationally coherent* mental states to the interpretee (Davidson 1970: 221). The link with interpretation means that mental states and their linguistic expressions hang together *as a whole*.

It is important to note that for this position what is the case about inner states or contents begins and ends with what can be attributed in interpretation; there is no further matter to be considered, no irreducibly *internal* mental content. Hence Cavell terms the position, which she holds in common with Davidson, *externalism* (1993: ch. 1, pt II).[2] She opposes Davidson's externalism to *internalist* (Cavell 1993: 12) approaches such as that of Descartes – and also, she more controversially contends, that of Freud (Cavell 1993: 46ff). Such approaches see mental content as essentially *private*. Freud counts as an internalist for Cavell because his idea of distinct unconscious primary process thinking means that there are mental operations which fall outside the public, normative network of motive ascription which for her, as for Davidson, is definitive of mind; an idea she thus finds unacceptable.

This is the aspect of her thinking which strikes deep into the Freudian conception, necessitating a wholesale rejection of primary process, the theory of instincts, and the metapsychology of the mental apparatus (Cavell 1993: 45–6; 74–6).

But Davidson's radical interpretation builds on a view of the mind which can be more loosely characterized: the idea that we employ a *natural competence* for making sense of each other interpretively by ascribing mental states which make (rational) sense of what we say and do. Acceptance of the existence of a natural common-sense psychological competence does not commit us further, to a position such as Davidson's which makes third-personal ascription *definitive* of mind. We can simply accept as a self-evident feature of our mental lives the fact that we naturally employ a vocabulary of mental-state attribution in the explanation of each other's actions, and use such an understanding of an ordinary human competence to found the kinds of ascription of unconscious motive met with in psychoanalysis.

For Davidson, rational mental states are *motives* – have efficacy in moving us to action – when they are the *causes* of those actions (Davidson 1963: 9). Because there are logical links among rational mental states, causal efficacy is transmitted via connections of content among such states. And because of such meaningful links, it is possible to establish causal connections between ideas and behaviour *interpretatively.*

Now, once we have the idea that causal connections can be attested by connections of content between the causes (ideas) and their effects (behaviour, or other mental states), we can raise the possibility that there may be *non-rational causal connections of content* which are likewise interpretable. But if, like Cavell and Davidson, we make rational connections of content *definitive* of mind, there will inevitably be a problem in accommodating a picture of the mind such as Freud's, which posits the existence of a distinct kind of mental activity – primary process – which is radically distinct from the essentially language-based rational mental processes. A position such as Davidson's must rule out such a possibility.

The looser, or more liberal, stance leaves the possibility open: it becomes an empirical matter. And from this more liberal standpoint there is a feature of common-sense psychology itself which points towards the need for something like the extension to psychoanalysis. The understanding of motive afforded by common-sense psychology has *gaps* in it; gaps which occur because of the existence of various sorts of irrational behaviour which are resistant to common-sense psychological explanation, yet bear features which cry out for interpretation through an *extended* psychology of motive. This is in effect Sebastian Gardner's position on these issues, in his book *Irrationality and the Philosophy of Psychoanalysis* (1993) and elsewhere (see Gardner 1995: 100).

A possible difficulty for the Cavell/Davidson view is that the kind of pre-linguistic mental content ascribed to infants in some versions of psychoanalytic theory, notably Kleinian theory, cannot be accommodated by what is essentially a conception which makes induction into a linguistic community a condition upon the possession of a mind. Gardner's position does not have this restriction, and indeed, he makes Kleinian theory a key element in his reconstruction of psychoanalysis (Gardner 1993: 10).

So our task now is to try to get a better idea of what is at stake in the differences between these versions of the common-sense psychology extension thesis when we give full force to the Kleinian picture of the mind. To begin with, let us assume that we accept that the evidence is in favour of that picture. This will incline us towards Gardner's philosophical reconstruction rather than Cavell's. But this can involve us in two difficulties. There may be conceptual inconsistencies in the Kleinian picture itself and there may be problems with Gardner's reconstruction of that picture. To tackle these difficulties we shall begin with the latter first, which will lead us in to an examination of some specifics of Kleinian theory.

What I hope to show is that the differences between versions of the extension thesis point towards a deep problem about how the mind engages with its objects. Different philosophical readings of psychoanalysis will rest upon different understandings of this relation between mind and object. To begin with, I shall attempt to indicate where the problem lies by looking at a paper by Jonathan Lear

(Lear 1995), a Critical Notice of Gardner's *Irrationality and the Philosophy of Psychoanalysis*.

Lear's main criticism of Gardner centres upon the charge that in explicating philosophically the Kleinian concept of *unconscious phantasy* Gardner uses an unacceptable notion of *pre-propositional content*. He quotes Gardner thus: 'What happens in repression is that a propositional mental state disintegrates into more primitive *pre-propositional components*; these are blocked from recombining in a propositional form and being manifested in consciousness' (Lear 1995: 869).[3] Lear calls this a version of the 'myth of the given . . . the idea of there being originary vehicles of meaning from which propositional content can develop' (ibid.). Later, on p. 875, he says:

> insisting that phantasy is *pre*-propositional . . . leads directly to the myth of the given. For now we have the idea of an Inner Picture – of breasts, feces [sic], food – before there is language through which these objects could be conceptualised. That is, we now need the idea of pre-propositional, originary vehicles of meaning.

This 'myth' poses a problem for how psychoanalysis is to be understood:

> It is, however, not at all easy for psychoanalysis to avoid some such developmental myth. Klein, for instance, wants to see unconscious phantasy as operative from the earliest stages of infancy, and she also conceives phantasy as constituted by representational content. I do not believe there is any coherent way to combine these two constraints; for together, they require us to take seriously the idea of *pre*-propositional content which . . . I believe to be incoherent. The form which the myth of the given takes here is the idea of originary content which is for the infant prior to its entry into the normative domain of propositional meaning. The important task which Gardner bequeaths to us is to formulate an adequate conception of the heterogeneity of the unconscious mental without having to rely on the idea of pre-propositional content.
>
> (Lear 1995: 870)

Lear proposes that unconscious phantasy should not be conceived in terms of content, but as a kind of *archaic mental activity* (Lear 1995: 875). The acquisition of representational content, whether propositional or pictorial, provides the material upon which this activity operates, by distorting the representational system, and undermining the prototypical relations between such representations, which are articulated by belief and desire and the holistic constraints which characterize them. This puts Lear in line with the version of the extension thesis developed by Marcia Cavell, for whom, as we have seen, content is necessarily characteristic only of language-based mental processes.

Lear's invocation of the 'myth of the given' fails to allow the possibility that there may be a different conception of mental content from that which can be derived from a consideration of language (though with the likelihood that there will be an active relation between the two kinds of content – the linguistic and the extra-linguistic). A kind of content which it makes sense to talk about because of the appearance of a new kind of public, intersubjective practice – psychoanalysis; yet a practice which points beyond the publicity of linguistic meaning towards *intrasubjective* sources of content.

The virtue of Lear's treatment is that it brings to a head an issue which arises from consideration of Kleinian theory. As I have mentioned, the notion of psychoanalysis as an extension of common-sense psychology gives rise to the following reflection: interpretation of others' behaviour, and of our own, through the positing of mental states such as belief and desire requires that there be logical relations between the beliefs and the desires ascribed in interpretation, relations in turn requiring a basis in language. But, as mentioned on p. 101 above, Kleinian theory extends mental life into earliest infancy: the literal *infans* period. What basis, therefore, can there be for legitimate description of what is going on in the infant using the terms of a mentalistic vocabulary which arises from the necessarily post-linguistic, inter-subjectively determined nature of the mind? This problem will remain *even if* we put aside Cavell's Davidsonian account of the mind in favour of Gardner's more liberal version.

Lear's answer is clear: the primordial heterogeneous unconscious mental does not include content. Content comes upon the scene with the acquisition of concepts in language. He must thus 'insist that phantasy primarily and primordially is mental efficacy' (Lear 1995: 873). This raises a problem which he does not tackle. According to the Kleinians themselves, as we shall see, the efficacy of phantasy manifests itself in terms of its phenomenology and its content. What the phantasy does to the mind depends on how the mind represents to itself what is happening to it: what it is *doing to itself.*

Lear apparently accedes to part of this picture. Yet he states that:

> If, on the one hand, one wants to preserve the rich phenomenology of the inner world, described by Melanie Klein and her followers, but, on the other one wants to insist upon the extraordinary power of phantasy to shape and organise the mind, one needs to link the primary sense of phantasy as activity with this . . . derivative sense of phantasy as activity on content.
>
> (Lear 1995: 874)

But if, as the Kleinians insist, phantasy operates in virtue of its contents; and if, as they also stress, it operates from birth, we are left with an explanatory and a temporal gap. There would seem to be nothing in virtue of which phantasy can operate at the earliest stage.

Marcia Cavell has little to say about Kleinian theory, but leaves us in no doubt where she would stand in this debate:

> Since Kleinians attribute very complex phantasies to infants, they would presumably hold that the infant's communications are meaningful to the infant as well as to us. Its cries are expressive of phantasies in which it thinks, for example, that it is spitting out its 'badness' into another. Depending on how early Kleinians think such phantasizing occurs, I may part company with them on this point.
>
> (Cavell 1993: 252, n. 11)

What, then, is going on in the very young baby, according to Cavell – at a time when, according to the Kleinians, phantasy life is in full efflorescence? For Cavell, the use of mentalistic terms to characterize infant behaviour is part practical necessity, part courtesy: 'We use a psychological vocabulary to describe infant striving and learning because it is the best available, and because as the child develops it becomes increasingly apt' (Cavell 1993: 54). Nevertheless, it is, strictly speaking, misplaced. To have a mind – i.e. to be the appropriate recipient of mentalistic descriptions of one's inner states – is to have gained entry into the propositional network of natural language. Infants, for Cavell, begin with biological needs which give rise to innate behaviour which is tailored to producing a change in the environment which will satisfy those needs. A hungry baby cries: it emits a signal which will, it hopes, bring about a feed. But the baby does not intend that its cry be understood as a demand for food; his signal is not a sign *for him*:

> His cries are meaningful to us, but not to him. What is initially a cry without meaning to the crier, not a sign intended to be understood in a particular way, becomes meaningful in part through the behaviour it produces in another.
>
> (Cavell 1993: 223)

So for Cavell the cry communicates the infant's need for food: but there is no *intention* to communicate. Yet the mother's response creates an interpersonal context within which the infant's discrimination of mother as a person and the sense of itself as a 'self' can develop in tandem, together with the language which will articulate the infant's emerging body of beliefs and desires, and its grasp of a shared, and therefore objective, world which provides the context for its understanding of self and other.[4] From this context, she thinks, phantasy emerges: as an imaginative reordering of reality in accordance with one's wishes. From this basis phantasy can be employed as a defence against anxiety – by representing the world as other than it is (see Cavell 1993: 187–8). Thus it is that Cavell concludes: 'prior to its communications with others the infant . . . has no real concepts at all; nor . . . does he have phantasies' (Cavell 1993: 223).

Intrinsic to the Kleinian view of phantasy is the notion of the *internal object*. The infant connects itself in phantasy with 'objects' upon which it acts and which act upon it. Cavell has a particular view of how such objects are to be conceived: 'thinking in the hard sense[5] is conditional on the child's real relations with others

106

... this thinking is in turn a presupposition for phantasizing about "objects" of any sort' (Cavell 1993: 40). Thus she is able to state: 'From the very beginning, Klein thinks, the infant has some rudimentary idea of other persons as psycho-physical entities, or "objects"' (Cavell 1993: 227). This, I think, is a misunderstanding. The Kleinian view of objects as they exist 'from the very beginning' is quite different.[6]

Cavell and Lear can be seen as agreeing that contentful, therefore mental, states – including unconscious phantasy – depend on the infant's entering the propositional network of language. Lear's objection to the Kleinian notion of pre-propositional content in unconscious phantasy is at one with Cavell's rejection of Freud's 'internalist' primary process. Lear is more concerned than Cavell with preserving the Kleinian picture of the mind, though. And as I have suggested (p. 105), for the Kleinians phantasy *is* directly revelatory of mental structure. However, Lear's insistence that phantasy is primarily a form of archaic mental activity which must be conceived of *apart* from content forces him to conceive of such determinations of mental state by content as derivative from phantasy in his primary sense of pure activity. This gives him his problem of how 'to link the primary sense of phantasy as activity with this . . . derivative sense of phantasy as activity on content'; the solution of which he defers to a projected 'detailed examination of the particular types of phantasy' (Lear 1995: 874); although he does not say how this sort of investigation might produce the desired result.

This, then, is Lear's statement of a difficulty which lies in the way of Gardner's reconstruction of Kleinian theory. Yet although he objects to Gardner's acceptance of primary unconscious content in the Kleinian theory of unconscious phantasy, he himself has no solution to the difficulty. It remains to be seen whether we can satisfactorily resolve it. Of course, the problem thus stated is ignored by the Kleinians, whose concerns are not philosophical. We can simply say that for them the idea that phantasy possesses efficacy for structuring the mind in virtue of its content constitutes a major breakthrough in psychoanalytic thinking. The task before us now is to clarify philosophically this notion of content – which must be *innate* content, given the Kleinian claim that phantasy exists from birth – and to see what such a clarified notion can contribute to a philosophical understanding of mental processes. Thus we shall begin to address the second difficulty which may lie in the way of the acceptance of what I called above (p. 103) the 'Kleinian picture of the mind': the possibility that Kleinian thinking on these matters is confused.

2

The primary and original content of unconscious phantasy, the Kleinians tell us (Rivière 1936: 37; 45), consists of the mind's relation to *internal objects*. So let us begin with a working definition of 'internal object', taken from R.D. Hinshelwood's *A Dictionary of Kleinian Thought*:

> This term denotes an unconscious experience or phantasy of a concrete object physically located internal to the ego (body) which has its own

motives and intentions towards the ego, and is in a greater or lesser extent of identification with the ego (a phantasy of absorption, or assimilation, to the ego). The experience of the internal object is deeply dependent on the experiencing of the external object – and internal objects are, as it were, mirrors of reality. But they also contribute significantly, through projection, to the way the external objects are themselves perceived and experienced.

(Hinshelwood 1991: 68)

We can extract a number of clues from this passage to guide further thinking on the topic.

1   The internal object is experienced as 'concrete': not as an image or 'mere' representation, but as an actual object inside.
2   Through 'identification' such objects are *constitutive* of the ego and thus of the sense of self; so the ego's structure is, through such objects, dependent on unconscious phantasy. This supports the contention, touched on in the previous section and to be examined shortly, that the mental apparatus operates through its *self-representations* (in the ego).
3   The internal object enjoys a sort of *priority in mental life*, both as the forerunner of later, more developed mental states, and as the bedrock upon which the structure of the mind is based.

So the internal object is the primary content of phantasy for the Kleinians, and therefore the original form of mental content. As we shall see in a moment, this is expressed in the Kleinian idea that unconscious phantasy is *innate*. So we are confronted with the concept of innate mental content, and it is this of which we must attempt to make philosophical sense.

If we are able do so, we can go some way towards the justification of Freud's ideas about the unconscious – the ideas which Cavell has castigated under the label of 'internalism'. The mental will have features which are more basic than those which define linguistically articulated and intersubjectively interpretable mind.

To confront the idea of innate content which gives subjective meaning to the earliest experience, we must enquire into the conditions under which the mind's relation to an object – in the form of the ego's relation to an internal object – first arises. Freud did not believe that the ego – which is the locus of selfhood – existed in earliest infancy (Freud 1914c: 76–7). For him, the neonate has no sense of self, just as for Cavell, the neonate – for very different and philosophically incompatible reasons – has no mind. To follow the Kleinian position on this matter is to claim that there is an innate sense of self, which necessarily exists alongside a sense of an object which is not-self. *A subject is a subject only in relation to an object*, from which it distinguishes itself and therefore gains a sense of self.

I now want to suggest that internal objects, and thus phantasy itself, have *a special relation to our embodiment*.

Before proceeding to a discussion of this claim, let us summarize the issue at stake. Mental life depends on mental content, as Cavell says. But Kleinian theory demands an account of content which does not confine it to what Freudians and Kleinians both would consider to be secondary-process thinking. Such content must be pre-linguistic ('pre-propositional'). It therefore cannot depend upon the social or interpersonal constitution of meaning: upon what is shared by speakers who are intelligible to each other because they enjoy access to a shared world. If the Kleinian claims are to be philosophically cogent, we must clarify the idea of a primary kind of meaning; and therefore also the idea of a primary and innate self, however rudimentary, *for* which the content can have meaning. Phantasies encountered in the analyses of children and adults can have complex representational content, describable in detailed propositional language, even though they are not represented propositionally in the mind. But let us remember that we are here concerned with the *origins* of phantasy in its earliest and most primitive manifestations – the mental endowment present from birth, according to the Kleinians. The Kleinian claim that there is an ego from birth (Segal 1989: 101) is a claim for the existence of a primordial self. To restate the point made above, for Freud, as for Cavell, there is no such primordial self. In this respect, Klein out-Freuds Freud as an 'internalist'.

So what can possibly explain the existence of such a primordial self? We can take a clue from Freud. But first note that the originary self, and its content, the internal object, must be *equiprimordial* if, as we have seen the Kleinians claim, content is *constitutive* of self: something of which, in turn, we must make philosophical sense.

The clue that Freud gives us is the suggestion that the ego originally derives from the sensations impinging upon the surface of the body. Such sensations give rise to a sense of the ego as *body-like*. This notion of a *bodily ego* (or 'body-ego') appears only once in Freud's work, in *The Ego and the Id*: 'The ego is first and foremost a bodily ego: it is not merely a surface entity, but is itself the projection [presumably in analogy to a *geometrical* projection[7]] of a surface' (Freud 1923b: 26). It can be summed up in a footnote by Joan Rivière added on Freud's authority to the 1927 version of her translation of this work:

> The ego is ultimately derived from bodily sensations, chiefly from those springing from the surface of the body. It may thus be regarded as a mental projection of the surface of the body, besides . . . representing the superficies of the mental apparatus.
>
> (Freud 1923b: 26)

This note is interesting, because it characterizes the ego on two levels of description: as 'representing the superficies of the mental apparatus' it is seen in structural, that is metapsychological, terms: a *theoretical* understanding of the ego's relations. As a 'mental projection of the surface of the body', however, it is a *representation in the ego*: the ego's representing of itself to itself, its taking of itself as its own object. *This, I claim, is the original object relation*, which makes the primordial sense of self, and therefore the original form of mental life, possible.

The distinction between the two levels of description, the theoretical and the phenomenological, thus breaks down in Kleinian theory. The phenomenology of unconscious phantasy[8] is what structures the mind – the mind is essentially its image of itself[9] – so a description of unconscious phantasy is at the same time a theoretical explanation of mental structure.[10]

The body-ego is an important idea for the Kleinians. Thus Susan Isaacs sees unconscious phantasy as necessarily bound up with bodily sensation (Isaacs 1948: 91); but there is no *temporally or conceptually separable* sensation which is then given a subjective meaning in phantasy. In discussion of the first version of her paper, delivered in 1943, Isaacs said that if sensations are psychical experiences, then from the beginning, phantasy and images[11] are: 'inherent in sensations and grow out of them' (King and Steiner 1992: 372).

In her paper *On the Genesis of Psychical Conflict in Earliest Infancy* (1936) Joan Rivière asserts that:

> From the very beginning of life . . . the psyche responds to the reality of its experiences by interpreting them – or rather *mis*interpreting them . . . This act of a *subjective interpretation of experience*, which it carries out by means of the processes of introjection and projection . . . forms the foundation of what we mean by *phantasy life*.
>
> (Rivière 1936: 41)

Such 'interpretation', I suggest, is the primordial experience of meaning, which is constituted in the subject–object relation. Its first manifestation is a concrete representation of the mind to itself as something *body-like*; an idea which is difficult to accommodate within the usual philosophical categories for conceiving such matters – as is the related concept of self-representation as constitutive of the mind.

In his paper 'The Bodily Ego' (1982) Richard Wollheim gives us some philosophical apparatus which helps towards such an accommodation. He argues that there are mental states which have efficacy in shaping the mind because of the way in which they represent the mind: that they are *self-representing* (Wollheim 1982: 67). That is: a mental state's being the state it is depends crucially upon its representing itself to the subject, its being grasped by the subject, *as* such-and-such. (An extra-psychoanalytic example Wollheim gives of self-representation is *make-believe*; states of make-believe could not exist unless they represented themselves as: 'not to be assessed against considerations of truth' [Wollheim 1982: 69]. Without this constraint they would simply be deviant beliefs – beliefs formed in a nonstandard way.) Furthermore, the self-representation of such states may depend upon their phenomenology. (The extra-psychoanalytic example here is memory. A memory's representing itself as a memory depends upon *what it is like* for the subject: its 'sense of pastness or familiarity' [ibid.].) Freudian explanation, Wollheim says, requires a particular set of such self-representing mental states; and the terms of such self-representation must be primitive and pre-propositional. How might they arise?

Freud, writing in *Negation* (1925h), traces the origins of a highly developed mental function, that of judgement, to the 'oral-instinctual' impulses: 'I should like to eat this' or 'I should like to spit this out' (Freud 1925h: 237). Wollheim sees this bodily way of representing mental activities as the necessary self-representation belonging to a special kind of mental activity: the formation of what he calls 'proto-beliefs' (Wollheim 1982: 69): belief-like states unconstrained by reality.[12] The formation of proto-beliefs depends upon the possibility that thoughts can be represented as something corporeal, something which can be put into or ejected from the body. 'A thought makes itself suitable for this kind of treatment by the way in which it represents itself' (Wollheim 1982: 70). We can make use of the idea of self-representation in proposing that the mind must represent itself (or be represented to itself) in a certain way in order to exhibit the meaningful – that is, contentful – relation of mind and object which entitles us to claim that mental life exists in such primitive phases of biological life.[13]

Curiously, despite placing greater weight on the concept of the body-ego than did Freud, Wollheim does not say anything about Freud's understanding of it. This is that it is, as Rivière says, 'ultimately derived from bodily sensations, chiefly from those springing from the surface of the body' (Freud 1923b: 26; see above p. 109). How are we best to understand this? Freud's thinking here is obscure; Wollheim's discussion can provide a clue for us to follow in expanding upon his hint. Thus it is not simply that mental states (constituting the ego) are represented as bodily: there is a representation of the ego itself as bodily. The ego contains a representation of itself which *unifies* it.[14] The representation derives from the body and is body-like: in particular it is represented as possessing a *boundary or surface*, and thus as having an inside and an outside. Furthermore, that the ego represents itself as a unified body in turn enables there to be a unified representation of the body in the ego. Unity of body representation and of ego go together. Thus the earliest motor activity of the infant, which, according to classical Freudian theory, is pre-egoic auto-erotic activity, and which would according to that theory produce only disconnected libidinal gratifications in the various erogenous zones, is in this perspective unified by the 'projection of a surface'.

But is it not a circularity to state that the ego derives its unity from a bodily representation of itself, and that a unified representation of the body is derived *from* the representation of that body-like unity of the ego? No. For if, as I have suggested, ego and object arise in this way *simultaneously* – are inaugurated in the same originary event – the ego *is* its object-relatedness. This is in effect to restate in psychoanalytic terms the (Brentanian) thesis of intentionality: that 'consciousness' (here the ego, in all its operations, conscious or unconscious) is *nothing but* its intentional relations to its objects.[15] *The primordial intentional relation is the relation to internal objects in phantasy*, since from the position I am developing these ego–object processes are *definitive* of mind. The mind is inaugurated in this grasp of the object, which is, in the first instance, the primordial unified body-*Gestalt*.

Now, the 'projection inwards' of the body surface in the establishment of the body-ego sets the boundary of the ego across which the projective–introjective processes – Freud's 'eating' and 'spitting out'[16] – can operate; and it is these processes which are fundamental to the mind's relation to its objects, and thus fundamental to its structure: 'When the ego receives stimuli from outside it absorbs them and makes them part of itself, it introjects them. When it bars them off, it projects them' (Heimann 1943: 125). So this original 'projection' of the body surface provides the ego with a representation of self-in-relation-to-not-self. Both self and not-self, ego and object, are dependent for their existence upon the way in which they are represented; and the fundamental feature of these representations is that they are *unified*. The representation of the ego itself must maintain a continuity across the various episodes of object-related phantasy; and the representation of the object must similarly maintain its identity, if it is to count as an *object*: as a stable locus of experience (albeit only more or less stable, at first, in line with the fragility of the early ego).

Freud's original suggestion that the body-ego is a 'projection' ('geometrical' projection) of the surface of the body inward upon the mental apparatus, creating a representation based on tactile sensations arising on the surface of the skin, gives the foundation of the body-ego but does not give all that is necessary for there to be a properly constituted ego from birth. Fundamental to the representation of the body-ego as a bounded volume is its phantastic function as a *container*, which has an inside and an outside, from which things can be expelled and into which things can be incorporated. Representations of the processes of incorporation and expulsion are needed to complete the picture. Such representations of bodily processes in phantasy are identical with the *mechanisms* of introjection and projection. The difference of terminology simply reflects the different levels of psychoanalytic discourse about unconscious processes. This is in line with what we have said about how Kleinian theory collapses the distinction between phenomenological description of unconscious processes and the theoretical account of mental structure. This in turn mirrors the most salient feature of the Kleinian understanding of the mind: that self-representation determines structure.

Projection and introjection are not to be viewed as simple mediators between outside and inside, in any naively realistic sense. These mechanisms are intra-psychic. Projecting part of oneself outside and locating it in an object, for example, can mean locating it in an object which is itself represented as inside (such as keeping parts of me safe by locating them in a good breast inside). Phantastic fears of attack from outside may be a phantasy of attack from an internal object. The transition from pleasure principle to reality ego does not mean a move away from an 'inner world' towards some unproblematic relation to an 'external world' which awaits the maturation of the individual in order to be grasped and adequately known. The external world has to be progressively constituted on the basis of projection and introjection of phantastic representations; representations which can *represent themselves* as being taken into an 'inside' or pushed into an 'outside'.

Freud's concept of the body-ego, plus the Kleinians' elaboration and Wollheim's elucidation of it, now enable us to see how the ego-at-birth is established as an original unity which is, from the beginning, the source of complex interactions with the outer world through the representation of an inner world of internal objects: not a 'representation' in the traditional sense made familiar from representational realism – a passive mirroring of an external reality which lies equally inert and self-identical before us – but a primordial apprehension of *meaning*, in which the ego/subject is actively engaged.

We have now seen that for the Kleinians the mind's structure (the 'apparatus') depends upon its phantastic representation. This presupposes that content is constitutive of phantasy, and is a way of saying that phantasy is constitutive of the mind. Hence, the operation of the mental apparatus is dependent upon the content of the foundational phantasies. We have given reasons for thinking that the primordial phantastic representations of ego and object are representations of unities.

Let us now assemble the following conclusions. At the heart of Freud's instinct theory is the conviction that the instincts cannot operate, and thus be the motors of action, without mental expression.[17] And mental expression involves meaning. Meaning, in turn, must be meaning for a subject. Mere 'stimuli' are meaningless.

Given Freud's model of an instinct-driven mental apparatus, plus the Kleinian notion of innate unconscious phantasy as the natural expression of instinct, we must think of the instincts as operating at birth. Conversely, the operation of the instincts at birth means that unconscious phantasy is active at birth. This involves internal-object relations; these in turn require the existence of an ego from birth:[18] a primitive subject of experience for whom the relation to internal objects constitutes *phantastic meaning*. Thus:

> An inner world comes into being. The infant feels that there are objects, parts of people and [later] people, inside his body, that they are alive and active, affect him and are affected by him.
>
> (Heimann 1952: 155)

3

Kleinian analyst Paula Heimann goes on to say that the inner world is the infant's: 'private replica of the world and objects around him' (ibid.); but this cannot be quite right. The inner world must come to reflect (more or less) the outer one, but this, as we have seen (p. 112 above), cannot be a *simple* reflection or corre-spondence. The outer or external world is an arena of socially shared meanings which arises from the interplay between instinctual need and the degree and quality of the provision which meets that need. In the process, the plasticity of instinct ensures that libidinal interest will eventually extend itself, if things proceed normally, across the whole range of social and cultural meaning. By being inducted into society, the individual is given a world of shared meanings within which she is located, but which is itself the outcome of a kind of meaning which arises from our shared biological endowment – unconscious phantasy:

In the interpersonal world there is no enduring 'thing in itself' to be discovered. To a major extent the external world is constructed and continually reconstructed by the individual and the group. A phantasy projection of an object into the external world is not an innocuous event; that phantasy may bring about an actual alteration of the object in the external world. . . . This amenability of the external world to being constructed from phantasy is an important factor to take into account when considering the question of *reality-testing*.

(Hinshelwood 1991: 302)

If unconscious phantasy – the primordial, innate kind of 'meaning' arising from the body – did not anchor the range of significance ('meaning') which could be expressed at the shared, social level of meaning, there would be no biologically-based restraint upon the social construction of meaning. For the Kleinians such innate bodily meaning in turn gives rise, through the phantastic dialectic of inner and outer made possible by the bodily representation of the ego/self, its projections, and its introjections, to shared, socially constructed meaning. But why should such a 'biologically-based restraint' matter?

The philosophical view of the mind with which we began, that of Cavell and Davidson, provides a universal account of what is definitive of the mental. It is able to claim universality because it settles upon a universal feature, rationality, as the definitive element. Rationally formed belief-states represent the world as it is (that is what it is for them to be rational), and we should aim to produce such states through our knowledge-gathering practices. So there is a link between knowledge of the world and a more fundamental capacity to find the world intelligible or meaningful; which is necessary in order to have experience of the world – *to have experience* – at all.

It is a commonplace that if meaning is exclusively a social construct, cultural relativism is likely to result. And such relativism will extend to knowledge, since epistemic practices are grounded in ontological commitments which arise from the way we understand our world. Traditionally, philosophical concern with relativism has taken the form of responses to *scepticism*. Relativism in the field of knowledge tends naturally towards scepticism. The traditional philosophical response to these difficulties has been through various kinds of *foundationalism*; the favoured version of foundationalism tending to determine how the basic intelligibility or meaning-fulness of experience is understood. Thus, for example, classical empiricism founds such meaning upon what is purely given in sense experience; but at the cost of accepting a *meaning-thin* picture of reality. The world we experience is stripped down to the minimum of intelligibility – passively observed regularities and their deducible connections, beyond which the cement of the universe is reduced to projected psychological associations. And this results, it can plausibly be argued, in a collapse back into scepticism. Empiricism 'mentalizes' our connection with the world, by confining it to the mind's passive reception of ideas, sensations or impressions (Locke 1975: 119; Berkeley 1975: 21; Hume 1975: 18).

114

Davidson is mentalistic too. But he overcomes relativism at the cost of *rationalist reductionism about the mind*: limiting what we take mind to be to what can be ascribed in acts of interpretation which aim at an ideal of rationality. It is a conception of the mind which has its own problems: for example in the explanation of irrationality.[19] It is the conception which motivates Cavell's anti-Freudian 'externalism'.

We have now seen that Kleinian theory puts this conception under pressure. Cavell and the Kleinians have in common the opinion that the world we inhabit is socially constructed. For Cavell, however, such an interpersonal world depends on the communality of language. For Klein it arises from modification through social interaction of a biologically derived repertoire of innate and primordially *internal* meaning: unconscious phantasy. This innate, unconscious meaning constitutes a universal in human nature, which constrains the social construction of our shared world. Ultimately, the world we inhabit depends upon meanings rooted in our embodiment, not upon the constructions of an impoverished – that is, secondary-process – mental activity.

This bodily – thus biological and transcultural – restraint on how a meaningful social world can be constructed puts the psychoanalytically informed philosophical view of the mind firmly on the side of those philosophical positions which develop a *meaning-thick* treatment of our relation to our world. Such positions as those of Kant, the German idealists, and the later post-Brentanian phenomenologists see our capacity to experience an intelligible world as dependent upon a rich inner reservoir of innate contents, conditions, principles or constitutive acts, which structure the self and its experience equiprimordially.

This alignment of psychoanalysis – especially Kleinian theory – with this broader perspective is the general philosophical fruit of a serious and sympathetic recon-struction of the psychoanalytic characterization of the mind which I announced at the beginning of the essay. It indicates a wealth of investigations yet to be undertaken.[20]

Notes

1 See, for example, Cavell (1993), Davidson (1982), Gardner (1995), Hopkins (1982), Wollheim (1991).
2 The term indicates that interpreter and interpretee share some true beliefs about the world. This is a necessary condition on interpretation. See Cavell (1993: 29).
3 See Gardner (1993: 104).
4 See Cavell (1993) ch 5 and 6. There is a link between the infant's pre-verbal experiences and later phantasies for Cavell, but it is a causal, not a meaningful, link: 'Long before we have reason to credit them with a network of concepts, children are acquiring fears, habits, styles of interpersonal relating, that are part of the causal history of their later thoughts' (Cavell 1993: 53).
5 That is, 'thinking' as anything stronger than a *façon de parler*.
6 The first objects are 'part-objects': not representations of whole persons but of bodily parts. See Heimann (1952: 154); Hinshelwood (1991: 378, 380).
7 This is not to be confused with the *mechanism* of projection operating in tandem with

115

introjection through incorporation and expulsion, which receives some discussion further on.

8 For justification of the concept of unconscious phenomenology, see Gardner (1993: 214–20).

9 See Wollheim (1968).

10 This point was made with great acuteness, albeit in the form of a criticism, by Edward Glover (1945).

11 Isaacs makes it clear that *mental imagery* and the phantasies based upon it are later developments, following on from the inherence of phantasy in 'bodily impulses' and 'the excitation of the organ' (Isaacs 1948: 94).

12 *Not* beliefs in which the usual processes of belief formation have failed to deliver truth, nor yet deviant beliefs (which may *happen* to be true), but belief-like states which are constrained by pleasurableness and painfulness in the same way that regular beliefs are constrained by truth and falsity.

13 It is important to realize that the primary phantasy establishing the body-ego is not a once and for all mental operation. It must be sustained throughout life as the bedrock of selfhood. Evidence for this lies in psychotic states, which severely disrupt ego functioning and the sense of the boundary between *me* and *not-me*. To elaborate:

The properties present in earliest phantasy must characterize phantasy as a whole, even if later phantasy acquires new properties through its links with more developed mental capacities. This must be the case if the unity of the concept of phantasy is to be maintained despite the differences in content between earliest phantasy and later phantasy. This unity is maintained because the content of later phantasy symbolically represents the content of earlier phantasy. But if earliest phantasy is bodily, and is definitive of later phantasy, a new question emerges. There are two possibile ways in which early and later phantasy may be related. The earliest phantasies, those of a necessarily bodily nature, may simply be necessary forerunners of later phantasy – they may provide a mere *genetic condition* for the possibility of phantasy in general. Or each manifestation of phantasy may necessarily require that the phantastic state represent itself in bodily form. Which of these ways best describes the situation?

It might seem, from Freud's idea of an original 'projection' inwards of the bodily surface, that this occurrence is a single, once and for all event. But no; as possibilities of psychotic breakdown suggest, once this representation is installed, at the origin of mental life, it must be maintained. This representation, the basis of integration and the unity of the subject, is constantly liable to disintegration under the pressure of instinct and intolerable reality.

This tendency towards dissolution of the ego requires the constant maintenance of a counter-tendency; the concrete expression of which is the continued operation of the phantasies which constitute the body-ego.

This way of understanding the situation enables us to approach a resolution of our problem: is bodily representation necessary for each episode of phantasy, or is it merely a condition upon phantasy in general? We can conclude that each episode of phantasy is dependent upon the background operation of the phantasies sustaining the body-ego, the ego's foundational representation of itself. I do not claim that this is a resolution. We can ask further whether the background phantasy and the occurrent, 'foreground' phantasy must share content. If not, then the background phantasy would seem to be relegated to the role of a mere causal mechanism. Here the notion of symbolic transmission of content may do some work towards the resolution.

14 'Klein saw the ego . . . as the experience it has of itself' (Hinshelwood 1991: 285).

15 Lest I be accused of confusing empirical theory with a priori conditions on the possibility of experience, I should emphasize that our task is to uncover the conceptual features of

Kleinian theory which imply what the nature of the mind *must* be, if it is given that the theory is true.

16 Strictly, description in such bodily terms applies to the *phantasies* of expulsion and incorporation through which the *mechanisms* of projection and introjection operate, though for the Kleinians this is a distinction without a difference. See the paragraph which immediately follows.

17 They are either *themselves* the 'psychic representatives of bodily processes' (Freud 1915c: 122) or they *require* such psychic representation (Freud 1915d: 152). Freud never clarified this issue. See the editor's introduction to Freud (1915c).

18 See Segal (1973: 13).

19 See Davidson (1982).

20 I would like to acknowledge the support of a University of London Trust Fund Studentship in the research which led to this essay.

References

Berkeley, G. (1975) *An Essay towards a New Theory of Vision*, in *Philosophical Works*, London: Dent.

Cavell, M. (1993) *The Psychoanalytic Mind: From Freud to Philosophy*, Cambridge, MA: Harvard University Press.

Davidson, D. (1963) 'Actions, reasons, and causes', in Davidson (1980).

—— (1970) 'Mental events', in Davidson (1980).

—— (1980) *Essays on Actions and Events*, Oxford: Clarendon Press.

—— (1982) 'Paradoxes of irrationality', in Wollheim and Hopkins (eds.) (1982).

Freud, S. *The Standard Edition of the Complete Psychological Works of Sigmund Freud*, translated from the German under the general editorship of J. Strachey in collaboration with A. Freud, assisted by A. Strachey and A. Tyson; editorial assistant A. Richards. London: Hogarth Press and the Institute of Psycho-Analysis (1966–1974).

—— (1914c) 'On narcissism' (*S[tandard] E[dition volume]* 14)

—— (1915c) 'Instincts and their vicissitudes' (*S.E.* 14).

—— (1915d) 'Repression' (*S.E.* 14).

—— (1923b) *The Ego and the Id* (*S.E.* 19).

—— (1925h) 'Negation' (*S.E.* 19).

Gardner, S. (1993) *Irrationality and the Philosophy of Psychoanalysis*, Cambridge: Cambridge University Press.

—— (1995) 'Psychoanalysis, science, and commonsense', in *Philosophy, Psychiatry, and Psychology*, 2(2), Baltimore: The Johns Hopkins University Press.

Glover, E. (1945) 'An examination of the Klein system of child psychology', in *The Psychoanalytic Study of the Child*, 1, London: Imago Publishing.

Heimann, P. (1943) 'Some aspects of the role of introjection and projection in early development', in King and Steiner (eds) (1992).

—— (1952) 'Certain functions of introjection and projection in early infancy', in Rivière (ed.) (1952).

Hinshelwood, R.D. (1991) *A Dictionary of Kleinian Thought*, London: Free Association Books.

Hopkins, J. (1982) 'Introduction' to Wollheim and Hopkins (eds) (1982).

Hume, D. (1975) *Enquiries Concerning Human Understanding and Concerning the Principles of Morals*, ed. L.A. Selby-Bigge, revision by P.H. Nidditch, Oxford: Clarendon Press.

Isaacs, S. (1948) 'The nature and function of phantasy', in Rivière, (ed.) (1952).

King, P. and Steiner, R. (eds) (1992) *The Freud–Klein Controversies 1941–45*, London: Tavistock/Routledge.

Lear, J. (1990) *Love and its Place in Nature: A Philosophical Interpretation of Freudian Psychoanalysis*, London: Faber and Faber.

—— (1995) 'The heterogeneity of the mental: a critical notice of Sebastian Gardner's *Irrationality and the Philosophy of Psychoanalysis*', *Mind*, 104(416), London: The Mind Association, and Oxford: Oxford University Press.

Locke, J. (1975) *An Essay Concerning Human Understanding*, ed. P.H. Nidditch, Oxford: Clarendon Press.

Rivière, J. (1936) 'On the genesis of psychical conflict in early infancy', in Rivière (ed.) (1952).

—— ed. (1952) *Developments in Psycho-Analysis*, London: Hogarth Press.

Segal. H. (1973) *Introduction to the Work of Melanie Klein*, London: Hogarth Press.

—— (1989) *Klein*, London: Karnac Books.

Wollheim, R. (1968) 'The mind and the mind's image of itself', in Wollheim (1973).

—— (1973) *On Art and the Mind: Essays and Lectures*, London: Allen Lane.

—— (1982) 'The bodily ego', in Wollheim (1993).

—— (1991) *Freud*, second edition, London: Fontana Press.

—— (1993) *The Mind and its Depths*, Cambridge, MA: Harvard University Press.

Wollheim, R. and Hopkins, J. (eds) (1982) *Philosophical Essays on Freud*, Cambridge: Cambridge University Press.

6

FREUD'S THEORY OF CONSCIOUSNESS[1]

Paul Redding

It is not unusual to read of the revolution in our understanding of the mind that has taken place in the last part of the twentieth century. After a period of behaviouristic dismissal of issues to do with either intentionality or consciousness, the explosive growth of the 'cognitive sciences' starting in the 1960s introduced ways of talking about the mind's intentional or 'representational' contents, while more recently increasing attention has been turned towards the effort to account for the 'what it is like' of consciousness. Against the background of this burgeoning body of work, the ideas of Freud have come to be dismissed by many as relics of a by-gone age. And yet a little probing reveals Freud not only as having had an interesting and sophisticated theory of the 'representational mind' but also of the 'what it is like' of consciousness. In fact, that most well-known aspect of Freud's work, the existence of the unconscious, might be seen as grounded in interlacing theories of mental representation and consciousness that have a remarkably contemporary hue.

In 1995, the philosopher Ned Block pointed to a confusion within recent discussions of consciousness between what he referred to as 'access' and 'phe-nomenal' consciousness: while a mental state has phenomenal consciousness if there is something that it is like to be in it, it is access conscious if it is 'poised for use as a premiss in reasoning . . . for rational control of action, and . . . for rational control of speech' (Block 1995: 231). On examination it can be seen that not only had Freud clearly appreciated this distinction, but that it was central to his understanding of the nature of his central discovery, that of the unconscious. This was because he came to ask questions about the *conditions* of Block's access consciousness, and to answer such questions in terms of a conception of con-sciousness like that currently known as the 'higher-order thought' (or HOT) theory (Rosenthal 1986; Gennaro 1995). For such a conception, a mental content, a perceptually given one, for example, is only access conscious if it is the object of some 'higher-order' concept or thought. But to pose questions of the *conditions* of consciousness is, of course, to open a conceptual space for mental contents that are *unconscious* in virtue of their failure to meet them. Such contents lacking access consciousness were what Freud came to think of as prototypically 'unconscious'. But, as we shall see, Freud wanted to hold on to a sense in which these contents were conscious, nevertheless: they were characterized by a type of 'unconscious consciousness' (Freud 1953–74, 14: 178). In Block's terms, they lacked access consciousness, but retained phenomenal consciousness.

It is far from my intention here to suggest a picture of Freud as an inspired genius who could anticipate future theories as if by magic. First, one could say that such conceptual innovations were prompted by his attempt to give an account of phenomena confronting him in the course of his clinical work, phenomena suggesting the existence of unconscious thought processes. But further than this, it can be claimed that the conceptual resources for his innovations were already available to him from the medical culture within which he had been trained. Freud, who had pursued a more conventional career within medical science until his mid-forties, was steeped in the neurological conceptions of the mind and consciousness of the late nineteenth century (Sulloway 1992, pt 1), and his developing understanding of the conditions of consciousness might be understood as having emerged *via* a transformation of an existing neurological conception of the nature of the mind–body relation – that of 'psychophysical parallelism' – under the impact of another neurological doctrine, that of the 'cerebral reflex'. Moreover, versions of the HOT account of consciousness were also extant within nineteenth-century thought, traceable at least to Kant's idea that 'intuitions without concepts are blind' (Kant 1933: A 51/B 75). While it may have indeed been the clinical evidence of unconscious mental states and processes that induced Freud to elaborate his theory of 'the unconscious', evidence for a pre-existing conceptual place for this notion can be found in his small pre-psychoanalytic monograph *On Aphasia* (Freud 1953). In what follows I suggest a pathway for the evolution of Freud's innovative theory of consciousness.

1 Two neurological doctrines

i *Psychophysical parallelism*

One nineteenth-century figure who seems to have influenced Freud both in his pre-psychoanalytic as well as his psychoanalytic work was Gustav Theodor Fechner, the founder of the discipline of 'psychophysics' and advocate of the psychophysical parallelist conception of the mind–body relation (Ellenberger 1993). Fechner had attempted to capture the relation between the psychological and neurophysiological spheres in terms of the idea of a single reality grasped from opposed subjective and objective points of view. Here he used an analogy which was later commonly repeated: the subjective mind and the objective body were related as were the concave and convex aspects of a single curved line.

> Both sides belong together as indivisibly as do the mental and material
> sides of man and can be looked upon as analogous to his inner and outer

sides ... What will appear to you as your mind from the internal standpoint, where you yourself are this mind, will, on the other hand, appear from the outside point of view as the material basis of this mind.

(Fechner 1966: 2–3)

In fact this was a doctrine with a considerable philosophical history. Fechner had taken the idea from the Schellingian 'transcendental anatomist' Lorenz Oken, and Schelling's talk of a *Parallelismus* between the body and mind, had clearly come from Spinoza (Lennig 1988). In England, the notion had been popularized by the physiological and psychological writings of George Henry Lewes, who was familiar with the work of both Schelling and Spinoza (Reed 1997). In *On Aphasia*, Freud affirmed such a parallelist conception of the relation of mind and brain: 'The relationship between the chain of physiological events in the nervous system and the mental processes is probably not one of cause and effect ... The psychic is ... a process parallel to the physiological, "a dependent concomitant"' (Freud 1953: 55). With this final phrase, which Freud rendered in English, Freud adverted to the influence on him of the English neurologist and aphasia specialist, John Hughlings Jackson (Forrester 1980; Rizzuto 1990, 1993). But Jackson also had advocated another idea that Freud embraced, and it was this idea which eventually undermined Freud's commitment to the parallelist conception of consciousness. Moreover, it was an idea that was implicated in the development of Freud's nascent HOT theory. This was the notion of the cerebral reflex.

ii The cerebral reflex

The doctrine of the cerebral reflex, like that of psychophysical parallelism, had roots deep into the nineteenth century. It postulated that the operations of the cerebral cortex, considered to be the seat of the mind's 'higher' rational operations, could be thought as continuous with the more mechanical 'reflex' operations of the nervous system's lower ganglionic centres or 'nuclei' of grey matter, of which the most basic were those located in the spinal cord and mediating spinal reflexes. In the late nineteenth century the cerebral reflex idea gained collateral support from Darwinism, the 'higher' cortical structures being seen as evolutionary developments of the simpler lower ones (Magoun 1960). But in fact the theory that the cortex worked on reflex principles continuous with the simple spinal reflex went back to the pre-Darwinian context of the early nineteenth century where it was supported by neurological thinkers influenced by German idealist nature-philosophy (Clarke and Jacyna 1987).

In England, early exceptional adherents to the German, distinctly anti-Cartesian, view of the mind–brain relation were Thomas Laycock and William B. Carpenter, both belonging to a circle of London-based, often Edinburgh-educated, physicians and biological scientists who in the 1830s and 40s became strongly influenced by German idealism and nature-philosophy.[2] From Carpenter, especially, the idea was popularized within evolutionary circles by Herbert Spencer and later in the century was applied in the explanation of symptoms of aphasia by Jackson, Laycock's former pupil.[3] Adopting the idea from Jackson, Freud used the notion in *On Aphasia* to challenge the views on the nature of cortical representation of his former teacher and director, Theodor Meynert. But in doing this he was *implicitly* challenging the associated parallelist conception of consciousness that went with it.

In his 1884 textbook *Psychiatrie* (Meynert 1885) Meynert described the spinal nuclei as operating reflexly but as controlled 'from above' by the cortex which worked on different principles. The cortex itself was thought as connected by *direct* afferent and efferent neural pathways with the body's sensory receptors and the motor nuclei of the spinal cord respectively. In general this fitted the psychophysical parallelist picture. In this, the body's sensory surfaces were conceived as 'mapped' on to the sensory parts of the cortex in a topographical point by point manner, and the basic elements of sensory experience were thought of as reflecting the patterns of stimuli at the body's surface. Accordingly, experience was thought of as constructed out of such atoms of 'sensation' according to the classical picture of an 'association of ideas', and actions as somehow assembled out of associations of muscular contractions.

In contrast, supporters of the cerebral reflex scheme understood cortical representation as *mediated* by lower reflex centres. Thus Jackson discussed such an ascending hierarchy of reflex centres as involving the 're-representation' (and 're-re-representation'!) of the sensory and motor periphery (Jackson 1931: 53). This allowed him to assert, in contrast to Meynert, that it was particular goal-directed *functions* that were represented neurally: 'nervous centres represent movements, not muscles' (Harrington 1987: 212). Following Jackson, Freud in *On Aphasia* contested Meynert's account of direct sensory tracks from receptors at the body's surface to the cortex, arguing that all afferent and efferent pathways to and from the cortex must pass through *intermediary* nuclei which subserve their own reflex arcs. This meant that Meynert's idea of any point-by-point mapping of sensation and muscle innervation on to cortical areas could no longer be maintained, and that the cortical representation of the body periphery had to be considered *functional* rather than *topographical* (Freud 1953: 52–4).

This appeal to a functional understanding of the nature of neural representation together with the associated abandonment of any ultimate distinction between lower 'reflex' and higher cortical associative functioning undercut the classical associationist character of Meynert's schema. For Meynert, the fixed nature of these primary projections to and from the cortex meant that such cortical areas could localize or correspond to fixed psychological elements (sensations) with identities independent of the associations into which they entered. With the functional construal of these processes, however, the separable identities of such postulated atomistic sensory and motor elements were lost. 'Is it possible, then, to differentiate the part of "perception" from that of "association" in the concomitant physiological process?' Freud asks, and answers bluntly: 'Obviously not. "Perception" and "association" are terms by which we describe different aspects of the same process . . . We cannot have a perception without immediately associating it; however sharply we may separate the two concepts, in reality they belong to one single process which, starting from one point, spreads over the whole cortex' (Freud 1953: 57).

It was the Jacksonian idea of cortical representation being functional and mediated rather than topographical and direct that allowed Freud to later adopt and adapt Jackson's major idea about the role played by the speech centre in cortical representation, an idea that was to have implications for Freud's psychoanalytic theory of the *Ich* or Ego. Thus not only were cerebral representations made up of 're-represented' sensory representations, the role of the speech centre in linking perceptual inputs to learned linguistic structures gave to these re-representations a linguistic or propositional form. It was the implications that this idea had for conceptions of the nature of consciousness that was to help shape Freud's later theory of consciousness from the starting point of the parallelist one affirmed in the aphasia monograph.

2 The paradox of the unconscious consciousness of repressed emotion

During the 1890s, Freud the aspiring neuroscientist became Freud the founder of psychoanalysis and by 1915 he had come to abandon parallelism as a general doctrine of the mind–brain relation because of its incompatibility with his notion of the unconscious. But what in fact had happened to the parallelist doctrine can be seen when we examine Freud's attempt to solve a puzzle which presented itself to the new psychoanalytic framework, the puzzle of whether or not from a psycho-analytic perspective *emotions* could be unconscious. It is here too that we see emerge quite clearly Freud's understanding of the difference between 'access' and 'phenomenal' consciousness.

In his paper, 'The Unconscious', Freud raised a paradox posed by the emotions for his distinction between conscious and unconscious mental contents. On the one hand: 'It is surely of the essence of an emotion that we are aware of it, i.e., that it should become known to consciousness.' And yet, on the other, psychoanalytic practice had led to speaking of 'unconscious love, hate, anger, etc'., with psycho-analysts finding it 'impossible to avoid even the strange conjunction, "unconscious consciousness of guilt", or a paradoxical "unconscious anxiety"' (Freud 1953–74, 14: 178). How could this be? How could there be an *unconscious* emotion if it was 'of the essence of an emotion that we are aware of it'?

One possible answer here would be to suggest the existence of some type of parasitic centre of consciousness embedded within, but unknown to, its 'host' consciousness – a position earlier put forward by Pierre Janet and William James in their theorizing about the psychopathology of 'multiple personality syndrome'. This, however, Freud explicitly rejected. Rather, Freud's way of responding to this paradox depended essentially on the distinction between Block's two senses of consciousness. A comparison with Block here might be helpful.

For Block, reflection on such abnormal states of mind as found in the medical oddity of 'blindsight' indicates the need to keep these two aspects of consciousness distinct (Block 1995: 233). Patients with blindsight seem to have a disturbance with the phenomenal consciousness associated with visual perception despite at least some retention of access consciousness there. Thus, for example, when asked, such a patient will correctly 'guess' the identity of some object in their visual field despite the fact that they have no awareness that they can *see* it. The prompt reveals their 'access' to the perceptual content despite the fact that there is apparently nothing 'that it is like' to have the perceptual experience.

In contrast, we might say that Freud's paradoxical cases of 'unconscious emotion' involve something like the reverse of blindsight. Here individuals would have the phenomenal sensation of the emotion but no 'access' to it, being able to neither act on it nor report it, even to themselves.[4] And this indeed is much how Freud approaches the paradox. An affective or emotional impulse is *necessarily felt*, but is capable of being misconstrued by virtue of being 'attached to another idea' after the one to which it had been originally attached had undergone 'repression'. Freud's idea seems to be the following. Say I feel guilty about some act, A. The idea 'attached' to the phenomenal state will be some kind of representation, a memory say, of that act about which I am guilty. This representation is repressed 'into' the unconscious. But *only* representations are susceptible to repression. Affects and feelings are not themselves 'representations' and subsequently they somehow persist phenomenally, but without their interpretative 'ideas', and can henceforth undergo various fates such as being 'reattached' to some other representation – I might feel guilty over some other trivial act B for which guilt is not warranted – or by being transformed into a type of qualitatively undifferentiated 'quota of affect', especially anxiety (Freud 1953–74, 14: 178).

Such an idea of repression as involving a differential loss of the access aspect of consciousness also seems to cohere with Freud's 'topographical' way of describing the situation resulting from repression. On repression the representation gets lodged in some region of the mind behind a 'border' preventing access to it. And if we ask, access by *what*, Freud's eventual answer given in his modified 'second topography' is access by the 'I' or 'ego', that mental agency associated with integrated propositional thought, which Freud seems to have developed on the basis of Jackson's idea of the 'speech centre'.

3 The ego and its access

It is with this account of the conditions for the 'access' consciousness of mental contents that Freud's theory of consciousness approximates the HOT theory, according to which mental contents must become subject to 'higher-order thoughts' before becoming fully conscious. As mentioned, a classical early expression of the HOT theory can be found in Kant, an authority whom Freud invokes in 'The Unconscious':

> The psychoanalytic assumption of unconscious mental activity appears to
> us . . . as an extension of the corrections undertaken by Kant of our views

on external perception. Just as Kant warned us not to overlook the fact that our perceptions are subjectively conditioned and must not be regarded as identical with what is perceived though unknowable, so psychoanalysis warns us not to equate perceptions by means of consciousness with the unconscious mental processes which are their object. Like the physical, the psychical is not necessarily in reality what it appears to us to be.

(Freud 1953–74, 14: 171)[5]

Freud's comments here on the conditions of access consciousness belong to a series of attempts to clarify these issues which started with the account of the secondary process in *The Interpretation of Dreams* of 1900, continued with his discussions of 'reality-testing' and the 'reality principle' in 'Formulations on the Two Principles of Mental Functioning' of 1911 and finally resulted in his theory of the ego in *The Ego and the Id* of 1923. Thus in the 1911 paper Freud described the necessity that the primary process be supplemented by a reality principle, which *cognitively* orientated the organism to the state of the external world (and not just the internal states of its own pleasure) and which articulated the organism's motor discharges with that world in a goal-directed way. With the formation of this new principle of brain functioning the infant could now 'form a conception of the real circumstances in the external world and . . . endeavour to make a real alteration in them' (Freud 1953–74, 12: 219).

For Freud this new type of functioning involves a directing of attention to qualities specifically given by the *outer senses*. 'Consciousness now learned to comprehend sensory qualities in addition to the qualities of pleasure and unpleasure which hitherto had alone been of interest to it' (Freud 1953–74, 12: 220). But in order to become relevant to the operations of a reality principle, such givens of external sense must, of course, be grasped *cognitively* – the organism's orientation to them has to be a matter of an '*impartial passing of judgement*, which had to decide whether a given idea [or representation, *Vorstellung*] was true or false', and *this* is achieved in terms of the demand for unity among these judgements – 'the decision being determined by making a comparison with the memory-traces of reality' (Freud 1953–74, 12: 221). Thus, for this to be possible, the organism must have some means of laying down memory traces, and so 'a system of *notation* was introduced, whose task it was to lay down the results of this periodical activity of consciousness – a part of what we call *memory*' (Freud 1953–74, 12: 220–1). Such an appeal to the unification of judgements within experience as the measure of objectivity has a distinctly Kantian ring, as for Kant, the cognitive question of the 'objectivity' of the mind's conscious representations turned on the question of their *justification* rather than, as Locke had thought, on that of their *genesis*. To focus on the question of justification means that the objectivity of appearances must be thought of as a matter *internal* to the realm of experience or appearance, not one concerning the relation of some experiential content to a 'thing in itself' beyond experience. That is, the question of objectivity had to become translated into the question of the coherence or unity among the mind's actual judgements or representations, a unity tied to that of the mind itself, the 'transcendental unity of apperception'.

But if *this* is what is meant by the ego's access to its mental contents, then it might also seem that there is a danger that Freud's topographical metaphor may lead us astray. Although we have spoken of representations 'losing' their access consciousness by being repressed 'into' the unconscious, it might be thought that this is more correctly put by describing such contents simply as *ceasing to be representations*. After all, to characterize a mental state as 'representational' is to characterize it in terms of its function of representing, and, it might be argued that from the perspective of Freud's Kantianism it is precisely the criteria of access consciousness that are themselves the *criteria* of representationality itself. Talk then of repression as involving the 'splitting off' of a representation from some affective state and removing that representation to some other place would then just be a metaphorical way of describing a process in which an initially phenomenally conscious representational or 'intentional' state simply lost this type of representational or intentional status (Lear 1990: ch. 2).

However, the topographical metaphor serves a further purpose in Freud's account. 'Unconscious' mental contents are for Freud, of course, not *simply* unconscious in this negative sense of lacking 'access consciousness' and the concomitant capacity to be integrated into propositionally articulated thought. They are unconscious in the further sense of belonging to a different system of mental functioning, one whose representations are subject to the 'primary process', a system Freud thought of as chronologically and organizationally prior to that 'secondary-process' characteristic of (access) conscious thought processes with their propositional contents.

In his *The Interpretation of Dreams* of 1900, a work which while undeniably psychoanalytic in its orientation still retained connections with his earlier neurological conceptions, Freud had attempted to explain the workings of the infantile system of mental processing neurologically in terms of immediate associations forged between innate reflexes. However, he theorized, during the course of its development the infant somehow acquired the capacity for those secondary, propositional, thought processes which came to 'inhibit and overlay' the more primitive system (Freud 1953–74, 5: 603). It was the idea of this second type of functioning which was to develop into the later theory of the 'ego' and which was linked to the acquisition of language. But again, this distinction between cortical and sub-cortical centres seems to have already been in place in Freud's Jacksonian neurological model in *On Aphasia* with its Darwinian distinction between evolutionarily more recent and older parts of the brain: 'The whole organization of the brain seems to fall into two central apparatuses of which the cerebral cortex is the younger, while the older one is represented by the ganglia of the forebrain which have still maintained some of their phylogenetically old original functions' (Freud 1953: 49–50).

As we have seen, for Jackson the speech centre, belonging to the most recently developed parts of the cerebral cortex, 're-represented' contents already 'represented' in older sub-cortical regions. Applying this idea of 're-representation' to Freud's theory, we might now describe the activity of the secondary process as somehow involving the linguistic re-representation of some content represented in some non-linguistic way at some lower centres. Repression, then, would involve the interference with or reversal of this process. Devoid of any specifically linguaform re-representation, a 'repressed' mental content would no longer be access conscious. But it may still function 'representationally' at 'lower' centres being related to other such representations and, say, manifested in speech and action, differently.

4 The fate of psychophysical parallelism

Freud's Kantian-HOT theory might be described as addressing the conditions under which mental contents can become *access* conscious, but what, we might ask, is the situation with respect to the subject's *phenomenal* consciousness? Here, I believe, we might gain some clues if we return to the question of Freud's original Fechnerian approach to consciousness. I have described Freud's rejection of the parallelist theory of consciousness as demanded by his discovery of unconscious mental content, and at first glance, this might seem to be because of the inability of psychophysical parallelism to provide a place for *unconscious mentality*. But this is not quite right. Freud seems to have maintained the parallelist approach precisely *with respect to* the contents of the unconscious. It had been because psychophysical parallelism approached 'consciousness' entirely phenomenally, that is *qua* realm of *sensation*, that Fechner had been able to speculate about a law-like relation between neural states and states of consciousness. In this way consciousness could be conceived in terms of its scalable *intensity* and supposedly correlated with the energetic dimension of underlying neural states. But with the development of Freud's more Kantian theme of the conditions of access consciousness, the scope of the parallelist doctrine became narrowed from being a doctrine of the nature of consciousness *per se*, to one applied to a limited and circumscribed realm – the 'unconscious consciousness' of *merely* phenomenally conscious states such as 'repressed' emotions. Thus, in 'The Unconscious' we find Freud, in differentiating affects from representations, describing the former in distinctly Fechnerian terms, construing them as the mental side of a single psychophysical reality: they 'correspond to processes of discharge, the final manifestation of which are perceived as feelings' (Freud 1953–74, 14: 178).

This Fechnerian conception of the unconscious mind is perhaps most explicit in works such as *Beyond the Pleasure Principle* from 1920 where Freud returns to speculation about the evolutionary development of the different mental systems. As has been pointed out by Henri Ellenberger, Fechnerian psychophysical thought had contributed to Freud's early 'energetic' conception of the mental processes, and one such Fechnerian element was a neurophysiological version of the law of conservation of energy, that Fechner had called the principle of constancy (Ellenberger 1993: 100–3). Combined with the parallelist idea of the mind–body relation the constancy principle yielded a theory of pleasure and pain. For Freud, it was the accumulation of energy produced by sensory stimulation in the organism above an optimum level that was experienced as pain while its subsequent reflex discharge in motor action was experienced as pleasure. It was in terms of such reflex discharges of energy that Freud had first described the system of the primary process in *The Interpretation of Dreams*.

In *Beyond the Pleasure Principle* Freud speculates about the evolutionary development of the sense organs. First, he notes the fact that embryologically the cerebral cortex develops from ectodermal tissue, that is, that layer of cells on the embryonic plate that is in general the source of the outer, protective skin of the body: '[T]he surface turned towards the external world will from its very situation be differentiated and will serve as an organ for receiving stimuli.' But Freud then construes the organism's original problem, as it were, as one of *too much* rather than too little stimulation, an idea which makes sense against his Fechnerian assumption that the accumulation of stimuli is, for the organism, essentially *painful*. Would it not be the case then that in the organism a 'crust' or 'shield' might have formed to protect it from the stimulation emanating from the powerful energies of its environment? '*Protection against* stimuli is an almost more important function for the living organism than *reception of* stimuli' (Freud 1953–74, 18: 26). This conception then guides Freud in his thought of how exactly to think of the operations of the external senses: 'It is characteristic of them that they deal only with very small quantities of external stimulation and only take in *samples* of the external world. They may perhaps be compared with feelers which are all the time making tentative advances towards the external world and then drawing back from it' (Freud 1953–74, 18: 27–8). Then, with very little explanation, Freud links this to the Kantian nature of conscious thought: 'This mode of functioning may perhaps constitute another way of providing a shield against stimuli' (Freud 1953–74, 18: 28).

But in contrast to this 'sampling' operation of external perception, the internal perception of endogenously generated stimuli lacks any such guard against excessive stimuli:

> [T]he difference between the conditions governing the reception of excitations in the two cases have a decisive effect on the functioning of the system and of the whole mental apparatus. Towards the outside it is shielded against stimuli, and the amounts of excitation impinging on it have only a reduced effect. Towards the inside there can be no such shield; the excitations in the deeper layers extend into the system directly and in undiminished amount, in so far as certain of their characteristics give rise to feelings in the pleasure–unpleasure series.
>
> (Freud 1953–74, 18: 28–9)

It is thus that the human organism deals with exogenously and endogenous produced stimuli in very different ways, and of the two, it is clear that it is the internal, endogenous system which works in a Fechner-like parallelist way. 'The excitations coming from within are, however, in their intensity and in other, qualitative, respects – in their amplitude, perhaps – more commensurate with the system's method of working than the stimuli which stream in from the external world.' In contrast, with their 'sampling' operations, external senses working as they do with relatively low energy states function in quite different, and apparently, non-Fechnerian ways. In contemporary cybernetic parlance, it might be said that for the external senses, effects are brought about, not by the flow of energy, but by the flow of 'information' that can be conveyed in the reduced flow of energy within the nervous system allowed by its 'sampling' mode of operation.

Conclusion: Freud at the close of the twentieth century

It is ironic, then, that in the last few decades there has appeared a very public and vocal group of critics of Freud, ready to dismiss him as having nothing relevant to say about the mind and as little more than a charlatan and a fraud. (For example, Crews 1993). These *ad hominem* attacks are often delivered as if the substantive debate over Freud's theories has been long settled against him and in favour of critics like the philosopher of science Adolf Grünbaum (Grünbaum 1984). But Grünbaum's critique is largely indifferent to any peculiarities of psychological knowledge, and is conducted with little reference to recent philosophical thought about the nature of mental content or consciousness. Precisely by appealing to current ways of thinking about intentionality, a number of defenders of Freud have criticized Grünbaum's levelling account, arguing that at the core of Freud's approach we find a sophisticated theory of mental content (for example, Hopkins 1988; Cavell 1993; Gardner 1995). But cutting across this, Freud also has what from today's perspective is a sophisticated and relevant theory of *consciousness*.

Notes

1   Portions of this chapter reproduce passages from Chapters 2 and 3 of my book, *The Logic of Affect*, published by Cornell University Press in 1999. I am grateful to Cornell University Press for allowing me to reproduce that material. I would also like to thank Stephanie Winfield, Michael Levine and a reviewer for Routledge for helpful comments on an earlier version.

2   On the origins and philosophical associations of the cerebral reflex theory and its subsequent role within neurological thought see Clarke and Jacyna 1987.

3   On Jackson see Dewhurst 1982 and Harrington 1987.

4   Block acknowledges the possibility of phenomenal consciousness without access consciousness, and, while considering William James's 'secondary consciousness' to fit into this category, does not consider Freud (Block 1995: 233–4).

5   While Freud construes the act rendering mental processes conscious on the analogy of an act of *perception* rather than thought – a clear misunderstanding of Kant – when we consider the general developmental trajectory of Freud's theory it is clear that it in essence closely resembles Kant's actual theory.

References

Block, N. (1995) 'On a Confusion about a Function of Consciousness', *Behavioral and Brain Sciences*, 18: 227–87.

Cavell, M. (1993) *The Psychoanalytic Mind: From Freud to Philosophy*, Cambridge, MA: Harvard University Press.

Clarke E. and Jacyna, L. S. (1987) *Nineteenth-Century Origins of Neuroscientific Concepts*, Berkeley: University of California Press.

Crews, F. (1993) 'The Unknown Freud', *New York Review of Books*, 18 November: 53–66.

Dewhurst, K. (1982) *Hughlings Jackson on Psychiatry*, Oxford: Sandford.

Ellenberger, H. F. (1993) 'Fechner and Freud', in *Beyond the Unconscious*, Princeton, NJ: Princeton University Press.

Fechner, G. T. (1966) *Elements of Psychophysics*, vol. 1, trans. H. E. Adler, New York: Holt, Rinehart and Winston.

Forrester, J. (1980) *Language and the Origins of Psychoanalysis*, London: Macmillan.

Freud, S. (1953) *On Aphasia*, New York: International Universities Press.

—— (1953–74) *The Standard Edition of the Complete Psychological Works of Sigmund Freud*, trans. and ed. James Strachey, London: Hogarth Press.

Gardner, S. (1995) 'Psychoanalysis, Science and Commonsense', *Philosophy, Psychology and Psychiatry*, 2: 93–133.

Gennaro, R. J. (1995) *Consciousness and Self-Consciousness: A Defense of the Higher-Order Thought Theory of Consciousness*, Amsterdam: John Benjamins.

Grünbaum, A. (1984) *The Foundations of Psychoanalysis: A Philosophical Critique*, Berkeley: University of California Press.

Harrington, A. (1987) *Medicine, Mind, and the Double Brain: A Study in Nineteenth-Century Thought*, Princeton, N.J.: Princeton University Press.

Hopkins, J. (1988) 'Epistemology and Depth Psychology', in S. Clark and C. Wright (eds), *Psychoanalysis, Mind and Science*, Oxford: Blackwell.

Jackson, J. H. (1931) *Selected Writings of John Hughlings Jackson*, vol. 2, London: Hodder and Soughton.

Kant, I. (1933) *Critique of Pure Reason*, trans. N. Kemp Smith, New York: Macmillan.

Lear, J. (1990) *Love and its Place in Nature: A Philosophical Interpretation of Freudian Psychoanalysis*, New York: Farrar, Strauss and Giroux.

Lennig, P. (1988) 'Gustav Fechner und die Naturphilosophie', in J. Brozek and H. Gundlach (eds) *G. T. Fechner and Psychology*, Passau: Passavia Universitätsverlag.

Magoun, H. (1960) 'Evolutionary Concepts of Brain Function Following Darwin and Spencer', in Sol Tax (ed.) *Evolution After Darwin, Volume II, The Evolution of Man*, Chicago: Chicago University Press.

Meynert, T. (1885) *Psychiatry: A Clinical Treatise on Diseases of the Fore-Brain Based upon a Study of its Structure, Functions and Nutrition*, trans. B. Sachs, New York: G. P. Putnam's Sons.

Reed, E. S. (1997) *From Soul to Mind: The Emergence of Psychology from Erasmus Darwin to William James*, New Haven: Yale University Press.

Rizzuto, A.-M. (1990) 'The Origins of Freud's Concept of Object Representation (*Objektvorstellung*) in his Monograph "On Aphasia", Its Theoretical and Technical Importance', *International Journal of Psycho-Analysis*, 71: 241–8.

—— (1993) 'Freud's speech Apparatus and Spontaneous Speech', *International Journal of Psycho-Analysis*, 74: 113–27.

Rosenthal, D. M. (1986) 'Two Concepts of Consciousness', *Philosophical Studies*, 49: 329–59.

Sulloway, F. (1992) *Freud, Biologist of the Mind: Beyond the Psychoanalytic Legend*, Cambridge: MA: Harvard University Press.

Part II

ETHICS

7

ARISTOTELIAN AKRASIA, WEAKNESS OF WILL AND PSYCHOANALYTIC REGRESSION[1]

Michael Stocker with *Elizabeth Hegeman*

I want to show why Aristotle saw akrasia as importantly a psychological or moral-psychological issue, not just an evaluative one. I will do this by showing how Aristotelian akrasia involves something very similar to regression – regression from adult, conceptualized forms of desire to developmentally earlier, non-conceptualized forms of desire. I will also suggest why we should see weakness of will as an importantly psychological or moral-psychological issue.

Aristotelian akrasia and what contemporary philosophers call weakness of will are often taken to be, near enough, the same phenomenon, raising the same questions and problems. Indeed, 'akrasia' is often translated as 'weakness of will' (sometimes as 'incontinence' or 'moral weakness'). But I think akrasia and weakness of will are significantly different.

One of the central questions contemporary philosophers ask about weakness of will goes something like (1) 'How, if at all, is it possible for people knowingly not to do what they think best?' But Aristotle did not ask – and for reasons having to do with differences between akrasia and weakness of will would not have asked – (1) about akrasia.

He did not think there was *one* such question to be asked about akrasia – since he did not think that akrasia was one, unitary phenomenon. He distinguished between *paradigmatic* and *non-paradigmatic* forms of akrasia, with subforms of the latter. And he asked different questions – different both from each other and also from (1) – about each. About paradigmatic akrasia, he asked something like (2) 'How, if at all, is it possible for people, *because of contrary, epithumetic (bodily) desire for epithumetic pleasure*, knowingly not to do what they think best?' About non-paradigmatic akrasia, he asked something like (2′) 'How, if at all, is it possible for people, *because of contrary, emotion-driven desires for certain sorts of pleasures*, knowingly not to do what they think best?' (I am mainly concerned with paradigmatic akrasia and (2). When concerned with non-paradigmatic akrasia and (2′), I will make that clear.)

Aristotle's question about akrasia – about each sort of akrasia – is, thus, doubly restricted. It is restricted just to *pleasures*. And it is restricted to just *some* pleasures.

He has been criticized for making these restrictions, for asking (2) instead of our more general (1), and – when the distinction between them is not simply ignored or dismissed out of hand – for distinguishing between (2) and (2').[2] But I think he had good reasons to approach akrasia this way. These reasons also point to how we should understand weakness of will. On my view, 'not doing what one thinks best' does not point to what Aristotle rightly finds important and troubling about akrasia, nor what we should find important and troubling about weakness of will. To get at these, we need to use psychology and moral-psychology to investigate the particular forms of desire akrasia involves.

I want to conclude this introductory section with a brief comment on how weakness of will is typically understood. Whether or not they think weakness of will problematic, philosophers differ over which evaluative notion (or notions) – e.g., best or right – is in question. Non-maximizers may well think *knowingly not doing what is BEST* entirely ordinary, unproblematic, and lacking any strong links to weakness of will. Those who deny the overridingness of the moral may well think this of *knowingly not doing what is RIGHT*. And so on. This issue is important for a full understanding of weakness of will and akrasia. But I think for present concerns we can and, for reasons of space, should, avoid it. I propose, therefore, that we read 'best' here and throughout as standing for whatever the relevant notion(s) is.

1 Paradigmatic akrasia

In this section, I give a characterization of paradigmatic akrasia. My concern here is not just to present what Aristotle says. It is also to help present his views on some important developmental issues that will help us see various of the psychological underpinnings of his discussion of akrasia. He says that 'The starting point of our investigation is the question of whether the continent man and the incontinent are differentiated by their objects or by their attitude', or both (*NE* VII.3, 1146b14 ff, trans. Ross and Urmson). He answers, 'Both':

> The man who is incontinent in the unqualified sense is neither concerned with any and every object, but with precisely those with which the self-indulgent man is concerned, nor is he characterized by being simply related to these (for then his state would be the same as self-indulgence), but by being related to them in a certain way. For the one is led on in accordance with his own choice, thinking that he ought always to pursue the present pleasure, while the other does not think so, but yet pursues it (VII.3, 1146a18 ff).

As already noted, akrasia is to be understood in terms of certain sorts of desire. Following the lead of this last passage, I want to urge that these desires are to be understood in terms of both *what* is desired and also *how* it is desired. Paradigmatic akrasia involves the desires that temperance, *sophrusune*, also involves (*NE* III.10). Both paradigmatic akrasia and temperance involve what is desired by animals and young children and is desired in the ways animals and children desire those things.

The objects of these desires – the *what* that is desired – are bodily pleasures that we share with animals: 'Temperance and self-indulgence . . . are concerned with the kind of pleasures that the other animals share in . . . [they involve] touch and taste' (III.10, 1118a23 ff). As will be discussed, these objects of desire are importantly preconceptual or non-conceptual. They differ from the conceptual, universal-involving objects of desire adults can have.

Let us turn now to the *how* of these desires. They are said to work on us directly, as if they directly move our bodily parts (VII.3, 1147a35). But they do not work the way mere, primitive urges or reflexes might be thought to work. To say that these objects work on us directly is to say, among other things, that they move us, and perhaps overcome us, but *not* via a universal, a principle, or an evaluation. This is desiring like, in ways typical of, an animal or young child, not a mature adult: 'self-indulgence would seem to be justly a matter of reproach, because it attaches to us not as men but as animals' (III.10, 1118b2 ff). 'And this explains why animals cannot be morally weak [akratic]: they do not have conceptions of universals, but have only the power to form mental images [*phantasiai*] and memory of particulars' (VII.3 1147b3 ff., trans. Ostwald).

We should note several contrasts here. One is a contrast with other objects of desire. 'That incontinence and continence, then, are concerned only with the same objects as self-indulgence and temperance and that what is concerned with other objects is a type distinct from incontinence, and called incontinence by a metaphor and not simply, is plain' (VII.6, 1149a21 ff., trans. Ross and Urmson). 'Victory, honor, wealth, and good and pleasant things of this sort' (VII.4, 1148a30) are among these *other* objects of desire. These objects are conceptually complex and require a considerable degree of maturity to be understood well enough to be desired. Because animals and young children lack the conceptual requisites, they cannot desire these objects.

Another contrast is with the attitudes of adults to these various goals. To help put this, the following sketch of a developmental story may be useful. When we are infants and young children, the desires and pleasures of touch and taste act on us directly in that we 'naturally' and 'without thought' like, desire and pursue such things as what is sweet and our mother's milk. As we grow older, we think about what we seek, what we like and what we do. This involves conceptualizing our goals, and also evaluating them. When we are adults, we can act on account of these principles, thoughts and evaluations.

Because Aristotle says so little on a subject that is so complex, it is exceedingly difficult to give an account of what in his view it is to think and act like a child on account of *phantasiai*, or like an adult, thinking and acting on account of principles, universals, and evaluations. But I can point to some things that may enable us to proceed, by indicating how *phantasiai* can account for akrasia.

We just read, 'And this explains why animals cannot be morally weak [akratic]: they do not have conceptions of universals, but have only the power to form mental images [*phantasiai*] and memory of particulars'. This might seem to allow for a relatively simple account of children's thinking – if we take 'they do not have conceptions of universals' as saying that children and animals lack *all* generalizations, especially all generalizations with *any* motivational force. This account may seem suggested by 'they . . . have only the power to form mental images [*phantasiai*] and memory of particulars'.

But there is no need to accept this suggestion, and there are good reasons not to. First, it does not lend itself to an account of akrasia. Second, it is too implausible on its face. And third, it seems to be based on the view that if universals do not figure in motivations or reasons, then these motivations and reasons can be only images or thoughts of particulars. I will take these in reverse order, leaving the first until the middle of this section.

Aristotle denies that the distinction between universals, on the one hand, and images or thoughts of particulars, on the other, is exhaustive. *Phantasiai* occupy a mid-range between them.[3] *Phantasiai* are not universals. But they are also not just of particulars: they apply to and take in more than one object. Why there must be such intermediate entities or states can be brought out by noting what is so implausible about the claim that because children and animals lack universals, they can, therefore, have only images, opinions, or thoughts of particulars. It is simply obvious that children and animals, too, form and use many sorts of generalizations. Both children and animals can and do learn from experience. One thing they learn is to see various particulars as tasty, because they seem like some other things that were tasty.

Pointing it out should be all the argument needed to show that children do learn this about a huge number of foods and other things they want to and do taste – perhaps starting with their learning to find a nipple.[4] So too, of course, for much else that they eventually learn. I think it also sufficient simply to point out that many animals learn this about different sorts of tasty or untasty plants and animals. So too, for much else they learn. Were all generalizations unavailable to such animals as dogs, or, for that matter, to children, we could not teach them: not even to keep off the furniture. For they would then be unable to recognize furniture in even the moderately accurate ways they do.

Further, both children and animals deploy in their own ways these generalizations in thinking and acting. Children, and not only when willful, certainly seem to show that they hold and act on such generalizations as 'Any sweet thing I want is mine for the taking'. And many hunting animals, such as lions, certainly seem to hold and act on something like, 'Any animal of a kind I have found tasty and catchable that I want to eat is mine for the catching'.

In brief, then, adults have and act on universal beliefs, including principles and evaluations. And they can do this in adult ways. These are ways that may resist ultimately satisfying characterizations, but are nonetheless clearly recognizable as different from the ways children and animals use their generalizations. As we might say with Aristotle, only adults can choose. Choice, *prohairesis*, involves having and using an evaluative 'principle', a universal belief, requiring, advising, or allowing the chosen acts and goals. We should note that choosing does not require having and acting on correct principles, but only having and acting on principles and universals. So, Aristotle says, 'For the . . . [self-indulgent person] is led on in accordance with his own choice, thinking that he ought always to pursue the present pleasure'.

What is important for us is that when people act akratically, the pleasures that overcome them do not work via, or even in accord with, principles and reasons, whether correct or not. Paradigmatic akrasia is not to be thought of in terms of a conflict between two principles, one telling the agent what is to be done and the other advocating what is akratic. More particularly, my suggestion is that in paradigmatic akrasia no work is done by principles and universals. Rather, akratics think and desire, and act upon *phantasiai*, in much the way children do. (As noted below, akratics must, in some sense, still have principles.)

The picture of a paradigmatically akratic act that I am suggesting, then, is this. The adult recognizes – perhaps as an adult would or perhaps as a child would – that something is sweet; the appetite, and in particular the desire for the sweet and pleasant thing, takes over and works directly, in much the same ways appetite does in children. (Why I say '*much* the same ways', rather than 'the same ways' is discussed below.) The appetite, or the person responding to appetite, is once again – as it always is in children – not under the control of principles and universals, not even to the extent of being guided by them or listening to them.

We might well wonder how this works and how it differs from what happens in good practical syllogisms or in non-paradigmatic akrasia. My answer is that in the case of paradigmatic akrasia, the sweetness and pleasure do not function as *reasons* for the tasting. The 'conclusion' of the appetite-'syllogism' is not 'I will taste this in that it is sweet and pleasant'. That 'reason' is not a reason, and that 'syllogism' is not a syllogism. Whatever results from it does not do so *as* a conclusion. It has no conclusion.

This can be put in terms of a passage from Book VII.9 of the *Nicomachean Ethics*: 'If anyone chooses or pursues this for the sake of that, *per se* he pursues and chooses the latter, but incidentally the former' (1151b1 ff). In the case of good syllogisms, we can describe the conclusion in terms of the universal, in terms of a justifying reason. Conclusions are not to be understood as telling us just something on the order of 'this act is to be done', but rather 'this act is to be done, in that —'. The blank is filled in with a principle or reason given in the good syllogism, which makes that conclusion a conclusion. In the case of paradigmatic akrasia, the sweetness and pleasure do not function as principles behind or reasons for the tasting. The 'conclusion' of the appetite-'syllogism' is not 'I will taste this in that it is sweet and pleasant'. It has no conclusion. And it is not a syllogism. Put in a related way, the conclusion of a syllogism – a real syllogism this time – could be 'I will taste this *in that it is sweet and pleasant*'. But where it is, we do not have a case of akrasia. Rather, we may have, for example, a case of self-indulgence or a case of well-chosen pleasure.

On my view, then, paradigmatic akrasia is not to be seen as a conflict between two incompossible conclusions of syllogisms, telling the akratic to do two incompossible acts. Nor is it to be seen as a conflict between two principles: here, between one telling that person to do what is good, and the other telling that person to taste what is sweet and pleasing. The objects of paradigmatic akrasia are the pleasures that temperance is concerned with and that children and animals pursue. Akrasia requires that these pleasures that overcome the akratic agent act directly, as they do in children and animals. In children and animals, there will not even be the materials for representing their psychic content and processes in terms of a practical syllogism. In adults, including akratic adults, there are such materials. But in akratic adults they may well not appear at all and may well not be used at all. If they do appear and are used, they do so as rationalizations, empty words, window dressing; or in child-like ways.

What is important about the *phantasiai* that are at work in and account for paradigmatic akrasia cannot just be that they are *phantasiai*. *Phantasiai* play roles in non-paradigmatic akrasia and also in totally non-akratic phenomena, too. It is – and this is my suggestion – that they are *phantasiai* with those objects, working in the ways that they do in children with those objects and those attitudes to those objects. To understand this, we do not need to investigate the very difficult, general interrelations between psychological objects and attitudes. Nor do we need to investigate the particularities of the interrelations between the objects and attitudes as they are found in paradigmatic akrasia; or as they are found in children and animals. It will be sufficient for us to recognize that there are important interrelations of the following sorts.

In children there are *phantasiai* that not only have those objects, but also that are taken up in ways appropriate to children pursuing those objects. This is not to be understood just in terms of attitudes, nor just in terms of objects. For philosophical purposes, we can make analytic distinctions between these objects and attitudes. But to understand what is happening in children, say, we must understand these as forming a complex. Children do differ from adults in what they desire. They also differ in how they think of, desire, and pursue what they desire. Further, their thoughts and desires help 'give' those objects the shape and attractiveness that, in those ways, children experience them as having. Paradigmatic akratics desire what children desire and they have and act on desires in the ways children do.

2 How paradigmatic akrasia involves regression: some relations between knowledge and akrasia

My suggestion is that paradigmatic akrasia involves a regression, a failure or loss of mastery and maturation and a return to what is developmentally earlier and more primitive. This helps explain why Aristotle thought that such akrasia and full knowledge are incompossible. It is not that regression, itself, is impossible. As Aristotle and we clearly recognize, regression is all too easy and all too possible. But what is not so clearly possible, if possible at all, is regression in areas where mastery and maturation *are still in play*. My suggestion is that we take Aristotle's claim of the incompossibility of paradigmatic akrasia and fully mature, adult knowledge as depending on the relations among mastery, maturity and regression. The impossibility is that of living, at once, both as a child and also as an adult. Or better, in order to give explicit recognition to the fact that adults can partially regress and partially remain mature and adult, we should say that what is impossible is living at once and in regard to the same matters both in an immature way and also a fully mature way.

The issues here go beyond what is conceptual of regression: that regression involves a going away from, perhaps a loss or a weakening of, mature mastery, and thus that it is conceptually impossible at once to be in a thoroughly regressed state and also maintain and show full maturity and mastery. The way they go beyond this is tied up with how being a mature adult goes beyond just a change in what is conceptually possible: that it is now conceptually possible to regress (a possibility 'enjoyed' only by those who have matured). Far more significantly, becoming and being a mature adult is a real and, indeed, a momentous achievement. It is becoming and being a person whose thinking, desiring, feeling and acting are, or can be, conceptual. The regression of paradigmatic akrasia is the abandonment or reversal of this achievement.

Another, very similar, way to see these issues is by contrasting the *non-*conceptualized or *differently* conceptualized ways children experience and understand with the conceptualized ways adults experience and understand. Here we could examine claims by various theorists that the differences are great enough to preclude anything like full and successful communication between people at these different developmental stages. These theorists claim that adults are unable to experience and understand the world, including themselves, in the ways they did when infants and young children.

The psychoanalyst Ernest Schachtel uses this to explain why adults cannot remember much, if anything, about their lives before they acquired language.[5] In a similar manner, the psychoanalyst Donald P. Spence argues that when a previously unformulated experience gets put into words, it gets shaped according to the narrative of the person doing the formulation, at the time of the narration.[6] Discussing cases where adults have seriously dissociated experiences – occasioned, say, by abuse, trauma and shock – the psychoanalyst Enid Balint writes, 'It is important to keep in mind that what is remembered by the patient but has never been thought – has never had words – must have been experienced by the patient in a different way from other events'.[7]

This allows that adults can retrieve memories laid down when infants. This also allows that adults can have experiences that are like infants' experiences that are not verbally conceptualized: that adults can have experiences that are 'understood' by them in non-conceptualized ways, much as infants 'understand' their experiences. Regression is one way – and for present concerns, an absolutely crucial way – that adults can have such experiences.[8]

Much, then, is allowed. But not everything is. One thing that is not allowed is that adults, using adult forms of understanding, can have access to infants' experiences and understandings or to infant-like experiences and understandings as had by adults who have regressed. Another thing that is also not allowed is that these latter experiences can be 'translated' accurately into non-regressed experiences and understandings as had by non-regressed adults.

Such talk of infant-like experiences might suggest that what I have said so far fits only animals, infants and very young children, and not also older children.[9] Perhaps this is right. But I think we can easily give a similar account showing that, as with infants, so with older children. Even older children's ways of thinking, experiencing and desiring are different enough from adults' ways to preclude full mutual understanding and make it impossible to think, experience and desire in adults' and older children's ways at once about the same issue.

Psychoanalysis and developmental psychology, not to mention the experience of many parents and children, give considerable support here. Children and adults think and reason in significantly different ways. To mention only some points, children's self-concept and adults' self-concept are significantly different; children and adults make distinctions between reality and fantasy in different places and different ways; children think far more concretely, and are far less able to think abstractly, than adults.

The pioneering psychoanalyst Sándor Ferenczi uses these differences to make a point that is at once conceptually, socially and morally important and disturbing.[10] He argues that this lack of comprehension explains a way adults manage to abuse children sexually without overt violence. Children are unable to understand adult genital sexuality and its attendant desires. Thus, as least initially, children misconceive those adult affectionate gestures and desires that do involve adult sexual genitality. They take these desires to be just like their own desires for tenderness and affection, as they understand these. And this incomprehension – whether or not it is recognized or exploited by the adults – allows adults to impose their adult genital sexual desires on children.

To the extent that there are these and other differences and problems of understanding between adults and children, we can go beyond the argument restricted to infants and also beyond the conceptual argument turning on the meaning relations between 'mastery' and 'regression'. These additional differences provide us with good grounds for agreeing with Aristotle's claim about the impossibility of paradigmatic akrasia when one has full, adult knowledge, used in full, adult ways. For these are grounds for holding that it is impossible to think, experience and desire, at once and in regard to the same issue, in both fully mature, adult ways and also in children's ways.[11]

It is important to note that this last way of putting my claim about akrasia does not depend on the possibility of regressed adults' experiences being exactly like infants' or children's experiences. For all I have argued or need to argue, it may well be that regressed adults' experiences are, despite being regressed, adult-like: that they are 'only' adult versions of, or near 'approaches' to, infant-like or child-like experiences.

This can be put in terms borrowed from Aristotle. He holds that people and various other animals can have some similar 'parts' of the mind (*psyche*), such as the arational or pre-rational, desiderative part(s). But this is a only a *similarity*. An animal's mind is not just like an adult's, with the sole difference that it lacks our rational parts – as we might imagine ours would be if just our reasoning parts were somehow excised, without affecting any other parts. The animal has its own particular sort of desiderative nature, as do humans. So too, we could say – now perhaps extending Aristotle's claim – that there is the same sort of similarity between children and adults. Both children and adults have desiderative or appetitive parts, which are arational or pre-rational. But a child's mind is not just like an adult's, except that it lacks adult rational parts. Nor is the child's desiderative part the same as the adult's.[12]

Correlatively, when an adult regresses – for example, in cases of paradigmatic akrasia – there is no need for the adult to do what may well be impossible: actually and literally regain a child's mind. That would require not only losing the adult rational parts, but also regaining the child's pre-adult arational or irrational appetitive and desiderative parts. It is sufficient for regression – and for paradigmatic akrasia – that the adult regresses to being child-like: to having *phantasiai* much like those had by children, had in ways much like the ways children have them.

Once again, we need to focus on both the *what*, the content, of the *phantasia* and also its *how*, the ways it is held and acted on. We need this to allow for akrasia. We also need it to allow that a child and a non-regressed adult could want and experience (much) the very same taste – say, of an apple. Moreover, it may be possible for an adult to have, at the same time, both preconceptual and conceptual understandings and desires. While having an infantile, preconceptual desire, the adult – perhaps while observing this in adult, conceptual ways – may have adult, conceptual desires of the 'same' object. After all, one goal in psychoanalysis is to experience, understand, and tolerate preconceptual desires.

This last raises questions about the strength of Aristotle's claim that paradigmatic akrasia and full knowledge are incompossible and of my argument in terms of regression in support of his claim. The issue turns on questions about what we might call 'double mindedness'. The central factual question is, 'Under what conditions, if any, is it possible for an adult to have regressed desires and understandings and also, at the very same time in regard to the very same issue, have fully mature, adult desires and understandings?' The central interpretational question concerns Aristotle's reasonableness in holding this is impossible and our reasonableness in answering it, no matter how we do answer it.[13]

One last point should be made. I have suggested that when an appetite-'syllogism' is in play – when, for example, an adult's *phantasiai* are much like and are working much like a child's – the right reason syllogism and its universals are not in play, if they are even there at all. This might be taken as suggesting a different and more standard account of akrasia than mine: akrasia is to be explained in terms of why the universal fails to be really and strongly in play but is, instead, in play only in a weak or deficient way, as shown, say, by a drunk uttering 'scientific proofs and verses of Empedocles'.

But I think that these accounts can be seen as complementary, not as rivals. My account needs to be supplemented with an account of what happens to the universals the akratic violates and thus has or had. This other account needs to be supplemented with an account of how akratics think. Each account must tell us why it is impossible both to have the universal in fully mature, adult ways and also to pursue pleasure akratically.

3 Why Aristotle was concerned with his, not our, question about akrasia

I now want to suggest why Aristotle 'restricted' his concern with akrasia to what is done *because of contrary desire for pleasure* – epithumetic desires and pleasures for paradigmatic akrasia, and emotion-driven desires and pleasures for non-paradigmatic akrasia. This will be to explain and justify why he asked his doubly restricted question about akrasia rather than, say, our (1), 'How, if at all, is it possible for people knowingly not to do what they think best?'

One way to explain and justify distinguishing between paradigmatic and non-paradigmatic akrasia and between both of these forms of akrasia and other ways of going wrong is by assessing the importance of distinguishing among their different sorts of objects and attitudes. For my part, I find both distinctions very important. To gesture to only one very large and important area, these distinctions help us see and understand our developmental history, including our transition from the sort or sorts of understanding animals, infants and older children have to those sorts only adults have. They also help us see the sorts of developmental stages, changes, challenges and failures we are subject to at different times of our lives.

Aristotle is clearly interested in these issues. Development is one of his central concerns: how we change from basically arational beings, to beings under the sway of infant desires, to the desire-led life of young children, and then to the desire-led and emotion-led life of older children, adolescents and young people, and finally to a fully mature, adult life of value, principle and character. This is to say that one of his central concerns is how we learn to be good by learning to think, by acquiring and using concepts and principles.[14] Often this developmental concern is discussed in terms of how pleasure and what we take pleasure in gets transformed from pleasures of touch or taste to pleasures based on value. And often this developmental concern is allied with a concern about how various shortcomings and vices can be cured.[15] All of these interrelated concerns involve issues about both what pleases us and about attitudes toward pleasure and pleasures: for example, what arouses our desire, what leads to action or longing.

These, then, are some reasons to distinguish among various sorts of akrasia. However, the question remains, why should we, or why did Aristotle, take epithumetic akrasia to be paradigmatic akrasia? This may, but need not, be merely a matter of classification. It can also reflect the reasonableness of seeing that sort of akrasia as especially troubling and as worse than non-paradigmatic akrasia.

Paradigmatic akrasia involves an especially troubling sort of regression – a return to the forms of understanding, experiencing, and desiring of animals, infants, or children. Character is such an achievement of maturation that 'adult character' is redundant and 'childish character' is, strictly speaking, contradictory. Adults who succumb to akratic, epithumetic desires do not so much show *bad* character as they show a lack of adult character: that is, a lack of character *simpliciter*.[16] As Aristotle put it, like self-indulgence, paradigmatic akrasia, 'attaches to us not as men but as animals' (III.10, 1118b2 ff).[17] Of course, it is bad – bad for us, as humans – to lack character. But this badness differs from that of having a bad character.

Non-paradigmatic forms of akrasia, such as acting from overkeenness, may also involve regression, perhaps to the impetuosity of young men:

> Young men have strong passions . . . their impulses are keen but are not deep-rooted . . . owing to their love of honor they cannot bear being slighted, and are indignant if they imagine themselves treated unfairly. While they love honor, they love victory still more . . . nature warms their blood as though with excess of wine.
>
> (*Rht*, II.12, 1389a3 ff., trans. Roberts)

As Aristotle also writes, talking about non-paradigmatic akrasia,

> Anger (*thumos*) seems to listen to reason to some extent, but to mishear it . . . For reason or imagination informs us that we have been insulted or slighted, and anger, reasoning as it were that anything like this must be fought against, boils up straightway; while appetite, if reason or perception merely says that an object is pleasant, springs to the enjoyment of it. Therefore anger obeys reason in a sense, but appetite does not.
>
> (*NE*, VII.6, 1149a25 ff)

These give us good pictures – even if not a detailed psychological and moral psychological account – of how Aristotle thought it is possible to be *non-paradigmatically* akratic. Such regression, too – which might be thought of as regressing to a state where one acts, not *just with* emotion, but *because of* emotion – is all too easy and all too possible. It also tells against a person's being fully good and fully mature.

But such regression and its attendant, non-paradigmatic akrasia do not show a return to primitive infantile or childish desire, emotion, and action – that is, forms of these that are not based on thought, principle, or evaluation. Nor do they show or involve the agent having and acting on base desires or showing a lack of adult character. Only adults or near-adults have the conceptual and reason-following capacities to understand and desire the objects of non-paradigmatic akrasia, 'victory, honor, wealth, and good and pleasant things of this sort'. This is even clearer in regard to *thumos* (anger) which 'seems to listen to reason to some extent' and in regard to *orge-* (anger), which involves thinking of something as a *slight*, not just as a harm, that is not just suffered, but is also *undeserved* (*Rht* II.2). Children, especially young children, do not yet have the concepts and the associated principles of undeserved slights. Nor do they yet have reason to mishear. Nor have they yet achieved the concepts and associated principles of 'victory, honor, wealth, and good and pleasant things of this sort'.[18] (To be sure, as shown in, say, their play and fantasies, children can have precursor-forms of these adult objects and concerns.)

These, then, are some reasons – and, on my view, good reasons – why Aristotle distinguished between paradigmatic and non-paradigmatic forms of akrasia. I want now to consider some reasons he 'restricted' his study of akrasia, why, that is, he asked (2), 'How, if at all, is it possible for people, *because of contrary, epithumetic (bodily) desire for epithumetic pleasure* – or (2') *because of contrary, emotion-driven desires for certain sorts of pleasures* – knowingly not to do what they think best?' rather than our more general (1), 'How, if at all, is it possible for people knowingly not to do what they think best?'

By asking (2), rather than (1), Aristotle does *not* consider various 'reasons' for weakness of will that contemporaries have considered. So, he does not consider not doing what is best on account of willfulness or orneriness; or because one wants to 'make a statement', or to take a 'moral holiday', or to perform an *acte gratuit*, or to thumb one's nose at morality, or to spit in its eye; or because one is a mean bastard who hates the good; or because one cannot be bothered or is all played out or is too tired or has lost heart; or because acting morally does not fit in with one's plans and goals; or because 'it seemed like a good idea at the time'; or for just no reason at all; or . . .

This heterodox, long, but still far-from-finished list suggests two interrelated points about weakness of will, as given by (1). First, the problem is not to find *one* way to have a weak will: there are all too many different ways to have one. Second, weakness of will is not one phenomenon, whether understood by ethics, psychology, or moral psychology; rather, it is, a collection of only somewhat similar phenomena. Putting these points together – in a manner that is joking, but certainly accurate enough in content – we could offer the following as an answer to the literal question posed by (1): the protocols of contemporary United States health insurance companies and the *Diagnostic and Statistical Manual, IV* recognize well over 150 distinct and billable ways for that.[19]

This complaint about the question some contemporaries ask about weakness of will cannot be levelled against Aristotle. He asked more specific questions about more specific psychological conditions and mechanisms.

Further, he does consider various *other reasons* for knowingly not doing what is best: *reasons* in that they tell why, even if they do not justify; *other* in that they differ from the reasons for paradigmatic akrasia or for non-paradigmatic akrasia, and also from the contemporary ones just given. He recognizes that there can be any number of reasons, with no organizing principle(s) – and in this way much like our reasons for weakness of will – for knowingly not doing what one believes *technically* best: for example, skilled doctors knowingly not doing what they know is medically best.[20] He also recognizes that *pain* can account for acting wrongly, knowingly failing to do what one thinks best. But if one acts on account of pain, then even if one knowingly does what is wrong, one does not act akratically. (I should say 'pain proper', to allow for pain that those too given to pleasure can feel on not getting their pleasures, and thus to allow for their akrasia.) Here we could recall Aristotle's statement that the moral faults 'relating to pleasures are incontinence [akrasia] and continence [*enkrateia*], those relating to pains softness and endurance' (VII.7, 1150a13 ff).

That Aristotle recognizes such other reasons for acting wrongly, despite knowledge, is very important for my argument. His use of excessive desire for both paradigmatic and non-paradigmatic akrasia, conjoined with his recognition of these other ways of knowingly acting wrongly, goes a long way towards showing that his concern with akrasia is not a concern just with knowingly not doing what one thinks best.

We can now explain and justify Aristotle's concern with akrasia, especially paradigmatic akrasia and why he 'restricted' it to what is occasioned by contrary desires for pleasures, especially epithumetic ones. In his discussion of akrasia in VII, he is concerned with the nature of good and bad people, with the real and pressing ways people go wrong, and with forms and grounds for praise and blame. These concerns are, of course, among the central concerns of the *Nicomachean Ethics*. His concerns with both paradigmatic and non-paradigmatic akrasia are part and parcel of his concern with excessive desire and the ever-present and ever-serious dangers of pleasure and excessive desire, especially for pleasure.[21] As said early in the *Nicomachean Ethics*, 'Now in everything the pleasant or pleasure is most to be guarded against . . . We ought, then, to feel towards pleasure as the elders of the people felt towards Helen' (II.9, 1109b7 ff). The point is worth repeating. In his discussion of akrasia, he is not interested in the conceptual connections – as moderns see them – between believing something best and doing or intending to do it. Rather, he intentionally and explicitly restricts his concerns with, his understanding of, akrasia to what is occasioned by contrary desires for pleasure, especially epithumetic ones, precisely because of the dangers – the moral and moral-psychological dangers – they pose to doing what one thinks best.

It would lead too far from the concerns of this work to discuss Aristotle's worries about pleasure, and why he distinguishes its moral dangers from other moral dangers. It would, among other things, involve showing why he thinks that pleasure and pain are not 'natural opposites'. This would be to show, as Aristotle might put it and as Elizabeth Anscombe did put it, that they do not function in ways differing just in terms of polarity. They are contraries, but not the way positive and negative are. They are far more like black and white, or even salt and pepper.[22]

Here we should remember that in *Nicomachean Ethics* III.1, Aristotle holds that pain can overcome us and that it can be more than anyone can bear. Such pain can thus excuse doing what, but for the pain, would be wrong. More strongly, it can excuse doing what is still wrong, even despite this overwhelming and excusing pain.[23] 'On some actions . . . forgiveness is [bestowed], when one does what he ought not under pressure which overstrains human nature and which no one could withstand' (1110a23 ff). Pain, then, can overwhelm us and excuse us. But there is no pleasure that can overwhelm us to the point where we are excused by it – where it gives us an excuse for doing what is or otherwise would be wrong (Cf. III.1, 1110b9 ff). This helps explain, and is also sustained by, his claims throughout Book VII of the *Nicomachean Ethics* that akrasia is not to be excused, and that it involves nothing, in itself, that provides an excuse.

4 The state from which regression and akrasia take place: some psychoanalytic comments

Although psychoanalysts rarely if ever refer to the concept of akrasia, some form of what Aristotle described and called akrasia is implicit in many psychological disorders recognized today. Many of the diagnostic categories in the *Diagnostic and Statistical Manual (DSM) IV* involve shifts down from, or away from optimal functioning, and an assessment of global functioning is one of the five axes included in the diagnostic process. Stocker has aptly posed the comparison of paradigmatic akrasia to psychoanalytic regression. I will examine some implications of this comparison, from the point of view of psychoanalysis. Both akrasia and regression imply an organism's dropping back or descent in function, down from a peak of development or of the attainment of maturity, integration, or control. Both strongly imply a more valued direction, and a strongly devalued direction, to a dimension of development we could roughly call functioning. Paradigmatic akrasia, as characterized by Stocker, has in common with regression that it involves 'the pleasures that temperance is concerned with and that children and animals pursue'. Both concepts imply or assume, in the notion of temperance, the capacity in the organism for a state in which the temperate choice might be made, and both imply the possibility of return to that state after the akratic episode. So, the desired and valued capacity for this optimal functioning does not disappear, it goes into temporary abeyance during the episode of akrasia.

How is this thinking about akrasia different from the familiar psychoanalytic emphasis on a conflict model? It seems that akrasia may involve a particular kind of conflict, such as whether to give in to a bodily desire. Akrasia is not just a matter of conflict, it involves going back to a form of childhood experience; regression may be a broader term, including many more different forms of experience, not always bad or loaded in the moral sense. If the question for the akratic person is, 'How could you, who know better, do such and such?' the question for the regressed person might be 'What provoked you to daydream all day, rather than working?' The regressed activity, in contrast to the akratic, might be a purely internal experience, and not necessarily harmful to the self or others.

Aristotle and modern psychoanalytic thought have in common a model of psychic development based on the attainment of a state of growth, maturation and development evolving partly from the unfolding of innate capacities and partly from the exercise of the will in conjunction with this unfolding. In other words, the nature of the mature person is different in kind from the nature of the less mature person. Thus the state from which the akrasia or regression takes place changes over the course of a person's development.

The state of development attained by the person matters to our understanding of both of these processes because the 'giving in' to pleasure (and indeed even the nature of what is pleasurable) involved in akratic behaviour is different depending on the level of maturity attained. In his important paper 'The Confusion of Tongues between Adults and the Child', Sándor Ferenczi makes the point that the child's desire and its goal are not the same as the adult's genital desire and its goal. The injury to the child that results from this 'confusion of tongues' comes from the adult's imposition on the child of just this difference between the adult's genitalized pleasure and the child's (now thwarted) desire for tenderness in kind. Thus, akratic regression does not involve different but equal or comparable subjectivities, as between adults, or even between children of different maturational levels. Both the akratic and the regressed person become more self-involved, more solipsistic and cut off from the experience of others; they lack an awareness of the other, the capacity for empathy, which they may otherwise be capable of.

This idea, that regression and akrasia are divisive of social connection in that they can introduce an incompatibility or discontinuity between persons, suggests that shared experience becomes more complicated in the face of both regression and akrasia: group or interpersonal akratic or regressive activities may exaggerate differences as people become more dissimilar in goal, or 'out of synch' with each other. The likelihood of miscommunication through the abandonment of shared ideals is increased. So, both states threaten social institutions, and those cultural forms which depend on consensus.

Akrasia and regression have in common the fact that they are subject to cultural variability in norms or individual character, rather than being fixed or absolute. For example, person A may indulge herself by postponing paying her bills until the lights get shut off; person B may binge on ice cream. What is regressive depends on the differences in personality or character, and may not be judged regressive by others; thus the notion of regression is quite variable and subject to cultural norms, since both what is 'mature' and what is devalued, or regressive/akratic, may vary over the course of time and according to cultural values. However, there is a difference between regression and akrasia which depends on a feature of psychoanalytic theory: akrasia is always bad, but regression can be useful, even necessary for further development or a creative leap, if it is partial or limited in scope. Regression in the service of the ego is a familiar term referring to an instance of creative humour, playfulness or artistic endeavour. It refers to a transcendent suspension of rational control or conventional thinking. Aristotle would probably not consider this form of regression a form of akrasia because it involves a more or less controlled or circumscribed expression which does nothing to disrupt the life or ongoing functioning of the person who engages in it.

Can the akratic ever recover? It is not clear from Aristotle's work whether he can; he may always be subject to infantile desires, even if the state abates or goes into remission. One does recover, however, from many forms of regression. It is even possible to recover from especially stubborn or resistant regressed states such as that of drug or alcohol addiction. Although Aristotle's moral tone is far more consistently judgemental than the more morally neutral medical model followed by modern psychoanalysis (indeed, the medical model has been criticized for its moral neutrality), it is interesting that many currently popular treatment methods emphasize strengthening of the will or the intention to overcome regressed behaviour. Cognitive behavioural methods of therapy, for example, employ such techniques as 'thought stopping' and 'thought substitution' even for such subjective states as depression, and hold the patient responsible to some degree for the success of the treatment inasmuch as he or she is diligent in applying these will-strengthening tactics to what are regarded now as bad habits of thinking about the self. Such terms as 'learned helplessness', one popular formulation of depression, and 'learned optimism' imply that educative efforts can and will pay off to ameliorate some affective states which had been previously dignified as existential despair or alienation. So we see that the beliefs a culture holds about its emotional life have powerful effects on the exceptional person within that culture. Depending on the narrowmindedness of the medical insurance carrier, it is now possible for a patient to be not only stigmatized for mental suffering, but blamed for it as well.

It is always interesting to speculate about what it means when there are similarities in disease/diagnostic categories in two different cultures, far removed in time and space. Dare we ask that if akrasia and regression have something in common, that we may be touching a bedrock of human nature? Is it possible that there is, in all cultures, some form of recognition when a person lapses from 'proper' functioning in some important and fundamental way? Perhaps it is so that, regardless of the content of the model of optimum personhood, there is a universal tendency to fail, to give in to temptation, or not to do one's best at all times, regardless of the cost or outcome in social terms.

Notes

1 This work continues the collaboration between Michael Stocker, a professor of philosophy, and Elizabeth Hegeman, a practising psychoanalyst and professor of anthropology, begun in our *Valuing Emotions* (Cambridge: Cambridge University Press, 1996). For extensive, general help with this work, I (Michael Stocker, the author of sections 1–3) thank Eric A. Brown, Norman Dahl, Deborah Modrak and Charles Young. For help with the psychological and psychoanalytic issues, I thank Elizabeth Hegeman (the author of section 4). I benefited from discussion of this work by the Wake Forest University philosophy department and a session at the 1997 meetings of the American Philosophical Association, Pacific Division. An earlier version of sections 1–3 of this essay appeared as 'Aristotelian Akrasia and Psychoanalytic Regression', *Philosophy, Psychiatry, and Psychology*, 4 (1997): 231–41.
2 See, for example, Donald Davidson (1969). See also Jonathan Lear (1988: sec. 5.4). Two recent works are notable exceptions: Sarah Broadie (1991) and John Cooper (1996).

I was heartened to find that we share many views on the nature, role and importance of Aristotle's paradigmatic akrasia in his ethics. Cooper's subdivides non-paradigmatic akrasia, and thus (2'), into non-bodily appetitive desires and spirited desires, primarily of *thumos* (often translated as 'anger'). I think that Cooper holds that these non-bodily appetitive desires are more bereft of reasons, more non-rational, than I do. (See n. 18 below.) Taking this up would lead too far from the main concerns of this essay, the nature of paradigmatic akrasia.

3 My thanks are owed to David Charles for discussion of many of the issues of this work and especially for emphasizing the importance of *phantasiai*, especially as discussed in the *Posterior Analytics*, II.19, the *Metaphysics*, I.1, and the *Physics* I.1. On *phantasiai*, see also Franz Brentano (1977); Kimon Lycos (1964); Martha Nussbaum (1978); and David Charles (1995).

4 See for example works by the psychoanalyst Daniel Stern, *The Interpersonal World of the Infant* (1985) and especially *Diary of an Infant* (1990).

5 See Schachtel in *Metamorphosis* (1984), especially ch. 12, 'On Memory and Childhood Amnesia', originally published as an article with the same title in *Psychiatry*, 10 (1947): 1–26.

6 In Spence's *Narrative Truth and Historical Truth: Meaning and Interpretation in Psychoanalysis* (1982).

7 In Enid Balint's 'Commentary on Philip Bromberg's "On Knowing One's Patient Inside Out"', *Psychoanalytic Dialogues*, 1 (1991), p. 425. See also two articles by the psychoanalyst Philip Bromberg (1991 and 1993) and two works by other psychoanalysts: Christopher Bollas (1987), especially under 'unthought known'; and Donnel Stern (1983). These issues have serious implications for the controversy over recovered memories, especially of sexual abuse, now hotly contested in the courts and the popular press, as well as in psychological theory and practice.

8 For an important psychoanalytic work on this, see Michael Balint (1979).

9 My thanks are owed to Eugene Garver for discussion here and elsewhere in this work.

10 In Ferenczi's 'Confusion of Tongues Between Adults and the Child', originally published in 1933 in German, translated and reprinted in *International Journal of Psycho-Analysis* (1949).

11 In 'Mad, Drunk, or Asleep? – Aristotle's Akratic', Justin Gosling (1993) offers an account of akrasia in terms of another somewhat similar sort of incompossibility: that of at once satisfying the akratic desire and the desire for the good. The text he uses for this is *NE* X.5, 1175b1–24, about the impossibility of satisfying competing pleasures at the same time. I am attracted to the simplicity of Gosling's very moderate account, but I do not think it goes far enough.

12 My thanks are owed to John Robertson for discussion here.

13 My thanks are owed to Amélie O. Rorty and Elizabeth Hegeman for discussion leading to these last two paragraphs. My thanks are also owed to Rorty, 'Where Does the Akratic Break Take Place?' in her *Mind in Action* (1988) and her essay delivered at the 1997 meetings of the American Philosophical Association, Pacific Division.

14 See, for example, Amélie O. Rorty (1974); Myles Burnyeat (1980); and L. A. Kosman (1980). My thanks are owed to Kosman for discussion.

15 My thanks are owed to Eric A. Brown for suggesting in correspondence that Aristotle's concern with the relative curability of intemperance and akrasia (VII, 2, 1146a31 and VII, 8) supports my understanding of why Aristotle is interested in akrasia.

16 To the extent that this developmental account is correct, we can question claims such as Bernard Williams's that Aristotle's seeing akrasia as a problem depends on his having an ethicized view of the soul (Williams 1993: 44–5). My thanks are owed to Samuel Levey for discussion here.

17 My thanks are owed to Norman Dahl here. He cites the discussion of Broadie (1991: 269–71). See also Cooper (1996: 90–5).

18 The disagreement, if there is one, between Cooper and me, as mentioned in n. 3, turns on the conceptual achievements needed for 'victory . . . '. On this and closely related matters – especially why Aristotle excluded epithumetic desires from emotions – see Stephen Leighton (1982): esp. 161–2.

19 I have been aided here by Kathleen V. Wilkes's arguments in *Real People* (1993) against the unity of consciousness. However, her (albeit very brief) comments on weakness of will seem to suggest that she sees it as one phenomenon.

20 See *Metaphysics* II.9, 1046b3 ff. My thanks are owed to Norman Dahl for stressing the importance of this passage.

21 Perhaps his own similar focusing explains John McDowell's describing the embracing of a conception of the good in terms of the *silencing* of contrary desires. This, however, does not fit cases we recognize (even if Aristotle does not recognize) of not acting well and even of weakness of will, occasioned by a *deficiency* of desire. Nor does it fit, e.g., NE III.7, 1115b10 ff., where Aristotle allows that a good person may have, without having to struggle against, contrary feelings and desires. For McDowell, see 'Are Moral Requirements Hypothetical Imperatives?' (1978) and 'Virtue and Reason' (1979). On deficient desires, see my 'Affectivity and Self-Concern' (1983) and 'Desiring the Bad' (1979). On *NE* III.7, see my *Plural and Conflicting Values* (1990: 75); and Broadie (1991: 308, n. 7).

22 I am indebted here to Anscombe and especially to her lectures on pleasure given at the University of Chicago during the 1965–66 academic year.

23 This is discussed in my *Plural and Conflicting Values*, esp. ch. 3, 'Dirty Hands and Conflicts of Values and of Desires in Aristotle's Ethics'.

References

Aristotle, *Metaphysics*.
—— *Nicomachean Ethics*, trans. W. D. Ross and J. O. Urmson, in Jonathan Barnes (ed.), *The Complete Works of Aristotle*, Princeton: Princeton University Press, 1984.
—— *Nicomachean Ethics*, trans. Martin Ostwald, New York: Macmillan, 1962.
—— *Physics*.
—— *Posterior Analytics*.
—— *Rhetoric*, trans. W. Rhys Roberts, in Jonathan Barnes (ed.), *The Complete Works of Aristotle*, Princeton: Princeton University Press, 1984.
Balint, Enid (1991) 'Commentary on Philip Bromberg's "On Knowing One's Patient Inside Out"', *Psychoanalytic Dialogues*, 1: 423–30.
Balint, Michael (1979) *The Basic Fault, Therapeutic Aspects of Regression*, New York: Brunner Mazel.
Bollas, Christopher (1987) *The Shadow of the Object: Psychoanalysis of the Unthought Known*, New York: Columbia University Press.
Brentano, Franz (1977) *The Psychology of Aristotle*, Berkeley: University of California Press.
Broadie, Sarah (1991) *Ethics With Aristotle*, New York: Oxford University Press.
Bromberg, Philip (1991) 'On Knowing One's Patient Inside Out: The Aesthetics of Unconscious Communication', *Psychoanalytic Dialogues*, 1: 399–422.
—— (1993) 'Shadow and Substance: A Relational Perspective on Clinical Process', *Psychoanalytic Psychology*, 10: 147–168.
Burnyeat, Myles (1980) 'Aristotle on Learning to be Good', in Amélie O. Rorty (ed.) *Essays on Aristotle's Ethics*, Berkeley: University of California Press.
Charles, David (1995) 'Aristotle and Modern Realism', in Robert Heinaman (ed.) *Aristotle and Moral Realism*, London: University College of London Press.

Cooper, John (1996) 'Reason, Moral Virtue, and Moral Value', in Michael Frede and Gisela Striker (eds), *Rationality in Greek Thought*, Oxford: Oxford University Press.

Davidson, Donald (1969) 'How Is Weakness of Will Possible?', in Joel Feinberg (ed.), *Moral Concepts*, Oxford: Oxford University Press.

Ferenczi, Sándor (1933) 'Confusion of Tongues between Adults and the Child', originally published in German, translated and reprinted in *International Journal of Psycho-Analysis*, 30 (1949): 225 ff. Reprinted in his *Selected Papers*, New York: Basic Books, 1955); and also in *Contemporary Psychoanalysis*, 24 (1988): 196–206.

Gosling, Justin (1993) 'Mad, Drunk, or Asleep? – Aristotle's Akratic', *Phronesis*, 38: 98–104.

Hegeman, Elizabeth (with Michael Stocker) (1996) *Valuing Emotions*, New York: Cambridge University Press.

Kosman, L. A. (1980) 'Being Properly Affected: Virtues and Feelings in Aristotle's Ethics', in Amélie O. Rorty (ed.), *Essays on Aristotle's Ethics*, Berkeley: University of California Press.

Lear, Jonathan (1988) *Aristotle: The Desire to Understand*, Cambridge: Cambridge University Press.

Leighton, Stephen (1982) 'Aristotle and the Emotions', *Phronesis*, 27: 144–74.

Lycos, Kimon (1964) 'Aristotle and Plato on "Appearing"', *Mind*, 73: 496–514.

McDowell, John (1978) 'Are Moral Requirements Hypothetical Imperatives?' *Aristotelian Society, sup. vol.*, 52: 13–29.

—— (1979) 'Virtue and Reason', *The Monist*, 62: 330–50.

Nussbaum, Martha (1978) *Aristotle's De Motu Animalium*, Princeton: Princeton University Press.

Rorty, Amélie O. (1974) 'The Place of Pleasure in Aristotle's Ethics', *Mind* 83: 481–97.

—— (1988) 'Where Does the Akratic Break Take Place?', in Rorty, *Mind in Action*, Boston: Beacon Press.

—— (1997) Paper delivered at the 1997 meetings of the American Philosophical Association, Pacific Division.

Schachtel, Ernest (1947) 'On Memory and Childhood Amnesia', *Psychiatry*, 10: 1–26. Reprinted in *Metamorphosis*, New York City: Da Capo Press, 1984.

Spence, Donald P. (1982) *Narrative Truth and Historical Truth: Meaning and Interpretation in Psychoanalysis* New York: W. W. Norton.

Stern, Daniel (1985) *The Interpersonal World of the Infant*, New York: Basic Books.

—— (1990) *Diary of an Infant*, New York: Basic Books.

Stern, Donnel (1983) 'Unformulated Experience', *Contemporary Psychoanalysis*, 19: 71–99.

Stocker, Michael (1979) 'Desiring the Bad – An Essay in Moral Psychology', *The Journal of Philosophy*, 76: 738–53.

—— (1983) 'Affectivity and Self-Concern', *Pacific Philosophical Quarterly*, 64: 211–29.

—— (1990) *Plural and Conflicting Values*, Oxford: Oxford University Press.

—— with Elizabeth Hegeman (1996) *Valuing Emotions*, New York: Cambridge University Press.

—— (1997) 'Aristotelian Akrasia and Psychoanalytic Regression', *Philosophy, Psychiatry, and Psychology*, 4: 231–41.

Wilkes, Kathleen V. (1993) *Real People*, Oxford: Oxford University Press.

Williams, Bernard (1993) *Shame and Necessity*, Berkeley: University of California Press.

153

8

EMOTIONAL AGENTS

Nancy Sherman

1 Introduction

We tend to think of emotions as things we suffer. We *fall* in love, we are *overcome* by anger, we are *struck* with grief. And what we suffer may be at odds with what we will. We may fall in love without wanting to, find ourselves angry when we wish we were forgiving, grieve long after we see its point. The point of much Ancient moral psychology is to lessen that conflict by bringing emotions under reason's rule. While classical psychoanalysis works toward conflict resolution, its method is by no means the top-down chastening method of ancient psychology. The problem is not simply that a harsh super-ego can make for a neurotic solution. It is that psychic conflict engages the unconscious. And the logic and mechanisms of unconscious mental life are distinct from those of conscious mentation. To work through psychic conflict requires working through mental layers that are more primitively organized than ordinary, conscious thought. To wag a finger, cajole, suggest, or persuade may simply not harpoon the right phenomena.

I want to consider conflict resolution through the lens of what I shall call emotional agency. Psychoanalysis shares the belief with the Ancients that many emotions can be modified, that we are not mere victims of our feelings. But its methods are revolutionizing. Through mechanisms of self-observation, transference and interpretation, the psychoanalytic presumption is that there can be movement on the emotional front – that an analysand will be able to modify, to some degree, how she loves, relieve some of her misplaced guilt or anger, better direct feelings of rivalry or competition. The process is slow, and affect or emotional change is less a matter of direct willing than indirect control, except, of course, that it is willful self-examination that sets in motion that process of expanding emotional agency.

The plan of the essay is this: I review Aristotle's conception of the emotions and his implicit account of emotional development and regulation. I compare his view with a more radical Stoic conception of emotional therapy. This will lead us to Freudian depth psychology and the claim that drives, defences and phantasy[1] underlie surface psychology, including many surface emotions. I next consider how analysis aims to loosen defences and enhance emotional agency through methods that try to avoid explicit persuasion and suggestion. I argue for a view of the analytic relationship as a mutual alliance that provides an arena for the development of emotional agency in analyst as well as analysand.[2]

2 An Aristotelian conception of emotions and emotional development

On an Aristotelian view, excellence of character is assessed both in terms of actions and emotions. The ideal is to hit the mean with regard to both: to make choices that are wise and to have and express emotions that are apt. As a consequence, the development of self falls, in no small measure, within the emotional domain, with due emphasis given to enlarging the range of emotions and cultivating capacities for their governance.

Emotions, according to this view, are cognitive. They are about something that we represent in thought. They involve a judgement. In the lingo of contemporary cognitive psychology, they are appraisal-based. This needn't exclude other features that are often thought to characterize emotions, such as feelings of pleasure and pain, or desires to act in specific ways. But those other features are subsidiary to the construal or thought content that identifies the emotion.

Aristotle limns the appraisal account in the second book of the *Rhetoric*. Anger, he says, laying out the paradigm, is based on the belief or construal that one has suffered an unwarranted injury.[3] This is accompanied by pain at the thought of the injury, and often a reactive desire to take revenge. Now Aristotle advances his theory in the context of a manual for orators intent on swaying a jury. In this sense, his psychological theory of the emotions is meant to have clear application for those whose business it is to change emotions. What the theory suggests is that emotional shifts are the result of cognitive shifts. Given the forensic context of the *Rhetoric*, persuasion becomes the instrument of change. To feel specific emotions is to take oneself to have reason to feel those emotions. The orator sets to work on those reasons.

Within the ethical corpus, Aristotle tells us little about the structure of emotions. This is odd given the important role he ultimately accords to cultivated emotions in the account of full virtue. We would expect something comparable to his analysis of action and choice, but are disappointed when we look. Still, what we do find in the *Nicomachean* is something about how emotions can be transformed. And here rational persuasion again is the preferred tool. So in *Nicomachean* I.9 emotions are said to be housed in the part of the soul that partakes of reason derivatively, and that can be made to be obedient and compliant with reason. In *Nicomachean* I.3. Aristotle similarly analogizes the lower part of the soul's compliance to reason with a child listening to the exhortations of a parent. The important discussion of friendship, and in particular, the best friendship among persons of good character, suggests that friends will act as mirrors and models for each other, but also, significantly, as rational interlocutors who will engage each other in practical reflection about the fit of their characters to the requirements of good living.[4]

Aristotle is not explicit about just how exhortation and practical reflection might transform evaluative contents. But compatible with his view is again a kind of *gestalt* shifting whereby individuals are encouraged to reconsider and reconstrue the appraisals implicit in emotions, on the view that to dislodge the emotion requires dislodging the judgement on which it rests. On this view, someone who experiences fear because he falsely believes there to be a suspicious object lurking in the distance is likely to undo the fear once he learns that the object is in fact not threatening. In a similar way, undue hatred, inappropriate joy, scorn, or envy can be undone by reconstruing the grounds on which the emotions rest. The background thought is that wise and discerning perception informs wise and discerning emotions. The emotions are informed by conscious belief and are changed by shifts in those beliefs. Rational discourse can resculpt emotions because the full cognitive content of emotions is of the same stuff as that discourse, and so, in principle, fully accessible to the reasoning process of that higher order function. There is a seamlessness in cognitive mental processes. The educability of emotions depends on the fact that reason, through the medium of its own language and organization, can reach deep into the lower parts of the soul and change those parts. In this sense emotions partake derivatively of reason and are responsive to its enlightenment. The channels of communication are already in place. It is simply a matter of opening ears and paying attention.

Psychic harmony, thus, results from a top-down exercise of reason. Emotion is chastened by reason, much like Plato's steeds, disciplined by the charioteer's reins. In the conflict between reason and conflictual emotions, the only story that makes real sense and that has authority is the one reason can tell. A conflict resolution that comes undone is a signal that reason must lecture louder, make its point more persuasively, undo an inappropriate emotional attachment or response by arguing it down.

At times, Freud might seem to talk in similar ways of psychic resolution. 'Psychoanalysis', he tells us, 'is an instrument to enable the ego to achieve a progressive conquest of the id.'[5] But the ideal analysed person, unlike the ideal of the Aristotelian *phronimos*, never fully conquers the steeds. For 'the rider', as he puts it, 'has borrowed its energies from the id'. To kill off the horse is to sap the person of its lifesprings.[6] The adaptive compromise requires not domination, but balance, where one agency of the mind is not 'favoured at the expense of the other',[7] nor conflict ever fully resolved. The oedipal complex, to appeal to that most famous of conflicts, is reworked throughout life, in the many ways we love and are vulnerable to loss.[8]

What Aristotle doesn't explore is why some emotions don't reform at the beck and call of reason, why they cling tenaciously in the face of a considered desire or willing (in Aristotle's term – a rational wish or *boulêsis*) to turn them around. Nor does he ground, in terms of the process of emotional development, the distinction he insists on between brokered deals that involve the inhibition of conflictual emotions, as in the case of the controlled or enkratic person, and resolutions that involve a more thoroughgoing transformation of emotion, as in the case of the fully virtuous or temperate person (the *sôphrôn*). How does one loosen the grip of certain disavowed emotions rather than merely suppress (or inhibit) them? Is persuasion the only instrument for either sort of resolution, i.e., that of control and that of transformation?

The Stoics carry the project of persuasion further. Like the Aristotelian, the Stoic holds that emotions are cognitive states, and more precisely, states identical with beliefs. But they are beliefs that are systematically false. For Stoic doctrine holds that the only proper and stable object of choice for happiness is virtue constituted exclusively by reason. Emotions, in contrast, are grounded in beliefs that objects of investment other than internal states of virtue (and reason) are worthwhile. So, for example, romantic love is an investment in a person who is separate from oneself and beyond one's full control. To love is always to be at risk of losing the object of love. It is to invest in what can't be fully conquered. Radical therapy, on the Stoic view, requires philosophical meditation and exhortation directed toward the end of extirpating emotion. It requires 'pushing the oars of dialectic', as Cicero puts it,[9] coming to believe in Stoic doctrine so that one will see and fully embrace the misconception in attaching to anything other than virtue itself. Thus, in the hands of the Stoics, reliance on rational discourse to loosen the grip of an emotion reaches new heights. From the point of view of psychoanalysis, the need for an alternative becomes all the more urgent.

3 Psychoanalytic theory and the depth of emotions

The question Ancient moral psychology leaves us with (though the Ancients never ask it) is, why doesn't persuasion work? That is, why doesn't rational discourse undo irrational emotions? Why can't we rid ourselves of akratic emotions by a direct act of will and belief? The questions underlie Freud's project.

First, it is important to recognize what Freud accepts from the Ancients. Unlike much early twentieth-century psychology, he allies himself with the Aristotelian view that emotions have cognitive or ideational content. But the caveat he adds is a revolutionizing one: ideational content may be unconscious. The story on which an emotion is grounded may be quite different from its surface rationale, both in content *and* structure. And it may be hidden. Rage at you may really be about rage at myself, fretful love may be grounded in hidden fears of inferiority, enmity may be a defence against too close an attachment, a love that shifts back and forth to all-out anger may repeat an archaic phantasy in which disappointment at a love object thoroughly annihilates that love. In all these cases cognitive depth runs deep. The psychoanalytic claim is that even if the layered meanings were to become intellectually transparent, so that through exhortation, lecture, or reflective discourse we could come to understand the deeper meaning of many of our emotions, emotional growth would still be wanting. For growth requires a 'working-through' whereby one regresses to more primitive levels of thinking and feeling. 'Regression in the service of the ego' (in Kris's famous phrase) allows for a breaking-down and rebuilding of the ego and its defences.[10] In contrast, enjoining through reason leaves the investments and defences that characterize emotions poised only for more repetition. As Freud puts it, 'Our knowledge about the unconscious material is not equivalent to *his* [the analysand's] knowledge: if we communicate our knowledge to him, he does not receive it *instead of* his unconscious material, but *beside* it; and that makes very little change in it'.[11]

Now not all emotions (or actions, choices and beliefs, for that matter) will mask other deeper mental phenomena. Sometimes a cigar is just a cigar and best dealt with as just that, whatever its perceived genesis. But the point of Freudian theory is that often there are deeper layers underlying surface phenomena – there is a world of the demonic and irrational, a world of regressed mental phenomena and processes that pressures more integrative functions. It is a world with infantile roots that we never fully grow out of, however much we domesticate its forces in our ordinary habits and ways. It is a world that we wouldn't fully want to grow out of, else our civilized layers would be desiccated, emptied of the wellsprings of raw passion, phantasy and the magical. A goal of analysis is to make parts of that subterranean world less shut off from what is conscious, so that what is conscious can breathe some of the life and depth that fuels that more primal world. Hans Loewald puts it well in *Papers on Psychoanalysis*:

> We may understand psychoanalysis and psychoanalytic treatment itself as an expression and utilization of the need to rediscover and reactivate the submerged communication channels leading from the origins of our lives to the solidified, alienated structures of behavior, automatic attitudes and responses, cultural institutions, conventions and beliefs, neurotic symptom formations, and defense systems and operations, which seem to have taken over and run their own inhuman course. (30)

I shall come to the topic of therapeutic change in the next section. For now, I want to explore the world of drives, defences and phantasy that underlie conscious mentation, and that underlie, on my view, an account of the emotions, such as Aristotle's. I take up Freud's theory of instinctual drives in order to demystify some aspects of the theory and show their bearing on the deeper structure of emotions. It also should be noted that drives and defences remain a constant feature of Freud's theory, through the transition from topographical to structural models. As is well known, the topographical model, distinguishing unconscious, preconscious and conscious processes comes to grief with Freud's discovery that the ego functions of defence, as well as super-ego trends, can be unconscious, and that unconscious processes thus extend to mental functions broader than those of the primitive id.

Like the ancient notions of *hormê* (impulse) and *orexis* (desire), Freud's notion of drive (*Trieb*) is a broad term meant to capture the basic stirrings of an individual, i.e., needs, wishes and urges. But unlike those ancient counterparts, drive is an unconscious motivational force.[12] It is an active force in the passive, non-willing ('it' or id) part of a person, not an intentional desire informed by a belief. Structurally, drive (and drive derivatives) in classical and contemporary psychoanalytic theory[13] are components of intrapsychic conflict that cause symptoms in conscious life. With drive, comes the idea of motives that remain hard to access because of defences that conceal them and the operation of a thought process discrepant with that of ordinary, rational thought.

Though a general notion of drive is present in Freud's earliest writings (under the various terms of 'endogenous stimulation', 'excitation', 'somatic sexual tension', 'wishful impulse') it is not until 1915, with the writing of 'Instincts and their Vicissitudes', that Freud formally grapples with the term, *Trieb*. From a physiological point of view, he argues, drive is an internal 'stimulus' or 'need' 'applied to the mind' that is satisfied not as external stimuli are, by 'actions of flight' or withdrawal, but by reduction of the tension they cause. Regulative here is 'the constancy principle' (itself derivative from mechanistic physiology) whereby an organism seeks to abolish the tension that drive creates. On this view, excitation is non-pleasure and a reduction of excitation, or discharge to prior levels of energy, is pleasure.[14] But there is another angle, Freud tells us, from which to consider drive. From this perspective, drive is not an organismic stimulus, but the 'psychical representative of it'. As such, drive is on 'the frontier', he says, between the mental and the somatic, not in the sense that it, more than other mental phenomena, has privileged connections to a neurological substrate,[15] but in the sense that its specific work is in psychologically *representing* somatic urges and needs. True, Freud never fully disambiguates the physiological from the more psychological account of drive, and in *Beyond the Pleasure Principle*, as we will see momentarily, he reverts to a more biological view of drive as a condition, not of the psyche, but of all living matter. Still, in 'Instincts and their Vicissitudes', we see Freud well aware of a non-reductive view of drive as a primitive mental form of motivation and impulse.

Freud emphasized that drive theory is a speculative artifice – 'our mythology', as he puts it in 1933: 'instincts are mythical entities, magnificent in their indefiniteness'.[16] In the earlier work, 'Instincts and their Vicissitudes', he puts the point less flamboyantly, that the concept of *Trieb*, like many concepts in science, is an abstract and indefinite convention to be revised and redefined as part of the theory-building.[17] His tinkering with the theory, and his constant shoehorning it into the existing terms of physiology, ethology, or speculative metaphysics shows up in the shifting series of dualisms that mark different stages of his views. The progression to the famous dual instinct theory is worth briefly reviewing: The sexual excitations documented in the early writings (e.g., the 'sexual soil' that gives rise to conflict) bifurcate in later writings into ego and sexual drives (in Freud's homier gloss, hunger and love[18]), with ego drives aiming at self-preservation and defence and sexual drives concerned with attachment to self and others. With *Beyond the Pleasure Principle*, the dualism ultimately shifts to a biological and cosmic pitting of *eros* against *thanatos*, with *eros* (formerly the sexual drive) becoming a global impetus for unification, and *thanatos* or the death drive becoming an 'urge inherent in organic life to restore to an earlier state of things',[19] expressed psychologically, Freud claims, in the urge to endure pain as well as aggression.

The discovery of the death drive, Freud maintains, marks a rejection of the supremacy of the constancy principle. Two phenomena lead him to this view. The first is his observation of war victims and their compulsion to repeat, in dreams and phantasies, their war traumas. Implicit, he claimed, is a desire to endure and return to an earlier state of pain, rather than to rid themselves of its tension. The second is, as Freud puts, a 'chance opportunity' of watching the invented game of his one-and-a-half-year-old grandson. The child would repeatedly make toys disappear, in one case, a piece of string on a reel, and then utter the word, *'fort!'* 'be gone'.[20]

Freud is not unaware that the phenomena underdetermine the interpretation: the repetition of disappearances or trauma and the distress that goes with it, he suggests, could equally be attempts at mastery rather than repetitions of unpleasure; the child's game could be as much anticipations of the pleasure of returns *'fort'* (as in Mommy returning) as repetitions of 'gones'.[21] Loewald makes the more critical point, that the postulation of the death drive does not in fact mark the rejection of the pleasure or constancy principle, but its reconstitution in the form now of an inherent drive whose aim is just to restore the organism to an earlier state of non-excitation.[22] A regulative principle of the nervous system now becomes a constitutive function of drive. In this sense, the death drive does not go 'beyond' the pleasure principle, but embraces it. It 'is nothing startlingly new in Freud's theory'.[23] What is new, Loewald insists, is the positing of an erotic principle that relates drive to objects, as more than just mediums for gratification. The point of *eros*, as Freud says, is that it 'establishes ever greater unities'; its aim is to 'bind together'.[24] Primitive drives now have some relatedness to the outside world and as such, are no longer representatives of only intrapsychic stimuli. The point is an important one: with the language of *eros*, Freud begins to conceive of instinctual drives as constitutively related to objects, and not just as urges that instrumentally require objects as mediums for gratification.

Regarding Loewald's first points, he may be right that with the death drive Freud reintroduces rather than breaks with the old constancy (pleasure) principle now organized as itself a drive. But this still buries aggression in a physiologically rooted system and obscures the newness of aggression as a *psychological* phenomena in the theory of drives. Freud certainly had ample clinical experience of aggression at this point in his practice, as evidenced in his discussions of sado-masochistic wishes, self-punitive trends of the super-ego, fear of loss and mutilation, clinical melancholia and so on.[25] This more than cosmological or biological speculations give weight to the notion of powerful and primitive feelings of rage. But we need to be careful here. Whatever the emphasis on clinical data, Freud never relinquished the distinction between basic mental drives and their expression or derivatives. And in contemporary drive theory that distinction remains, as well as the basic dualism between sex and aggression.[26] But the emphasis in contemporary theory is even more clearly on experience-near phenomena and the varied expression and fusion of wants and urges in the clinical setting. This seems to be a welcome advance.[27]

I have taken up Freud's conceptualization of drive theory, not primarily for exegetical purposes, but to set us on the way of understanding the mental layers that underlie surface emotions. In this regard, one point emerges as seminal. And that is that drives are *primitive mental representations* of needs, rages and longings in relation to self and others. It is not just that we are impinged upon by stimulation (internal or external), but that that stimulation is represented and those representations, however immature or primitive, continue to influence how we feel and act. Surface emotions may not be fully understood or changed unless we appreciate their relation to those more primitive ways of seeing and feeling the world.

What are those more primitive ways of seeing and feeling the world? Freud claims that a drive is composed of an affective state with ideational content, as well as a wish that aims at fulfilment.[28] But the ideational content might be radically distinct from that of an ordinary emotion and wish-fulfilment distinct from ordinary desire satisfaction. To see this consider, again, the appraisal model of ordinary emotions. On this view, an emotion like hate is grounded in beliefs or propositional attitudes about the offensiveness of the target object, accompanied often by a desire to harm it through certain instrumental means and beliefs about the efficacy of those means. But when Freud speaks of an instinctual urge, such as the Rat Man's unconscious hatred for his father, its unconsciousness (and inaccessibility) is tied up with the fact that the hatred is not grounded in thoughts about the offending object that can easily enter into ordinary rational discourse.

On one interpretation, the instinctual feeling, as a primitive emotion with infantile roots, is not simply an unconscious analogue of a conscious emotion, but a different kind of emotion with a more primitive representational structure. The view is put forth by Sebastian Gardner, who argues that the primitive structure is non- or pre-propositional: the Rat Man's hatred is directed not at a state of affairs – the father under a certain description, e.g. as hated because of certain beliefs about him and loved in virtue of others, but just as the father, a particular, whose unconditional and total character is to be hated. It is the total nature of the response and the incapacity for ambivalence or a composite attitude that warrant its repression:

> The Ratman's infantile hatred is not hatred of his father as one who administers punishment, but of his father tout court; yielding a response of matching crudity: a wish for his father's annihilation. Uninformed and unmoderated by judgement, the hatred is not in touch with thoughts about its cause that would make it appropriate . . . Insulated in the unconscious, such emotions may survive into adulthood with their infantile character intact and without loss of potency. When they do so, they can not be combined in ambivalent formations, since these presuppose a coordinated network of thoughts . . . It follows that ordinary emotional ambivalence is a rational luxury denied to the Ratman.[29]

The interpretation exploits a Kleinian development of Freudian theory. According to Melanie Klein, the earliest emotional responses of an infant are pre-ambivalent, with objects experienced episodically in mutually exclusive ways, as either all-out good or bad, i.e., as thoroughly objects of either love or aggression. Ambivalence is an achieved state that allows for a composite attitude toward a given individual. With that achievement, one and the same object can be both loved and hated, with the good object surviving the revengeful attacks on the bad.[30] I shall say more about this when we turn to phantasy. For now, the point to focus on is the all or nothing character of this infantile and unconscious emotion, and the extremity of the wish or impulse that accompanies it.

This is one way of conceiving of primitive feelings. But some primitive feelings might be structurally more like ordinary appraisal-based emotions, yet still primitive in the sense that they are based on early perceptions that have been frozen in time, and have not had the opportunity for correction of distortion and more realistic assessment. The Rat Man's hatred for his father is based on his childhood perceptions of beatings and childhood fear of parental authority. The primitiveness of his feelings may have less to do with non-ambivalence than simply with the fact that the construals constitutive of those feelings have been shut off from the assessment of more mature reflective capacities. Part of what is involved in analysis is the revisiting of early conflictual positions with the eyes of a more mature and reality-based observing ego, so that resolutions that are maladaptive from a current adult perspective can be reopened and reworked.

The Rat Man's hatred for his father is puzzling to the Rat Man, for it's inconsistent with what he takes his feelings to be. So Freud says, 'he wondered how he could possibly have such a wish [for his father's death], considering that he loved his father more than any one else in the world'.[31] This is the emotion he identifies with and endorses. At work, is a defence system. When gratification of drive is too costly because of conflict with other mental states, drives are warded off or defended against. Defences, then, represent the mechanisms by which we flee from the anxiety of the prospect of certain gratifications, in the Rat Man's case, the fear of his parricidal wishes and their consequences. In Freud's later theory, anxiety is an early-warning system that signals the prospect of threats so that defences can be mobilized pre-emptively.[32] Defences include repression, but also, familiarly, denial, splitting, reaction formation, projection, introjection, identification with the aggressor, sublimation and so on.[33] They are unconscious operations, linked with the ego's drive for self-preservation. The emphasis is on 'unconscious'. It is not that the Rat Man intentionally decides to escape the terror of fulfilling his parricidal impulses (such that we could schematize his defence activity in a practical syllogism where the defence is represented by an instrumental belief/minor premise for fulfilling a desire captured in a major premise). It is that the mind strategizes ways to flee the impulse unconsciously. There is no presumption of truth, no concern about justificatory warrant in the use of these instruments of flight and avoidance. To avoid the conflict posed by drive gratification through unconscious defence is not a disguised exercise in the ordinary psychology of propositional attitudes of belief and desire. Rather, it is an exercise of unconscious mentation which has a logic of its own, and which is distinct from conscious efforts at self-deception.[34] Equally, to speak of defence mechanisms is not to dedicate a specific class of entities to that function; rather, it is to call attention to the defensive ways the mind uses thoughts, desires and emotions to avoid others. It is to call attention to a function.

In a very real sense, all defences are denials, just ways of saying 'no'.[35] The genius of psychoanalysis is to note that the mind does this in incredibly resourceful ways. So, surface emotions can be 'reaction formations', that is, reversals of underlying feelings into their opposites – the Rat Man's hatred turns into love, fear is denied by counterphobia, love becomes enmity. A woman who finds intimacy and longing hard to tolerate may defend against them by contemptuous disparagement, or by belittling herself at moments when she begins to feel tenderness. Identification with the aggressor, captured by the thought – 'If you can't lick 'em, join 'em' – is one way the five-year-old oedipal boy, rivalrous of his father's intimacy with his mother, defends against his feelings of competition and fears of revenge. Emulation becomes a way of transforming competitive and aggressive feelings. Equally, an emotion felt towards others can be introjected inwards on to oneself, just as what is felt in oneself can be projected outward on to others, so that hatred of another, becomes in a self-victimizing way, her hatred of me. The defence mechanism of projective identification, first introduced by Melanie Klein,[36] is a composite of projection and introjection. An unwanted part or aspect of self (or internalized representation of another) is projected outward on to others, with an unconscious intention to pressure that object to be like that part. The extruded aspect is then reinternalized after it has been modified or 'metabolized' by the other. So a hostile boy might unconsciously induce his father to be the bearer of his hostility so he can be rid of it himself or at least see it mirrored at a safe distance and predigested for easier intake. The father's aggression felt in the boy's presence is not fully understood unless it is seen in the context of this projection.

There is a third element that underpins ordinary emotions, on the psychoanalytic view. And that is phantasy. Defences, as well as drives, often work through phantasies and what Freud calls the 'primary-process' mentation of phantasy and dream-thought. The idea, developed in *The Interpretation of Dreams*, is that in dreaming as well as phantasy the unconscious engages in a level of mentation that constructs wish-fulfilments and defences without regard to truth, tense, reality testing, or principles of non-contradiction.[37] This more primitive mentation coexists with 'secondary-process' thought – the familiar type of rational, waking-life thinking that is bounded by reality-testing and considerations of what is possible and what is not.

Phantasies that rely on the omnipotence of thought can provide ways of warding off the anxiety of fulfilling certain wishes or needs. So Freud thought that a young child's hallucinatory phantasy of a breast may, for a while, ward off hunger before more instrumental strategies are sought. A patient may protect against the fear of fully disclosing herself through free association by harbouring phantasies of safety in the analytic setting. An anorexic girl's unconscious phantasy that her body is really her mother's, compounded with unconscious hatred of her mother, may give cause for punishing that body through starvation.

At work in this last example is the mechanism of displacement, a defence habit characteristic of the dreaming mind, in which one object is substituted for another – the girl's body for her mother's in order to conceal the real object of anger while still allowing aggression to do its work. Similarly, Little Hans's oedipal anxiety of his father is displaced on to a phobia of horses, allowing him to be with his father and yet avoid the easier substitute father. Again, the work of displacement is not a conscious chosen instrument to resolve conflict. It is not that the above anorexic chooses her body as a vehicle of punishment over her mother's, or that Little Hans makes a conscious choice of horses as his substitute object. Contingent chains of association provide the material. Condensation is a second principle of dreamwork operative in phantasies. What the mind constructs is a meld or composite that distorts elements of the real objects of wishes or fears. Dreams are notorious for this process. In the famous Irma dream, Freud recounts that the principal figure in the dream was his patient Irma, as she appeared in real life. But his examination of her by the window was derived from another patient whom he wished she were, while her specific medical condition, as well as her name, recalled that of his eldest daughter, about whose health he had been anxious. Toward the end of the dream, the patient morphs into one of the children whom he had recently examined in the neurological department of the children's hospital.[38]

Condensations and displacements through phantasy allow drives to work under conditions of concealment. Objects become enough unlike their replacements to escape repression, but like enough to provide some gratification of drives.[39] Again, the phantasy, as an element of primary-process mentation, does not aim at truth of fit. Unlike holding a belief, in phantasizing, judgement about the truth is suspended or, better, never enters as part of the cognitive frame.

Kleinian theory notoriously pushes phantasy back to the earliest moments of mentation and instinctual urge.[40] On Klein's view, libidinal and aggressive drives have an essential relatedness to objects represented by unconscious phantasies. The infant at the breast, with each suck of mother's milk, takes in images of a good object – a 'good breast', just as the hungry and raging infant incorporates a 'bad object' – a 'bad breast', devoured, scooped out, bitten. As we saw earlier, according to the Kleinian view, the all good and all bad introjections are part of the early, pre-ambivalent vocabulary of positive and negative emotions. The primitive mechanism of splitting, of keeping the good from the bad, is a defence that sets in with the threat of the onset of ambivalence. If the breast that feeds is also the breast that frustrates, then the good can be savaged by the bad and one's own badness (or greed) can be persecuted for the spoilage. Splitting is a way of warding off the persecutory anxiety. The positions are never once and for all passed beyond. Like most developmental stages, they are returned to in one form or another.[41] Much can be said about Kleinian theory, both critical and exegetical. I touch on the theory here as simply another way of getting at the notion of primitive psychological representation that psychoanalytic theory posits as part of early emotional or drive experience.

With these structures elaborated, we are in a better position to return to the question the Ancients leave unanswered, of why some emotions don't respond to reasonable persuasion and argument. In part, according to the picture we have elaborated, it is because they are underpinned by primitive drives and regressive defences that present a regressed reality discrepant with the demands of reason. Consider the following pared-down example: a father overreacts to his son's poor academic performance on a school test, knowing all the while that he is overreacting, but yet his scorn and anger don't abate. True, he says to himself, the test is a small part of the child's overall academic profile; it was a careless error that caused the poor grade, and anyone can slip up that way without it reflecting badly on overall effort or ability. Yet the rational voice (his or that of others) does not dislodge the voice of disappointment and shame. From a psychoanalytic view, one supposes there are underlying fears and wishes that fuel the disappointment, and resistances that prevent them from fully surfacing and being assessed by more rational considerations. In this particular case, the father's fear is that he will himself fail in a world where he has made academic success the only escape route from the deadened life of his family. Anxiety about his potential failures and depressed and self-punishing feelings about past shortcomings get repeated in a projection on to the son. The phantasy that he will not escape his origins if he academically slips up is passively relived on the screen of the son. Rationally, he doesn't believe the archaic construals on which his fears rest nor would he consciously settle on the adaptations he has defensively constructed. But he neurotically repeats the drama, unable to own it and then let it go.

For purposes of expedience, I have come at this as an outsider. And I have interpreted wholecloth. This is neither the psychoanalytic process nor the way resistances are weakened. In the section that follows, I discuss aspects of the psychoanalytic process important for promoting emotional agency.

4 Emotional agency in the psychoanalytic process

I have spent time going over elemental parts of classical Freudian theory in order to examine the cognitive and affective depth that underlies surface emotions. A common rebuke of psychoanalysis is that in positing the unconscious it leaves the human diminished in agency and autonomy. The force of this essay is to argue against this. Still, the charge brings to the fore the question of how human beings, given the psychoanalytic view of them as 'creatures in conflict, burdened by their past, and operating in ways that exceed their awareness',[42] they can become masters rather than victims of their lives.

The broadly shared view of the psychoanalytic process is that emotional transformations depend upon working through transference and its resistances. Transference, in its most general sense, is the ordinary process of constructing meaning in light of the past, of living the here and now through the structures and habits of past relationships and ways of standing in the world. All human relationships are based on transference, in the sense that they carry their histories with them. They are repetitions, re-editions. Freud's critical claim, however, in his early papers on technique, is that the compulsion to repeat stands in the way of remembering.[43] The analytic process is one of trying to regain memory by self-consciously observing repetitions and enactments. Through reliving in the immediate clinical relationship (the so called 'transference neurosis'), the habits and defences of the mind are exposed under the watchful eye of analyst and analysand. Through the art of well-timed and carefully titrated interpretations, the analyst helps the analysand to come to core insights about conflictual needs and longings that have led to compromises that no longer work. It is often the breakdown of these brokered deals that bring a patient into analysis.

The transformation process requires an induced regression that exposes infantile feelings and early developmental positions. Through the fundamental rule of free association, the secondary-process restraints of logic and ego organization are relaxed. Other conditions, such as the use of the couch, restriction of normal actions and deprivation from the facial cues of the analyst, are meant to further promote the regression.[44] With channels to the unconsciousness and past opened, the patient can move more easily between primary-process thought and the more organized and mature structures of secondary mentation. Jealous rages and incestuous impulses, unbearable losses and self-persecution for their perpetration, once recorded and defended against by the child, may now be relived and refelt. The hope of analysis is to experience those feelings in parallel track, as the child but also as the adult, able to assess those feelings with empathy, but also for what they are. Emotional agency becomes a matter of reintegrating the past with the present, of owning the past – mixing our labour with it – so that it is no longer alien or otherwordly. To use Loewald's metaphor, in analysis we are like Odysseus roaming the underworld, hoping to turn the ghosts that haunt into familiar ancestors that 'live forth in the present generation'.[45] The ghosts become cut loose from the demonic shadows when they are allowed to taste the blood of recognition, of remembrance.

On the traditional view, the analysand works through the transference of symptoms and compromise formations on the blank screen of the analyst. Clinically neutral and abstinent, the analyst deprives the analysand of many of the usual responses that her emotions provoke, and so forces the analysand to observe in an uncontaminated way her own psyche and its way of constructing the world. The model is of an anonymous analyst who can act as a mirror for the analysand's projections and constructions. In the more contemporary reworking of this paradigm, the human side of empathy, underscored by Kohutian self-psychology, is given some due, but primarily as an element of the framing condition of the analysis – i.e., in the working or therapeutic alliance that establishes a viable clinical relationship with the analyst.[46]

The model of the non-judgemental analyst has considerable attraction. Freud himself came to it after his own early method of hypnosis ran afoul by putting the power of suggestion and the authority of a surrogate super-ego figure in the role of clinician. The early studies on hysteria, written by Freud and Breuer while still under the influence of the suggestive model, read like Sherlock Holmes detective stories, where Freud, as Holmes, knows just what he is in search of and succeeds in convincing the patient to concur. But compliant concurrence, like chastening, is not a working-through. It is a way of being imposed upon that has its price.

The point of the neutral analyst is to push back the work on to the analysand and her process of discovery and self-exposure. To be neutral is to not judge, but also to not bite at the bait as most of the actors in the analysand's world do. Of course, just as all suggestion cannot be eliminated, so too on this view, some degree of projective identification is unavoidable: the cunning of the analysand is to manipulate, to get the most guarded and neutral observer to bite. But these are moments to be wary of and avoided as much as possible. The analyst must lash himself to the mast, be a predictable and stable object against which the analysand (and analyst) can see the vicissitudes of the analysand's transference. If and when the empress needs to see she is wearing no clothes, she will see her nakedness all the more clearly through the reflecting mirror of the analyst.

The mirror or blank screen metaphor has come in for its share of criticism in contemporary theory. The rise of interpersonal theories and 'two-person psychologies' emphasizes that despite training and psychological flexibility, no analyst is anonymous or invisible in the psychoanalytic process. There are always two people in the room. As Owen Renik puts it, 'we can put our hands over our eyes, if we want; but we will not disappear'.[47] As such, forbearance and silence are less ways of disappearing into blankness than ways of processing an analysand's material through countertransferential thoughts and feelings, reveries, regressions to the past, subtle enactments, and so on.[48] Moreover, to have those responses is to have the epistemic cues requisite for tracking what the analysand is feeling and experiencing. The problem is not with the practical goal of neutrality, but with the notion that the analyst achieves it through washing himself of emotional responsiveness, as the blank-screen metaphor implies. Epistemic sensitivity to others requires the input of emotions. Moreover, an emotional responsiveness that tracks salient circumstances is conceptually distinct from explicit emotional reactiveness and expression, however difficult they are to separate in practice and however useful subtle emotional enactments may themselves be for fully recording the import of an emotion. The point is that as a metaphor, the blank screen simply doesn't capture what the analyst must do to follow a patient's drift and unconscious meaning. Mirroring back the patient's words and meanings has its place, but one gets there not by being epistemically or emotionally blank. This is not to say that the analyst should be 'busy' with emotional engagement. There is something to be said for the Buddhist ideal of meditative quiescence, in which the mind is emptied of frantic desire and argument. But the point of that emptying is not to become blank, but precisely to be in a position to notice reveries and passing thoughts without getting hooked on them.

I shall say more about these issues shortly as I develop some themes in a more two-personed, relational model of treatment.[49] For the moment, a crucial point is that the analysand's development of emotional agency takes place concurrent with an ongoing process that involves the analyst's own emotional growth. Though the analytic relationship is established for the sake of the mental health of the patient, it is a mutual journey that can achieve its goal only when the analyst as well as the analysand are open to meeting the challenges and revisiting the conflicts of emotional development.

Psychoanalysis viewed as a shared voyage between two persons can take many shapes. A common model is the parent–child relationship. Though not a relationship of equality, there is clear mutuality in the earliest relationships of parent and child, with the sensitive parent trying to match her responses to the affect levels and intensities of the child, but also to regulate affects when they become rageful or fragmenting and to stimulate them when they need stretching. Daniel Stern's work stands out here in documenting the empathetic synchronies the infant and parent establish as they try to couple and forge a stable bond.[50] The analytic relationship shares something in common with this process of merger and empathetic identification and attunement. Moreover, analytic couples each have their own personalities, just as child and parent dyads have their respective chemistries, and matches and mismatches. In both spheres, some relationships will require hard work to become and stay coupled, others are more natural fits. Also, like the parent, the analyst can be conceived as a co-facilitator of emotional change, offering new objects to be internalized for self-regulation as well as safe opportunities for expanding horizons.

The synchronies of the early child–parent relationship are heuristic for analysis. But the analogy with the parent–child relationship is relevant simply because the latter is a prototype for a context in which emotional development takes place. The parallel with analysis is especially apt when we focus on the child on the verge of language. Just as the newly linguistic child learns to identify and differentiate emotions through the talk that often accompanies play, so analysands in the context of a daily hour devoted exclusively to self-examination work on experiencing and labelling the emotional currents of their lives. Through clarifications and interpretations that work in the analysand's own idiolect and metaphors, the analyst helps to bring to awareness emotions that hover on the edge of consciousness. As Thomas Ogden puts it, analytic dialogue is a mutual process 'in which the analytic pair elaborates and modifies the metaphors that the other has unself-consciously introduced'.[51] Of course, any labelling process can be defensive – a premature rush to rationalize a fury or cringe that is still archaic and inchoate, disconnected from rational, secondary-process thought. A good analyst will analyse the defence and work through at the level of primary process, just as she would a dream and its twisted logic of contingent associations, displacements and morphed images. Indeed, the point of working with certain metaphors that emerge in analytic dialogue is that they resonate with primary process. Body metaphors and concrete visions can at times seem almost to be the things they are about. At such moments, the gap between language and raw experience feels unmediated, without filters or protective layers. To experience in this way is to be distanced from rational organization and its niceties and yet to open reason's door to a new source of lifeblood and energy. Conversely, to dwell in the world of archaic experience is to partially purge it of its demons by making sense of it through language and rational capacities.

Robert Winer has recently warned of the limitations of the parent–child model – that it reintroduces authoritarian elements into analysis as well as encourages some of the omnipotent fantasies and eroticization that the oedipal child brings to the parent, and the parent in turn (as analyst now) covertly conspires to satisfy.[52] These are serious concerns, which in the context of our previous discussion, bring to mind the unworkable elements of an Aristotelian model of psychic harmony achieved through top-down rule and compliance to the wise elder. Still, despite these limitations, the parent–child analogue underscores a crucial aspect of emotional development, which we have not yet touched on and which ought not be obscured by concerns about misplaced authority. And this is that the child, even pre-verbally, is an emerging emotional agent, who in the context of the 'good-enough' relationship with parents, struggles to find ways of experiencing and regulating emotions that put her more rather than less in charge of her emotional life. Developmental research is rich here, and the subject of another essay.[53] But a few points can be touched on. The three-month-old infant needn't be viewed as a passive bundle of pleasure and distress, but an agent who tries to stimulate pleasure in her own environment, cooing and smiling most vigorously from the mobiles she manipulates, and from the smiles she herself elicits from her mother. Similarly, when the toddler ventures out into the big world on her own, but then discovers there are bigger guys out there and that the world is no longer her oyster, she emotionally reconsolidates, or 'refuels' by scurrying back into her father's arms. This, as Margaret Mahler describes it, is one way the child actively uses parental resources to negotiate separation and individuation.[54] The even younger child, not yet independently mobile, also finds ways to mediate what is potentially threatening and joyous in the world by glancing back, or 'referencing' parents' facial responses to see how they react to those novel objects. Social referencing, in Emde's terms,[55] is another way in which the child unconsciously figures out, and regulates, what to feel and when, given environmental realities and parental resources. Indeed, the child of poker-faced parents is deprived of the cues that help regulate her own emotions. Again, the cuddly teddy bear or favoured blankie, which in Donald Winnicott's words provides a 'transitional object'[56] for a child to invest in when parents are not available, is another coping skill the child adopts to prevent psychotic rage and fragmentation. With the onset of language, the child takes a giant leap into the world of emotional agency, finding a new way to share a world with parents and to control and identify what earlier could only be acted out or experienced diffusely.

Of course, the renegotiating of emotional agency in the analytic setting will take a very different course. The point is not that the above developmental stages are recapitulated (though some may be, such as the use of the analysis as a transitional space), but simply that just as the child develops the skills of emotional agency in the context of a 'good-enough' parental relationship, so too, by analogy, it is plausible to think of the analysand as becoming a more robust emotional agent in the context of the 'good-enough' clinical relationship.

Still, the parent–child pair is not the only model for an analytic relationship, conceived of as mutual and a context for emotional growth. Winer's own choice is marriage:

> Both marriage and treatment offer developmental second chances. The seasons of marriage – pairing, developing a sexual/somatic bond, moving to threeness with the addition of children, identifying with the children through the various stages and conflicts of childhood, suffering the losses of the children's emancipation, rejoining at midlife, bearing the losses of aging – offer the chance to find new solutions to the oldest problems. This can also be said for the seasons of therapy.[57]

Winer develops the details of the metaphor in a compelling way, though I cannot map those parallels here. Rather, in the space remaining, I want to follow a suggestion that the marriage metaphor evokes, and that is that the collaborative work of analysis involves mutual growth and development, in the way that a good marriage does. In many ways, the point is uncontroversial, as unnovel as saying that analysis requires that the analyst be analysed and continue a self-analysis, in some fashion or other, throughout life. But the point I want to make is about the analytic process itself – that it requires the recognition of mutual transferences and regressions, countertransferences and enactments, shared moments of mourning and loss, not as disruptions which take the treatment off course, but as constitutive features of analysis, which when properly analysed, move the treatment along. They are part of the vicissitudes of analysis, and a reflection of the fact that analysis is a human pursuit – however artificial and rigidly constrained – conducted by an analyst who is 'not a machine in absolute self-control'[58] nor a sage who has once and for all found permanent psychic harmony. There are always residues, shadows of conflicts, and potentials for recrudescences, however subtle and controlled the bubblings may be. Unlike various notions of ideally impartial and neutral persons in moral theory – e.g., Hume's judicious spectator, Smith's ideal observer, or Rawls's parties to the original position – the ideal of the analyst is meant as a model for real-life practice. It is not an idealized reconstruction (or at least not meant to be), in the way much moral theory is.[59]

But this means that the analyst's transferences, like the patient's, will have their influence and will, at some level, be a constitutive part of the analysis and its mediations. Emotional vulnerability, or responsiveness, is not just to what patients project, but to one's own lurking issues and unfinished business. The effect of mutual transferences on the analysis is illustrated by a vignette James McLaughlin offers, and whose main points I briefly summarize:[60]

Mrs P. sought analysis because of a 'pervasive sense of never having been in charge of her life'. Her style of narrative within the analysis was to offer 'running monologues' about her frustrations in life. They were masterpieces of ambiguity that left the analyst frustrated in his attempts to make sense of her drift. His response was to offer only intermittent interventions at moments when he thought he could really make sense of the ramblings. Each intervention was warded off by

Mrs P., with the best being met with a defensive 'yes, but'. The pattern continued with the analyst retreating to a 'dogged silence', followed by infrequent but assertive sorties, and the patient volleying back that she didn't understand or agree with the points, 'reducing to fragments' the analyst's 'best efforts to see and make sense'. The analyst was well aware that Mrs P.'s intolerance for his judgements was rooted in her relationship to her father and his overbearing critical solicitude. He was bothered by his own insistent tone as he heard himself speaking in the analysis, but the mutual enactment continued for some time unaltered.

The stalemate broke when in a moment of reverie, the analyst caught himself taking on and off his bifocals. This was the 'madeleine' that lit up an old conflict of his own simmering in the analysis. As a child he suffered from severe myopia that went undiagnosed for some time. When he finally got corrective lenses, the world was transformed. There was family lore about his attachment to his glasses and 'the expansive changes their magic made'. Fiddling with his glasses pinpointed his blind spot, so to speak. The 'well-known and dull' conflict between being blind and longing to see and be understood was rekindled by his unconscious identification with Mrs P. and her sense of being lost and bumbling in the world. His declamations were defensive retreats from the frightening and shameful feelings he once felt of being adrift, without vision or focus. Becoming aware of the dynamics of this stalemate and the contributions of his own regression were necessary for moving the analysis along.

I draw on one further vignette, offered by Robert Winer, as another illustration of the mutual transferences that are ubiquitous in analysis:

> A middle-aged patient told me that she and her older brother had coped with the misery of their childhoods through a nightly experience in which he read to her and then engaged in sex play, which included intercourse. This had ended at her brother's insistence when she was 7 because he had become afraid of impregnating her. She had never forgiven him for stopping.
>
> In psychoanalysis, my patient found the limitations of the therapeutic relationship intolerable. She peeked inside my car, watered my waiting-room plants, stole food from the kitchen adjacent to my waiting room, and contorted herself on the couch wishing that I would anally penetrate her. I found her relentlessly demanding. Two years into the treatment, to my astonishment, I discovered that I was not certain that this woman would not succeed in seducing me, despite my lack of conscious sexual attraction to her. She was, after all (indeed!), old enough to be my mother. I discovered that we shared a belief that the appeal of incest was irresistible. The dawning awareness that she would actually not be able to seduce me was followed by my realization that she was perfectly capable of destroying the treatment. This double recognition allowed me to move the treatment forward.[61]

As Winer reflects, he identified with the patient's conflict and incestuous feelings, and it was only when he 'must have finally been able to feel an attraction to her – that is, to finally have stopped defending against feeling it' that he 'could register the seduction and then take my measure of it. I could master the experience when I stopped blocking it . . . Had I been able to keep enough distance from her not to feel her incestuous demand in the first place, I believe that I would have ultimately been of less use to her.' Here it is not only the patient whose emotional mastery is at stake, but the analyst's. The treatment hangs on it, and on the active and ongoing task of working through the conflict. The claim is not that his vulnerability to this patient's seductive desires was necessary, but that given that he was attracted, recognizing it was important for preventing further resistances and enactments on his own part.

These illustrations suggest that the analyst, within the analytic relationship itself, is not outside the very process of emotional transformation and growth. And though analysis is different from most other relationships of mutuality and intimacy – be it marriage or Aristotelian *philia* – in having as its end the well-being of one individual and not both, the analytic pair cannot do its work unless both use the analytic relationship as a chance to emotionally grow.

Notes

1 Following the psychoanalytic convention, I use 'phantasy' to refer to unconscious constructions and 'fantasy' to refer to conscious daydreams, reveries and the like.
2 For further discussion of issues of emotional agency, see Sherman (1999).
3 *Rhetoric*, 1378a30–32.
4 See my discussion of *philia* in ch. 5 of Sherman (1997).
5 Freud 1923, XIX: 56. Or as it as often put, where the id went, the ego shall now go.
6 Freud 1933, XXII: 77; see De Sousa (1982) 158–59.
7 Freud 1931, XXI: 218.
8 See Loewald (1979).
9 Cicero, *Tusculan Disputations*, 4.9
10 Kris (1952).
11 Freud 1916, XVI: 436–8.
12 And in the early writings, restricted to internal stimulation. The term differs from ethological notions of instinct in that Freud is less interested in what is innate than in the transformations or 'vicissitudes' of instinctual impulses as a result of environment and learning. It also should be noted that by 1915b (XIV: 178), Freud concludes that strictly speaking there are no unconscious emotions, and that when we use the term, we use it only loosely. The rationale here is that affects are discharges of which we have to have some lively feeling, in a way that is not required for an idea or intention. Freud is, at best, tentative about this linguistic point, and I shall continue, as he does, to speak of unconscious drives and feelings.
13 See Brenner (1982); also Boesky (1998).
14 The constancy principle shares something in common with the Stoic goal of *ataraxia* – freedom from disturbance, though Freud draws his notion from mechanistic physiology of the nineteenth century: the nervous system impinged by stimuli seeks to rid itself of that stimuli.
15 This is Brenner's criticism of 'frontier concept' (1982). See Loewald (1971: 118) for a more congenial account.

16 Freud 1933, XXII: 95
17 Freud 1915a, XIV: 117–18; 124.
18 Freud 1933, XXII: 95.
19 Freud 1920, XVIII: 36.
20 Ibid.: 15.
21 Ibid.: 16–17.
22 Loewald (1971: 122).
23 Ibid: 124; see Lear's (1998) discussion of this.
24 Freud 1940, XXIII: 148.
25 For example, Freud's *Mourning and Melancholia* (1917)'; *Three Essays on Sexuality* (1905); 'The Cases of "Little Hans" and the "Rat Man"' (1909), to name just a few.
26 See De Sousa (1982: 150), however, for the argument that there is no real basis for distinguishing one instinct from another, since Freud maintains that in repression, 'the force repressed and the repressing force can have the same source'.
27 Boesky (1998).
28 See, for example, Freud 1915b, XIV: 177–8; 1900, V: 463.
29 Gardner (1993: 97–8). Contrast Suppes and Warren (1982) who propose a propositional model of the unconscious.
30 Gardner (1993: 146).
31 Freud 1909b, X: 180.
32 Freud 1926, XX. In the early theory, (e.g., 'The Neuro-Psychosis of Defence') anxiety is the result of the defence of repression. More specifically, it is the leaking of repressed libido. The economic theory of drive is in full force: if libido is not discharged, then even though repressed (i.e., its ideational content is severed from the affect), the energy of the drive remains constant, with anxiety leaks as tell-tale signs of that bottled up energy. See 1894, III.
33 See Anna Freud (1966).
34 See Gardner (1993) for a helpful discussion of the literature on the distinction between acts of self-deception and unconscious acts of defence.
35 Brenner (1982: 7).
36 Klein, 'Some Notes on Schizoid Mechanisms' (1946) .
37 See the instructive discussion of Linda Brakel (forthcoming).
38 Freud 1900, IV: 292.
39 Lear (1998: 121).
40 See Ogden (1990: 13–14) on the notion of Kleinian phantasy as a hard-wired deep psychological structure.
41 See especially, Klein (1952: 69) and (1957: 144).
42 Robert Winer (1994: 29).
43 Freud 'Remembering, Repeating and Working Through', 1914, XII: 151.
44 For discussion of induced versus non-induced regressions, see Aron and Bushra (1998).
45 Loewald (1960: 249).
46 Greenson (1965); Zetzel (1956).
47 Renik (1995: 469).
48 Joseph Sandler (1976) points to a similar idea in his notion of 'free-floating responsiveness' and 'free-floating attention'. 'By "free-floating attention" I do not mean the "clearing of the mind" of thoughts or memories, but the capacity to allow all sorts of thoughts, daydreams and associations to enter the analyst's consciousness while he is at the same time listening to and observing the patient', 44. Thomas Ogden (1997) describes a similar phenomenon in the notion of reverie as an avenue to what Freud called 'catching the drift' in the analytic relationship: 'I include in the notion of reverie', Ogden writes, 'the most mundane, quotidian, unobtrusive thoughts, feelings, fantasies, ruminations, daydreams, bodily sensations, and so on that usually feel utterly disconnected from what the patient is saying and doing at the moment.'

49 Some might object that the drive theory outlined earlier does not lend itself to a more mutual and relational view of therapy. I don't believe this to be the case, though I cannot argue the point here.
50 Stern (1985).
51 Ogden (1997: 719).
52 Winer (1994: 64).
53 Sherman (1999); also for a discussion of the developmental literature on empathy, see Sherman (1998).
54 Mahler, Pine and Bergman (1975).
55 Kimmert, Campos, Sorce, Emde and Svejda (1983).
56 Winnicott (1971).
57 Winer (1994: 80).
58 Sandler (1976: 45).
59 I consider the comparisons more extensively in Sherman (1995).
60 McLaughlin (1991).
61 Winer (1994: 79).

References

Aristotle (1984) *The Complete Works of Aristotle*, Revised Oxford Translation, 1 and 2, Princeton: Princeton University Press.

Aron, Lewis and Bushra, Annabella (1998) 'Mutual Regression: Altered States in the Psychoanalytic Situation', *Journal of the American Psychoanalytic Association,* 46: 389–412.

Boesky, Dale (1998) 'The Concept of Psychic Structure', *Journal of the American Psychoanalytic Association,* 36 Supplement: 113–35.

Brakel, Linda (forthcoming) 'Phantasy and Wish: A proper Function Account for Human A-Rational Primary Process Mediated Mentation'.

Brenner, Charles (1982) *The Mind in Conflict*, Madison, CT: International Universities Press.

Cicero (1964) *Tusculan Disputations*, trans. J.E. King. Cambridge, MA: Loeb Classical Library, Harvard University Press.

De Sousa, Ronald (1982) 'Norms and the Normal', in R. Wollheim and J. Hopkins (eds), *Philosophical Essays on Freud*, New York: Cambridge University Press.

Freud, Anna (1966) *The Ego and the Mechanisms of Defense*, Madison CT: International Universities Press.

Freud, Sigmund (1974) *The Standard Edition of the Complete Psychological Works (S.E.)*. London: Hogarth Press.

—— (1894) 'The Neuro-Psychosis of Defence', *S.E.* III.

—— (1900) *The Interpretation of Dreams*, *S.E.* IV–V.

—— (1905) *Three Essays on Sexuality*, *S.E.* VII.

—— (1909a) 'Analysis of a Phobia in a Five-Year-Old Boy', *S.E.* X.

—— (1909b) 'Notes Upon a Case of Obsessional Neurosis', *S.E.* X.

—— (1914) 'Remembering, Repeating and Working Through', *S.E.* XII.

—— (1915a) 'Instincts and their Vicissitudes', *S.E.* XIV.

—— (1915b) 'The Unconscious', *S.E.* XIV.

—— (1916) *Introductory Lectures on Psychoanalysis: General Theory of the Neurosis*, *S.E.* XVI.

—— (1917) *Mourning and Melancholia, S.E.* XIV.

—— (1920) *Beyond the Pleasure Principle, S.E.* XVIII.

—— (1923) *The Ego and the Id, S.E.* XIX.

—— (1926) *The Problem of Anxiety, S.E.* XX.

—— (1931) 'Libidinal Types', *S.E.* XXI.

—— (1933) *New Introductory Lectures on Psycho-Analysis, S.E.* XXII.

—— (1940) *An Outline of Psychoanalysis, S.E.* XX.

Gardner, Sebastian (1993) *Irrationality and the Philosophy of Psychoanalysis*, New York: Cambridge University Press.

Greenson, R.R. (1965) 'The working alliance the Transference Neurosis', *Psychoanalytic Quarterly*, 34: 155–81.

Kimmert, M., Campos, J., Sorce, F., Emde, R., and Svejda, M. (1983) 'Social Referencing: Emotional Expressions as Behavior Regulators', in R. Plutchik and H. Kellerman (eds), *Emotion: Theory, Research, and Experience.* vol. 2. *Emotions in Early Development*, Orlando: Academic Press.

Klein, Melanie (1946) 'Some Notes on Schizoid Mechanisms', in *Envy and Gratitude and Other Works 1946–1963*, New York: The Free Press, 1975.

—— 1952 'Some Theoretical Conclusions Regarding the Emotional Life of the Infant', in *Envy and Gratitude*.

—— 1957 'Envy and Gratitude', in *Envy and Gratitude*.

Kris, E. (1952) *Psychoanalytic Explorations in Art*, Madison CT: International Universities Press.

Lear, Jonathan (1998) *Open Minded*, Cambridge, MA: Harvard University Press.

Loewald, Hans (1960) 'The Therapeutic Action of Psychoanalysis', in *Papers on Psychoanalysis*, New Haven: Yale University Press, 1980.

—— (1971) 'On Motivation and Instinct Theory', in *Papers on Psychoanalysis*.

—— (1979) 'The Waning of the Oedipal Complex', in *Papers on Psychoanalysis*.

Mahler, M., Pine, F. and Bergman, A. (1975) *The Psychological Birth of the Human Infant*, New York: Basic Books.

McLaughlin, James (1991) 'Clinical and Theoretical Aspects of Enactment', *Journal of the American Psychoanalytic Association*, 39: 595–614.

Ogden, Thomas (1990) *The Matrix of the Mind*, Northvale, NJ: Aronson.

—— (1997) 'Reverie and Metaphor: Some Thoughts on how I Work as a Psychoanalyst', *International Journal of Psycho-Analysis*, 78: 719–32.

Renik, Owen (1995) 'The ideal of the Anonymous Analyst and the Problem of Self-Disclosure', *Psychoanalytic Quarterly*, 64: 466–95.

Sandler, Joseph (1976) 'Countertransference and Role-Responsiveness', *International Review of Psycho-Analysis*, 3: 43–8.

Sherman, Nancy (1995) 'The Moral Perspective and the Psychoanalytic Quest', *The Journal of the American Academy of Psychoanalysis*, 23: 223–41.

—— (1997) *Making a Necessity of Virtue*, New York: Cambridge University Press.

—— (1998) 'Empathy and Imagination', in *Midwest Studies in Philosophy*, 22.

—— (1999) 'Taking Responsibility for our Emotions', *Social Philosophy and Policy*. Also in Paul, Miller and Paul (eds) *Responsibility*, New York: Cambridge University Press.

Stern, Daniel (1985) *The Interpersonal World of the Infant*, New York: Basic Books.

Suppes, Patrick and Warren Hermine (1982) 'On the Generation and Classification of Defense Mechanisms', in R. Wollheim and J. Hopkins (eds) *Philosophical Essays on Freud*, New York: Cambridge University Press.

Winer, Robert (1994) *Close Encounters*, Northvale, NJ: Aronson.

Winnicott, D.W. (1971) 'Transitional Objects and Transitional Phenomena', in *Playing and Reality*, New York: Penguin.

Wollheim, Richard (1993) *The Mind and its Depth*, Cambridge, MA: Harvard University Press.

Zetzel, E. (1956) 'Current Concepts of Transference', *International Journal of Psycho-Analysis*, 37: 369–76.

9

MORAL AUTHENTICITY AND
THE UNCONSCIOUS

Grant Gillett

> You brood of vipers, How can you say good things when you are
> evil? For from the fullness of the heart the mouth speaks. A good
> person brings forth good out of a store of goodness, but an evil
> person brings forth evil out of a store of evil. I tell you on the day
> of judgement people will render account for every careless word
> they speak. By your words you will be acquitted and by your
> words you will be condemned.
>
> Matthew 12: 34–7

Freud is commonly perceived to have triggered a widespread re-evaluation of
the human mind which highlighted the role of a domain of sub-rational mental
states and events in motivating and indeed causing many of our conscious mental
acts. The interplay of this sub-rational content itself obeyed chaotic and irrational
principles based on causal efficacy and the emotive force attached to that content
(the primary process). This interplay shows itself in the individual's attitudes
to self and others, and the crucial forces involved, on Freud's account, arise from
events and dispositions acquired and moulded pre-rationally and very early in the
individual's history. Freud never advanced his theory as a reason to undermine
the idea that human beings are responsible for their actions in relation to the
requirements of morality but I will argue that his theoretical orientation does have
the effect of casting doubts on a number of cognitivist accounts of human moral
judgement. I will then look for a conception of the subconscious which allows us
to formulate a substantive idea of moral authenticity as a narrative product of a
lived human life.

Thesis: moral authenticity

A conception of moral authenticity is difficult to formulate but seems to have
something to do with sincerity. Sincerity is a matter of saying without 'common-
or-garden' deception what is on your mind. But authenticity tends to go beyond this
in that it also seems to involve significant gains in dealing with inner conflict and

self-deception because the notion of inner harmony seems to be an appealing feature of authenticity (at least of the virtuous kind). If we extend this we can make a reasonable attempt to provide a conception of moral authenticity as being true to one's reflectively endorsed moral beliefs where reflection has also had a significant hand in dealing with the inconsistencies, incontinence and self-deception that is endemic in human personality. Having said this we must firmly correct the possible misconception that all or most moral beliefs are rational and reflective in their creation and formulation but hold on to the idea that a certain kind of reflective endorsement is central in their being the beliefs of an authentic person. Such reflection is, however, not necessarily rational or logically coherent even though there must be some kind of considered judgement about the moral contents involved. At the minimum we should be able to defend some notion of acceptance and endorsement that allows moral attributions, for instance of praise and blame, to be grounded in the domain of the agent's conscious attitudes and responsibility for self. That claim seems a fairly modest requirement for any theory of moral judgement to call itself cognitivist rather than wildly emotivist in its inspiration.

We can arrive at the role of cognition or reflection from any number of paths. Aristotle, for instance, thought that our moral character was the result of training which inculcated moral sensitivity or perception, the development of good dispositions, and reflection upon those dispositions.[1] Kant aimed to ground our moral nature purely in our being as rational agents, arguing that reason provided us with the perfect rational maxim – the categorical imperative – which we could then universalize because the only consistent attitude towards it was to will that it should be binding on all rational beings. Mill and the utilitarians also argue that our dispositions ought to be governed by the rational principle of utility (suitably generalized) if we are to act morally. The principle of utility is not, however, an instinctive part of our response to a situation and requires some reflective distance from our immediate intuitions. We might also pursue a path suggested by Nagel who argues that as good as it gets in moral reasoning is to reconcile a fairly objective view of our own actions, given all the interests involved in a situation, with the internal view of one's own motives and intentions.[2] A substantial conception of moral authenticity might, on this account, be linked to the idea that the authentically moral or virtuous being has an inner reflectively mediated harmony of motivation and action so that he or she enjoys peace in the self.

Michael Smith develops, from a Humean foundation, a rationalist theory of intention and action which has points of convergence with the present view of authenticity.[3] However, he then formulates, at the end of his inquiry, a radically anti-Humean thesis that moral motivation is entirely grounded in a rational desire for coherence in one's set of propositional attitudes. To do this he helps himself, in addition to the belief/desire psychology which represents contemporary Humeanism, to the *prima facie* plausible thesis that any agent has a motive to have the most coherent set of beliefs and desires that he or she can achieve. One might object that such a model is so untrue to normal human psychology that it is not to be taken seriously or even that it has disadvantages for a successful adaptation to the vicissitudes of life. Smith does seem to assume a remarkable degree of transparency in the attitudes and reactions that motivate any given agent. However, his view should not be too lightly dismissed as we can see by considering certain, other, plausible sources of support.

Firstly, it embodies a normative view which coheres very well with the common intuition that we are all backsliders, to a greater or lesser degree, from our ideal or most endorsable character. This leads to the common-sense notion that morality is an ideal that most of us apply and that we acknowledge the deficiencies within our own psychology in the light of it.

Second, he can claim support from an evolutionary account of mind in that the holding of a coherent propositional attitude set rather than a confused one would, one might think, lead to an effective and maximally adaptive set of action plans in a given domain of activity.

Smith's maximal coherence view is also independently appealing to anyone who subscribes to a folk-psychological model which links PAs according to principles of rationality and particularly the Davidsonian variants that stress the normative role of rational coherence.[4] Again the teleological appeal of such a view is that it entails that in any given situation some combination of beliefs and desires would be able to be exhibited which would lead to the formation of a relatively unconflicted intention. In service of his project, Smith introduces the notion of a normative reason such that, to say that we have a normative reason to @ in certain circumstances is to say that, if we were fully rational, we would want that we @ in C.[5]

On this basis, a rational requirement – to achieve a maximally coherent set of beliefs and desires – generates a reason for action or change of desire and becomes (effectively) a categorical imperative for those who find themselves disposed to be rational. The idea that agents who have developed reason as their most sophisticated adaptive device in an informationally challenging environment should have such a motivation seems independently plausible, or at least not implausible, particularly when we claim that it is a prescriptive norm and not a descriptive constraint on an adequate philosophically informed psychology. If Smith succeeds then he could claim moral authenticity was an ideal to be approximated by any agent who would strive to act in accordance with all his reasons including normative reasons. Of course, it does not require that the relative weights of members of the maximally coherent PA set remain invariant over time and circumstance. Smith's account would also clinch the relationship between authenticity and harmony in that the normative reason, if acted on, moves one towards maximal coherence between one's desires and beliefs.

We can, however, excuse ourselves from appeals to authority here and go some way towards a similar conclusion about reason and morality by noting that moral judgements are subject to argumentation and rational debate. Therefore, however we construe moral argument, a case can be made that moral appeals address themselves in no small measure to the rational, conscious and deliberative self. The conclusion seems plain: morality is that which controls, moderates and curbs our amoral or even immoral natures and imposes the rule of reflectively moderated sensibilities over our baser instincts. It follows that a moral agent should strive to be authentic to this aspect of self. Such authenticity allows the person to hold self-consistent positions on moral issues because these positions have been subject to reflection and rational criticism, even if crucially informed by emotional and cultural commitments. The result is an agent who moves with assurance and inner harmony through the moral challenges of life.

This is a reassuring conclusion because it seems to secure our practice of holding people accountable for their moral choices. The two critical features of the view are an overall integrity of character or inner harmony and some kind of reflective endorsement of the dominant reasons for action which move that character. If moral authenticity has this inherently reflective aspect then conscious and deliberatively formed intentions are central in the picture and moral praise and blame rest on a secure foundation in moral psychology.

However, the picture is not so clear and distinct as it is here painted because hardly any moral theorists have ever held that reason can go it alone in relation to moral action (although Kant veered remarkably close to that view).

Hume had argued that in moral judgements there is an ineliminable appeal to sentiment or sympathy. Kant found this unpalatable in that sentiment was a species of emotion and therefore, in relation to reason, pathological and not an intrinsically rational determining ground of the will. But although he was acutely aware of the need to exclude the moral will from pathological causation, he never in fact provided an adequate account of the moral incentive. He argued that the fundamental determining ground of the will was pure reason in so far as the agent was acting morally but acknowledged that there must also be a subjective determining ground of the moral will. He was led to extol awe and respect (for the purity and rationality of the categorical imperative) as that subjective ground.

Even when Kant, like Plato and Aristotle, affirmed the possibility of self-love, he put a rational constraint on it in that it was properly restricted to a love of the self in so far as it acted in accordance with the dictates of pure practical reason.[6] Kantian self-love was therefore as thoroughly rational in its commitments and origins as any other feature of the human mind. In fact his remarks are reminiscent of some of Freud's observations about the stern and relatively austere role played by the super-ego as a paternalistic voice in the mind. Suffice it to say that many have not found Kant's observations about purely rationally motivated respect to be an adequate account of what we mean by moral thinking and its role in our psychology.[7]

We can deepen our hesitation about Kant's account by reflecting on the fact that our feelings are engaged not only to incline us toward a certain conclusion but also in understanding what is at stake in a moral decision. Here an example makes the situation clear. I might say that I authentically believe that children should not be abused or treated violently. If I were asked why I thought this, I might produce a number of rational considerations based on the harm to the child and the undesirability of a society in which violence and cruelty go unchecked. But, in a sense that is quite prior to those considerations, the evil involved is intuitively self-evident. The wanton cruelty involved in physical abuse of a child is just palpably wrong. In fact I would be likely to say to someone who could see an adult gratuitously injuring a child 'Can't you just see that that is wrong?'[8] This is, of course, a fairly straightforward appeal to the moral intuitions or moral sense of the other. It is uncontentious that such intuitions are part of my nature as a moral agent and that if I were to deny them I would be acting inauthentically. In fact if we were to turn the spotlight on my moral reasoning we would find that, at root, many of our deepest moral convictions rest on just such intuitive foundations. If we examine apparently self-evident moral propositions such as 'To inflict gratuitous harm on another is wrong' or 'Love is better than hate', we would find that they have an intuitive appeal which is much deeper than reason.

There are three other ways that we might argue for an intuitive, non-rational, or significantly sub-rational basis for moral psychology and therefore for the intuitions that seem to lie at the heart of many of the moral convictions we come to endorse.

First there is the whole idea of moral perception as a deep orientation towards a *way of seeing* something rather than a rationally determined attitude to a state of affairs. Nussbaum has argued eloquently for this understanding of the fundaments of moral judgement.[9] More recently, DesAutels has likened ways of seeing which reveal moral aspects of situations to *gestalt* shifts such as that involved in Wittgenstein's duck–rabbit phenomenon. She remarks, '*gestalt* shifts are common and unavoidable and they play a significant role in the mental processes used to perceive particular moral situations'.[10] She discusses Gilligan's rejection of the levels of rational development at the heart of Kohlberg's moral theory. Gilligan notices the fundamental importance of focus phenomena whereby subjects shift the pattern of saliencies to which they are responding and so come to alter their moral judgements about a given situation.[11] Such perceptual shifts are clearly not the kind of thing that occur as a result of formulating reasons and believing in certain propositions. It is therefore plausible that they, like other perceptual phenomena, arise at a sub-rational level and are driven in part by deep-seated sympathies and interests and not by explicit conscious reasoning. This is not to say that the moral persuasion that results from such *gestalt* shifts is independent of rational criticism and possible endorsement. Again, however, there is a kind of ambiguity in rational reflection such that it depends on the focus of deliberation exactly how the reasoning goes. The aspects of a situation that get emphasized the way in which they are seen, and their relevance to the moral situation are all dependent on one's way of looking at things. Imagine, for instance, that the child being beaten had just been cheeky to his father. Under these circumstances one can imagine moral judges with one set of prejudices stressing the need for children to learn respect, the way in which it is so irritating to be defied, spare the rod and spoil the child, and so on, while a different group would talk about the abuse of power, the propagation of violence, and the inherent abhorrence of violence in general and cruelty to a child in particular. We all realize that these irrational or arational dispositions ought to be subject to rational reflection but if Freud is to be believed, that process of reflection might be subject to rather than corrective of such sub-rational forces.

Second, the very ancient source quoted at the outset puts moral weight on character dispositions which show themselves in the thoughts that find expression in unguarded moments. The claim is that each of us will give account for every careless word he or she utters and, again, these are precisely *not* the kind of things that get expressed as a result of conscious rational deliberation but rather exhibit sub-rational features of the self.

Third, my incentive in morality, on Smith's analysis, comes out as a fairly monistic and rational disposition, but it does not seem like that when I attend to the phenomenology of intention and action. Most of the time I seem more conflicted and ambivalent than Smith might be taken to suggest. I am sure Smith means his account to be a conceptual exploration of a possibility that moral thought, in its ideal form, might turn out to be reason-driven despite the persuasive Humean idea that reason is conceptually the slave of passions. However, in everyday life we might find a great deal of plausibility in Hume's account in that he does stress the need for arational and emotive forces to move us whatever our rational capabilities. The weakest claim that looks plausible here is that, for real people and real moral decisions, purity is not the norm, forces within us that do not have primarily rational credentials have a significant influence on our moral judgements, and a credible theory of moral authenticity ought to accommodate that fact.

Ancient authorities also yield a fairly realistic acknowledgement of the prevalence of mixed motives. Luke has Jesus saying 'Love your enemies and do good to them, and lend expecting nothing back; then your reward in heaven will be great' (Luke 6: 35) which hints at a widespread prudential or self-serving motive for charity rather than a pure love for others. Matthew's Christ says 'Take care not to perform righteous deeds in order that people may see them' (6: 1), thereby recognizing the mixed motives that often overdetermine our good deeds. St Paul in his letter to the Romans admonishes us to be sincere but in another passage in the same letter says 'If your enemy is hungry, feed him; if he is thirsty, give him something to drink; for by so doing you will heap burning coals upon his head' (Romans 12: 20). This may be good advice but the motive veers close to out-and-out vice and, even if it is meant to be taken to refer to the conscience of an enemy who unexpectedly meets charity, the remark, once again, reminds us of the mixed motives with which the most seemingly virtuous act can be done. One need not believe that such motives are fully conscious to find it plausible that they are part of the cause of moral actions as performed in the real world by mere mortals such as us.

The last indication of the role of subconscious mental acts and orientations in moral thinking is the guilt that seems an intrinsic part of moral agency and subjectivity. Freud, of course, made a lot of this force in the human psyche. The fact that guilt at my own, perhaps private, moral failings arises unbidden and then is not entirely responsive to reason or rational negotiation betrays the fact that its origins are not in the rational domain of consciousness and self-determination. Again we seem forced to conclude that a significant aspect of moral experience depends on the unconscious and sub-rational aspects of mind and it remains a challenge to reconcile this with a robust notion of reflectively endorsed harmony of character.

These concessions to the role of character, or a domain of non-rational mental dispositions, in moral judgement are not threatening if we can conceptualize moral authenticity as arising from an integration or endorsement by the rational subject of traits within the self that are judged to be admirable and worthy when submitted by second-order reflection and self-evaluation.

However, this move will not save us from the Freudian *coup de grâce* which threatens the idea of moral authenticity as traditionally conceived.

Antithesis: the Freudian deconstruction of morality

Freud elaborated a detailed theory of the mind and its system of psychic formations. What is more the content in the subconscious mind formed interacting complexes whose causal effects were subject not to reason and reflection but to the primary process, an altogether irrational mode of operation. Therefore, if we were to find that subconscious and sub-rational features of the self were the source of moral attitudes and judgements, then this would unseat a robust conception of reflective authenticity as a consciously organized set of mental acts characterizing the person concerned.

Freud posited the existence of an unconscious system (Ucs.) as distinct from the preconscious (Pcs.) or conscious (Cs.) systems. Cs. is the system of rationality and the voluntary control of behaviour[12] conforming to the requirements of a cognitivist theory of mental acts and moral judgements. Cs. and Pcs. are both divisions in the ego which also elaborate the super-ego as the residue of cultural norms and parental authority. The super-ego, although produced by the ego, is quasi-autonomous in that it has 'the capacity to stand apart from the ego and master it' (Freud 1986: 469). The super-ego is also the locus of the ego-ideal or the idealized expression of the identification of the child with the parents. It is here we must look to understand our moral nature. 'The super-ego is the vehicle of the phenomenon that we call conscience' (Freud 1940: 42) and it issues imperatives to act and to feel thus and so. Freud explicitly insinuates Kantian language here in describing the action of the super-ego.

As the child was once under the compulsion to obey its parents, so the ego submits to the categorical imperative of its super-ego (Freud 1986: 469). However, the move is not in service of a conception of the moral agent as the supreme realization of human reason but in service of quite another doctrine because the sense of 'categorical' that Freud makes use of is not the Kantian sense at all. The Kantian sense invoked the claim that the supreme moral claim was categorical and not hypothetical in that it did not depend upon prior conditions or interests of the agent as a psychological subject. It was therefore unqualified by 'if' clauses which could be disputed on the grounds of the soundness of the motives being served because the imperative derived purely from the nature of a human being as a being of reason. Freud's super-ego issues categorical imperatives in the sense that they are unconditionally demanding. Therefore, if they are subjected to dispute or rational negotiation, the very fact that the agent seeks to moderate them in this way is likely to cause guilt and psychic effects because the subject has not whole-heartedly endorsed them. This feature of Freudian imperatives shows that they owe their origin to something less reasonable than the reflective ego, indeed that they draw on more primitive and coercive forces.

There are two paths by which the contents of the id can penetrate into the ego. The one is direct, the other leads by the way of the ego-ideal (Freud 1986: 476). The ego-ideal is paradoxical in nature because in it a transformation occurs. 'What has belonged to the lowest part of the mental life of each of us is changed, through the formation of the ideal, into what is highest in the human mind by our scale of values' (Freud 1986: 459).

This deeply paradoxical relationship between the id and the super-ego entails a much deeper connection between the instinctive self and the emotive content of morality than envisaged by, say, Williams or Urmson.[13] The distinctness of the contents of the ego-ideal from the contents of our conscious ego can profitably be analysed further in trying to understand Freud's challenge to our post-Enlightenment conception of morality and what we ordinarily call virtue and vice.

'If anyone were inclined to put forward the paradoxical proposition that the normal man is not only far more immoral than he believes but also far more moral than he knows, psychoanalysis, on whose findings the first half of the assertion rests, would have no objection to raise against the second half' (Freud 1986: 472).

If we unpack this remark we will grasp the nub of the problem.

Freud here trades on the two-way directedness of moral attitudes – attitudes toward others and attitudes towards self. If a person were living in a state of moral authenticity one might expect these to coincide. She would be comfortable with herself because there would be no significant divergence between her moral attitudes towards others and her deep character dispositions and orientations, and all of the psychic elements concerned would evince virtue in the way they viewed human beings. However, the possibility of living in such a harmonious state is problematized by Freud's exposition of the paradox.

He argues that the id is totally non-moral even though the ego strives to be moral. In order to make the ego moral when it is constantly being influenced by the id, the super-ego must be cruel. Thus the more one checks the (id-originating) aggressive and exploitative tendencies of the ego, which seeks to derive satisfaction from others at minimal cost, the more one must turn the full power of the super-ego against oneself. One is thus in the paradoxical position of being unable to be kind to oneself and to others at the same time. One must choose between internal hostility and self-hate or immoral dealings with others and the elusive harmony of moral authenticity comes to seem an unattainable ideal. Of course, we do not have introspective and conscious awareness of this deep disharmony but we do find ourselves stirred in a disturbing, irrational and uncompromising way by moral demands which arise within the self.

We can now pose a significant philosophical question about moral attitudes based in the following argument. (1) An individual's moral attitudes and behaviour arise from deep character dispositions rather than the results of explicit conscious reasoning. (2) Deep character commitments are not straightforwardly revisable in the light of reason and not readily accessible to the ego. (3) Deep character commitments plausibly originate from instincts found in Ucs. and are ingrained in the super-ego. (4) Ucs. contains psychic formations with dubious origins which are not under the control of the agent and potentiate hidden and not-so-hidden inner conflicts. (5) The psychic complex which makes up a personality cannot have anything like harmony or authenticity in its moral dealings with the world and itself and is not under rational control. (6) One is not responsible for one's own moral attitudes or actions based on them. (A conclusion which Freud denies.)

This argument seems to undermine the idea of moral authenticity prevalent in common-sense views and many Anglo-American theories of ethics. In fact Freud would go further and defend the following claim.

In as much as I act morally I act as a result of hostility against myself as a result of subconscious forces curbing my natural tendencies. I will argue that the weakness lies in the way in which premises 2, 3 and 4 are taken to license 6. In order to license the crucial move, these premises must be taken to embed the thesis that the Ucs. is an origin of psychic states which cause conscious attitudes and behaviour and that this causation works in one direction only. It is this reading that defeats the attributions of responsibility to the agent and it is here that Freud's deterministic system is vulnerable. If one could argue that, in fact, the ego or our conscious deliberative self did have a formative role on the subconscious motivations which influence our moral judgement then, despite the conflict, we would have a route whereby it is possible that the self could be brought into harmony in the service of a deliberatively endorsed set of character traits and orientations.

Freud does not deny the possibility although he considers the effects of the ego to be very limited. He gives us some *entrée* into such a line of reasoning in his discussion of the role of speech in the formation of psychic configurations in the super-ego. 'Having regard, now, to the importance we have ascribed to pre-conscious verbal residues in the ego, the question arises whether it can be the case that the super-ego in so far as it is *Ucs.*, consists in such word-presentations and, if it does not, what else it consists in. Our tentative answer will be that it is as impossible for the super-ego as for the ego to disclaim its origin from things heard; for it is a part of the ego and remains accessible to consciousness by way of these word-presentations (concepts, abstractions). But the *cathectic* energy does not reach these contents of the super-ego from auditory perception (instruction or reading) but from sources in the id' (Freud 1986: 473). Freud is here conceding that the super-ego and the psychic processes operating within it have a partial origin in the interchanges of speech and remain open to speech although the emotive or cathectic weightings and therefore, to a large extent, the motivating forces playing a crucial role in the work of the super-ego arise from the id. Freud also believes that material coming first to primitive awareness or impingement on the subject is only admitted to the domain of conscious thought and reflection after negotiating two boundaries: the first into Pcs. and the second into Cs. The second process of transition from the pre-conscious ego content into full consciousness is said to be intimately involved with speech.

'This is the work of the function of speech, which brings material in the ego into a firm connection with mnemic residues of visual, but more particularly of auditory perceptions' (Freud 1940: 46).

If, once this has begun to occur, the material is repressed then it returns to Ucs. and operates there. Such material crucially involves cathectic energy to do with the oedipal conflict and the internal identification with the father or (to broaden the case beyond the male psyche) the mother so prominent in the formation of the ego.

Before we attempt to get reason and reflection into dynamic interplay with the contents and processes in the super-ego we need two further pieces of the puzzle to be in place. The first is the recognition that words, units of speech, are not just propositional in nature. Freud himself says 'the unit of the function of speech is the "word", a complex presentation, which proves to be a combination put together from auditory, visual and kinaesthetic elements' (Freud 1986: 179).

It would be ludicrous to claim, in view of all of Freud's other writings that words did not give rise to a complex set of associations to do with feelings, images based on the context of hearing the word, the sound associations of the auditory stimulus, and all the other sensory concomitants gradually accumulated over multiple presentations of the word. Some of these would be expected to fade but others may well remain as more or less enduring associations of the word. Any given presentation of the word would therefore, depending on its psychic moment in the experience of the subject, tap into and modify this complex pattern of associations.

The second piece of the puzzle requires the concession that the consciously apprehended word may have an effect on the Ucs. through the complex pattern of associations it invokes. This is independently plausible in the light of holistic or network-based theories of word meaning but it also seems to follow from Freud's own views. However, it has the effect of rendering the flow of causal influence two way between Ucs. and Cs. and not just one way. That is the pivotal point in the present argument. Is there any reason apart from those rehearsed to suppose it to be true? I think there is.

One reason is based in the realization that consciously apprehended word meanings change the mind in non-propositional ways. Think back to the discussion of *gestalt* shifts and recall how easy it is to spoil a puzzle picture or other pattern-recognition task by telling somebody the answer or dropping a key word into the conversation: for instance, 'Think of a dalmation'. In such a case it is clear that the word does allow the mind to do something that its cognitive processes were finding difficult to achieve otherwise. Or think, for instance, about how a chance word, say, 'She is a bit precious' may work away at a less than conscious level and transform your attitude towards somebody over time. As a final example notice the way that an astute colleague, by just dropping a word into the conversational 'pot' to simmer away in your mind for a bit, might direct your mind on to the resolution of an *impasse* in your thought after you had thought that all had been said and done. In each case the conscious entertainment of a certain thought does bring about an arational and to some extent subconscious transformation in experience.

In fact Freud should welcome this suggestion because it gives us a philosophical hold on the part played in the resolution of psychic conflicts by rethinking and reinterpreting one's emotional disturbances within the process of therapy. An astute therapist might, by dropping words into the conversation which have suggestive links to common sources of conflict, allow the mind to recall, rehearse and rework tracts of psychic content which have a distorting or disturbing effect on the psyche of the person in therapy. This need not be a process of reflective or rational reconstruction based on a systematic review of content but of the sparking of new associations and the shift of cathexes which allows an inner transformation in the way that one psychically relates to the self and others.

Synthesis: the dynamic negotiation of self

Recall that we need an account of moral authenticity conceived as a thoroughgoing commitment to the things regarded as good by the agent. Such an orientation makes the moral commitments and morally relevant actions of the subject a product or expression of the total self so that there is a natural sense in which one can be said to be responsible for moral judgements and actions. Since Plato and Aristotle such a thoroughgoing psychic integrity has also been thought to involve a harmony in the soul, a belief that seemed to be threatened by Freud's account of the super-ego. Freud not only argues that the self is lacking in the kind of unity or integrity needed to attribute moral authenticity in this strong sense but also suggests that, in fact, moral excellence is concomitant with a deep-seated hostility to the self.

I now need to construct a plausible account of moral psychology which rescues our pivotal intuitions about the relationship between moral authenticity and a substantial integrity of the self secured by an interplay of reason and emotion. I have begun by arguing that discourse, as consciously entered and experienced by the subject, plausibly affects what Freud calls Ucs (a concession that Freud himself makes). But here we need to do a little further work on what we call the contents of Ucs. Cavell makes a plausible case that the contents of Ucs. and the psychology of the primary process that Freud believes to hold sway there cannot be so unambiguously given determinate psychic content as is often thought.[14] Freud constantly talks as if there were determinate thoughts, wishes, desires, attitudes and motives in Ucs. while holding that they do not obey the normal laws of propositional association and connection. But this is a deeply problematic claim. Think, for instance, of a thought that my father is an ideal figure whom I should strive to be like and who represents all that is perfect in humankind and try and hold it contemporaneously with the thought that my father is a cruel monster who is waiting to mutilate and diminish me. Freud vacillates between the idea that such thoughts and fears are chaotic and fluid, able to transform in their nature and condense and merge into one another, and the idea that they have a determinate content which explains behaviour in the style of more familiar intentional explanations. This ambiguity cries out for some kind of resolution which I think is forthcoming if we follow some of Cavell's suggestions in this area (1993: 175ff). She argues that primary process does indeed involve a primitive and ill-formed mental order which is not nearly as unambiguously articulate as ascriptions of propositional attitudes such as belief, desire and so forth might suggest. She argues that this inherently indeterminate content and somewhat more formed ideas which we are motivated not to be fully aware of form the dynamic unconscious. She also contends that the residue of childhood impressionistic ideas 'or rather unrevised childhood readings of events, together with childhood beliefs and passions, may be preserved as a motivating force in the adult mind' (1993: 176). If we combine these claims with what I shall call the *narrative integrity claim* we can get a different view of adult moral psychology.

The narrative integrity claim

A human subject is constantly revising and editing their conscious life narrative and memories of events to effect maximal narrative integrity. Cavell remarks 'Many things happen to an infant before it has thoughts in any real sense of that word; causes of all sorts have been operating on him from the beginning affecting his ways of going about things in ways we can only guess' (1993: 101). As we reach adult life, the proportion of causes acting on our psyche that we do not clearly encompass within a coherent narrative of conscious experience may get less but they never stop happening. The formation of psychic states from this material is sensitive to the conscious narrative or self-telling subjectivity of the agent, which, in itself, reflects all the unresolved conflicts in one's cumulative history. In this history the psyche has been configured under the influence of speech from parents and significant others such that certain significant words and meanings have become part of the narrative self. On this basis new information is organized and connected with what Freud calls 'mnemic residues' building layer upon layer of habits and attitudes just as one might build a city by a haphazard growth of streets, houses, and points at which human activity has carved out certain niches for itself. Just as a city takes on character, so does a personality with no uniform or rational plan to which it conforms. Freud posits that the more primitive always conforms the more recent, sophisticated, and complex. In fact, we might plausibly argue that the process goes both ways with discursive formation of the self reaching deep into the soul at certain moments and operating fairly near the surface at others.

In all this the self, at every level, is under some pressure to achieve narrative integrity, a slightly less sanitized orientation than that suggested by Smith's overall coherence constraint among one's propositional attitudes. Habits of perception, emotional response, reactive attitudes, styles of reasoning, moral intuitions, desires, beliefs and so on are invariably fixed and fluid interactions with one another under the relentless moulding influences of relationships and discourses which impinge upon one's personal trajectory. Choices change one's trajectory, and therefore the discourses one encounters, and those discourses change one's ability to conceive and make certain choices. These choices in turn yield moral judgements which influence one's trajectory and the position one takes up in the discourses that one encounters.

For any thinker who takes a broadly Aristotelian view of mind and body, all of this ongoing dynamic is faithfully tracked and variably stored in neurocognitive networks which are subject to bottom-up and top-down influences. The higher centres which are structured according to linguistic forms and the lower centres giving rise to instinctive forces interact with each other to affect behaviour and the connections configuring excitation paths. The resulting processes realize what we all encounter as the evolving psyche. The result is a subject who is truly and radically a joint production of the external and the internal, the individual and the social, and for whom neither can be given precedence. Brains exist solely to facilitate the preservation of all these influences in a way that may be used to direct and organize behaviour and the successful negotiation of the many challenges in life.

Where does this leave the concept of guilt, so prominent in Freud's theory? I think it casts guilt in the role which it has always occupied. Guilt is initially determined as a result of the cultural means used to induce conformity to the expectations of others who play a key role in the structure of values that one will inherit (Freud 1985). In the healthy adult, guilt is transformed so that it is produced by a recognition of the failure of authenticity on a particular occasion. One feels guilt when one acts in a way that does not cohere well with one's commitments and self-positioning on some issue. If we invoke the narrative integrity claim, it is a failure to do well the task one has set oneself. It might therefore be expected to be most pronounced in those who do have some clear idea of the kind of narrative integrity that is worth striving for and who do not realize that this may be unrealistic. Thus one might expect pathological guilt in those cases where the individual concerned had undertaken a task which was bound to prove too demanding or where the person lives with inner expectations that are bound to cause conflict and failure. Ultimately this person would tend to be increasingly paralysed by guilt because there is no way that the (unattainable) goal of narrative integrity in accordance with some conception of the self can be attained. Under that psychically crippling condition, all steps forward are steps toward failure. This may, of course, occur more frequently in those who are striving to identify with a father who has high attainments and is perceived to hold even higher expectations of the subject.

This production of an integrated self-narrative is ethical in the sense that it results from a series of what Foucault calls aesthetico-political choices.[15] Any person is discursively inscribed with certain response patterns which create a sense that certain things are intrisically appealing or to be accepted and these desiderata are, to a significant extent, determined by relations of power. But the effects of these relations and the multiple discourses through which they are expressed are by no means unambiguous in the tendencies they create. For instance, if we recognize the inherent conflict between the discourse of nurturing, being nurtured, feeding and valuing food on the one hand and the discourse of abstinence, thinness and female beauty on the other and that these are applied to every girl and young woman, we can immediately see how discursive forces might cause cathectic conflict. To some extent it rests with the individual subjectivity how exactly the inscriptions on the individual body will be disposed. Those inscriptions themselves potentiate discursive techniques and those techniques transform the situations in which the individual puts herself and finds herself (pun intended). The more the individual acts in accordance with the narrative integrity claim the more comfortable and competent will be the dispositions of the self. The more self is evaluated in a way that is sustainable and consistent with the evaluations applied to others, the less conflicts, guilt and prejudice would be predicted to arise. The more that occurs, the more true it will be to say of that individual that she is acting authentically or that her moral judgements and actions reflect an inner harmony or assurance. And this achievement is a product of rational (broadly speaking) or at least discursive negotiation.

We can illustrate and summarize many of the points about the subtle interplay of speech and the subconscious or emotive conditioning influences on moral judgement by borrowing the example DesAutels herself borrows from Stephen Covey.

Covey finds himself a passenger on the subway. Some children enter with their father. Covey is increasingly disturbed by the disruptive and uncontrolled behaviour of the children, finally exasperated to the point where he admonishes the father to control them. The father apologizes and, in a distracted way, as if returning from a reverie, explains that he and his children have just come from the hospital where his wife, their mother had died an hour previously.[16]

DesAutels remarks upon the *gestalt shift* which alters Covey's moral attitudes at this point. It is indeed a very good example of just the kind of thing that is intrinsic to many moral judgements and therefore serves as an excellent source of enlightenment about the interaction of rational and arational influences in moral psychology. The rationally apprehended situation engages immediately with the felt reaction and the orientation of the ego is adjusted, all without deliberation or extended reflection. Just such instances and moments of enlightenment, though not perhaps quite so dramatic as Covey's, are a familiar part of our day-by-day moral experience. There are relations between the discursively formed level of self narrative and the moral attitudes which position one's evaluations and at times these are quicksilver. At other times they are slow, a creeping displacement or takeover of an initial response by some contradictory or undermining thought. The mind uses moments of experience and the slow insistence of a word or a meaning to transform the self and introduce greater subtlety and fluid coherence into one's narrative. Contra Freud, this is neither chaotic nor totally driven by forces which the cultured self would want to disown. In the best of lives moral authenticity and the discursive creation of self does not result in any monolithic and maximally rational set of moral intuitions, reactions and attitudes but is properly sensitive to all the ills to which flesh is prone and does justice to what a sensitive appreciation of life reveals as being of worth. Being true to that kind of dynamic (and slightly messy) self-narrative, it seems to me, is what moral authenticity is all about.

Notes

1 Tobin (1989).
2 Nagel (1986).
3 Smith (1994).
4 Davidson (1980).
5 Smith (1994: 181).
6 Kant (1997: 62ff).
7 Williams (1985).
8 Gillett (1994).
9 Nussbaum (1990).
10 DesAutels (1996).
11 Gilligan (1982).
12 Freud (1940, 1986).
13 Urmson (1994).
14 Cavell (1993: 167).
15 Foucault (1984: 354ff).
16 DesAutels (1996: 130).

References

Cavell, M. (1993) *The Psychoanalytic Mind*, Cambridge, MA: Harvard University Press.
Covey, S. (1989) *The Seven Habits of Highly Effective People: Restoring the Character Ethic*, New York: Simon and Schuster.
Davidson, D. (1980) *Essays on Actions and Events*, Oxford: Clarendon Press.
DesAutels, P. (1996) 'Gestalt Shifts in Moral Perception', in L. May, M. Friedman and A. Clark (eds), *Minds and Morals*, Cambridge, MA: MIT Press.
Foucault, M. (1984) *The Foucault Reader*, P. Rabinow (ed.), Harmondsworth: Penguin.
Freud, S. (1940) 'An Outline of Psychoanalysis', *International Journal of Psycho-Analysis*, 21: 27–84.
—— (1985) 'Civilization and its Discontents', in *Civilization Society and Religion* (The Penguin Freud Library, vol. 12), London: Penguin.
—— (1986) *The Essentials of Psychoanalysis* (ed. A. Freud), London: Penguin.
Fulford, K.W.M., Gillett, G.R. and Martin-Soskice, J. (eds) (1994) *Medicine and Moral Reasoning*, Cambridge: Cambridge, University Press.
Gillett, G. (1994) 'Women and Children First', in K.W.M. Fulford, G.R. Gillett and J. Martin-Soskice (eds), *Medicine and Moral Reasoning*, Cambridge: Cambridge University Press.
Gilligan, C. (1982) *In a Different Voice*, Cambridge, MA: Harvard University Press.
Kant, I. (1997) *Critique of Practical Reason*, ed. M. Gregor, Cambridge: Cambridge University Press.
May, L., Friedman, M. and Clark, A. (1996) *Mind and Morals*, Cambridge, MA: MIT Press.
Nagel, T. (1986) *The View from Nowhere*, New York: Oxford University Press.

Nussbaum, M. (1990) *Love's Knowledge*, Oxford: Oxford University Press.

Smith, M. (1994) *The Moral Problem*, Oxford: Blackwell.

Tobin, B.M. (1989) 'An Aristotelian Theory of Moral Development', *Journal of Philosophy of Education*, 23(2): 195–211.

Urmson, J. (1994) 'Morality: Invention or Discovery', in W.K.M. Fulford, G.R. Gillett and J. Martin-Soskice (eds), *Medicine and Moral Reasoning*, Cambridge: Cambridge University Press.

Williams, B. (1985) *Ethics and the Limits of Philosophy*, London: Collins.

Part III

SEXUALITY

10

FREUD ON UNCONSCIOUS AFFECTS, MOURNING AND THE EROTIC MIND

Amélie Oksenberg Rorty

'It is surely of the essence of an emotion that we should feel it, that is, that it should enter consciousness . . . For . . . feelings, and affects to be unconscious would be out of the question.'[1] As coming from Freud, the view that there are no unconscious affects is astonishing. After all, according to popular understanding, it is Freud who – if anyone – has insisted that a person can love or hate without recognizing his condition. 'It may happen that an affect or emotion is perceived but misconstrued. By repression of its proper presentation (i.e., its ideational content), it is forced to become connected with another idea . . . Its ideational presentation undergoes repression.'[2] Certainly Freud's case studies present the best evidence for the persistent and canny substitution of one presentation for another, cases where someone is ignorant, and perhaps even systematically, willfully ignorant, of the true objects of his affects. In some cases one object is substituted for another: the clerk's (forbidden) hatred of his father is expressed by his hating his boss. There also appear to be cases where one affect is substituted for another: sons who hate the father whom they believe they love, fathers whose fear for their daughters' safety are a transposition of their own sexual attachments, colleagues who harbour murderous hatred for one another under the surface of elaborate respect or jovial banter. Even in his analysis of non-pathological cases, in the account of the aetiology and specificity of adult love – its origins in the family drama that characteristically fix the objects of love – Freud appears to allow that we can be persistently and systematically ignorant of our affects. What, then, could he mean by denying that there are unconscious affects? Is it a defensible claim within his system? Is it a defensible claim independently of that system?

Although Freud would consider most psychological states that are normally classified as emotions to be affects, his notion of *Affekt* is both broader and narrower than the folk-psychological notion of emotion. It is broader in that it includes conditions which, like irritation, surliness, and excitation, are feelings and sensations that need not have characteristic proper objects. It is narrower in that some basic psychological conditions standardly considered emotions in folk psychology – love, for instance – are, on Freud's classification, sometimes direct manifestations of instinctual drives and sometimes by-products of the frustration of those drives. When love is the direct expression of libidinal energy, it need not be experienced as an affect; if it is felt, or is accompanied by feelings, those felt libidinal energies would be physiologically and phenomenologically distinguish-able from the longing feeling associated with the affect of love.[3] Freud sometimes treats an affect as an independent, self-contained psychological event with a specific sort of aetiology and function in releasing or expressing blocked libidinal energy. But sometimes he treats it as essentially and identificationally conjoined with an idea: an affect is then the felt qualia of the idea, the 'charge' of the idea a dynamic force with a functional role that can be phenomenologically experienced.

Sometimes several problems are better than one: by rubbing them together, one can generate a bit of light. Freud's surprising doctrine on unconscious affects becomes somewhat less puzzling if we put it together with three other surprising views. I want first to try to make sense of the claim that there are no unconscious affects, relating this view to Freud's discussion of the phenomena of identificational mourning. With a fuller account of the Freudian canon of explanation in hand, we can understand Freud's concerns about whether affect-laden memories of childhood seduction are fantasized or real. Finally, we should be in a better position to reconsider whether the presumed submergence of affect during the 'latency' period is self-deceptive.

1

Freud's chronicles of the unacknowledged rage of a son against his father, a daughter's denial of her jealousy of her mother, chronicles of (what appear to be) self-deceptive – or at the very least systematically misunderstood – affects, do not, on his understanding of the matter, constitute examples of unconscious affects. Although these psychological conditions are often misdiagnosed, although someone can often be mistaken about the true target or object of her feelings, and can even substitute one feeling for another, she experiences her condition affectively. To understand Freud's distinction between an affect, its object, its aim and its function, we need, alas, to sketch one of the mainsprings of classical Freudian theory: the theory of drives. It is an almost ludicrously simple theory, resting on an almost breathtakingly simple image that provides the model – a sometimes Procrustean model – of endogenous action.

Behaviour has its origin in – sometimes Freud speaks of it as a manifestation of – a set of drives. The most basic, most general drive is that of organic survival: it is expressed in a host of more specific drives, for food, for bodily maintenance, and for protection. Each of these generates and sometimes is expressed in yet more specific, intentionally individuated and identified motivating forces. Although drives have proper satisfactions and proper objects, they are the most general and plastic energetic origins of action. Their energies can be directed and redirected,

196

and the objects that satisfy them are substitutable and fungible. The drive for nourishment has food as its natural object, eating as its natural expression, and digesting as its natural satisfaction. But even in this basic, simple process, satisfying the original drive allows latitude for substitution: synthesized chemicals can serve as food; intravenous feeding can bypass the usual forms of eating and digesting. Indeed drives are sufficiently general and plastic to allow even contrary realizations and expressions ('The Antithetical Sense of Primal Terms', *S.E.* 11: 153). Hunger can manifest itself not only by imagining elaborate feasts but also by elaborate rituals of refusing food. In themselves, drives are blind. They do not carry their own interpretations: a person need not be consciously aware of their aim or objects. All behaviour – even such a mechanical, physically caused behaviour as hiccuping – can be given intentional significance by an agent. A person can treat such behaviour *as if* it were voluntary, and thus elicit defensive reactions against forbidden behaviour and thoughts.[4] Although actions are identified by their intentional descriptions, and the same piece of behaviour can, under different intentional descriptions, designate distinctive actions, at least some actions have standard or fundamental normative intentional descriptions.

The prolonged, physically and psychologically vulnerable dependence of infancy produces acute psychological problems whose resolutions require, and are expressed in, a vast range of symbolic activities and attitudes. An infant's dependence on those who feed and nurture it generates problems – and images – that centre around ingestion and incorporation. The problems of nourishment are followed by those of muscular control, expressed in the struggles for physical and psychological power and mastery.[5] Each of these sets of problems is double-faced: the organism is itself affected not only by the objects with which it interacts but also by its own activity in interaction. Not only the food digested but the processes of digesting affect the organism. This double-faced character of the expression of drives makes activity and passivity coordinate: every event experienced as a passive response can also be experienced as an outcome and expression of the organism's own activity. This Spinozistic inheritance has obvious consequences for Freud's theory of affects: when the natural expression of a drive is blocked, the body undergoes a set of physiological modifications that are experienced as affects, that is, as a set of distinctive sensations. For Freud, as for Spinoza, an affective reaction can be transformed into an active expression of an endogenous drive when the person's intentional description of her behaviour connects it to her libidinal energy. In any case, the consequences of organic interaction with the environment do not remain localized at the point of interaction: every modification is the 'active cause' of changes that are individuated by their aetiology.

These elaborations are consequences of Freud's attempts to combine a mechanistic model with an organic one: his psychodynamic theory borrows heavily from, and attempts to unify, Aristotle's psychology with Hobbes's mechanism. He wants to combine the advantages of Hobbes's functionalist identification of psychological states with an Aristotelian intentionalist identification of actions. He adopts and develops Aristotle's view that genetically and socially determined psychophysical development – the acquisition of habits of action and of mind – affects the intentionality of actions and interactions. He adopts and develops Hobbes's mechanistic account of motivational energy as a quantum of force with direction and momentum. Following the mechanistic picture, Freud characterizes an organism as a homeostatic system functionally organized to preserve its quantum and balance of energy. The system is constructed in such a way that it discharges the excess energy produced by invading stimuli. Because psychic energy is neither created nor destroyed, substitute channels are found when direct reactions to stimuli are blocked.

On this model, the energetic force of psychological states is distinguishable from their ideational contents. Identifying actions that have been determined by vectorial resolutions of forces does not require reference to their intentionally described energetic origins. Part of our problem in interpreting Freud's claim that there are no unconscious affects is the problem of reconciling an Aristotelian intentionalist with a Hobbesian extensionalist identification of psychological activities – the problem of giving an account of the relation between the intentional object of a psychological state and its functional role.

Identifying psychological states requires four parameters or variables:

(a) the impetus – the amount of energy;
(b) the aim – the character of the satisfaction involved;
(c) the object intentionally described;
(d) the source.

('Instincts and their Vicissitudes', *S.E.* 14: 126)

Because these identifying factors are independent of one another, transformations can occur in one without affecting the others. So, for instance, the object of a psychological state can be replaced by a symbolic substitute without affecting the impetus; and the impetus can be reconstructed – reapportioned within the psychological field – without affecting the aim. Much of the Freudian canon of explanation consists in the set of rules governing the transformation and substitution of libidinal energy: the strategies of drive satisfaction. For our purposes, the significant rules can be characterized as rules for the transformation of energy and rules for the translation of ideational content. The rules for the transformation of energy are formally elegant, involving simple spatial redirections. The direction of the energy can be internalized or externalized; its charge can be changed from positive to negative; the relation can be active or passive ('Instincts and their Vicissitudes', *S.E.* 14: 126). The rules for the translation of ideational or intentional content are much more complex: they permit idiosyncratic symbolization from sources lying in an individual's psychological history, as well as in standard cultural allusions.

The energetic force of a drive remains constant until it is expressed or discharged. It is directly discharged when it is expressed in the sort of behaviour that characteristically brings the satisfaction that is its instinctual aim. When the direct expression of a drive is blocked, its redirections will have an affective charge, no matter what form they take. Dreams, fantasies, symbolic ritual acts, or sublimated activities – indirect expressions of a blocked drive – carry an affective charge that releases the original energy. And it is *that* – the affective charge – which can't be unconscious. Affects just are the by-products, the effects of blocked or frustrated drives. They are a kind of psychophysical explosion, a feeling that expresses and releases the energies of the pent-up drive.

> An affect . . . represents that part of the instinct which has become detached from the idea . . . [It] corresponds with processes of discharge the final expression of which is perceived as feeling . . . Affectivity manifests itself essentially in motor (i.e. secretory and circulatory) discharge resulting in an (internal) alteration of the subject's own body without reference to the outer world.
>
> ('Repression', *S.E.* 14: 91, 111)

It is precisely their being felt and experienced that releases the force of the drive, and that identifies the psychological condition as an affect.

We are now in a better position to see why Freud thinks that his examples of unacknowledged hatreds, displaced loves and transformed angers are compatible with his insistence that there are no unconscious affects. The *affect* – the feeling – is (virtually by definition) consciously experienced as such. But all the surrounding material – the original drive, the object, the direction, even the tonal quality as positive or negative, active or passive, projected or introjected – can be transformed, displaced, or substituted to fit the rest of the person's psychological condition: to avoid what is forbidden, to follow habitual, encoded symbolization, and so on. It is about all of this surrounding material, rather than about the presence or absence of the affect, that a person can be self-deceived. 'The ideational material has undergone displacements and substitutions, whereas the affects have remained unaltered' (*The Interpretation of Dreams, S.E.* 4–5: 461).

Sometimes Freud speaks of affects as distinctive, non-intentional psychological states, those which succeed in discharging the energy of blocked drive in a specific way: by felt somatic modifications that have no reference to the outer world. But sometimes he says that all indirect expressions of frustrated drive – even those which, like dreams, fantasies and ritual actions, are essentially attached to an ideational content – carry an affective discharge. But what distinguishes a direct from an indirect release of a drive, particularly if drives are plastic and fungibly satisfiable? What differentiates the redirected or sublimated satisfaction of a drive from an indirect expression of its frustration? Why introduce affects as special events at all? How do they differ from other forms of release? Why wouldn't fantasies, dreams and redirected activity be sufficient to release the energy of a drive? And why can't someone be mistaken about whether she is in an affective condition?

As long as someone can deny the translation or symbolization of an ideational content or deny that an energetic drive has been transformed, then affects

– individuated by their ideational content – can be as unconscious as anything else. The affect is then not identifiable independently of the ideational content to which it attaches, any more than the ideational content is fully identifiable independently of its aetiology. This is the solution that follows the Aristotelian intentionalist strand in Freud's thought. But following the mechanistic, functionalist Hobbesian line – a line that Freud considers necessary for the possibility of the redirection and transformation of psychic energy – requires him to separate the energy of a psychological state from its ideational content. And it is this, the mechanistic rather than the organicist version of his theory of drives, that leads him to insist on the impossibility of unconscious affects.

There is a set of related problems: if the affect just is the experience of discharged energy that has been blocked, then there can be no question of its appropriateness to its object or even to its cause. It is not even clear how qualitative distinctions among affects are identified. To the extent that affects just are 'motor discharges', they can be distinguished from one another only by the non-intentional sensations associated with their various physiological conditions. 'The release of affects as a centrifugal process directed towards the interior of the body and analogous to the processes of motor and secretory innervation' only allows a non-intentional criterion for the differentiation of affects (*The Interpretation of Dreams*, S.E. 4–5: 467–8). But if affects are only identifiable and distinguishable by physically based, non-intentional sensations, then an affect cannot be used to recover a repressed idea. When Freud speaks of the inappropriateness of an affect, or of the singular absence of an appropriate affect, however, he clearly envisages a closer connection between its energy and its content. ('If the affect and the idea are incompatible in their character and intensity, one's waking judgement is at a loss' [*The Interpretation of Dreams*, S.E. 4–5: 459–61]. Indeed only if there is a proper connection between an affect and its idea is there a reason to repress or displace the idea, to replace the real with a manifest content. And only if there is a proper connection can an affect be used to 'give us a pointer as to how we can find the missing (i.e., the censored or repressed) thoughts . . . The affect [helps us] seek out the idea which belongs to it but which has been repressed and replaced by a substitute' [ibid.].) At least in *The Interpretation of Dreams*, Freud means to make the close connection between an affect and its ideational content a pivotal diagnostic and therapeutic tool. Because the affect remains the same when the idea is changed, it can be used to recover the original idea; when the idea is again connected to its original affect, some affective disorder can be corrected. Nowhere is Freud's struggle between the mechanistic-associationistic and the cognitive-intentional views sharper than in the tension arising out of his attempts to explain how an affect that has become detached from an idea can be used to recover the repressed idea.[6]

2

Before the situation improves, it must get worse. It might seem that either every psychological state is affective (because it involves the transformation and redirection of blocked drives) or there are no purely affective states (because drives are always somehow expressed). If every case of successfully redirected energy that requires patterned ignorance and misdescription involves the suppression of material that is also implicitly recognized, then self-deception lurks virtually everywhere. Or self-deception is nowhere, because the mechanisms that explain denial, or repression, or the censorship of unconscious material do not represent the activities of *the self*. There is no such single entity. If on one hand 'the self' is a complex whole, composed of more or less integrated subsystems, it does not, *as that whole*, deceive itself: one subsystem systematically misleads others. If on the other hand the 'self' is the well-developed ego, then there is no self-deception, because the ego is the subsystem that attempts to integrate all others. If affects are just the non-intentional sensations consciously experienced as the result of blocked drives, then self-deception could only consist in an attempt at verbal denial – a denial manifestly invalidated by the rest of the person's behaviour. But if affects are also identified by their ideational content, then self-deception can only involve systematic misdescription or misidentification of the object of the affect.

Freud's discussion of mourning – and his puzzling failure to connect two sorts of identificational imitation – provides an illuminating example of his indecision about how to resolve the problems that emerge from his views on unconscious affects. In discussing the connection between mourning and identification, Freud observes that the mourner often takes on the *persona* – the habits and gestures, intonation patterns and sometimes attitudes – of the person she has lost. He speculates that this identification attempts to recreate the lost object.[7]

Though it is basic to the explanatory canon, the term 'identity' is rarely characterized with any precision: it is vaguely used to cover a wide range of senses. Freud's use of the term can be reconstructed, in such a way as to give us some understanding of what it is for a set of traits, ideals and habits to be central to a person's identity. What Freud treats as structure can be interpreted in dynamic and defensive terms. A trait, object relation, attitude or belief, concern, or ideal is central to a person's *identity* when it is essential to her survival as the sort of person she is. The preservation and expression of that trait (attitude, concern, object relation, ideal) is motivationally central: a threat to it directly mobilizes the strategies of defensive manoeuvres exercised in self-preservation, without requiring any other pleasure-bound, pain-avoiding motivation. Exercising, enhancing, defending, promoting and expressing those traits (etc.) is constitutively and directly motivating independently of any other satisfactions or ends. As it stands, this rough characterization allows that someone might be mistaken about what is essential or central to her identity, either falsely believing that a trait (etc.) is central when it is not, or falsely believing that a trait (etc.) is not central when it is. At least some traits essential to a person's identity can be extensionally identified; sometimes that identification can significantly differ from the person's own conception of what is essential to her identity, even when the behavioural expression of the two are the same. Yet understanding the systematic pattern of a person's actions and thoughts requires not only understanding what is effectively identificational (in the sense sketched above) but also her conception of what is essential to her, including active ideals that she tries, but fails, to realize.[8]

Freud does not draw the obvious consequence of his theory: the hidden proper object of mourning is the self that has been diminished or transformed by the loss. The reason he does not draw this consequence is that when mourning is expressed as an affect, it does not have a proper object. The energy released at the frustration or blockage of a drive bears no representational relation to the objects or aims of the original drive; nor does it represent the causes of its repression. Freud does not face the problem of why those forms of mourning that recreate, internalize and act out the life of the lost object are not experienced or felt as affects. On the one hand, such mourning is surely fused with felt grief. On the other hand, it might seem as if identificational mourning does not conform to the conditions of affectivity: it is externally and representationally rather than internally directed. In that case the fact that the mourner can be systematically unaware of reproducing the lost object, and can even deny the loss, does not disconfirm Freud's claim that there are no unconscious affects. When mourning is expressed by assuming and acting out a lost identity, it is not expressed as an affect. Perhaps Freud can have it both ways: the two forms of mourning – the affective and the behavioural – might be psychologically fused while being analytically distinguishable.

Still there is a problem. Identifying with the lost object, the mourner defends herself by recreating and imitating what has been lost. What was necessary or essential to her identity is magically preserved. This defence must be disguised to be successful, particularly in that, all along, the real but obscure object of mourning is the dear self, whose identity has been threatened by the loss. Following this line of thought would lead Freud to preserve the strong connection between an affect and its object: for it is precisely by imitating and preserving the lost object that damage to the self is avoided. *For this process to work successfully, the person must be systematically unaware of what she is doing*. For if she were fully conscious of the fiction, she would not succeed in defending herself against the threat to her identity. Presumably Freud would have to argue that insofar as mourning is behavioural, it can be unconscious or self-deceptive; but insofar as it is affective, it cannot be.

The labyrinthine intricacy of Freud's view appears even more dramatically when, after the first account of the phenomena of mourning, he remarks that the mourner's attempt to incorporate the lost object is very similar to the sort of identification and imitation that newly married women make: they often acquire and imitate their husbands traits, opinions and gestures (*Mourning and Melancholia, S.E.* 14). He notes, without developing the matter, that there appears to be an asymmetry in the acquisition of traits when couples live together. The woman tends to identify with and imitate the man; rarely does the man take on the traits of the woman. Surprisingly, Freud simply mentions this as yet another form of identification, without exploring the possibility that far from being an independent phenomenon, this type of imitative identification is an instance of self-deceptive mourning.[9] Why does Freud conjoin the two phenomena without connecting them and without elaborating or explaining his observation? Why did he introduce this phenomenon of wifely imitation in the middle of a discussion of the identificational processes that take place in mourning?

In the course of describing and analysing this process of identificational mourning, Freud remarks that the choice of a sexual object appears not only to influence the development of the ego of women, but also to affect their character, that is, their identity. There seems, he says, to be an intrusive relation between identification and object-choice. Women tend to imitate and identify with the objects of their attachments even when the cathexis is anaclitic and not particularly loving.

Of course there may be many other explanations for this imitative identification. Characteristically, the woman is socially and economically dependent on her husband. Especially when there is a marked difference in age, the wife is often formed by her husband (cf. Freud's educative letters to his fiancée) and formed for him (cf. Rousseau's highly influential *Emile*). Without being aware of doing so, the woman may well be placating or complying with or wooing (those whom they experience as) their superiors. But because there is good reason to think that there is overdetermination in this area, I want to explore the possibility that such imitative identification is mourning, with the affect submerged or denied. Our question will then be: is the woman self-deceived when she is unaware of, and would deny, her mourning?

Freud believes that we acquire our conceptions and expectations of love from our early experiences: the particular tonal character of parental nurturing serves as the paradigmatic model for all that we later consider to be affectional bonding. Characteristically, the kind of love that newly coupled men receive from their women tends to include the sort of attentive nurturing they received from their mothers.[10] Standardly, men are fed and preened by wives who follow maternal patterns down to the details of attending to clothing. But unless they are narcissistic types, women rarely receive this sort of attention, even when they are well loved. Standardly and conventionally, a man's ardour is greater before sexual partnership is established, while a woman's affections are more strongly bonded afterward. On Freud's account, this difference is a function of the differences between male and female genital development: male genital drives are physically developed in adolescence, while female sexuality only matures with experience. Once the couple are established sexual partners, the man not only receives sexual satisfaction: he also reliably receives the kind of nurturing care on which he comes to depend, and which he associates with love. As long as he receives both kinds of attention, he need not experience any affect of love or longing.

But the woman's story is somewhat different. Although in the best cases, her awakened genital drives are satisfied, her need for nurturance is not. Even though the man provides for her financially, he does not actually tend or attend to her as he did during their courtship. But since the woman also formed her conceptions and expectations of loving bonding from parental nurturing, she experiences her husband's bonding as incomplete. She has lost the man who courted her. This is why many women are puzzled by what seems to them as their husbands' withdrawal, while men are puzzled by what seems to them to be their wives' excessively clinging emotionality. The men cannot understand why their women fail to recognize that love is thoroughly expressed in action and in sexuality, in satisfaction rather than in longing. Freud provides the materials for explaining the phenomena. To the extent that some of her needs for nurturance – needs she associated with physical bonding – are frustrated, the newly married woman experiences longing love as a mode of mourning. To the extent that her sense of herself has been bound up with her husband, her identity is threatened by what she experiences as a loss. She often tries to woo her husband back by what is usually counter-productive clinging – the sort of clinging a child evinces when it experiences the withdrawal of a parent – or, like other mourners, she attempts to identify with, and to recreate, the suitor she has lost. The more helpless she is to express that love effectively, the more powerfully felt it becomes.

If the newly wed wife is mourning, she is usually either systematically unaware of, or self-deceived about, the true nature of her affective condition. She may well have reason to deny that her diffuse longing and its accompanying identificational imitation are varieties of mourning, deflections of her sense of diminished identity. If she finds that her continued expressions of melancholic love distance her husband, she may repress the feeling as well as the expression. Yet her imitative identificational behaviour may express mourning, as well as the acknowledgement of power. If there are such cases of repression, Freud's denial of unconscious affects must, at the very least, be hedged.

3

Freud's difficult vacillation over the theory of childhood seduction – the problem whether adult reports of childhood seductions are bona fide memories on whether they are fantasies – also provides an argument that Freud should accept rather than reject the existence of unconscious affects.

Setting aside those cases of actual physical seduction, does it follow that all other cases of reported childhood seduction are phantasies based on wish, subjected to the usual set of projective transformations? No; I believe it does not follow. The very large area that combines reality, interpretation and phantasy provides ample documentation of self-deceptive or unconscious affects.

This, I believe, is a naturalistic story about parent–child seductive interaction. In the course of giving their children physical and nurturing care – bathing them, combing their hair, dressing them and so on – parents often come to form an erotic attachment to their children. Finding them delectable, seductive, they may often have erotic phantasies and wishes of which they are only marginally aware. They might simply wish to extend and prolong their caresses and in an obscure way want to arouse the child to return caresses. Though such wishes and phantasies would normally be suppressed and not overtly enacted, still the parent's arousal may be sufficient to change her or his expression and gestures in a subtle but observable way. An intent that is not expressed in overt action can nevertheless be observably manifest to a sensitive child. A child might not only notice but respond to such subtle changes in the features of an erotically aroused adult. The child would of course not understand the latent intent, because it would have no way of assimilating this to other experiences. The event would present something unknown and frightening, both because it is unknown and because it carries an unassimilable, responding, excited charge. Particularly because the subtle traces of erotic arousal sometimes can superficially resemble the subtle traces of repressed anger, the child might find the undigested, uninterpreted, unacknowledged experiences difficult and unresolvable. Frequently repeated, sometimes highly charged, such experiences might be strong enough to produce anxiety requiring working out in dreams and fantasies whose own internal psychological momentum might magnify it.

Once the child acquires the categories and concepts of sexual life, new explanations can retrospectively be applied to the unabsorbed eroticized experience. The stories of childhood seduction can sometimes fall in that important area between phantasy and reality: the child has correctly recognized the latent and submerged content of an interaction, and has done so at a time when it cannot mark the all-important distinction between an intention that is overtly expressed in behaviour and one that is psychologically real but behaviourally sublimated or repressed. Since the distinctions between mood, intention and action are learned only gradually, and are indeed always being reinterpreted, it is not surprising that the child confuses a real tonality with a realized action. In the absence of any correcting experience, the adult continues the child's confusion, reporting something that falls between memory and phantasy.

What has this to do with unconscious affects? It suggests, though of course it does not prove, that an adult who has reworked such erotically charged experience is recounting and reporting affectively charged memories that can, but need not be, experienced affectively. Sometimes, indeed, it can be just the very deadpan *absence* of affect in situations that, presumptively, are strongly affect-laden that reveals the person's psychological struggles. If it is genuinely possible to report and behaviourally manifest the absence of affect in situations that appear in every respect to conform to the model of blocked – affectively redirected – energies, it would seem that a person could be self-deceived about whether she is affected, as well as about *what* affects her.

4

Yet again, things must get worse before they get better. Before trying to resolve Freud's problems about unconscious affects, let us see what the mystery of latency can contribute to the story.

The apparent blankness of the latency period presents a puzzling lacuna in Freud's account of the psychodynamics of development. Why should there be such a long dormant period at a time of important physical and intellectual change? Following the general dictum that all psychophysical and intellectual changes are psychosexually significant, it seems implausible that this period should be developmentally blank, centred primarily on consolidation. As Anna Freud was later to suggest in her account of intellectual development, thought processes can become affectively charged to express and release psychodynamic conflicts. A child's success in developing a powerful, affective and richly subtle intellectual and imaginative life depends on her being systematically unaware of the psycho-sexual functions of those processes, of the ways her thought expresses and releases psychodynamic conflicts. But systematic ignorance – patterned repressive discrimination of attention – requires scanning for forbidden material, which involves implicit admission of its import. The success of sublimated activity appears to depend on denials and repressions of affect that are suspiciously like self-deception. And if the intellectualization of libidinal processes and conflicts is not affectively experienced, then not only ideas but also affects themselves can be unconscious.

The latency stage occurs between the end of the anal stage and the beginning of the genital stage, after habits of psychophysical self-control and mastery have been developed and consolidated. The activities of the oral stage – introjection and projection, absorption and rejection – have been integrated and expanded on to a larger somatic and psychological field. Before puberty focuses on the issues of genitality, a person's central psychological work consists in developing charac-teristic intellectual patterns of thought, imagination and phantasy: it is the period for the formation of psycho-intellectual strategies for elaborating, transforming and gratifying instinctual processes. The metaphors central to the earlier stages remain: seeing is a way of absorbing and introjecting the world, imagining is a way of mastering and controlling it, speaking and writing are expressions, expulsions, explosions. The eye and the mind become eroticized during the latency stage. What we cannot have, we can imagine. What we cannot destroy, we can deconstruct. It is the stage for the development of thought at the service of defence. But it is also the stage in which thought, imagination and phantasy come to be sources of – and not merely avenues for – independent autoerotic satisfaction. The child develops habits of categorization and association, characteristic narratives of symbolic thought and action, patterns of substitute gratification. Rituals of play and games form expectations of roles and attitudes: life is seen as combat, adventure, or exploration; one's role is that of leader, follower, or observer; the world affords opportunities or frustrations: events unfold with fateful necessity or largely by accident and chance; other players are comrades or kinfolk, mysterious strangers, allies, enemies, superiors or inferiors, primarily men or primarily women, or indifferently men or women. Communication is largely verbal or non-verbal, direct or symbolic; the tone is playful, devious. ironic, or serious. The primary strategies of defence are intellectual or physical, political or aesthetic. (Of course these alternatives are meant to be suggestive rather than exclusive or exhaustive.)

Why didn't Freud recognize the eroticization of the eye and the mind, of language and modes of communication? Of course in one sense it was he who introduced this idea: thought is a means toward, and eventually itself becomes, a form of

206

gratification: the redirection and satisfaction of instinctual drives. Phantasy and the imagination originally provide substitute gratification; but when they have become eroticized, they provide direct as well as substitute satisfaction. When Freud discusses the eroticization of thought, he dampens the distinction between the energy of a psychological state and its content ('Instincts and their Vicissitudes', *S.E.* 14). But even though his analyses of scoptophobic and linguistic disorders amply document the eroticization of the eye, language and the imagination, his commitment to one version of the Hobbesian mechanistic model prevents his accepting the consequences of his insight. While Freud gives an account of general somatic eroticization, the erogenous zones include the mouth, the anus and the genitals, but not – except in pathological cases – the eyes and ears. Freud's continued commitment to the mechanization of the biological model – the buildup and release of energetic charges – explains his surprising failure to connect his theory of the development of erotically charged intellectual processes with his theory of the role of erogenous zones in psychodynamic development.

With considerable strain and some Procrustean cutting, Freud can interpret his theory of the activities of mouth, anus and genitals within his mechanistic model: the mouth devours and spits, the anus constricts or defecates, and genital tension mounts and is orgastically released. Here the problems of theory become dramatic: what are the criteria for *release*? Do eating and defecating really conform to the excitation-and-release model? Each seems to involve a different model of release. In any case, however wide the latitude of the mechanistic model of excitation, accumulation, tension and release, the eroticized eyes, ears and mind do not follow it.

We might try to combine the two strands of Freud's theory by distinguishing the phenomenological from the ontological enterprise.[11] The separation of an affect from its ideational content, required by the Hobbesian approach, is introspective and phenomenological; the connection between the two, required on the Aristotelian view, is ontological and conceptual. This would be a pretty solution if it were true. But does an introspective-phenomenological account really reveal the separability of an affect and its content? The phenomenological feel of affects seems content-bound and variable with the details of the individuation of their objects: someone's affective feelings toward (just this) newborn child are radically different from his affective feelings toward that child when she is six, or ten, or twenty. And these are different from his affective feelings toward his brother's children at six, ten, and twenty. And these again are different from the affective feelings one has toward the children of one's friends. Introspectively, affective feelings are protean indeed: but protean because they are bound up with, rather than disconnected from, their ideational content, which itself varies with the psychodynamic role played by that ideational content.

We can distinguish affect types (rage, love, or fear, for example) from individuated ideas-and-affects identified by their aetiology and functional roles (for instance, a child's particular fear of a particular church spire on a particular occasion). The former permit the substitution of objects and allow for functionally equivalent replacements (hate for love, gratitude for envy); the latter do not. Even though an affect type is characterized by associated typical intentional objects (sibling jealousy, for instance), it can be detached from its particular objects (brothers, sisters). The minuet graces of transformations (the change of charge from positive to negative, from active to passive, from projective to introjective) and the rich thesaurus of translations of objects (the substitutions of sons for brothers, kings for fathers, gloves for mothers, church spires for kings) all take place on the level of affect types. Only on that level is it possible to reidentify 'the same' affect under its transformations and 'the same' content under its translations. But individuated affects are radically transformed by every transformation: someone's horror of a particular church spire just is different from his horror of his maternal uncle's beard at a particular time, under particular circumstances. This is not important news: it is a trivial consequence of the discernibility of distinct individuals.

Freud can retain the advantages of the physiologically orientated mechanistic model – the advantages of accounting for the redirection of energy from one content to another – with the advantages of the cognitive model according to which individual psychological states (and the behaviour and actions that express them) are intentionally identified. The mechanistic model applies at a general level, the level of typical description: at that level, ideational contents of psychological states are substitutable; indeed it is sometimes just their substitutability that allows them to play their appropriate functional roles. Sometimes psychological states themselves – and not merely their ideational contents – are functionally substitutable. So, for some (but not for all) purposes hate can play the same functional role as love, love the same role as envy. The stringency of conditions for the reidentification of a psychological state varies with the level of detail at which its functional role is described. So, for some purposes, an affect can be identified by its generalized functional role: for this purpose, hate need not be distinguished from love. But for other purposes – purposes that require a more detailed and individuated description of functional roles – the two affects are distinguished. *When the functional role that a psychological state plays essentially requires its having a specific intentional content, then the affective charge of the state cannot be separated from its ideational content. When the functional role of a psychological state can be played without any particular intentional content (and perhaps even without any particular type of intentional content) then it can be identified independently of that intentional content.* Because the criteria for reidentification need not reduce to the criteria for individuation, a psychological state can be identified at different levels of generality for different explanatory purposes. So, for some explanatory purposes, it can be separated from the particular intentional contents that individuate it, and for others not.

When affects are identified independently of their intentional contents – when they are identified by their functional roles most generally characterized – they cannot be unconscious. They cannot be unconscious because at that level of generality, there is nothing to them but their affective feel: no affective feel, no affect. At *that* level of generality, affects are not individuated, not even as affect types: characterized so generally, the functional role of hate is not distinguished from that of love. But when affects are identified by their intentional contents, a person can be as self-deceived about her affect as she can be about its intentional content. If the content is translated or substituted, so can the affect be; if the content is repressed, so can the affect be. One of the attractions of this solution is that it gives us a way of saying that at one level of description – as playing a generalized functional role – an affect cannot be unconscious, but at another level of description, it can be. Is it the same affect which, at one level of generality, is unconscious, and at another level, is not? The answer depends upon the generality of the question. At a general level of reidentification – one which allows the substitution of intentions *salve functione* – 'the same affect' can, under one description, be unconscious, and on another, not. But, strictly speaking, affects individuated by their intentions cannot be both conscious and unconscious.

Acknowledgements

Ronald De Sousa, Lawrence Friedman, Brian McLaughlin and Ruth Nevo contributed useful comments on this essay. An earlier and shorter version of the essay appeared in *Hebrew University Studies in Literature and the Arts*, vol. 14, no. 1, ed. R. Nevo and L. Besserman, under the title 'Mixing Memory and Desire: Freud on Unconscious Mourning'. Another version appeared under the pseudonym of Leila Tov-Ruach, 'Freud on Unconscious Affects, Mourning and the Erotic Mind', in Brian McLaughlin and Amélie Oksenberg Rorty (eds), *Perspectives on Self-Deception* (University of California Press, 1988).

Notes

1 'The Unconscious' (1915), vol. 14 of the *Standard Edition of the Complete Psychological Works of Sigmund Freud*. Henceforth, all references to this edition will be given in the text as *S.E.* Freud's use of the term *Affekt* derives from Spinoza's *affectus*, a reactive modification contrasted to the active expression of *conatus*.

2 Ibid.: 110. Without systematically distinguishing them, Freud sometimes speaks of the *idea* (*Idee*), sometimes the *concept* (*Begriff*) or *content* (*Inhalt*), sometimes the *object* (*Objekt*) of psychological states. In all cases, he is referring to intentional objects.

3 Since Freud sometimes suggests that drives are themselves *felt*, and that their being felt is part of their operation, he owes us an account of the difference between the felt experience of the expression of a drive and the felt experience of its frustration.

4 The Talmudic strand that Freud shares with Spinoza is central here: a mechanistic account of behaviour is compatible with an open-ended and revisionist intentional, ideational, or cognitive description of that behaviour.

5 Freud is greatly indebted to Rousseau's account of the effects of dependence: it produces a kind of anxiety that in turn generates a cycle of vulnerability to, and defiance of the powers and opinions of others.

6 Brian McLaughlin (in correspondence) has suggested this formulation for the difference between the two strands in Freud's theory: 'A given state is an affect in virtue of having a functional role F [that of releasing the energy of a blocked drive]; that state is a state

of *love* in virtue of having a functional role, F′; it is a state of *loving one's mother* by virtue of having a functional role F″. Being in any affective state is essentially open to consciousness. Any F″ state is also F′; and any F′ state is also F. But an F state need not be F′; nor need an F′ state be F″. So while being in an affective state F is essentially open to consciousness, a person might be in F′ or F″, without being aware of being in a certain type of affective state and without being aware of the particular content of that state.' (Though essentially aware of being in some sort of affective state, a person can mistake his anger for love, and his anger for his father as an anger for his boss.)

Ronald De Sousa (in correspondence) has suggested that there might be interesting parallels between this aspect of Freud's theory – the view that affects are sensed experiences of physiological changes – and the James Lange account of emotions as the sensations of bodily states.

7 Mourning at death is, of course, not the only kind of mourning. There are losses in separation, alienation, the death of affection, even in the perception of dramatic or radical change in the objects central to a person's identity. There are even losses of phantasy objects and losses of phantasy relations. Whatever is perceived or experienced as the kind of loss that affects a person's conception of what is essential to her sense of herself presents an occasion for mourning.

8 Clearly it is not necessary that a person loves what she mourns or that she loves what she takes to be centrally identificational. Someone can, for instance, mourn the transformation of a family home or neighbourhood which, in childhood, brought pain and misery; or she can mourn the loss of a hated enemy. Her sense of herself, her identity, had been bound up with him, or with her hatred of him, even though she not only hated the villain but hated hating him.

9 This interpretation of the gender-linked asymmetry of mourning is borne out by the differences between the mourning of widowers and that of widows: widowers who have lost their primary nurturers, as well as their friends and partners, often suffer affective debility and disorientation, while widows who must learn how to manage their financial affairs appear to suffer in more straightforwardly practical, less affect-ridden ways. Of course when such practical difficulties are symbolically highly charged – as often they are – they become affectively laden.

10 Freud took marriage to be the central model of the kind of bonding he described. But of course the phenomena are more general: even men and women who form relatively bracketed and short-lived alliances exemplify all the patterns Freud characterizes as marital. It is not always the *woman* who follows the pattern Freud describes: it can be Marcel in relation to Albertine, one male homosexual to another, or a nurturing man to a narcissistic woman. But even such variations on the standard type exemplify the plot Freud sketches, when the suitable substitutions are made.

11 Cf. Ann Thompson, 'Affects and Ideas in Freud's Early Writings' (unpublished paper).

References

Freud, S. (1900) *The Interpretation of Dreams, Standard Edition of the Complete Psychological Works of Sigmund Freud*, ed. James Strachey, 24 vols, London: Hogarth Press, 1953–73, *S.E.* 4–5.
—— (1910) 'The Antithetical Meaning of Primal Terms', *S.E.* 11.
—— (1915) 'The Unconscious', *S.E.* 14.
—— (1915) 'Repression', *S.E.* 14.
—— (1915) 'Instincts and their Vicissitudes', *S.E.* 14.
—— (1917) *Mourning and Melancholia, S.E.* 14.
Thompson, Anne, 'Affects and Ideas in Freud's Early Writings', unpublished paper.

11

LOVE AND LOSS IN FREUD'S
MOURNING AND MELANCHOLIA
A rereading

Jennifer Radden

Introduction

Mourning and Melancholia is one of Freud's most revered works. Yet it is deeply ambiguous and opaque. In particular, we leave it unsure of the extent to which melancholic states are part of the human condition, rather than rare forms of mental disorder. It is clear that melancholia is a condition of loss, but mystery attaches to the question of what is lost and whether adult states relive or merely mimic earlier infantile experiences. In addition, we remain uncertain of the relation between melancholia and hysteria, as of that between melancholia and mania. The notions of the ego-ideal, the super-ego and the part played by ambivalence also remain vague and unresolved. I would be the first to grant the resonance and charm of the essay. Who can resist the image of the shadow of the object falling across the ego, or fail to be intrigued that 'a man must become ill before he can discover truth . . .' (Freud 1917: 156)?[1] Here, however, I want to examine not only the brilliance and appeal of *Mourning and Melancholia* but its strange opacity.

In the following pages is a discussion of the ambiguities in this text which allow us to wonder whether Freud's melancholia is a universal propensity, or even a universal experience. I note two later and influential psychoanalytic theories, those of Melanie Klein and Julia Kristeva, which develop on, and exploit, this ambiguity. I also identify what is innovative in Freud's essay. Some importantly new ways of portraying melancholia *are* to be found in *Mourning and Melancholia*, which diverge quite markedly from both the psychiatric thinking of Freud's own era, and from the much earlier, more literary tradition of writing about melancholy. But alongside these new ideas are older associations and assumptions apparently derived from that earlier tradition. The curious compound that results, I suggest, accounts for some of the puzzling and elusive aspects of the piece. (It probably also accounts for some of its special appeal.)

Innovations such as Freud's bold theory of narcisissism and introjection have been widely adopted by later neo-Freudian thinkers, and widely credited. But less commonly recognized to be Freud's original contribution are two constituents of melancholic states, loss and self-loathing. In addition to offering a diagnosis of the essay's opacity, I draw attention to these insufficiently acknowledged innovations in *Mourning and Melancholia*.

The discussion which follows falls into three sections. In section 1, I discuss the seeming ambiguity which has allowed neo-Freudian interpretations to portray melancholia as very widespread or even a universal propensity, and I note some of the implications of that reading. In section 2, I identify aspects of Freud's essay which seem to harken back to earlier traditions about melancholy and melancholic states. While not new to Freud, these elements reflected a tradition absent in the writing of Freud's contemporaries, I show. The purpose of this discussion is twofold. By identifying the residue from past traditions on melancholy, I will be able to isolate those of Freud's own innovations which I believe have been neglected. These, the notions of melancholia as a condition of loss, and as comprising self-critical attitudes, are explored in section 3. Despite its echoes of past writing on melancholy, Freud's was also a thoroughgoing reconstruction of melancholia, and I want to elucidate the extent and depth of that reconstructive effort. Also in section 3, I note the influence of Freud's loss model on twentieth-century analyses of melancholia and clinical depression, analyses in which it has been appropriated, but misunderstood and even trivialized.

One last preliminary: until rather recent attention by contemporary theorists outside analytic philosophy and psychoanalysis, commentaries on Freud's writing have more often quoted from than thoroughly analysed *Mourning and Melancholia*. Philosophers have not provided much by way of systematic analysis of this particular text either, in comparison with their close examination of other writing of Freud's, and the philosophical analyses which do exist differ widely in their view, and use, of this work. For those who cast melancholia as a form of neurotic or unresolved grief, and a failure of proper mourning, this is an essay about melancholia understood as a rare, pathological condition (see Mitchell 1974; Cavell 1993). For those who read the introjection, identification and narcissism Freud introduces here as a feature of all mourning, it is an essay about narcissism and (normal) mourning (see Rorty, in this volume). For those directing their attention to the splitting of the ego proposed by Freud as the source of later melancholic states, it is merely the first intimation of the super-ego concept (see Wollheim 1971).

Those within the fields of literary, feminist and cultural studies have shown a welcome interest in Freud's essay, and their recent work provides a sustained and illuminating commentary (Schiesari 1992; Enterline 1995), Nonetheless, this work also, I show, fails to recognize and acknowledge the extent of Freud's innovative reconstructive effort.

1 Melancholia as loosely bounded and ambiguous

In drawing attention to the blurring of the boundaries around melancholia, let me comment briefly on Freud's term 'melancholiac'. The essay begins with a warning.

Even in descriptive psychiatry, Freud remarks, 'the definition of melancholia is uncertain; it takes on various clinical forms . . . that *do not seem definitely to warrant reduction to a unity*' (Freud 1917: 152, my emphasis). In light of this admission, Freud may be judged to speak of 'melancholiacs' incautiously. Uncertain over the extent to which melancholia constituted a recognizable unity or 'syndrome' in the medical or psychiatric sense, and stood as a permanent or semi-permanent ascription, we might today suppose he would better have referred to 'those suffering melancholic states'. Such niceties may not have troubled Freud or his translators as much as they do us, however. In the psychiatry of his time, the term 'melancho-liac' had begun to acquire a narrower meaning. But in the long tradition of writing about melancholy which preceded Freud, 'melancholiac' refers indifferently to those suffering occasional melancholic states and to those permanently afflicted with a more serious disorder.

Several aspects of Freud's account seem to contribute to a blurring of the difference between melancholic states as rare disorders and as more common propensities. To understand these, it is important to distinguish the object of melan-cholic states from their occasion: Freud appears to adhere to a structure whereby an affective state is over or about some object (which may itself be unconscious), while often precipitated by another state of affairs which is merely its immediate occasion. First, then, the 'object' of melancholic states is vaguely specified, suggesting that our primal narcissistic object choices dispose us all to subsequent melancholic states; second, the occasions of melancholia are not only (adult) loss of a loved one, but every possible kind of human suffering; finally, melancholia is somehow linked with two other universal propensities, mourning and conscience.

Who or what is the object?

To understand the notion of the object in Freud's analysis it is necessary to examine the machinations by which, according to Freud, love of another may be transformed into melancholic self-accusation. The narrative of loss and transformation in *Mourning and Melancholia* goes this way:

> First there existed an object-choice, the libido had attached itself to a certain person; then, owing to a real injury or disappointment concerned with the loved person, this object relationship was undermined. Then . . . the free libido was withdrawn into the ego and not directed to another object . . . [where] . . . it served simply to establish an *identification* of the ego with the abandoned object. Thus the shadow of the object fell upon the ego, so that the latter could henceforth be criticized by a special mental faculty like an object, like the forsaken object. In this way the loss of the object became transformed into a loss in the ego, and the conflict between the ego and the loved person transformed into a cleavage between the criticizing faculty of the ego and the ego as altered by the identification.
>
> (Freud 1917: 159)

Who or what is the object? Freud's specification is loose, even careless. In the case of the 'deserted bride' he points out, it may be the missing groom (155); in other cases it may be an ideal or an idea, rather than a person (155). What is more, we cannot always know what the object is, because it may be unconscious.

This is an important qualification. As in mourning, melancholia starts with the loss of an object of love, but *the patient may not consciously recognize what that object is.* Then, 'This, indeed, might be so even when the patient was aware of the loss giving rise to the melancholia, that is when he knows whom he has lost but not *what* it is he has lost in them' (Freud 1917: 155). In contradistinction to mourning, in which 'there is nothing unconscious about the loss', Freud concludes, melancholia is 'in some way' related to loss of an unconscious love-object (Freud 1917: 155). Moreover, he later emphasizes that this unconscious aspect of melancholic states is of the greatest importance: what is conscious, a conflict as he says between one part of the ego 'and its self-criticizing faculty' is insignificant. What is 'essential' is the unconscious part (168).

Is the object ever – or always – the mother, or the image of the mother? Remarks in the succeeding pages of Freud's essay suggest that if the object is not the mother, then nonetheless the process of narcissistic identification which allows the ego to incorporate the other in melancholia is a process in every way analogous to 'the way in which the ego first adopts its object', i.e., first adopts its mother-image. The ego 'wishes to incorporate this object into itself, and the method by which it would do so, in this oral or cannibalistic state, is by devouring it' (169). This process, described as the 'regression from narcissistic object choice to narcissism' (161), which marks melancholia, is also found in the progression by which the ego 'first adopts an object', i.e., in normal object-relational, or interpersonal, development.

Melancholia is 'in some way' related to loss of an unconscious love-object, but how? What remains opaque is the extent to which adult suffering is not only like the early loss of the mother but also over, or about, that loss. Adult melancholia at the least mimics, but perhaps even re-enacts, the psychic incorporation of the mother by the infant.[2] If all melancholiacs resort to regression from narcissistic object-choice to narcissism, then our primal narcissistic object-choices apparently dispose us all to subsequent melancholic states. The distinction blurs between melancholy as part of the human condition and melancholia as an infrequently occurring mental disorder.

What are the occasions for melancholic states?

Freud's essay introduces a sustained analogy between normal mourning over the loss of a loved one and melancholia, and interpreters of Freud have sometimes cast melancholia as a form of unresolved and inappropriate grief. But melancholic states arise on occasions both related *and unrelated* to adult grief. Indeed Freud asserts that for the most part the occasions giving rise to melancholia extend beyond the clear case of a loss by death. They include '*all those situations of being wounded, hurt, neglected, out of favour, or disappointed, which can import opposite feelings of love and hate into the relationship or reinforce an already existing ambivalence'* (Freud 1917: 161, my emphasis). Almost any kind of disappointment may rekindle the infantile experience of loss which marks melancholia.

This is merely to extensively rewrite the range of possible occasions for melancholia; it is not, of course, to say we all experience melancholic states when such occasions arise. Nonetheless, even for Freud, melancholic states are now potentially associated with almost every kind of human suffering and this passage encourages us to regard melancholia as an aspect of the human condition. As adults we all experience some form of suffering and distress, and we all have experienced early loss, the enactment of which may be occasioned by such suffering and distress.

Melancholia is portrayed as a pathological condition. But mourning is also a quasi-pathological condition, Freud makes clear. That mourning does not *seem* to us pathological, he insists, 'is really only because we know so well how to explain [it]' (Freud 1917: 153). If a tendency to melancholic states parallels normal mourning in being an aspect of the human condition, then partial recognition of this deeper parallel between mourning and melancholia – not only are they each conditions of loss with eerily similar psychic and behavioural manifestations, they are also each universal, though pathological, propensities – may have motivated Freud's development of other comparisons between the two states of melancholia and mourning which I explore in section 3 of this essay.

Freud wrote little on melancholia after the 1917 essay. At the outset of *Mourning and Melancholia* he notes that the various clinical forms of melancholia in descriptive psychiatry 'do not seem definitely to warrant reduction to a unity' (Freud 1917: 152). We can surmise that this doubt over its unitary status dampened his interest in the alleged syndrome of melancholia. If melancholia were without clear boundaries, then it would not readily submit to close theoretical analysis of the kind to which Freud would wish to subject it. When melancholia recurs in his writing (it is in *The Ego and the Id*, published in 1923), the processes which were earlier used to explain it are recognized to have much broader application. The universal feature allied to the early splitting and introjection revived in melancholia has become moral development, conscience and character. *Character formation results from the splitting of the ego and the emergence of the super-ego.*

Looking back at the time of his earlier work, Freud now remarks: 'we did not [then] appreciate the full significance of this process [splitting and introjection] and did not know *how common and how typical it is.* Since then we have come to understand that this kind of substitution has a great share in determining the form taken by the ego and that it makes an essential contribution towards building up what is called its "character"' (1923: 18, my emphasis).

By this later analysis a distinction not remarked in the 1917 essay provides Freud a means of separating the melancholiac from the normal person. Early loss and early object relationships are the source of all adult character, but the nature and resolution of that loss determines what kind of character ensues. In the *normal* person the super-ego is present, but not unduly strong. In the melancholiac, by contrast, are the self-critical attitudes which received such stress in the 1917 essay. Now 'the excessively strong super-ego . . . rages against the ego with the merciless violence' (Freud 1923: 43). Not only is this criterion for separating the melancholiac absent from the earlier work: because Freud attributes conscience to the same processes explaining melancholic states, even in this later work melancholic states seem at risk of being seen as a common and central part of our human condition – as common and central, perhaps, as is the conscience which springs from the same source.

Klein and Kristeva

Thus far I have employed an interpretive contrast between presenting melancholic states or propensities as rare and pathological, and as common and normal. But this alignment is explicitly collapsed by Freud when he regards mourning as both common and pathological or quasi-pathological. And in the influential neo-Freudian interpretations and developments of Melanie Klein (dating from the 1930s and 1940s), and Julia Kristeva (1970s), we find melancholia, also, portrayed as common while still pathological.

The roots of the developmental stage which Klein termed the 'depressive position', a stage she judges of paramount importance to psychological develop-ment, can be found in Freud's discussion of mourning and melancholia, and in Freudian ideas of introjection and identification. The depressive position is the distressed state with which the infant responds to the loss associated with the early, and inevitable, separation from the mother such as that occurring during weaning. The experience of all infants, the depressive position is nonetheless a neurotic or disordered condition of which Klein remarks that 'it is a melancholia in *statu nascendi*' (Klein 1935: 345).[3]

The depressive position, then, which is sometimes reactivated in adult life, is universally experienced. We are all mothered and weaned, we are all frustrated and disappointed by, and ambivalent over, our first 'object'. Moreover, not only other adult neuroses and excessive grief but all and any adult mourning reactivate the depressive states of infancy. Echoing Freud, Klein remarks that the mourner is in fact ill, 'but because this state of mind is common and seems so natural to us, we do not call mourning an illness' (Klein 1935: 354).[4] This means that not one but two different aspects of the Kleinian analysis suggest melancholia or depression as universal states or propensities: the infantile experience of the 'depressive position' and the 'illness' undergone in all adult mourning.

Carrying forward Freud's best-known innovation in *Mourning and Melancholia*, his theory of projective identification, or introjection, Klein employed the same concepts as Freud in describing the infant's psychic incorporation of the mother. But Klein also elaborated. Hatred and rage, as well as love, are directed toward the other; bad as well as good aspects of the other are incorporated. In later writing, Klein still represented feelings as clustered around the depressive position, but

216

the depressive position became an affective structure, reflecting differences in ego integration. (Psychoanalytic theories have continued to cast the depressive position as a mode of relating to objects based on ego integration. Rather than an infantile stage to be overcome, the depressive position is a relatively mature psychic achievement. Fluctuation between the depressive and more primitive paranoid-schizoid modes, on this elaboration, is a central factor in psychic life [Bion 1963].)

In a controversial development Julia Kristeva also inherits Freud's model of infantile 'mourning' for the maternal object. But Kristeva's analysis construes this experience of early loss in such a way as to render melancholia or depression a universal state or propensity, at least for women. We are all alike subject to the loss of the object, she explains, and thus inclined, as Freud believed, to incorporate or 'introject' the other. But due to the identification with the same-sex mother peculiar to the female infant, combined with a universal matricidal drive, there is a proneness to depression peculiar to women. The 'inversion of matricidal drive', which in the male child is transformed into misogyny, takes a different course in women. For the female infant, 'the hatred I bear her [the mother] is not oriented toward the outside but is locked up within myself. There is no hatred, only an implosive mood that walls itself in and kills me secretly, very slowly, through permanent bitterness, bouts of sadness' (Kristeva 1989: 29).

For the woman, on Kristeva's account, avoidance of this painful depression may be impossible in heterosexual development. The extent to which homosexual adjustment is women's only way to avoid melancholia and depression is left ambiguous. Nonetheless, the broad meaning of Kristeva's analysis is apparent: for women at least, melancholic states may be next to inevitable.

Freud's essay invites speculation over the commonness or even universality of melancholic states, and these Kleinian and Kristevian developments on Freud's work offer a certain resolution on the matter. Melancholic states are human nature for Klein; for Kristeva they are women's nature. Although I cannot deal with them in any detail here, the implications of adopting either analysis are clearly profound. If melancholic states are part of human nature, then two features attaching to this century's conception of clinical depression seem to be thrown into question, the 'medicalization', by which it is construed on the model of symptom clusters or syndromes in clinical medicine, and its gender association. Even if melancholic and depressive states are part of women's nature, as Kristeva suggests, then at least their construction as medical diseases and as abnormal must become problematic.

2 The older tradition

In allowing the distinction between common and uncommon states to remain unresolved, Freud's work echoes a long, earlier tradition of writing on melancholy, melancholia and melancholic states. (These three variations are not distinguished in any systematic way in that tradition.) There, rather than a limited disorder in some adults, melancholy is often portrayed as a condition common to all, an 'inbred malady in every one of us' in Robert Burton's words.

And, while a remarkably innovative work, *Mourning and Melancholia* is strongly evocative of earlier writing on melancholia. Freud's exemplar of the melancholiac was Hamlet, and, as this suggests, he was familiar with the rich vein of European traditions around melancholy. (Freud was an attentive student of European literary traditions, reading several languages including Shakespeare's and Burton's English.)[5] These traditions originated in the humoral theories of the Greek physicians, and flowered in works of the Renaissance such as Ficino's *Three Books on Life*, Burton's *Anatomy of Melancholy*, and literary and artistic representations like Hamlet, and Durer's engravings on Melancholia.[6]

At least three features of this older tradition appear to have found their way into Freud's essay. The first: the categories of melancholy and melancholia elude definition. The second, melancholy is characterized by groundless fear and sadness (fear and sadness 'without cause'). The third element of the tradition: melancholic states have a glamorous aspect. The melancholy man (and it is a man, as contemporary writing has emphasized (Radden 1987; Schiesari 1992)) shows artistic genius and intellectual greatness; moreover the melancholy man knows states of passion and exaltation not allowed to other mortals. I shall take these three characteristics in turn and show how they match, and may be reflected in, Freud's thinking in *Mourning and Melancholia*.

Melancholic states as undefinable

Consider the passage quoted earlier in which Freud remarks that the definition of melancholia is 'uncertain', and melancholia takes on various clinical forms, that 'do not seem definitely to warrant reduction to a unity' (Freud 1917: 152). This phrasing affirms so much in past writing on melancholy that it reads like a self-conscious allusion to such writing. Again and again we find this theme of melancholy eluding capture because of the multitude and variety of its forms. (The tower of Babel, Burton remarks, 'never yielded such confusion of tongues as this Chaos of Melancholy doth variety of symptoms' (Burton 1621: 395).

Related to this issue of melancholy's elusiveness, is ambiguity in the term 'melancholy'. We in the twentieth century are inclined to separate melancholia as a mental disorder from melancholy as a temporary or more long-lasting state or trait in an otherwise normal person. Yet until the end of the nineteenth century saw the advent of psychiatry in something like the form we know today, this distinction was rarely stressed in writing about melancholy and melancholic states. It is not merely that the borders between mental disorder and normalcy were recognized to be vague and uncertain. Nor is it that floridly disordered states were not encountered, or not included in the category of melancholia, for they were. It is rather that due to certain unifying factors, on the one hand, and in the absence of a set of disciplinary interests and purposes associated with psychiatry, on the other, the divisions and categories which today seem so obvious went without remark. The humoral theories served to unite all forms of melancholy as disorders and manifestations of the black bile (Foucault 1973; Jackson 1986). In a late nineteenth-century shift the hitherto encompassing category of melancholy divided, leaving a sharper distinction between the despondent moods and temperamental differences of essentially normal experience, on the one hand, and the clinical disorder known as melancholia or clinical depression, on the other. But this shift resulted only when a complex set of distinctions such as those arising from seventeenth- and eighteenth-century faculty psychology combined with developments in medical thinking and practice to lay the base for a distinct science of psychiatry (Radden 1987, 1996).

Just as the distinction between melancholy as part of the human condition and melancholy as an infrequently occurring mental disorder is blurred in the earlier, pre-psychiatric and pre-Freudian tradition, so *Mourning and Melancholia* reaffirms the elusive and encompassing nature of melancholy expressed in the older tradition.

Fear and sadness without cause and the unconscious object of loss

The second theme from pre-Freudian writing on melancholy which seems to make its way into *Mourning and Melancholia* concerns the traditional characterization of melancholy as groundless fear and sadness. (To speak of fear and sadness 'without cause', is not to deny that the fear and sadness were occasioned by something, but to deny that their 'object', i.e., what these feelings are about or over, is known to their subject.) Freud's analysis of melancholia as a state of loss parallels these older accounts in two ways: it emphasizes the subjective and affective, and it introduces a phenomenologically objectless mental state, a mood.

First, in contrast to the prevailing psychiatric ideas of his time, Freud's analysis of melancholia as a condition of loss, is a subjective and affective one. The somatic and behavioural elements of melancholia rather than the subjectivity of melancholic states, were more commonly emphasized in the psychiatric thinking of Freud's contemporaries. Freud's recognition of the growing emphasis on the behavioural and somatic in his time is conveyed by his opening remark that melancholia takes on a variety of clinical forms, some of them suggesting somatic rather than 'psychogenic affections' (1917: 152). But his qualification aside, Freud's analysis nonetheless offers melancholia as a 'psychogenic affection', characterized, just as Burton's had been, by references to its sufferer's affective subjectivity.

The second parallel is between Freud's particular, and, I will insist, new, emphasis on the subjectivity of melancholia in terms of *loss*, and earlier accounts in terms of fear and sadness without cause. The characterization of melancholy subjectivity as fear and sadness without cause is found as early as Hippocratic and Aristotelian writing, and is a recurring theme for as long as a century after Burton.[7]

Familiar and long lived as they are, however, fear and sadness without cause introduce ambiguity as symptoms of melancholy. In particular, the phrase 'without cause' is a confusing one. Does it mean without any cause, or is it elliptical for without sufficient cause, it is necessary to ask? Some commentators have read Burton and those who followed him to mean the latter (without sufficient cause), rather than the former (without cause) (Jackson 1986). Others have emphasized the former, and in so doing highlighted that the subjective state is a nebulous and pervasive mood rather than an affective state with any more sharply delineated cognitive content.

The philosophical distinction sometimes maintained between moods and emotions is the one identified here. If fear and sadness are *without sufficient cause*, then they are still accompanied by 'intentional objects' – that is they are over or about something which the sufferer understands to be so or to exist (Gordon 1986). But their objects do not appear to warrant the degree of feeling attributed to them. (An example would be excessive fear over a clearly minimal danger, or excessive distress over a trifling event.) In contrast, if melancholic fear and sadness are *entirely without cause*, then they are not over or about anything in particular (in one sense, they are so pervasive as to seem rightly judged about everything). If so, then they are moods. This distinction is not one made explicit until the sharpened focus on the cognitive content of emotions which came with Brentano's theory of intentionality at the end of the nineteenth century (Brentano 1874/1955). (Brentano's theory, it is worth remembering, was one with which Freud was familiar).[8] Nonetheless, its retrospective application suggests that Renaissance and later writing about melancholia is concerned as much with nebulous, pervasive and non-intentional *moods* of fear and sadness (no cause), as with the *emotions* of fear and sadness in excess of their occasions (without sufficient cause).

In *Mourning and Melancholia*, we saw, Freud makes an important qualification about the object of the loss suffered in melancholia: the object may be unconscious in melancholia, as may some aspect of the object's *meaning*. By allowing this, Freud has linked his analysis with traditional accounts of melancholic states. There is something, the sufferer knows not what, toward which his nebulous mood of loss is directed. An affective mood state, *a sense of loss without a (consciously recognized) cause* now makes up part of melancholic subjectivity. (I emphasize this to point out that Freud is not suggesting that every aspect of the loss is unconscious. Some aspect, the sense or *mood* of loss, and even sometimes some recognition of its object, may be an item of conscious awareness.)

Freud characterizes the symptoms of melancholia as 'Painful dejection, abrogation of interest in the outside world, loss of the capacity to love, inhibition of all activity, a lowering of the self-regarding feelings to a degree that finds utterance in self-reproaches and self-revilings, and culminates in a delusional expectation of punishment' (1917: 153). Of the characterizations of the earlier eras, only the affective state of sadness ('painful dejection') remains part of that subjectivity. With his strong – and innovative – emphasis on melancholic subjectivity characterized by *moods of (often) objectless loss*, rather than groundless fear, and in addition to groundless sadness or dejection, Freud has at the same time revived the earlier Renaissance tradition and rung significant changes upon it.

JENNIFER RADDEN

Brilliance and inspiration and the compensations of mania

Melancholy's link with genius, creative energy and with exalted moods and states is the third feature of earlier accounts which can be found in Freud's essay. This is an alignment which traces back to Aristotelian writing.[9] Reawakened and transformed during the Renaissance, the 'glorification of melancholy' gathered strength from the new category of the man of genius. It waned during the early eighteenth century, only to be revived with the Romantic movement. Now the suffering of melancholy was again associated with greatness; again, it was idealized, and the melancholy man was one who felt more deeply, saw more clearly and came closer to the sublime, than ordinary men (Klibansky et al. 1964).

By the time Freud wrote *Mourning and Melancholia* much of the lustre had left melancholia. Nonetheless, as Juliana Schiesari has pointed out, there are signs that it was only with difficulty that Freud relinquished the associations with inspiration, genius and exaltation (Schiesari 1992). For Freud, as for the earlier tradition, Schiesari argues, the figure of the melancholic is a male one. (Schiesari's own theory is that in the gender economy of our patriarchal structures men suffer melancholia while women merely mourn. Other contemporary theorists such as Jacques Lacan and Luce Irigaray have also precluded women from the satisfactions of melancholic expression, although for slightly different reasons than Schiesari's).[10] For Freud also, the glamorous Hamlet is the developed case example. The interests of patriarchal ideology and of psychoanalysis, remarks Schiesari, are both served by the mad prince, 'When Freud refers to Hamlet, he signals the fact that a well-known *male* character such as Hamlet is indeed [in contrast to the unnamed female patients referred to in the essay], a *nameable* subject and a subject of literary and psychoanalytic interest precisely because the canon legitimizes his "neurosis" as something *grand . . .*' (Schiesari 1992: 59, my emphasis).

For Freud, finally, melancholia provides inspiration and a privileged knowledge. The melancholic 'has a keener eye for the truth than others who are not melancholic' (1917: 156) This and similar remarks of Freud's seem on their face most notable examples of an uncritical embrace of the earlier romantic traditions. On the other hand, the observation rings curiously true, today, in light of empirical studies showing the unsurpassed realism of the mildly depressed, and the consistent link between accurate appraisal, mild depression and low self-esteem (Taylor and Brown, 1988).

The boundary separating melancholia, the mental disorder, from other dejected states and melancholy dispositions was sharpened with the advent of modern psychiatry in the late nineteenth century. And as this occurred, something of the tradition of associating melancholy with creative energy and brilliance re-emerged as a focus on the connection between melancholy and the more enlivened states of mania. 'Cyclical insanity', otherwise known as *folie à double forme* or manic depression, became a central category.

Freud also, is alert to the suggestion that manic moods are melancholia's twin and compensation. We see this in remarks on mania at the end of *Mourning and*

Melancholia. These remarks constitute no more than a 'first sounding' (Freud 1917: 164), and Freud calls off the investigation in the very last paragraph of the essay. Moreover, he earlier resists the assumption that all melancholia has the capacity to transform into the joy, triumph and exultation which as he says 'form the normal counterparts of mania' (Freud 1917: 164). Nonetheless, the essay ends with an allusion to mania. Narcissism remains, but melancholia will end. After the work of melancholia is completed, mania is possible (Freud 1917: 169–70). So, supported this time by the more orthodox German psychiatry of his day, Freud also seems to glimpse in mania the balance and compensation for the bereft states of melancholia.

3 The new

Several aspects of *Mourning and Melancholia* deserve the title of innovations, both relative to Freud's own earlier writing and when judged from the perspective of psychiatric writing about melancholia in his own time. Best known is the elaborate theory of narcissism, identification, decathexis and ego 'splitting'. But his notion of melancholia as loss is another innovation, as is his association between melancholia and expressions of self-loathing and self-criticism, and the discussion which follows focuses primarily on the identification of melancholia with loss and self-loathing, as it is the status of these, *as innovations*, which has been ignored.

Loss and self-loathing

Most contemporary writing about melancholia and depression, not only within psychoanalysis but in much contemporary psychology and psychiatry as well, presupposes the link between melancholia and loss. Recent theoretical attention to melancholy and depression within feminist psychoanalysis, literary criticism and cultural studies, for example, treats loss as an inevitable component of those conditions (Kristeva 1982; Irigaray 1991; Schiesari 1992; Enterline 1995). A passage from Julia Kristeva will serve to illustrate: depression, she remarks in *Black Sun*, 'is the hidden face of Narcissus . . . I discover the antecedents to my current breakdown in a loss, death, or grief over someone or something that I once loved' (Kristeva 1989: 5).

But to a great extent this modern framing is attributable to Freud. Melancholia takes on stronger connotations of loss, as it does themes of self-loathing, only in – and after – Freud's essay. Indeed, through its emphasis on the theme of loss and self-critical attitudes, Freud's writing on melancholia may be seen to have *reconstructed* melancholic states. From a condition of humoral imbalance and a mood of despondency, melancholia has become a frame of mind characterized by a loss of something – and also by self-critical attitudes. As the result of Freud's work the latter aspects of melancholic subjectivity, hitherto granted little importance, become attenuated, elaborated and central. Far from the nebulous and pervasive mood states of Elizabethan melancholy, Freud's melancholiac experiences self-directed emotional attitudes of criticism and reproach which Freud regards as definitive of melancholia. Dissatisfaction with the self on moral grounds, as he says, is 'in the clinical picture . . . the most outstanding feature' (Freud 1917: 157).

My thesis here concerning Freud's reconstruction of melancholia as loss and self-loathing represents a significant departure from some interpretations. Recent writing on melancholy and melancholia from cultural and literary studies, in particular, explicitly notes and emphasizes an alignment between melancholy, melancholia and loss (or lack) in the earlier traditions going back to the Renaissance. There is some force to this interpretation. Undoubtedly for Ficino and Burton, as also for Shakespeare, melancholy was a narcissistic condition; moreover, it was recognized to parallel normal grieving. Nonetheless, while conceding certain similar themes in earlier writing, I think it a mistake to overemphasize these similarities. It is implausible because Freud's ideas on loss in *Mourning and Melancholia* can be shown to derive seamlessly from earlier work on melancholia and loss in the letters to his friend, Wilhelm Fliess, written in 1902, and these earlier ideas bear less resemblance to Renaissance accounts of melancholy. It is also wrong because it depends on an inexact translation whereby 'loss' (literally, in German *Verlust*) becomes 'lack', which is not an equivalent of 'loss' or of *Verlust*. (And this is a difference, we shall see, which is significant.) The influence of Renaissance accounts of melancholy and melancholic states is not absent from *Mourning and Melancholia*. In various ways his essay reveals Freud's familiarity with the category of melancholy known through the writing of earlier eras. But in the case of his notion of melancholia as a condition of loss, Freud's idea is his own.

The theme of loss in *Mourning and Melancholia* is foreshadowed in comments on melancholia to be found in letters to Fliess. This series of letters to Fliess during their intense ten-year correspondence and friendship in which they shared observations and hypotheses are a valuable source for Freud's earliest theoretical developments. In light of these letters, we can identify two stages in Freud's thinking about melancholia, loss and mourning. In the first stage, found in letters written in 1902, Freud identifies the loss he sees in melancholia as a lack of sexual excitement. Normal mourning is the longing for something lost; in melancholia this something lost is 'loss in instinctual life'. Thus he says 'melancholia consists in mourning over a loss of libido'.[11]

At this early stage Freud identifies the loss of libido or (sexual) 'anaesthesia', which at the first stage he sees as inviting melancholia, as predominantly a characteristic of women – although for reasons of cultural and not biological difference. (Women, he observes to Fliess, become 'anaesthetic' because they are brought up to repress sexual feeling, and because they are often required to engage in loveless sex.) Despite this, and the fact that the medical psychiatry of his time had already established a gender link between women and melancholia or depression, Freud does not in *Mourning and Melancholia* present melancholia as a women's disorder. (He does not do so, arguably, precisely because of the influence on his thinking of the Renaissance tradition in which melancholia is associated with the man of genius.)

By the 1917 paper Freud has developed both his notions of projection and identification, and his understanding of narcissism. Now, two new themes predominate. First, melancholia represents loss of the 'object', that is, another person: the mother, or mother-image. And second, self-accusation and self-hatred have become a *central characteristic* of the melancholic state, and the sole characteristic allowing us to distinguish melancholia from normal mourning (Freud 1917: 153). The attitudes of self-accusation and self-abasement represent a form of rage toward the once-loved object, now redirected toward one part of the ego by another. Having incorporated the object, the self attacks that object within it. The conflict between the ego and the loved person or object, as he puts it, results in a schism 'between the criticizing faculty of the ego and the ego as altered by the identification' (159). (This last conclusion Freud derives from his observation that there is a quality of disingenuousness about the protestations of the patient: 'we get the key to the clinical picture – by perceiving that the self-reproaches are reproaches against a loved object which have been shifted on to the patient's own ego' [158].)

The parallel between the despondent frame of mind of melancholia and the frame of mind found in the normal mourning occasioned by the loss of loved ones was not Freud's invention, as I have said. We know that writing about melancholy had repeatedly drawn such parallels, at least since Elizabethan times. In addition, Freud attributes to his follower Karl Abraham recognition of the importance of this parallel between melancholia and normal mourning. Yet the standard comparison likening the despondent mood and characteristic dispositions of sorrow, lethargy and low interest in normal mourning to melancholic states was merely Freud's starting point. He constructed a more elaborate parallel. The mourner has *lost* something (someone, that is) and grieves his loss; thus, the melancholic also must have suffered a loss.

The operative term is 'loss' notice, not merely 'lack'. The two words (loss and lack) are sometimes interchanged in contemporary discussions of these ideas, such as Schiesari's. But this represents a distortion of Freud's intent and leads, I believe, to a failure to recognize the originality and importance of Freud's loss theory of melancholia. Let us see why, and consider James and Alix Strachey's decision to render the German *Verlust* not into the English 'lack' but into 'loss' in the English edition of Freud's work which – importantly, since Freud was a fluent speaker and reader of English – Freud himself authorized and oversaw.

The German *Verlust* was Freud's consistent choice in passages discussing this aspect of his analysis. This word translates literally as ' loss', and 'loss' was the Strachey's consistent choice, as a glance at these passages in the German will reveal. The German *fehlen* corresponds most closely to our 'lack' in the English sense of 'lacking' something. ('I lack courage', 'Something was lacking'.) *Fehlen* is not found in these German passages, nor does 'lack' occur in the translation.

By contrasting the two English words 'lack' and 'loss' we can perhaps see some of what was at stake in the Stracheys' choice. We may *lack* many things including qualities (tact) and particulars (money), and including things we have never had (stamina). But we *lose* particulars (persons, sets of keys); and we only lose particulars we have once possessed, in some sense of that term. The 'loss' we associate with grief is loss, not lack. A particular love, once known to us ('possessed'), is gone. The loss Freud attributes to the melancholic parallels the loss of mourning. Although not always recognized as such by its sufferer, the object lost (the mother or mother-image) is a particular, once possessed. Recognizing this, the Stracheys and Freud relied on the English word best able to convey not only the literal meaning of *Verlust* but the broader theoretical context within which the term was embedded: Freud's sustained analogy with mourning. (For illumination on the sensitivity with which James and Alix Strachey approached the task of translating Freud, see Meisel and Kendrick 1985.)

We can now summarize the two stages of Freud's lack/loss theory. At first, in the 1895 unpublished letter and writing to Fliess, Freud proposes that the lack, or want, is of libido. There is no hint here that the object of lack is personified (i.e., that it is a loss). Only later, in the essay, does he complete the parallel with mourning; now the lost object is not libido but another person, or, more exactly, the distorted idea of another person (the *imago*).

The formation of Freud's loss theory of melancholia may now be traced. The parallel with mourning, itself triggered by a long literary tradition on the subjective mood states of melancholy and also, apparently, by Abraham's work, directs Freud through a series of recognitions: first that melancholia must be identified in terms of lack, eventually that it must be the loss of someone. Only then come the ideas of self-accusation and self-loathing which form a central and much-repeated theme in *Mourning and Melancholia*.

These attitudes, also, are something rather new. They are to be found neither in the clinical psychiatry of Freud's own time, I shall now demonstrate, nor in the writing on melancholic states from earlier eras.

Self-accusation and self-loathing are absent from the portrait of melancholia found in the elaborate case summaries of Kraepelin, and in more casual clinical references from his era. Kraepelin notes self-accusation as a feature of *one* kind of melancholia, but it is not treated as a central feature. (In the more severe *melancholia gravis* Kraepelin notes that ideas of sin and self-reproach are often present, but so also are ideas of persecution. The less severe *melancholia simplex*, which is arguably closer to the kind of disorder suffered by the patients Freud describes in his essay, is for Kraepelin characterized as much by world loathing as by self loathing: '*everything* has become disagreeable to him [the melancholic patient]' [1921: 76, my emphasis].) Kraepelin's findings are mirrored in William James's more casual observations on melancholic states from the same era. James identifies what he calls the sense of sin as only one of three themes found in milder forms of melancholia (those, that is, which 'fall short of real insanity') in *The Varieties of Religious Experience*: he lists as well the vanity of mortal things, and the fear of the universe (James 1902: 158). So rather than a central theme, self-accusation is merely one of three possible themes characterizing the melancholic frame of mind.

Although it has widely been accepted as central to depressive subjectivity as the result of Freud's influence, self-accusation is not a theme associated with melancholic subjectivity in writing from the Renaissance. Garrulous, complaining, self-obsessed these melancholiacs were, but not self-hating. In a tradition deriving from as far back as the Greek physicians and Aristotle, the subjective moods of melancholy and melancholia were identified as groundless mood states of sadness and fear; less central characteristics included disinterest, despair, inertia and dullness, moreover, but not self-loathing.

Interestingly, recent cross cultural studies of depression from our own era also fail to reveal any emphasis on guilt and self-accusation in the symptom idiom of other cultures (Ihsan Al-Issa 1955; Kleinman and Good 1986).

We must conclude that Freud's listing of the 'distinguishing mental features' of melancholia in *Mourning and Melancholia* includes some which are widely accepted, consonant both with more recent and empirical, and older and more literary, accounts, and others which are new. 'Painful dejection, abrogation of interest in the outside world, loss of the capacity to love, inhibition of all activity' (Freud 1917: 153) – these correspond to the traditional and modern psychiatric notions of melancholic subjectivity. But 'a lowering of the self-regarding feelings to a degree that finds utterance in self-reproaches and self-revilings, and culminates in a delusional expectation of punishment', do not. These attitudes of self-loathing and self-reproach became and remain today central parts of the symptom description and symptom idiom of melancholia and depression, transforming melancholic and depressive subjectivity. And it is to Freud that a great measure of this transformation is due.

The influence of Freud's loss analysis of melancholia is also evident in later twentieth-century analyses, where it is a commonplace in medical, behavioural and psychoanalytic theories of depression that 'loss' is a constituent of depression. But Freud's account of that 'loss' is today identified with clinical depression, an oversimplified loss model wherein 'loss' conveys any lack, any disappointment, any sorrow and any source of suffering. There is no place for Freud's separation of loss from lack: any lack is a 'loss'. The influential 'learned helplessness' model of depression is identified as a loss theory (Seligman 1975), for example. But although it is trivially true that helplessness corresponds to a deprivation of opportunity to act, the state of helplessness identified by Seligman implies no loss of a personified object of the kind intended by Freud. In other theories, moreover, depression is defined as a loss of self-esteem, of self, of relationships, of agency, and even, rendering such accounts entirely circular, a loss of hedonic mood states.

Conclusion

In this essay I have explored some of the unresolved and confusing elements in Freud's essay on mourning and melancholia, offering an explanation of those elements, and of the essay's resonant appeal, by analysing it as the effort of a brilliant innovator enmeshed in his history and culture. Much in the essay is breathtakingly new, I have argued; the rest is breathtakingly old.

The rich complexity of *Mourning and Melancholia* stimulated theoretical writing important even today within object-relations psychology and psycho-analysis. Melanie Klein's 'depressive position' remains a central category within these fields, and Julia Kristeva's recent loss analysis of women's depression is today influential among feminist theorists and those working in cultural studies. Nonetheless, the fate of melancholia as a mental disorder has not been what Freud's innovative and striking reframing at the start of this century deserved. Increasingly, even in his own era, melancholia the category came to be subsumed under and eclipsed by the broader diagnostic grouping of clinical depression. With this change, the connotations from earlier eras' writing on melancholy dwindled in medical and psychiatric analyses. Left was a disorder of abject despair. Clinical depression had become a condition identified with feminine subjectivity, and with a set of metaphors conveying oppression, wretchedness, apathy, and, others have suggested, with mute suffering. It also came to be a condition identified by its bodily and behavioural symptoms.

The fortunes of the two particular features of melancholia discussed here, loss and attitudes of self-criticism and self-loathing, have differed widely. Evidence from cross-cultural psychiatry suggests that it is a culture-bound, and thus an apparently fragile association by which Freud found melancholia to express itself in attitudes of self-loathing and self-criticism. Yet self-loathing and self-criticism continue to be elevated to the status of central symptoms in accounts of clinical depression. Loss, on the other hand, has been transformed. In twentieth-century writing about Freud's essay, as we have seen, a failure to distinguish the narrower 'loss' from the broader 'lack' has led to a misinterpretation of Freud's analysis and obscured its originality. More significantly, an oversimplified loss model wherein depression is understood in terms of 'loss', and 'loss' now conveys a lack or want of any kind, has come to dominate a range of theories of clinical depression. A failure to honour Freud's careful separation of loss from lack renders many of these claims little better than trivially true.

Acknowledgements

I am grateful to Michael Levine, an anonymous contributor to this volume, Joan Fordyce, Neal Bruss, David Flesche, and to members of PHAEDRA, Jane Martin, Janet Farrell-Smith, Ann Diller, Beebe Kipp Nelson and Barbara Thayer-Bacon for helpful criticism and commentary on this essay.

Notes

1 All pages references are to the *Standard Edition* (Freud, 1917/1967). That there is no authoritative interpretation of Freud's essay is part of my thesis. For the sake of those readers who may not be familiar with this work, however, let me provide one, brief, interpretation of it. When some adults (melancholiacs) experience despondency and

inertia notably like that experienced during mourning, a disappointment or loss undergone in adult life has reignited an unresolved early loss. That unresolved early loss was marked by the psychic incorporation of the simultaneously loved and hated other, or mother. There was a splitting of the ego or self into two parts, one judging and the other judged, and as a result the melancholiac, unlike the mourner, reveals attitudes of self-loathing and self-criticism.

2 For useful explication of the notions of narcissism, 'splitting' and projective identification introduced in this passage, see Bruss (1986), Bollas (1987), Wollheim (1984, 1971), Cavell (1993), Mitchell (1974).

3 Klein's (often-criticized) development of these ideas goes like this. 'In the very first months of the baby's existence it has sadistic impulses . . . The development of the infant is governed by the mechanisms of introjection and projection. From the beginning the ego introjects objects "good" and "bad", for both of which the mother's breast is the prototype – for good objects when the child obtains it, for bad ones when it fails him. But it is because the baby projects its own aggression on to these objects that it feels them to be "bad" and not only in that they frustrate its desires: the child conceives of them as actually dangerous – persecutors who it fears will devour it . . . compassing its destruction by all the means which sadism can devise. These imagoes, which are a phantastically distorted picture of the real objects upon which they are based, become installed not only in the outside world, but, by a process of incorporation, also within the ego' (Klein 1935: 262).

4 Klein's account of mourning is as follows. 'Mourning the subject goes through a modified and transitory manic-depressive state and overcomes it, thus repeating, though in different circumstances and with different manifestations, the processes which the child normally goes through in his early development' (Klein 1935: 354).

5 Did Freud read Burton? I surmise that he probably did, based on his love of English literature (he apparently restricted his leisure reading to English for a decade of his life), and his affinity for Shakespeare. See Jones (1953–7/1961), also Gilman, Birmele, Geller and Greenberg (1994), and Gay (1990, especially ch 4, *Reading Freud through Freud's Reading*). But he would not need to have read Burton to have absorbed the features of the tradition discussed in this essay; they are recurrent and inescapable themes in a great part of the best in English literature from Chaucer to the novelists and poets of the nineteenth century.

6 For a thorough discussion of the ideas in this tradition see Klibansky et al. (1964) and Jackson (1986).

7 Well into the seventeenth century, we find Thomas Willis offering an explanation of the fear and sadness of melancholia without challenging their centrality as symptoms. (This is in *Two Discourses Concerning the Souls of Brutes*, published in 1672.)

8 Freud is known to have attended more than one philosophy course taught by Brentano at the University of Vienna between 1874–5 (Jones 1953–7/1961: 59–60).

9 It is believed to have probably been one of Aristotle's followers, most likely Theophrastus, who penned the famous section on melancholy in the *Problematica* which begins by asking why all brilliant men suffer melancholia.

10 See for example Lacan (1982), Irigaray (1991).

11 Even earlier than these letters to Fliess, Freud analogized melancholia to mourning and introducing the notion of a loss of libido. In an unpublished letter dated January 1895, Ernest Jones informs us, Freud defined melancholia as grief at some 'loss', probably of libido, and emphasized the link between melancholia and sexual anaesthesia. Reference to this letter is found in Jones (1953/1961). In it Freud offers a quasi-physiological explanation of the link between melancholia and sexual anaesthesia, which Jones conveys as follows: 'When the libido loses strength, energy is correspondingly withdrawn from associated "neurones", and the pain of melancholia is due to the dissolving of the associations' (245).

References

Bion, W. (1963) *Elements in Psycho-Analysis*, London: Maresfield Reprints.

Bollas, C. (1987) *The Shadow of the Object: Psychoanalysis of the Unthought Known*, New York: Columbia University Press.

Brentano, F. (1968) *Psychologie von empirischen Standpunkt*, ed. Kraus, Hamburg: F. Meiner.

Bruss, N. (1986) 'Validation in Psychoanalysis, and "Projective Identification"'. *Semiotica*, 60(1/2): 129–92.

Burton, R. (1621/1927) *An Anatomy of Melancholy*, ed. Floyd Dell and Paul Jordan-Smith, New York: Farrar and Rinehart.

Cavell, M. (1993) *The Psychoanalytic Mind: From Freud to Philosophy*, Cambridge, MA: Harvard University Press.

Enterline, L. (1995) *The Tears of Narcissus: Melancholia and Masculinity in Early Modern Writing*, Stanford: Stanford University Press.

Ficino, M. (1489/1989) *Three Books on Life, A Critical Edition and Translation* by Carol Kaske and John Clark. Binghampton, NY: Medieval and Renaissance Texts and Studies.

Foucault, M. (1973) *Madness and Civilization: A History of Madness in the Age of Reason*, New York: Vintage.

Freud, S. (1917/1957) *Mourning and Melancholia*, in *Collected Papers*, vol. IV, pp. 152–70, authorized translation under the supervision of Joan Rivière, London: Hogarth Press.

—— (1923/1966) *The Ego and the Id*, trans. Joan Rivière; revised and newly edited by James Strachey, London: Hogarth Press and the Institute of Psycho-Analysis.

Gay, P. (1990) *Reading Freud: Explorations and Entertainments*, New Haven: Yale University Press.

Gilman, S., Birmele, J., Geller, J. and Greenberg, V.D. (eds) (1994) *Reading Freud's Reading*, New York: New York University Press.

Gordon, R. (1986) 'The Passivity of Emotions', *Philosophical Review*, 95: 371–92.

Ihsan Al-Issa (1995) *Handbook of Culture and Mental Illness*, Madison, CT: International Universities Press.

Irigaray, L. (1991) *The Irigaray Reader*, edited with an introduction by Margaret Whitford, Oxford: Blackwell.

Jackson, S. (1986) *Melancholia and Depression*, New Haven: Yale University Press.

James, W. (1902) *The Varieties of Religious Experience*, New York: The Modern Library.

Jones, E. (1957/61) *The Life and Work of Sigmund Freud* edited and abridged in one volume by Lionel Trilling and Steven Marcus, New York: Basic Books.

Klein, M. (1935/1975) *Love, Guilt and Reparation and Other Works*, London: Hogarth Press.

Kleinman, A. and Good, B. (1986) (eds) *Culture and Depression: Studies in the Anthropology and Cross-Cultural Psychiatry of Affect and Disorder*, Berkeley: University of California Press.

Klibansky, R., Panofsky, E. and Saxl, F. (1964) *Saturn and Melancholy: Studies in the History of Natural Philosophy, History and Art*, New York: Basic Books.

Kraepelin, E. (1899) *Lehrbuch der Psychiatrie* Leipzig: Abel.

—— (1904) *Lectures on Clinical Psychiatry*, authorized translation, New York: Hafner.

—— (1921) *Manic Depressive Insanity and Paranoia*, trans. R. Mary Barclay from the eighth edition of the *Textbook of Psychiatry*, vols 3 and 4, Edinburgh: E. and S. Livingstone.

Kristeva, J. (1982) *Powers of Horror: An Essay in Abjection*, trans. Leon Roudiez, New York: Columbia

—— (1989) *Black Sun: Depression and Melancholy*, trans. Leon Roudiez, New York: Columbia University Press.

Lacan, J. (1982) *Feminine Sexuality: Jacques Lacan and the École Freudienne*, trans. Jacq§ueline Rose, ed. Juliet Mitchell and Jacqueline Rose, New York: Norton.

Lloyd, G. (1979) 'The Man of Reason', *Metaphilosophy*, 10(1) (Jan.): 18–37

—— (1984) *The Man of Reason: 'Male' and 'Female' in Western Philosophy*, Minnesota: University of Minnesota Press.

Lutz, C. (1986) 'Emotion, Thought, and Estrangement: Emotion as Cultural Category', *Cultural Anthropology*, 1: 287–309.

Meisel, P. and Kendrick. W. (eds) (1985) *Bloomsbury/Freud: The Letters of James and Alix Strachey 1924–1925*, New York: Basic Books.

Mitchell, J. (1974) *Psychoanalysis and Feminism: Freud, Reich, Laing and Women*, New York: Basic Books.

Radden, J. (1987) 'Melancholy and Melancholia', in David Michael Levin (ed.), *Pathologies of the Modern Self: Postmodern Studies in Narcissism, Schizophrenia and Depression*, New York: New York University Press.

—— (1996) 'Lumps and Bumps: Kantian Faculty Psychology, Phrenology, and Twentieth Century Psychiatric Classification', *Philosophy, Psychiatry and Psychology*, 3(1): 1–14.

—— (1998) 'Melancholy, Melancholia and Depression: Contemporary Reflections', unpublished essay.

Schiesari, J. (1992) *The Gendering of Melancholia: Feminism, Psychoanalysis, and the Symbolics of Loss in Renaissance Literature*, Ithaca and London: Cornell University Press.

Seligman, M. (1975) *Helplessness: On Depression, Development, and Death*, New York: W.H. Freeman.

Taylor, Shelley and Jonathan Brown (1988) 'Illusion and Well-Being: A Social Psychological Perspective on Mental Health', *Psychological Bulletin*, 103: 193–210.

Willis, T. (1683) *Two Discourses Concerning the Souls of Brutes*, trans. S. Pordage, London: T. Dring, C. Harper and J. Leigh.

Wollheim, R. (1971) *Sigmund Freud*, New York: The Viking Press.

—— (1984) *The Thread of Life*, Cambridge, MA: Harvard University Press.

12

LUCKY IN LOVE

Love and emotion

Michael P. Levine

Many psychologists, philosophers and others who eschew claims of psycho-analysis to be scientific also regard psychoanalysis as having little insight or validity. However, the view of psychoanalysis that has been on the ascendancy among philosophers, who see it as essential to explaining and interpreting behaviour, is that it is an extension of common-sense psychology. This 'extension' view has it roots in assessing the significance of questions about the scientific status of psychoanalysis.[1] As David Snelling points out (this volume), there are different versions of the extension view. These different versions do not, in my view, fall neatly into a division between those who see the extension as basically formal – psychoanalytic explanation as similar in type or structure to common-sense psychological explanation – and those who see the extension as primarily substantive – that is, as extending the realm of beliefs, desires, motivations, phantasies and other mental states (intentional or sub-intentional) that must be taken into account when explaining otherwise seemingly inexplicable actions, feelings and thoughts.

Given the rise of the 'common-sense psychology extension view' it is perhaps worth remembering that, at least substantively, the distance between ordinary common-sense psychological explanation and psychoanalytic explanation often appears so vast that it may be implausible, at least in the first instance, to see the latter as an extension, even a profound extension, of the former. If one can speak of common-sense grounds for rejecting psychoanalysis, it is certainly not because, for example, the success rate of psychoanalytic practice is questionable; rather it is because what Freud tells us about little girls' penis envy; the oedipal complex; or about the causes of psychical impotence ('Where they love they do not desire and where they desire they cannot love')[2] sounds so utterly implausible – so far removed from ordinary (or even extraordinary) explanation.[3] The world that psychoanalysis presents to us is a world utterly different from the world of common sense – although it is also familiar (cf. Freud 1901b).[4] This is so despite the fact that the everyday world with its ordinary occurrences is, along with clinical data, the principal resource of psychoanalysis. In this essay I want to show how psychoanalysis transforms our understanding of the philosophical dimension of a few problems about love and emotion – and also of ourselves.

1 Loving individuals for their properties: or, what was the colour of Yeats's mother's hair?

In 1884 Freud (1960), twenty-eight years old and love-smitten, wrote a letter to the woman he was to marry two years later. 'When we meet again you may be disappointed on finding that I look different from the lovely picture your tender imagination has painted of me. I don't want you to love me for qualities you assume in me . . . in fact not for any qualities; you must love me as irrationally as other people love, just because I love you, and you don't have to be afraid of it' (Freud to Martha Bernays, 16 January 1884). On one level Freud can be seen as expressing a feeling that is common when one is passionately in love – that of wanting to be loved unconditionally. Even if one does not strictly desire to be loved independently of certain properties one possesses, then at least one does not want to be loved in virtue of (or because of) such properties since they may prove ephemeral. The desire for unconditional love is a feeling that is perhaps familiar from adolescence and one that psychoanalysis, and I think Freud, would later recognize as having its roots in infantile experience. Similarly, the desire to be loved 'just because I love you', along with the distinctive belief/feeling that you *must* love me since I love you,[5] are feelings rooted in infancy and childhood but operative in varying degrees in adult life.

However, the extent to which this letter to his fiancée is consonant with Freud's later views on love is unclear. Freud continues to believe that love is irrational, and he of course believes that people *think* that they love people in virtue of certain qualities possessed by the beloved – even though there is ample *everyday* (i.e. not psychoanalytically interpreted) experience to the contrary.[6] Nevertheless, what he says about the nature of the object-choice in love being either narcissistic or anaclitic; about the overvaluation of the sexual object; and about psychosexual development generally, implies that the reasons one thinks one has for loving someone are, put simply, not the real reasons – they are not even close. This, in part, is why love is seen by Freud as irrational. Whether or not Freud is right in telling Martha that she does not have to be afraid of loving him in the way he is asking to be loved is another question. It is a philosophical and practical question having to do with the implications of a psychoanalytic analysis of love. There may be grounds for being afraid (very afraid) even if (or alternatively *because*) one cannot choose the kind of person one falls in love with, that is, even if one can do little to effect a change in one's object-choices of love.

For the most part, philosophers continue to neglect psychoanalytic theory in analysing love.[7] But if a psychoanalytic account is anywhere near the truth; if it can give a more adequate explanation of commonplace (and uncommon) but puzzling phenomena that occur in love/sex relationships than non-psychoanalytic accounts, then this neglect is serious.

In one form or another, the issue that has been prominent, if not dominant, in recent philosophical discussions of love (Brown 1997; Hamlyn 1978; Kraut 1986; Lamb 1997; Nussbaum 1997; Rorty 1986; Williams 1973b) is whether or not romantic love involves loving a person 'for their properties', or in a sense difficult to elucidate, for 'themselves' alone.[8] I shall argue that loving a person always involves loving them for their properties; that as far as the object of love is concerned there is nothing else, no self-alone, to love apart from properties that a person more or less uniquely instantiates. (I doubt this begs any important metaphysical questions, about the nature of the self that cannot safely be ignored. It is the object of love rather than the nature of the self that is of concern.) Furthermore, I contend that this unique instantiation of a particular set of properties over time and in relation to oneself really gives those, like the woman in Yeats's poem, who want to be loved for themselves alone and not for their properties, all that they really want.[9]

Once sorted out, all of this is, I believe, rather straightforward. What is significant is the controversial point relatively undiscussed by philosophers – which is that the properties we ordinarily identify as those in virtue of which we love someone, are not the properties in virtue of which we love them. The actual properties or reasons in virtue of which we love have little to do with the ostensible properties that lovers cite as the reason or grounds for their love. In large part, this is what makes love so strange; so alternatingly or even concurrently disappointing and satisfying. Nevertheless, in the end, this too comes as no surprise to anyone who accepts some of the core psychoanalytic pronouncements on the nature of love.

2 Love and the individual

Roger Lamb (1997) has recently discussed a problematic implication of the view that people love people in virtue of their properties. The implication is that contrary to the ideology of love, even though love is an emotion of attachment, the object of romantic love is fungible (cf. De Sousa 1980b: 293). In other words, contrary to expectation as well as ideology, if one loves X for their properties, then one may be rationally constrained, all things being equal, to love anyone else with relevantly similar properties. Lamb is right in claiming that persons are loved for their properties rather than for themselves alone, but mistaken in the implications he draws from this.[10]

Lamb (1997: 24) says,

> [O]ur taking up of attitudes towards others is typically a function of various properties . . . those others manifestly have, or are believed to have . . . attitudes are *universalizable*. This is to say that if we adopt some attitude towards someone we know, in virtue of the fact that that person . . . is believed by us to have a certain property or set of properties, then *we* . . . are *constrained* to extend the same attitude-type towards *others* . . . believed by us to have, the same (or relevantly similar) properties. . . . However, the constraint at issue is not always a socially sanctioned one,

nor is it necessarily one with moral credentials . . . if Smith adopts some attitude towards Jones in virtue of Jones' evidencing some property, F, then Smith is *rationally* constrained, *ceteris paribus*, to extend the same attitude-type towards others similarly evidencing the property [or rather '*not* to resist any natural inclination he or she may have to extend the same attitude-type towards others having those properties' (p. 44)] . . . How, we will want to know, can she – *in consistency* – adopt some attitude towards Jones in virtue of Jones' *having* property F, but fail to extend the same attitude-type towards another plainly having the same property?[11]

One case in which the constraint at issue is not a socially or morally sanctioned one is the case of erotic love. 'Love' is usually alleged to be 'particular' (i.e. non-universalizable). Consider the following (Lamb 1997: 25). 'You love S . . . in virtue of the fact that S manifestly has properties $F_1, \ldots F_n$. Now as it happens there is someone else ["J"] who also manifests properties $F_1, \ldots F_n \ldots$ The question for us to consider is not whether you do . . . nor, indeed, whether you ever will – love J. You may, but you may not. Rather the question to consider . . . is whether, all other things remaining equal, you are under any rational constraint to love J (as well as S).'

Much, but not all, of what appears to make the universalizability of love problematic is forestalled as soon as one sees that the properties in virtue of which one loves another are often (virtually) uniquely exemplified. If you love a person because of their generosity it is not just because of their generosity *simpliciter*, but because of their generosity as exemplified along with their other properties. These other properties combine with generosity to make the exemplification of generosity rather unique to a particular person. The exemplification of a property and loving a person because of it are highly contextualised. Being generous is not like having a certain amount of money in one's pocket. It is rather like wearing a particular suit of clothes which everyone wears differently. The fact that everyone exemplifies properties in their own way and in conjunction with their other properties is the commonplace that undermines the significance of the issue of universalizability in relation to love as Lamb presents it. It demystifies one aspect of the question of whether we love someone for their properties or for themselves alone; and it makes a non-starter of the question of whether loving a person for their properties implies that one is constrained to love others with the same properties. On this analysis, loving someone for their properties *just is* to love them for themselves since no one else exemplifies the properties the beloved has as they do.[12]

The distinction that one is really after is not between loving someone for themselves as opposed to loving them for their properties. Rather it is between loving someone for properties that are regarded (by themselves or by the lover or both) as integral to them, instead of loving them for properties exemplified superficially and which are not significantly connected (in their own mind, or by the lover or both) to enough of their other qualities.

There are three notions in play: (1) loving someone purely for themselves, unmediated by properties of any sort; (2) loving them for properties, but for (deep and historical) properties that *de facto* particularize them; and (3) loving them shallowly for universalizable properties. Those whom I am arguing against draw a false dichotomy between (1) and (3). They also mistake (2) for (1), even though (1) makes no clear sense. When I say (above) that 'loving someone for their properties *just is* to love them for themselves alone' I am referring to (2), not (1).[13]

Lamb (1997: 35, n. 20; 41–2) appears to recognize this point when he says 'you may seriously question whether there is any reason to think: because you (admittedly) love S in virtue of her being $F_1, \ldots F_n$, and are an avowed universalist, it follows that you love her "*just* as an" $F_1, \ldots F_n$'. On my view you do not love her '"*just* as an" $F_1, \ldots F_n$'. You love her as having those properties in relation to some of her other properties. Insofar as you do tend to love someone for a few properties, properties not particularly related to other significant aspects of the person, that love will be shallow – albeit perhaps desirable under certain circumstances nevertheless. People do not object to being loved for their properties – not really. What they object to (sometimes) is shallow love. Thus, McTaggart's (1921–7, 2: 153–5) claim that 'Love is for the person, and not for his qualities, nor is it for him in respect of his qualities . . . It is for him' is confused. There is nothing to love a person for or about except in respect of properties, imagined or real, that evoke the emotion, and there is nothing demeaning to the nature of love or the beloved in this. Being loved for one's properties *is* to be loved for oneself. Concerning 'shallow love', what needs to be asked is whether shallow love is 'love'? Can a phenomenon be characterized as love without reference to its objects, history, context, on the basis of surface phenomenology alone?

The 'historicity' of love as a psychological attitude, its 'dynamic permeability' in Rorty's terms, is significant for understanding the complex nature of the properties in virtue of which one loves. These properties have a historical and relational dimension. Not only do these properties unfold as one gets to know the person one loves, but the properties are themselves altered and exemplified differently as a result of the loving relationship.[14] The exemplification of such properties requires time since they are properties-across-time. They are not synchronic but diachronic. Thus, the reasons and ways in which X loves Y are not only a function of Y's properties, but of X's relation to Y which affects those properties – and so on. This too is commonplace and is recognized as such in the realization that being loved changes one and has ramifications for the relationship.[15]

In its most extreme form, the problem allegedly introduced by the universalizability of love is that of supposing one to meet a twin who has properties identical to those in virtue of which you love and no other relevant interfering properties. But given the relevance of historicity in defining the properties in virtue of which one loves, this is a pseudo-problem. The imagined situation cannot come to pass except in cases of extremely shallow love. Even if the twins started out with more or less the same properties, the fact that the properties in virtue of which X loves Y actually changes the properties of Y through the dynamically permeable nature of the relationship – and so the basis of the historical love relation itself – will mean that X need not (under the constraint of universalizability), and ordinarily will not (under ordinary psychological and social constraints) love Y's twin. Not having had the same historical relationship with X, the twins will no longer be identical in the significant respects.

Because the properties in virtue of which X loves Y are historical, and so relational, the counterfactual possibilities that pose a problem in the abstract cannot really do so. If you meet Z who has properties similar to Y in virtue of which you love Y, you are under no constraint to love Z too – especially if you already love Y. The most one could say is that, *ceteris paribus*, X is inclined to love Z, where '*ceteris paribus*' might mean (but would not necessarily mean) that X does not already love Y, since if he did then his attitude towards Z might be altered.[16]

Of course there are people who love extremely shallowly – people who will love just about anyone with a good mind or good body – where these are the only properties in virtue of which they love someone, and where they ignore other properties a person has that might 'defeat' such love. Practically speaking, only in such cases will the rational constraints that appear to follow from the universalizability of love be operative.

Consider an objection by a person S who wishes to defend the particularity of love and thinks it necessary to reject the universalizability of love in order to do so. S wants to be loved for herself. Lamb (1997: 41–2) says,

> S is operating under the assumption that if an attitude is universalizable, then it cannot be the case that the intentional object of such an attitude is an individual, *simpliciter* – that it must be that the object of a universalizable attitude is something rather more complex, something like 'the individual *only as an* instance of a kind', where what happens in such a case is that 'a *universal* . . . enters into [the] intentional object and provides the true object of attention' . . . the rather curious idea appears to be that if an attitude is *universalizable*, then its object is in some way a *universal*!

Is Lamb right in dismissing the objection? If the attitude is universalizable, then why *should* one suppose 'that the intentional object of such an attitude is an individual, *simpliciter*' rather than 'something rather more complex, something like "the individual *only as an* instance of a kind"'? We have seen that if the intentional object of an attitude such as love is an individual *simpliciter* then there is no reason for supposing that that attitude will be universalizable. No matter how identical in properties any other individual Y may be to S, the fact that one loves S *simpliciter* means that there will be no logical constraint on the person to love Y as well as S. S is correct in her assumption. If one is not 'loving an individual only as an instance of a kind', but in their particularity, then insofar as the person's particularity enters into one's attitude that attitude will *ipso facto* fail to be universalizable in any meaningful sense. It will be universalizable only when two people are identical in every way – including in the history of their relationship with the loving person. If an attitude is universalizable, then *whether or not* its object is a universal (which depends on one's account of universals among other things), its object is not an individual *simpliciter*. The objection stated in terms of universals is not amiss, but there is no need to raise the issue of universals to state or to sustain the objection.

Lamb (1997: 42, n. 32) says, 'There is the strong suggestion . . . that Scruton [1986: 96] supposes that the particularity of the objects of love is possible only on the condition that love is not universalizable'. If this is what Scruton is suggesting he is right. Lamb is confusing the particularity of the object of love with the fact that what one loves, if love is universalizable, is not the individual *simpliciter* but the individual as a bearer of certain properties. What it is that one loves if love is universalizable is not the individual *simpliciter* (what would that mean?), but the individual in virtue of their instantiation of the properties that one loves in virtue of – in whatever individual they may be instantiated. If the reason you love X is because of his real estate – you do not love X in his particularity. You love X in virtue of his property. The 'in virtue of' makes all the difference. It is an individual you love, but you do not love her *qua* 'herself', *qua* 'individual' if you love her simply in virtue of her homes and gardens.

Consider the objection further. Lamb (1997: 42–3) says,

> [I]t is perfectly possible to despise some aspect of someone's character without . . . despising the person . . . In such a case, we might say, 'Well, I don't despise James, you understand, but I do find his cowardice completely contemptible'. On the other hand, it is obviously just as possible to despise *James* (himself), in virtue of his cowardice. And here, it is not that I despise some complex, e.g., '*James as a coward*'. It is quite simply *that* I despise *James*. And this situation is untouched by *my* being a universalist.

Is he correct? Can one despise James in virtue of his cowardice, and only in virtue of that, without despising some complex such as 'James as a coward'? It is James one despises all right, but in so far as James is despised in virtue of his cowardice and only that, then although it is the particular 'James' one despises, it is only in so far as James, in his cowardly particularity, instantiates cowardice that he is despised. It is that complex 'James as a coward', that is despised. That is what is important; not whether or not the object of the attitude is a universal. Contrary to Lamb, in so far as James is despised (purely and simply) in virtue of his cowardice, the universalist – in despising just James – despises the complex '*James* as a coward'. This means that one is also committed to despising anyone else who is a coward *qua* coward, though one may not despise either James, or anyone else who is a coward, overall.

If one insists on putting the matter in terms of universals then, contrary to Lamb, there are grounds for claiming 'that if an attitude is *universalizable*, then its object is in some way a *universal'*. Universals are instantiated in particulars. But the attitude towards the particular instantiating the universal is better described as the universal itself rather than the particular instantiating the universal, in so far as the attitude towards the particular is not sustainable in the absence of the instantiation of the universal in that particular.

What needs to be reiterated is that one never loves a person merely in virtue of some simple property x – unless one is God or, on an uncharitable reading, Don Juan. One loves someone in virtue of a complex set of properties many or most of which are relational and 'historical' in character. The idea that we love *de re*, that we love a person 'for themselves' rather than for their properties, is an illusion fostered by the complexity of the set of properties, a set largely unbeknownst to both the lover *and the one they love*, that someone is loved in virtue of. There are reasons for fostering such an illusion, and for why the properties in virtue of which we love someone are largely unknown to us and to them. These reasons are, in my view, far more interesting and significant than the question of whether love is universalizable, or whether we love someone for themselves alone.

Lamb (1997: 44) thinks his view on the universalizability of love has a 'practical corollary'. 'To the extent that . . . [one agrees] with the logic of the universalist's position, then . . . they are *themselves* under a constraint not to let jealousy get in the way of the newly developing loving relationship.' Just as you should not prevent yourself from loving someone else who has the same properties in virtue of which you love the person you do, you should not let your jealousy get in the way of letting your lover develop new loving relationships with those who have relevantly similar (love-provoking) properties to yourself. But even if the universalist is technically under such a constraint, it is a constraint that, even apart from psychological reasons, could be practically realized only in cases of shallow love – only where one loves merely in virtue of a (trivial) property or two. The reason the constraint would not ordinarily be realized is not because being jealous is, or may be, out of one's control. A logical constraint would hold even if one cannot adhere to it, or adhere to it only imperfectly. Instead, it would not hold because the set of properties in virtue of which X loves Y, where the love is not shallow, cannot, for all intents and purposes, be replicated. Repeating the history of a loving relationship with someone new – where that history is itself crucial to the properties in virtue of which one loves – is not a possible task, let alone an easy one, as anyone who has tried to do it is aware. That it is *nevertheless* a task that, according to psychoanalytic theory, we not only try to undertake but do undertake (i.e., loving relationships are frequently anaclitic)[17] should be a cause of interest as well as of consternation. Lamb's logical constraint would only hold if the new lover was identical in every way (except perhaps spatio-temporally) to oneself – that is, if the 'new lover' was not a new lover at all. At any rate, one can probably be jealous (as well as envious) of oneself, even if under a logical constraint not to be.

3 Why love is strange

When we love someone it is in virtue of some complex set of properties that we love them. Love *de re* is a misguided notion, not a romantic illusion, that has its roots in the fact that we are by and large ignorant of why we love and in virtue of what properties we love. An insistence on being loved for oneself rather than for one's properties is also based on confusing the grounds of concern for the constancy and endurance of love. There are frequently plenty of reasons to be concerned, but a failure to be loved *de re* (for 'oneself alone') should not be the source of such concerns. One can be a universalist and still claim to love and be loved (to some extent) for oneself since, lets face it, there isn't anyone else around exactly like you with properties defined in part in relation to one's beloved. This should do little however to assuage one's concerns about endurance and constancy. The properties in virtue of which one loved yesterday need not be those in virtue of which one will love tomorrow. That is only part of what makes love so darned difficult.

There is more. If psychoanalytic theory is more or less correct, the properties that people often sincerely cite as those in virtue of which they love someone are not the actual properties one loves in virtue of, nor are they the reason one loves. (I have already cited Pataki's reasons for why this view may have to be qualified.) Depending on just whose psychoanalytic theory one is employing, some love is engendered by infantile phantasy and is best explained in terms of some combination of phantasy along with instinct, projection, narcissism, complexes, guilt, and more generally, an individual's psychosexual development.[18] The properties that one actually loves someone in virtue of, and *why* one loves someone in virtue of those properties and not some others – for example, properties that one might intellectually regard as more worthy of love – are a function of these and other psychoanalytically identified factors.[19] This is not the place to argue for the truth, or near truth of such theory in any of its forms.[20] But if it is right, then love is not only different from what we ordinarily take it to be, it is also stranger.[21]

At this point the important question is whether the psychoanalytically identified grounds for love imply that the reasons for love ordinarily cited are not really the operative ones. The psychoanalytic answer is that they are not – to a degree. Just as Freud's account of the psychoanalytically discovered reasons for religious belief do not strictly entail but do strongly imply that the reasons people ordinarily give for such beliefs are not the real reasons; so too psychoanalysis implies the reasons people ordinarily cite for loving people are not the real reasons. This does not mean that one does not in fact like it that X is generous or beautiful or may be attracted to X, on some level, in virtue of X's exemplification of such features. It means that what one does find attractive, not simply intellectually appealing . . . or appalling, is a function of psychical states that psychoanalytic theory regards as determinative. This gives rise to the most worrying question of all. To what extent can we affect or decide whom we love and why? There is no univocal psychoanalytic response to this question – just as there is no univocal common-sense response. For Freud, however, the suggestion seems to be the one that many regard as pessimistic. We have little control over love itself, and what we decide to do in relation to love (where we have more control) is usually peripheral to the love itself. Furthermore, Freud's considered opinion is that unless how or who we love is debilitating, it might be best to leave it alone.

This does not mean that relationships cannot be worked on and improved, although it should be remembered that, no matter how earnest partners are, what usually passes for working on the relationship is not really that at all but more of the same – seeking various kinds of satisfactions. And it does mean that whatever one does in this regard is likely, though not necessarily, to be at a level independent of the determinative features in a relationship that psychoanalysis claims to uncover. (It is possible to address issues like projection, narcissism and guilt in relationships.) This is like saying that people in loving relationships are unclear about what makes them work, and know that they do not know – a claim which to many will seem obvious. Are these conclusions as pessimistic? This is a difficult question but to some they might actually be reassuring. These conclusions do not undermine choice in love or the hard and sometimes useful yakka that is part of a committed relationship. They do show that choices are determined in certain ways, and that for all of one's best efforts it is better to be lucky in love than to have to excessively work at it.

Briefly consider some common phenomena that can be used to support the psychoanalytic view that the reasons we think we love someone are not the real reasons. First, there is the overvaluation of the sexual object that Freud discusses (e.g., 1912d). When one is in love with someone in a certain way they are frequently blinded to the beloved's faults and exaggerate their virtues. ('Love is blind.') Frequently, one is aware of this only in retrospect and even then only partially – although one may experience intimations of overvaluation while in its grip. When no longer smitten, previously unnoticed faults become startlingly apparent. A lover may come to wonder, with considerable puzzlement, how they could have loved *that* person at all. Narcissism, wish-fulfilment and projection may also play a role in this. In a sense, *all* love is unrequited love for Freud, since even if the beloved loves back, their love will be subject to the same types of exigencies and vicissitudes as those of their lover. Their love too will be subject to narcissism, projection, and overvaluation. Lover and the beloved are both constructed/reconstructed objects. Stories about love potions and being under love spells illustrate the 'mysterious' but widely recognized fact that why and who and how we love seem beyond our ken and control.

Next, consider the fact that people are often repeatedly attracted to a certain type of person – whether or not, or how many times, a relationship with that type fails – and *even*, in some cases, where one does not like (though one may well 'love' – or love and hate) the person one is attracted to. Psychoanalysis has an explanation for this in terms of the anaclitic nature of the object-choice. A dependent need to revive attachment to the mother is one way of repeating a mistaken choice; a need for suffering or revenge may be others. (Psychoanalysis also explains baby-talk among lovers in terms of regressive tendencies and the desire to be loved unconditionally.) Then there is the related case that people (especially men) frequently bemoan the fact that despite their strong desires (i.e. intellectual but not affective desire), efforts and beliefs, they are not sexually attracted to the person(s) they love – but instead to those they don't love or regard as inferior; or that as love grows sexual attraction diminishes. The psychoanalytic explanation here is in terms of the oedipal complex and subsequent incest barrier (cf. Freud 1905d; 1912d).[22] Incidentally, Freud's (1912d) account of psychical impotence also explains why so-called erotica can never do the job of pornography in terms of eliciting sexual excitement, where (for the sake of argument) pornography as opposed to erotica is taken as involving an element of debasement. There are of course other explanations of these features of our love life, just as there are alternative explanations of neurotic symptoms and hysteria. Psychoanalysis claims that its explanations are the most adequate and that they are not *ad hoc*.

An account of love that specifies caring for the other for their own sake, desiring their company and enjoying it, and taking an interest in their projects, an account along just these lines, describes an emotion found among creatures only remotely similar to ourselves. None of these features of love figure prominently in Freud's account. It is odd, though understandable, that people accept such seemingly weighty and fanciful accounts – ones that preclude their own love as experienced, as ever counting as love. Compare the above version with Santas's summary (1988: 117) of Freud's account of types of love.

> The central thesis of Freud's theory of love is that all love is a derivative of the sexual instincts. The nuclear case is sexual or 'romantic' love, where the love-object is a person of the opposite sex and the aim is sexual union; these are the 'normal' object and (intermediate) aim of the sexual instinct. All other kinds of love including self-love, familial love, friendship, and the love of humanity, love of concrete objects and abstract entities, are formed by displacement of the normal object or by inhibition or by deflection of the normal aim. The first task of a theory of love is to explain . . . the central case of sexual love. Freud tried to do this by describing the main observable characteristics of sexual love – exclusive attachment and overvaluation – and by constructing genetic explanations of these characteristics on the basis of his theories of the libido and psychosexual development . . . The remaining task . . . is to explain . . . all other kinds of love . . . Freud tries to show that all these other attachments are derived from the sexual instinct and are formed through the mechanisms of object displacement, repression or inhibition of aim, and deflection of the normal sexual aim.

But for Freud the pristine nuclear case is never found, or if it is, it is transitory and effervescent. What Santas refers to as the 'other kinds of love' are often, in varying degrees, constitutive of the nuclear case. (See Freud 1905d, 1910, 1912d, 1921c.) Santas is mistaken, or has oversimplified matters, if he thinks, as might be indicated in the above quotation, that deviation from sexual instincts is all there is to Freud's view of love.

An idealized account of love that fails to capture salient features will be conceptually egregious and phenomenologically flawed. On Freud's view, no account of erotic love can succeed if it fails to mention narcissism, projection, displacement and wish-fulfilment, along with relevant features of a child's psychosexual development.[23] Just as an account of morality that fails to ground itself in an adequate conception of human nature must fail; so too, if psychoanalytic theory is right, any account of love or other emotions that ignores the psychoanalytic extension (and in many ways defence of) folk-psychology, will be anaemic. However, the substantive extension of folk-psychology begins to fail here. A narcissistic attachment, say, which is really an attachment to a part of oneself projected into another, is not easily teased out from common-sense psychology. The idea that I can love myself in loving another seems remote from common-sense psychology.

Along with the ideas that (i) infants are sexual beings whose development must be understood psychosexually, and (ii) that there is a continuum instead of a radical discontinuity between the neurotic and normal, one of the most important things Freud seeks to explain, connected to i and ii, is the nature of love. Freud thought that to begin to understand love one had to have recourse to his theories of libido, psychosexual development and other of his metapsychological and psychoanalytic views. But he also thought that understanding love was unlikely to help much in terms of people loving more wisely or more successfully. And the notion that we could improve our love lives by better understanding ourselves was one of those wish-fulfilling phantasies that Freud mercilessly rejected.[24] Perhaps one way that better understanding can help improve our love lives, along with other significant aspects, is to help lower our expectations. This too would be rejected by Freud. It is his considered view that our expectations, remarkably, will remain intact. On Freud's view, self-deception is constitutive of human nature and it is just about omnipresent. Most paradigmatic acts of repression, involving as they do the intentional suppression of what is known, are instances of self-deception.[25] Freud could never seriously consider the suggestion that there might be a fully integrated or ideal self that was rarely self-deceived.[26]

Labouring under a misconception about the nature of love has practical consequences. As A.S. Byatt (1990: 425) says, 'the expectations of Romance control almost everyone in the Western world, for better or worse, at some point or another'. But this is only half the story. The age we live in determines how we love and think of love; but it is also true that love determines the age. How we conceptualize emotions has personal and interpersonal ramifications. Misunderstanding love may not only place a practical burden on the one taken in; it may also prevent or alter one's experience of something closer to the real thing, or something that better serves our well-being. There is a story about Charlie Chaplin entering (incognito) a Chaplin look-alike contest to promote one of his new films. He came in third. In my view, this is precisely the story Freud tells us about love. We are compelled to dress it up

– to enter it in contests. Apart from a more holistic account of love (and other emotions), true love, like the real Chaplin, will place behind fancy imposters. It may be possible to alter our emotional lives by thinking about the emotions differently. Freud suggested as much – along with what this might involve.

4 Emotion; rationality; well-being

I have been discussing not so much the nature of love but a particular aspect of the irrationality of love – ways in which it misleads us as to its objects and causes. Love itself, even erotic love, is probably not an emotion but a complex of various emotions, beliefs, desires and commitments. Nevertheless, much of what may be right concerning the implications of psychoanalysis for understanding love can be applied to emotions in general.

On a common-sense view emotions will generally be rational if they are appropriate in the circumstances. Additionally, Amélie Rorty (1986) has argued that although emotions cannot be rational in the narrow sense of being logically derived from accepted premises, they can be deemed rational in a broader sense as 'appropriately formed to serve our thriving'.[27] However, the common-sense view and Rorty's broader view are not altogether independent. When particular emotions are triggered by certain perceptions, beliefs and desires, they are triggered in part precisely because having those emotions in those circumstances usually does appear to serve our thriving – at least *prima facie*. This is part of what 'appropriateness' in the circumstances appears to consist in. If they did not seem appropriate, if they did not seem generally conducive to well-being, then other emotions would be had, ones that would better serve us – or so we assume. This does not mean that each time we have an emotion it will be rational in Rorty's broad sense. It means that far from being grounds for supposing that particular emotions will not be rational, the fact that such emotions are automatic responses is reason for supposing they are generally rational.

But on a psychoanalytic view, 'appropriateness in circumstances' is not even a *prima facie* reason to suppose that instances of emotion are rational – or at least not rational on a more fundamental level. The psychoanalytic view rejects what Sebastian Gardner (1992: 36) calls the 'rationalistic account' which 'holds that emotions are direct and sufficient outcomes of complexes of belief . . . beliefs which identify the emotion's kind, cause, and object and reflect its normative framework'.[28] Psychoanalysis gives us reason to believe emotions are irrational in significant respects, no matter how appropriate they appear to be in the circumstance and irrespective of whether they serve our thriving.

A particular instance of an emotion is *prima facie* rational because it matches paradigm scenarios in which the emotion was learned and refined. It is appropriate to those relevantly similar situations in which it was learned to be appropriate. But if the reasons we have the emotions we do, when we do, are fundamentally irrational, then this undermines grounds for believing emotions are overall rational. If the reason you have emotion x in situations like y is because of genetic disposition, infantile phantasies, desires or frustrations relating to one's body, then perhaps x is fundamentally irrational after all. It does not matter if it corresponds to learned scenarios or serves one's well-being. The emotion's aetiology may undermine its overall rationality instead of enforcing it. If the more basic reason for my jealousy or envy or gratitude, is not just a partly learned disposition for the emotion combined with the socialization that reinforces the disposition, but instead is due to infantile phantasy, then this would undermine reasons for supposing a particular emotion to be *prima facie* rational because it occurs in the right sort of situation.

Given a psychoanalytic account of their aetiology it is often not plausible to see emotions as rational in some important ways, including and perhaps *especially* in the sense of serving our well-being. We are not, if Freud is anywhere near the truth, the rational creatures, emotionally or otherwise, we take ourselves to be. That emotions are fundamentally irrational is perfectly compatible with David Sach's claim (1982: 93) that Freud maintained a 'persistent adherence . . . to the idea that, between any person's emotions or affects and the causes or objects thereof, there always obtains an actual proportionality or real appropriateness, no matter how discrepant or incongruous those relations may appear to be, and regardless of the person's mental condition . . . [whether] psychotic, neurotic, or normal'. Once the aetiology of emotion is psychoanalytically understood, 'actual proportionality or real appropriateness' between an emotion and its cause does not underwrite the emotion's rationality, but its irrationality.

In discussing the philosophical implications of Melanie Klein's account of the emotions, Gardner (1992: 42, 44) says:

> The first general law that governs the formation of phantasy directs it towards producing an ideal situation in which the distribution of badness and goodness on the 'map' of self and world is such that all goodness is coincident with the ego and all badness external to it. This 'a priori' of phantasy is the basic condition which determines when configurations of psychological states do and do not call for phantastic solutions [p. 42] . . . [T]he consciously recognized and self-ascribed state of emotion is a *historical descendant* of an earlier kind of state, which is one of phantasy. The philosophical claim is that a state of emotion is fully intelligible only in terms of such an ancestor-state. So, even, when an emotion occurs in adult life and is adjudged appropriate, appearing not to indicate any kind of unconscious activity, it remains true that it is at least derivative of an infantile and phantastic prototype . . . an emotion is a thought-like power to determine phenomenological properties . . . the thought from which this power is derived is an unconscious, phantastic thought . . . [and] to each emotion-kind there corresponds a particular kind of phantastic thought [p. 44].

Phantasy itself seems to be the product, at least in part, of wish-fulfilment – depending on what one means by both of these terms. I assume that the philosophical claim to which Gardner refers is that an ancestor state of phantasy is necessary, but not sufficient, to make an emotion 'fully intelligible'. The claim that an emotion is 'fully intelligible' in terms of its ancestor state would be to overstate the significance even of phantasy. To show that emotion is rooted in phantasy, to explain it in terms of the phantasy and even to explain the phantasy as Klein has done, would still not suffice to show why the infant has that particular phantasy or emotion and not some other. Even if psychoanalytic theory does tell 'us what *kind* of phantasy is its [an emotion's] ancestor-state' and even 'what particular phantasy currently underpins it' (Gardner 1992: 44), it will not have made an instance of an emotion 'fully intelligible'. It is not even clear what 'full intelligibility' or a complete explanation would be. But if basic emotions such as envy and gratitude are derivative in the manner Klein describes then they are fundamentally irrational.[29]

Although questions relating to moral responsibility for one's emotions have been discussed (Sankowski 1977; Blum 1980: 188–90; Schlossberger 1986; Oakley 1993), the more basic issues concerning the implications of the irrationality of the emotions for morality are unclear and have not received much attention from moral philosophers. Whether or not people are responsible for their emotions and how such responsibility impinges upon morality are important questions. But how the basic irrationality of emotions may impinge upon morality is an issue that cannot be glossed in addressing these questions. Justin Oakley (1993: 187) claims that '[S]ince people do have morally significant features which they are not responsible for having, morality does not presuppose responsibility . . . the moral significance of our emotions does not depend on establishing our responsibility for them' (cf. Williams 1993, ch. 3 'Recognizing Responsibility'; Sherman, ch.8 in this volume). But whether or not we are responsible for our emotions, Oakley's claim does not take into account the issue of whether the irrational nature of the emotions might in any way mitigate their moral significance. If, as is now widely believed (cf. Williams 1973a; Oakley 1993), Kant is mistaken and emotions do play a crucial role in moral motivation and other aspects of our moral lives, then the irrationality of emotion may have significant negative ramifications in our moral lives and important implications for moral theory. At least, it is not apparent how the ramifications could be positive. How can irrational and automatic emotional responses be related to a person in a morally significant sense? Can Kant seek support for his view on the radical independence of morality and emotion from psychoanalysis?

Whether particular instances of emotion are rational, and if so in what sense, is one question; and (contrary to Rorty 1986) whether they generally serve our thriving is, for various reasons, quite another. Because this latter question involves thinking about what it means to thrive; about the nature of the good life; speculation about emotional possible worlds; and even theories about the nature of happiness; it is a mistake to regard the question as basically empirical. This is surely not the best of all possible worlds emotionally speaking for reasons beyond those entailed by the fact that this is not the best of all possible worlds. What does psychoanalysis have to say about whether or not emotions generally serve our thriving? McCullagh (1990) claims that particular emotions are not generally rational because they are not rationally arrived at, and so he concludes that they are not formed to serve our thriving. This does not follow. May not particular emotions serve our thriving even if, on a psychoanalytic account, they are not rationally arrived at, and even if they are fundamentally irrational?

Particular instances of emotion are instances of generic emotions, and if a generic emotion is formed so as to serve our thriving, then it is possible, but unlikely, that the majority of instances of that emotion will not serve our thriving, unless they consistently occur inappropriately. They might consistently be inappropriate if people continually muddled the salient features of emotion-provoking scenarios, or if people are unduly influenced by wishes and desires or consistently mistaken in beliefs and judgements constitutive of the emotion. Even then it would have to be shown that the resultant emotions did not generally serve our thriving. Perhaps wishes and excess desires and muddled scenarios function positively in some lives. After all, even emotions that we may recognize as ill-formed and inappropriate may at times serve us well. Whether they do so depends on extrinsic factors (e.g., how others react) as well as intrinsic ones. Maybe it is better overall in terms of thriving to have emotions that are often not rational rather than no emotions, or mostly rational emotions. At any rate, if – as Klein does – one takes emotion to be rooted in phantasy and so fundamentally irrational, then there is a sense in which emotions are always the result of muddled emotion-provoking scenarios, confused desires, and the like. This is so even if Freud was right in maintaining, as Sachs (1982: 93) claimed he did, 'that, between any person's emotions or affects and the causes or objects thereof, there always obtains an actual proportionality or real appropriateness, no matter how discrepant or incongruous those relations may appear to be'.[30] As I have said, the 'actual proportionality or real appropriateness' between an emotion and its cause or object does not underwrite the emotion's rationality. It does not show that emotions are not the result of, or do not stand in a historical relation to, infantile unconscious phantastic thoughts.

If a generic emotion is rational in Rorty's sense then, despite exceptions, most instances of that emotion will serve our thriving. If our emotional lives serve us well, then most emotional occurrences, including disquieting ones, will be rational in that they serve us well. They are, after all, simply instances of those generic emotions 'appropriately formed'. Other particular instances of emotion may not be rational because they may be instances of generic emotions that undermine well-being. Whether there are more rational generic and particular emotions, in Rorty's sense, than there are irrational ones is a perplexing question. If the answer is affirmative, it is not obviously so.

Most instances of a generic emotion would not have to serve our thriving for particular counterparts to do so. Most particular instances of an emotion may not be so conducive, but in the cases where they are, they may be so conducive to well-being that they overall out-weigh negative instances of the emotion. Thus, rage may not ordinarily be conducive to our thriving, but in those few cases where it is, it may be so crucial that overall it is better to be able to instantiate rage than not. It is *probably* true that most particular instances of an emotion are conducive to our thriving (but see below). And they are so conducive because the generic emotion they instantiate also tends to be so conducive. So all things being equal the 'rationality' (in Rorty's sense) that a particular emotion has, will simply be an instance of the rationality of the generic emotion it instantiates. A particular emotion may be conducive to our thriving even when its generic counterpart is not, and vice versa, but this will usually not be the case. It is not clear whether this could usually be the case. That is, it is not clear whether only particular emotions could be rational in the sense of serving our well-being while their generic counterparts never, or infrequently did.

I said that it is probably true that most particular emotions are conducive to our thriving, but I am not convinced. The question of whether emotions generally are conducive to well-being is more fundamental and more interesting than whether they are rational. It is not something that can be decided experimentally by showing, for example, that more emotional people are 'happier' than less emotional ones – though this might be relevant. It might be thought that if our emotions did not generally serve us well, then biologically or psychologically, we would have developed different ones. But this is not clear. For one thing, assuming emotions to be an artificial rather than a natural class, we may be on our way towards a different understanding of ourselves upon which various new emotion types may supervene. Furthermore, it may be that our biological and emotional well-being diverge at all levels, including the most basic. Emotions may serve the former without concomitantly serving the latter. It seems that our biological and emotional well-being are (i) only contingently related, and (ii) related in *extremely peculiar* ways. These two claims are independent of one another. The cost–benefit calculation of natural selection might well have established some mechanisms, including mechanisms that relate to the emotions, that save the members of some species in extremity, though they hinder them in small ways when the situation is not critical. If the environment is favourable, we could imagine that most members of the species never encounter the critical conditions in which the mechanism would save them, and so experience it only as an obstacle to living. This relation would perhaps be peculiar, but it is not contingent.

There are, however, various ways, some significant and some less so, in which our biological and emotional well-being are peculiarly related. I am thinking about diet, sex, work, play, relationships, responsibilities – take your pick. When they become problematic, psychoanalysis seeks to explain aspects of these curious relations. Even the emotionally well-adjusted may not benefit in terms of their well-being from being fortuitously emotionally attuned. There is the daunting prospect that the emotionally well-adjusted may be those whose emotions are least conducive to their well-being. Psychoanalysis takes this possibility seriously.

If the emotions are integrally related to morality, in terms of character and virtue, then it appears they serve our well-being. But this is not uncontroversial. Alternative emotions, or as Kant claimed, no emotion whatsoever, may better serve morality. Perhaps a very heightened sense of compassion would make a difference to the moral state of things. If so, would such a morally improved state be more conducive to our emotional and physical well-being? Insofar as emotions are integral to morality they seem necessary to well-being. But the question remains as to whether the emotions we have are those most conducive to well-being. *Prima facie*, it seems many emotions are not generally good for us. Emotion breeds many kinds of discontent – including emotional discontent. Some discontent is good for us, but does such discontent *usually* serve our well-being?

5 Are there emotions not worth having?

Which emotions, if any, generally impede our thriving so that it would be better to wean ourselves from them if we could? If there are emotions we would be better off without, shouldn't we try to get rid of them? There are, for example, people that try not to love. However, even emotions people think they could better do without, and could often do better without (e.g. envy, rage and jealousy), may overall enhance well-being. Given the way they may relate to one's overall complement of emotions, it is far from clear that excising envy, greed and malice from one's psychic economy – rather than bringing them to consciousness, recognizing them in their disguises, containing and mitigating them – would be a good thing. Psychoanalysis aims only at the latter. A notion of 'well-being' plays a role in deciding which emotions to eliminate if one could. But the answer is not a straightforward function of one's idea of eudemonia. Does a psychoanalytic account of emotion have implications for this issue? The question of the manipulation of emotions is central to psychoanalysis. It arises and is highlighted when psychoanalytic theory meets practice.

Sebastian Gardner suggests that despite their fundamental irrationality, emotions serve our well-being; or at least it makes no sense to suppose we can excise them – whether or not they serve thriving. He says (1992: 48) 'If emotion does have a profoundly irrational aspect, ought we not try to excise it from our lives? This would make sense only if it were thought that people should aspire to live in a world stripped of emotional qualities and that they could prise themselves apart from their deepest sources of motivation. We would not know how to begin to act on either of these assumptions.' But Gardner begs the question – several questions – here and his assertion appears to be independent of psychoanalytic considerations. After all, at least one central task of psychoanalysis is to manipulate or realign emotions – which in some cases amount to excision. Why shouldn't we try to excise emotion, or a great deal of it, from our lives? Is it really impossible for people to 'prise themselves apart from [some of] their deepest sources of motivation'? Would it not be desirable, even morally desirable, if they could? Doesn't psychoanalytic practice demand nothing less in some cases? Perhaps Gardner's claim that it makes no sense to talk about excising emotion reflects not so much the belief that one would not know how to act on either of his stated assumptions, but rather the view that despite their irrationality, emotions serve our thriving and happiness. Even if psychoanalytic theory is in general agreement here, in many contexts it also denies this.

Gardner talks about excising all emotion from our lives, but of course there are a number of middle positions concerning the desirability of excising emotion. For example, one can maintain that excising irrational emotions that have particularly deleterious effects is desirable; and most would hold that it is desirable to excise them in some circumstances. Some psychoanalytic theory might allow that it is possible to replace certain phantasies from which certain emotion-kinds are derived with more desirable and beneficial phantasies from which other and unknown emotion-kinds might be derived. Perhaps this can be done by changing child-rearing arrangements or abandoning the nuclear family as some feminist psychoanalytic theory suggests. By considering cases in which it would be desirable to excise emotion from our lives we are given an intimation or foothold into knowing what Gardner claims we cannot know; namely, how to begin to act on the assumptions he claims are necessary to make sense of the question of whether we ought to excise emotion. We can begin to consider what it would be like to live in a world stripped not of all emotional qualities but of some of them. We can consider what it might be like to prise ourselves apart from at least some of our emotional sources of motivation. Isn't this precisely what psychoanalysis asks of its patients? At any rate, given that all emotion has an irrational aspect, but that much emotion appears to be clearly beneficial, the natural question is not whether we ought to excise *all* emotion from our lives, but which emotions, if any, can and should be excised.

As Gardner (1992: 49) notes, Kleinian psychoanalytic theory 'does not entail the undesirability of emotion. Rather it suggests the desirability of one's emotional life being structured by, and characteristically manifesting attainment of, the depressive position' instead of being 'structured by the paranoid-schizoid position' which is responsible for the 'undesirable emotional states that constitute human bondage'.[31] He says, 'given that we live in, and cannot want not to live in, an emotionally characterized world, what should be aspired to is a condition in which emotion contributes maximally to psychological integration and malforms belief as little as possible'. This view however is completely compatible with holding that some emotions can and should be excised or altered. The question as to which emotions, if any, *can*, let alone *should*, be excised – in particular cases, but especially in general – is made more complex when relations among emotions are considered.

The names of individual emotions, how they are classed and spoken about, suggest it is possible to delineate those that are desirable from those that are not. But emotions have conceptual and emotional relations to one another that may prevent such culling on conceptual as well as practical grounds. They are dynamically interrelated. Let's call this view 'emotional holism'. Emotional holism is deflationary. Jealousy, for example, might be ingredient in many instances of love, and necessarily so. Or consider 'hate' which is, after all, sometimes said to be close to love. This may have to do with the phenomenological content of the affective component, or the evaluative or wilful components in love and hate. But one who says that hate is close to love could be making another point, one that is conceptually suggestive about love in particular and emotion in general. They may be putting forward a view of the relation amongst various emotions that would belie some of the more common and less complex accounts of those emotions. They may be emotional holists.

The idea that emotions are interrelated in ways that prevent strict individuation of emotion-kinds, or instances of particular emotions, in terms of common-sense or folk-psychological classification, can be found in psychoanalytic theory's emphasis on (i) the source of emotion in phantasy, and (ii) its narrative understanding of emotions. Thus, Gardner (1992: 46) says

> emotion-kinds occupy roles in typical sequences, and this permits a relational identification of an emotion in terms of what precedes and what follows it in the model narrative set out in psychoanalytic theory. This contrasts with our pre-psychoanalytic 'atomism' about emotions: we do not ordinarily . . . suppose that emotions have a deep organization which interrelates them . . . we ordinarily take emotions on a one-off basis, seeking immediate environmental cues for each instance of emotion. Psychoanalytic theory improves on this 'shallow' view.

In terms of individuating emotion-kinds, Gardner (1992: 45–6) notes that 'although psychoanalytic individuation of emotion-kinds must of course remain *roughly* within the parameters set by our ordinary classification, the important possibility is created that two different instances of emotion may be regarded as exemplifying different emotion-kinds despite an identity of feeling and conscious belief across cases, since this remains compatible with a difference in content at the level of phantasy'. According to the psychoanalytic view of Melanie Klein's to which Gardner is referring, it is on the level of phantasy that emotion-kinds are primarily to be individuated – which is not to say (Gardner 1992: 46) that psychoanalytic theory 'denies the reality of ordinary psychological distinctions'. The possibility Gardner cites is important not just theoretically, but for psychoanalytic practice where correctly locating an emotion vis-à-vis the correct emotion-kind (as psychoanalytically determined) may be crucial.

Justin Oakley (1993: 14) has defended the view that emotions are 'dynamically related complexes of cognitions, desires and affects'. If so, it is reasonable to suppose that emotions are themselves interrelated in terms of these complexes. This suggests a more complicated understanding of emotion than perhaps Oakley depicts since each emotion would have to be understood in terms of others. This affirms what we already know about the complexity of emotions. They are permeable and constantly run up against one another. Oakley's view about emotions such as love, may be truncated if one takes the dynamic nature of an emotion to be intra-emotional as well as related to the components that are 'individually necessary, and when dynamically linked, jointly sufficient for an emotion'. Thus, despite Oakley's insightful account about the nature of emotion, his Aristotelian account of love, for example, is an abstraction that will not ring true to those in love – not even those who labour under the illusion of the 'old high way of love'.[32] Rorty (1985: 349) attends to the complexity of emotions when she says 'evaluations, [and] appraisals are rarely reducible to a sharp contrast between polar attitudes of either favouring, or disfavouring . . . The ways in which they appear within the intentional component of emotions is far more subtle than a yea or nay towards some aspect of an object.'

Oakley, I think, treats emotions as a natural kind rather than an artificial class. But as Rorty (1985: 343–4) says, 'Distinctive conditions were introduced into the class of emotions for different reasons at different historical periods. The artificial class *emotions* intersects with other equally artificial classes: passions, feelings, sentiments [etc.].' Oakley's characterization of love may stem from his regarding the class of emotions as natural. One who sees the class of emotions as artificial is likely to take the relations among them as essential to their characterization, and is also likely to reject Aristotle's non-holistic, essentialist, description of the emotions. Klein's view that emotion-kinds are primarily individuated on the level of phantasy is, I take it, compatible with a view that regards emotions, as ordinarily identified, as an artificial class. Klein's psychoanalytic view is a corrective to what Gardner refers to as the shallow view. It is on the side of emotional holism.

Acknowledgements

Versions of this essay were presented at Rhodes University and the University of Cape Town. My thanks to the audiences for useful discussion and to Margi La Caze, Roger Lamb and William Lycan. Earlier versions of sections of this essay have been published as 'Rational Emotion, Emotional Holism, True Love, and Charlie Chaplin', *Journal of Philosophical Research*, 24 (1999), pp. 489–506; and 'Loving Individuals for their Properties: Or, What Was the Colour of Yeats's Mother's Hair?', *Iyyun: The Jerusalem Philosophical Quarterly*, 48 (1999), pp. 251–67.

Notes

1 The best known exponent of this 'extension' view is Jim Hopkins (1982; 1988). Hopkins (1988: 59) says 'Grunbaum has made no case against the view . . . that much of Freud's reasoning can be regarded as cogently extending common-sense psychology. If Grunbaum has missed something about connection between content and wish-fulfilment, and if what he has missed constitutes reason to accept Freudian claims, then his conclusions systematically understate the support for Freudian theory'. Also see Gardner (1993; 1994); Cavell (1993).
2 See Freud (1912d), 'On The Universal Tendency to Debasement in the Sphere of Love'.
3 The real grounds for rejecting Freud's views practically out of hand are, according to Freud, more complex. See, for example, Freud's explanation in Freud (1916–17) *Introductory Lectures on Psychoanalysis*, Lecture I.
4 For an excellent summary of the weird (non-commonsensical) world Freud presents us with see the opening paragraph of David Sachs's essay, 'On Freud's Doctrine of the Emotions', in Wollheim and Hopkins (1982), pp. 92–105.
5 William James discusses this in his *Principles of Psychology*.
6 For reasons related to what he describes as the 'obscurity of Freud's treatment of love', Tamas Pataki (correspondence) has raised important queries regarding my claims that (i) Freud believes love to be irrational, and (ii) that the reasons cited for love are not even close. He says, 'Although it is difficult to reconcile Freud's various pronouncements on

the libido theory between 1905 and 1920 the general drift seems to be something like this. In this early phase (e.g. 1905d, 1912d, 1915c) Freud distinguishes two currents of object-libido, affectional and sensual. The former current is object-directed from the first, precedes sensual object-libido and leans upon – is anaclitic to – some of the self-preservative or ego-instincts. It appears to come in two phases, first as a primary attachment to the self-preservative instincts of nourishment and then later, in latency, as "mitigation" of auto-erotic libido. Freud suggested, implausibly, that except for a momentary experience of erotic attachment to the breast the child's erotic activity is primarily auto-erotic or narcissistic until it unifies its component sexual instincts at puberty when the sensual object-libido arrives. Later, with the new duality of instincts introduced in *Beyond the Pleasure Principle* (1920g) Freud dropped this distinction between the two currents of object-libido and derived all the affectional, and indeed the attachment drives formerly attributed to the ego-instincts, from the aim-inhibition, sublimation (or, later, neutralization) of what were originally erotic or sensual drives. Although Freud always made it clear that love is a combination of sensual and affectional currents (e.g. 1915c, 1921c: Ch 12) he sometimes suggested that love had more to do with the affectional, aim-inhibited drives than the sensual ones. Thus in *Group Psychology and the Analysis of the Ego* (1921c: ch. 8) he says: "The depth to which anyone is in love, as contrasted with his purely sensual desire may be measured by the size of the share taken by the aim-inhibited instincts of affection". And the aim-inhibited drives and their derivatives – or on the earlier theory, the derivatives of the earliest affectional current of libido and aim-inhibited or sublimated sensual libido – are by and large nothing other than our everyday conscious and pre-conscious motives, assessed as rational or not in the usual ways. So the reasons for this kind of love, were it to exist in pure form, could be pretty close to the reasons ordinarily cited, and the emotions transparently rational. Where repressed sensual or affectional-attachment currents are at work, we have a different issue.'

There are a number of ways to respond to this – none of them wholly satisfactory. A response that would be too easy perhaps is to say that the aim-inhibited instincts never do exist in a pure form. The affectional current is never wholly divorced from the sensual but is instead grounded in it. Another, but related, way to respond would be to say that Freud uses 'love' in several different ways, and that when he sharply distinguishes 'love' from sensual desire as he does (above), he is referring to a type of love that people think exists but does not really exist. More directly, there is the question of whether the fact that instincts of affection are aim-inhibited, neutralized, or sublimated sexual drives, itself undermines the rationality of love, or the claim that the reasons ordinarily given for why we love are close to the real reasons.

7   There are important exceptions – especially among philosophers with psychoanalytic training such as Lear (1990); De Sousa (1980a and b; 1987) and Neu (1999). Lear's interpretation of psychoanalysis's account of love seems to me to be well removed from Freud's. Lear (1990: 143) describes his own project as follows. 'I have been inquiring what the world must be like, given the psychoanalytic understanding of human existence. The inquiry is into the conditions of the possibility of psychoanalysis. Or rather, it is an inquiry into the conditions of the possibility of human existence (given the psychoanalytic understanding of what it is to be human). It is an internal metaphysics because it is working within the concepts of psychoanalysis, trying to deduce their metaphysical implications.'

8   Reference is often made to W.B Yeats's poem 'For Anne Gregory' (*The Collected Poems of W.B. Yeats* (New York: Macmillan, 1956), p. 240). Cf. Lamb's (1997: 46–47) discussion of the yellow-haired woman's desire to be loved 'for myself alone and not my yellow hair'. Also see Shakespeare's Sonnet 116 from which Amélie Rorty takes the title of her essay (1988) by altering Shakespeare's lines 'love is not love which alters when it alteration finds'.

9 See Steven E. Boer and William G. Lycan (1986: 155–6). Delaney (1996) reaches some of the same conclusions.

10 Although it is Lamb's essay I discuss in detail, what I say is applicable, *mutatis mutandis*, to Nussbaum (1997) and to the discussions cited of what one loves when one loves a person. I choose Lamb's essay to discuss because I think it most clearly presents the problem.

11 Lamb (1997: 39) later reiterates the objection. 'What appears to threaten our rationality as lovers is the conjunction of our loving in virtue of properties believed by us to be possessed by those loved, yet refusing to extend this most important of attitude-types towards others who admittedly have just the same (or relevantly similar) properties. If such refusal is detected in a less important attitude, e.g., in liking, or admiring, we are commonly and rightly open to criticism.' Lamb (25, n. 4) cites Scruton (1986: 96) as one who claims love is not universalizable and Max Scheler (1913: 149) as one who observes 'approvingly' that it is not universalizable.

12 Williams's (1973: 81) distinction between 'token-person' (i.e. a 'place-holder of predicates' in Lamb's terms) and 'type-person' is not relevant to (non-superficial) love, where a token-person, described in enough detail, tends to converge with the type-person.

13 William Lycan helped me sort this out.

14 Cf., De Sousa (1980b: 293). 'The ideology of love is . . . directly contrary to the general desirability of emotional fungibility. For the properties on which human attachment is based are not qualitative, but historical.' But De Sousa has overstated his case. Such properties are both historical and qualitative.

15 Cf. Rorty (1988).

16 Cf. Lamb's discussion (1997: 39–40) of universalizability 'across possible worlds, but not within world'.

17 Charles Rycroft (1970: 6). 'Freud . . . distinguished two types of object choice: narcissistic and anaclitic . . . anaclitic object-choice occurs when the choice is based on the pattern of childhood dependence on someone unlike himself . . . the implication is that the man rediscovers a mother and the woman rediscovers a father . . . Alternatively . . . in anaclitic object-choice the sexual choice follows a path laid down by the self-preservative instinct.'

18 Pataki (correspondence) says: 'the earliest current of affectional libido which is anaclitic to the self-preservative instincts is not conceived by Freud as engendered by phantasy and subject to the vicissitudes, or at least not in the same way, that the erotic or sensual trends are. Freud says: "It springs from the earliest years of childhood; it is formed on the basis of the interests of the self-preservative instincts" (1912d). It seems to be conceived as a basic attachment to mother and others, not derived from auto-erotic or sensual object libido, which follows hard on the attachment to mother of the dependent, nourishment seeking self-preservative instincts. Except in the middle period when it was submerged in Eros, this primary affectional current was considered an important component of love. It is less clear whether the ego-instincts which antecede and base them form a component of love. In 1915c Freud says: "We do not say of objects which serve the interests of self-preservation that we love them; we emphasize that we need them, and perhaps express an additional, different kind of relation to them by using words which that denote a much reduced degree of love – such as, for example, 'being fond of', 'liking' or 'finding agreeable'."'

19 Given this psychoanalytic account of love, it is an interesting question as to whether all 'love' should be regarded as, in a sense, shallow or superficial. I am inclined to think that it should not be. Rather, it suggests an understanding of love very differently from how it is ordinarily understood. See Levine (1999) for a related discussion.

20 Alan Soble (1997: 65) claims, 'A quite ordinary (and true) thought is that when x loves y, x wishes the best for y and acts, as far as he or she is able, to pursue the good for y.' Soble is right in seeing this as a quite ordinary claim. However, even apart from anything

that psychoanalytic theory has to say about love, it is so blatantly false one wonders how Soble can regard it as a truism.

21 W. H. Auden, from 'Heavy Date'. *The Collected Poems of W.H. Auden* (New York: Random House, 1945):

> Slowly we are learning,
> We at least know this much,
> That we have to unlearn
> much that we were taught,
> And are growing chary
> Of emphatic dogmas;
> Love like Matter is much
> Odder than we thought.

22 More complex cases can be considered as well. Cf. De Sousa's discussion (1980b: 293–4), with explicit reference to psychoanalysis, of 'two sorts of self-deceptive possibilities' in regard to 'attachment emotions'. 'One is that a desire for fungible sexual satisfaction, because it advertises itself as "love", should be experienced as nonfungible ("I feel that I love you forever"). The other is its converse 'an ideology constructed out of the desire to avoid the dangers of the former ideology, which denies the need for nonfungible attachments, or even their possibility'. Cf. De Sousa (1980a; 1987).

23 I am claiming that hatred, narcissism, etc. are components, not contaminants of love. Narcissistic infatuation may not have anything structurally in common with mature dependent love, but, when one loves, these various aspects may each have their role to play (cf. Freud 1915c). Tamas Pataki (correspondence) suggests: 'Perhaps love is nothing like a natural kind and there are just a lot of different phenomena with little in common except a surface phenomenology and a common name.'

24 Bouveresse (1995: xi) says, 'Freud reconfigured the paths to this knowledge ['the Socratic adage "know thyself"'] by teaching us that we should look for the truth about ourselves, not in the "ego" of the philosophers but in aberrations, dreams, caprice, phobias, bungled actions, and so on.' Yes. But Freud didn't hold out much hope that such knowledge would result in big differences to how one lives. This is not meant to deny that a degree of self-understanding achieved in therapy may well relieve one of the pathological forms of love and other neuroses.

25 Contrary to what I take Freud's view to be, some philosophers deny the intentionality of repression and/or self-deception – or at least all cases of it. Pataki (correspondence) says that 'repression probably covers several distinct processes some of which may be non-intentional and others intentional, and depending on the scope ascribed to self-deception, some not involving self-deception'.

26 Freud's view is therefore at odds with those of Fingarette (1969) and Marcia Baron (1988) and Jopling (1996). To say that self-deception is constitutive is not to say that one should not try to eliminate instances of it. But it does mean that one must be selective. Not all instances of self-deception are harmful – indeed, probably few are. It is implausible to suppose that most cases of self-deception ramify negatively in one's life to the extent that Fingarette, Baron and Jopling do. Furthermore, even leaving psychoanalysis aside, I do not think that they appreciate the extent of self-deception in ordinary lives.

27 See Levine (1999); McCullagh (1990); De Sousa (1980a; 1987). I continue to discuss instances of emotion, or emotional behaviour, as rational or irrational but I agree with Amélie Rorty that questions about the rationality of emotion are generally not well formed. She says (1985: 351): 'Emotions are not as such either rational or irrational. Nor are particular emotion types as such rational or irrational. Even if we know that a person has been rational or irrational in having a particular emotion, in a certain way, at a certain time, in a certain context, we only have the slenderest, and not the most significant or

interesting parameter for evaluating its reasonableness, its appropriateness, its desirability.'

28 Gardner (1992: 35). See Gardner's essay for a critique of the rationalistic account of emotion in favour of the psychoanalytic theory that sees emotion as 'a kind of mental state which cannot be understood apart from – for the reason that it is derived from – the kind of mental state that psychoanalytic theory refers to as phantasy'. Some issues require clarification. If some emotions develop from phantasy but now operate independently of it (i.e., the relation is developmental and historical but not current), then is the rationality of such emotion undermined by its relation to phantasy? It seems to me that the rationality of an emotion is undermined whether its relation to phantasy is (i) developmental and historical or (ii) current – though it is more seriously challenged in the latter case than in the former. It also seems to me that i and ii are integrally related. If an emotion's relation to phantasy is historical and developmental then it must also be current.

As Amélie Rorty (1985) has pointed out 'rationality' has a variety of meanings. However, in the current context no particular specialized definition of rationality is needed. Gardner (1992: 49) says 'What the rationalistic account [of emotion] is right about is not the causal explanation of emotion, since this is not in fact a process of syllogistic practical reasoning; what it correctly models is the non-causal, normative relations that constitute the concept of appropriate emotions.'

29 See Melanie Klein (1957), or, for a brief account of Klein's theory of envy and gratitude see Gardner (1992: 42–3). Gardner (1992: 43–44) assumes 'that Klein's account of envy and gratitude can be generalized to other emotions'.

30 Cf. Lear (1990: 131). 'In his [Freud's] discussion of dreams, he says that an idea and the emotion attaching to it are merely soldered together . . . What he meant was that an emotion can be detached from the idea to which it is appropriate and then be attached to any idea whatever . . . this detachment only occurs at the manifest level of consciousness. Once we consider the deeper, latent content of a dream, it emerges that an emotion is indissolubly attached to its appropriate idea. Similarly with the sexual drive and the sexual object.'

31 The 'Depressive Position' 'describes the position reached . . . by the infant . . . when he realises that both his LOVE and Hate are directed towards the same object – the MOTHER'. The 'Paranoid-Schizoid Position' is 'a psychic configuration . . . in which the individual deals with his innate destructive impulses by (a) SPLITTING both his EGO and his Object-Representations into Good and Bad parts, and (b) projecting his destructive impulses on to the bad object by whom he feels persecuted' Charles Rycroft (1970: 32,111–12).

32 Yeats (1956: 79) from 'Adam's Curse':

> I had a thought for no one's but your ears:
> That you were beautiful, and that I strove
> To love you in the old high way of love;
> That it has all seemed happy, and yet we'd grown
> As weary hearted as that hollow moon.

References

Auden, W.H. (1945) 'Heavy Date'. *The Collected Poems of W.H. Auden*, New York: Random House.

Baron, Marcia (1988) 'What is Wrong With Self-Deception?', in B. McLaughlin and A.O. Rorty (eds), *Perspectives on Self-Deception*, Berkeley: University of California Press, pp. 431–49.

Blum, L.A. (1980) *Friendship, Altruism and Morality*, London: Routledge and Kegan Paul.

Boer, Steven E. and Lycan, William G. (1986) *Knowing Who*, Cambridge, MA: Bradford Books/MIT Press, ch. 6.

Bouveresse, Jacques (1995) *Wittgenstein Reads Freud: The Myth of the Unconscious*, Trans. Carol Cosman, Princeton: Princeton University Press.

Brown, Deborah (1997) 'The Right Method of Boy-Loving', in Roger E. Lamb (ed.), *Love Analyzed*, Boulder, CO: Westview, pp. 49–63.

Byatt, A.S. (1990) *Possession*, London: Vintage.

Cavell, Marcia (1993) *The Psychoanalytic Mind: From Freud to Philosophy*, Cambridge, MA: Harvard University Press.

Delaney, Neil (1996) 'Romantic Love and Loving Commitment: Articulating a Modern Ideal', *American Philosophical Quarterly*, 33: 339–56.

De Sousa, Ronald (1980a) 'The Rationality of Emotions', in Amélie O. Rorty (ed.), *Explaining Emotions*, Berkeley: University of California Press, pp. 127–51.

—— (1980b) 'Self-Deceptive Emotions', in, Amélie O. Rorty (ed.), *Explaining Emotions*, Berkeley: University of California Press, pp. 283–97.

—— (1987) *The Rationality of Emotions*, Cambridge, MA: MIT Press.

Fingarette, H. (1969) *Self-Deception*, London: Routledge and Kegan Paul.

Freud, Sigmund (1953–74) *The Standard Edition of The Complete Psychological Works of Sigmund Freud*, trans. and ed. J. Strachey, London: Hogarth Press.

—— (1960) *The Letters of Sigmund Freud*, selected and edited by Ernest L. Freud, translated by Tania and James Stern. New York: Basic Books.

—— (1901a) *On Dreams*.

—— (1901b) *The Psychopathology of Everyday Life*.

—— (1905d) *Three Essays on the Theory of Sexuality*.

—— (1910) 'A Special Type of Choice of Object Made by Men' *(Contributions to the Psychology of Love I)*.

—— (1912d) 'On the Universal Tendency to Debasement in the Sphere of Love' *(Contributions to the Psychology of Love II)*.

—— (1915c) 'Instincts and their Vicissitudes'.

—— (1916–17) *Introductory Lectures on Psychoanalysis*.

—— (1917e [1915]) *Mourning and Melancholia*.

—— (1920g) *Beyond the Pleasure Principle*.

—— (1921c) *Group Psychology and the Analysis of the Ego*.

Gardner, Sebastian (1992) 'The Nature and Source of Emotion', in Jim Hopkins and Anthony Saville (eds), *Psychoanalysis, Mind and Art: Perspectives on Richard Wollheim*, Oxford: Blackwell, pp. 35–54.

—— (1993) *Irrationality and the Philosophy of Psychoanalysis*, Cambridge: Cambridge University Press.

—— (1994) 'Psychoanalytic Explanation', Samuel Guttenplan (ed.) *A Companion to the Philosophy of Mind*, Cambridge, MA: Blackwell, pp. 493–500.

Grünbaum, Adolf (1984) *The Foundations of Psychoanalysis: A Philosophical Critique*, Berkeley: University of California Press.

Hamlyn, D.W. (1978) 'The Phenomena of Love and Hate', *Philosophy*, 53: 5–20.

Hopkins, Jim (1982) 'Introduction: Philosophy and Psychoanalysis', Introduction to Richard Wollheim and Jim Hopkins (eds), *Philosophical Essays on Freud*, Cambridge: Cambridge University Press, pp. vii–xlv.

—— (1988) 'Epistemology and Depth Psychology: Critical Notes on *The Foundations of Psychoanalysis*', in Peter Clark and Crispin Wright (eds), *Mind, Psychoanalysis and Science*, Oxford: Blackwell, pp. 33–60.

Jopling, David A. (1996) '"Take Away the Life-Lie . . . ": Positive Illusions and Creative Self-Deception', *Philosophical Psychology*, 9: 525–44.

Klein, Melanie (1957) 'Envy and Gratitude', In *Envy and Gratitude and Other Works 1946–1963, The Writings of Melanie Klein*, vol. 3, ed. Roger E. Money-Kyrle, London: Hogarth Press.

Kraut, Robert (1986) 'Love De Re', *Midwest Studies in Philosophy*, 10: 413–30.

Lamb, Roger E. (1997) 'Love and Rationality', in Roger E. Lamb (ed.), *Love Analyzed*, Boulder, CO: Westview, pp. 23–47.

Lear, Jonathan (1990) *Love and its Place in Nature: A Philosophical Interpretation of Freudian Psychoanalysis*, New York: Noonday Press.

Levine, Michael (1999) 'Rational Emotion, Emotional Holism, True Love, and Charlie Chaplin', *Journal for Philosophical Research*, XXIV: 489–506.

McCullagh, Behan C. (1990) 'The Rationality of Emotions and of Emotional Behaviour', *Australasian Journal of Philosophy* 68: 44–58.

McTaggart, John (1921–1927) *The Nature of Existence*, vol. 2, ed. C.D. Broad, Cambridge: Cambridge University Press.

Neu, Jerome (1999) *A Tear Is an Intellectual Thing: The Moral Significance of the Emotions*, Oxford: Oxford University Press, forthcoming.

Nozick, Robert (1974) *Anarchy, State and Utopia*, New York: Basic Books.

Nussbaum, Martha C. (1997) 'Love and the Individual: Romantic Rightness and Platonic Aspiration', in Roger E. Lamb (ed.), *Love Analyzed*, Boulder, CO: Westview, pp. 1–22.

Oakley, Justin (1993) *Morality and the Emotions*, London and New York: Routledge.

Rorty, Amélie, O. (1980) 'Explaining Emotions', in Amélie O. Rorty (ed.), *Explaining Emotions*, Berkeley: University of California Press, pp. 103–126. Reprinted in *Mind in Action*, pp. 103–20.

—— (1985) 'Varieties of Rationality, Varieties of Emotion', *Social Science Information*, 24: 343–53.

—— (1986) 'The Historicity of Psychological Attitudes: Love Is Not Love Which Alters Not When It Alteration Funds', in *Midwest Studies in Philosophy*, X: 399–412. Reprinted in Amélie O. Rorty, *Mind in Action: Essays in the Philosophy of Mind*, Boston: Beacon Press, 1988, pp. 121–34.

Rycroft, Charles (1970) *A Critical Dictionary of Psychoanalysis*, London: Penguin.

Sachs. David (1982) 'On Freud's Doctrine of the Emotions', in Richard Wollheim and Jim Hopkins (eds), *Philosophical Essays on Freud*, Cambridge: Cambridge University Press, pp. 92–105.

Sankowski, Edward (1977) 'Responsibility of Persons for their Emotions', *Canadian Journal of Philosophy*, VII: 829–40.

Santas, Gerasimos (1988) *Plato and Freud: Two Theories of Love*, Oxford: Blackwell.

Scheler, Max (1913) *The Nature of Sympathy*, trans. Peter Heath (1954), London: Routledge.

Schlossberger, Eugene (1986) 'Why We Are Responsible for Our Emotions', *Mind*, 95: 37–56.

Scruton, Roger (1986) *Sexual Desire*, London: Weidenfeld and Nicolson.

Soble, Alan (1997) 'Union, Autonomy, and Concern', in Roger E. Lamb (ed.), *Love Analyzed*, Boulder, CO: Westview, pp. 65–92.

Williams, Bernard (1973a) 'Morality and the Emotions', in *Problems of the Self*, Cambridge: Cambridge University Press, pp. 207–29.

—— (1973b) 'Are Persons Bodies?', in *Problems of the Self*, Cambridge: Cambridge University Press, pp. 64–81.

—— (1993) *Shame and Necessity*, Berkeley: University of California Press.

Wollheim, Richard and Hopkins, Jim (1982) (eds) *Philosophical Essays on Freud*, Cambridge: Cambridge University Press.

Yeats, W.B. (1956) *The Collected Poems of W.B. Yeats*, New York: Macmillan.

Part IV

CIVILIZATION

13

SUBLIMATION, LOVE, AND CREATIVITY

Marguerite La Caze

Before the problem of the creative artist analysis must, alas, lay down its arms.

Sigmund Freud, 'Dostoevsky and Parricide'

1 Introduction

Sublimation is considered to be one of the great lacunae in psychoanalytic theory in that the process is never fully explained by Freud. Yet Freud's concept of sublimation is essential to understanding the workings of the libido, the nature of creativity, and Freud's views on women and love. These questions are linked together in an interesting way. Examining his work on the question of women and sublimation can illuminate these links and help to develop a more comprehensive understanding of sublimation. Freud thought that women had lesser and more passive libidos, and so a lesser capacity to sublimate than men, and thought it followed from these limitations that women will be naturally less creative, but not less loving than men. This is why the connection between love and creativity is also important to explore – to see whether there really is a disjunction between the two. First we need to understand what Freud says about sublimation in general.

2 Sublimation

The fundamental idea behind sublimation is a familiar one: when sexuality is sublimated, it is transformed into something higher and finer, more 'sublime', such as art or intellectual and scientific achievement, or work in general. Freud says that the sexual instinct, as opposed to other instincts such as hunger, is particularly able to contribute to professional activity of various kinds because of its capacity for sublimation. Sublimation is defined as 'the power to replace its [the sexual instinct's] immediate aim by other aims which may be valued more highly and which are not sexual' (*S.E.* XI: 78).[1] Sublimations are the activities in which a person engages or the products that result from sublimation. According to Freud, most people are able to direct a significant part of their sexual energy into their profession: 'Thus a person of this sort would, for example, pursue research with the same passionate devotion that another would give to his love, and he would be able to investigate instead of loving' (*S.E.* XI: 77). Such redirection tends toward socially appropriate ends.

Sublimation differs from fixation, which is not at all useful for civilization because it remains fixed on its original aim. It is also distinct from perversions in being (at least in some cases of sublimation) the transformation of them. For Freud, the existence of sublimation in any particular case is confirmed by sexual interests in childhood and by a lack of sexuality in adulthood. The sexual instinct consists of different component instincts, some of which are suitable for sublimation, and some not. The strength of the sex instinct varies from person to person, or at least the amount of it which can be sublimated, rather than repressed or expressed. While sublimation is a desirable outcome and better than repression, it is important to keep in mind that everyone needs some direct sexual satisfaction, otherwise they become ill (*S.E.* IX: 188).

Sublimation has to be understood by examining the relationship between sexuality and the search for knowledge in early childhood. In children, both the thirst for knowledge and the sexual instinct are exemplified by their constant questioning. The craving for knowledge is itself an instinct (*S.E.* XI: 77).[2] Freud argues that any instinct that is particularly intense must have had a sexual reinforcement; and in the case of children's sexual researches the sexual instincts support the search for knowledge. The instinct for knowledge uses the energy of scopophilia – the love of looking. He claims that most children engage in infantile sexual researches to find out where babies come from, possibly in order to discover how to avoid the awful event of the arrival of a sibling. Children are sceptical about fables of storks and so on, and speculate that birth has something to do with eating, defecating and the father's relationship to the mother. Freud believes that the inevitable failure of these researches due to children's sexual immaturity and the discouragement of adults often has a deleterious effect on future intellectual pursuits.

There are three possible outcomes and types of thinkers which emerge from this failure to discover where babies come from for the instinct for research.

The first result is neurotic inhibition. In such a case, curiosity, like sexuality, is permanently inhibited and intelligence is limited. Such an inhibition of curiosity is reinforced by a religious education (usually) or indeed, any education which enforces ignorance in sexual matters. This outcome is a very common one, presumably. As we will see, Freud thought that most women would be this type of thinker.

The second outcome is neurotic compulsive thinking: sexuality and intelligence form an alliance and intellectual effort is coloured by sexual satisfaction and anxiety. Research becomes sexual but remains brooding and ultimately unsatisfied. Hamlet has been given as an example of this type.[3]

The third and rarest outcome is an extraordinary capacity for sublimation: sexuality is sublimated into curiosity and attached to the instinct for knowledge and it does not lose its intensity. In this case research becomes sexual, without being neurotic. Of course, there is still some repression, because sexual themes are avoided (*S.E.* XI: 79-80). The central example here is Leonardo da Vinci (1452-1519). Given that creative art is seen by Freud as the highest form of sublimation, we need to understand the workings of sublimation in that case.

3 Leonardo as a paradigm case

A deeper understanding of the workings of sublimation can be gained by examining Freud's paper *Leonardo da Vinci and a Memory of his Childhood* which contains an extensive discussion of sublimation.[4] Not coincidentally, it is also one of his most complete treatments of the life of an artist and the nature of creativity. For Freud, Leonardo is a paradigm case of the third type of individual mentioned above, who has a great capacity for sublimation of sexuality into curiosity, because he had a highly developed instinct for research coupled with a minimal sexual life. He succeeded in sublimating his libido into research – he converted his passion and love into a thirst for knowledge (*S.E.* XI: 74).[5] At this point, Freud explicitly models the conversion of psychical forces on physical conversions, and concludes that there must be a loss in both cases. In Leonardo's case, the substitution of knowledge for passion means a loss of love in his life, and his intellectual curiosity even takes over his artistic impulses at certain periods of his life. Freud thinks this high level of curiosity shows that the instinct for knowledge must have been very strong in Leonardo's childhood and that it was supported by sexual instincts, and so substituted satisfaction for some of his sex life. Leonardo is a good example for the discussion of sublimation. Due to the range of his talents, his case gives us some sense of the wide variety of forms of creativity.

Freud speculates that Leonardo escaped the full force of the repression which operates in most people's lives because of his early sexual curiosity. This precocious wondering meant that much of his sexual instinct could be sublimated into 'the general urge to know' (*S.E.* XI: 32). However, sublimation does not account for all of his sexual instinct – a small part of his libido was manifested in an ideal love for boys, and some was fixated on his mother in his unconscious. Freud thought that his love of boys was a result of his identification with his mother – that he loved little boys as his mother loved him. Leonardo also shows some elements of obsessional neurosis – for example, in his detailed listing of the costs of his mother's funeral. At certain periods in his life, Leonardo was able to reach what Freud considers the highest level of sublimation. He believes that Leonardo had two important creative periods – in his early years of painting and later when, as Freud speculates, he met the woman whose smile reminded him of his mother. This second peak is exemplified in certain paintings, such as the *Mona Lisa* and *Madonna and Child with St Anne* (Louvre, Paris), which Freud finds particularly important for understanding Leonardo, well as being his greatest artistic achievements.

On the other hand, in Leonardo's case, there was also regression – his artistic sublimation moved back to earlier sublimation in research. The endless drawings of human anatomy and Leonardo's sketches of flying contraptions can be taken as signs of this regression. Freud argues that Leonardo's creative activity contained aspects of unconscious instincts in the form of 'insatiability, unyielding rigidity and the lack of an ability to adapt to real circumstances' (*S.E.* XI: 133). For example, he worked very slowly, dissipated his talent in different activities, tried unlikely experiments such as a new method of fresco painting, and was dissatisfied with his work, regarding them all as unfinished, including the *Mona Lisa*.

4 Forms of creativity

There are interesting insights here regarding the differences between intellectual work and other types of creative work – like painting, for example. For Freud, there is a hierarchy whereby one moves from sex to science (in the general sense of research) to artistic creation.[6] He thinks that art is the better form of sublimation, because it is further away than scientific research from the original impulse to know and the sexual impulse in the sense of being a greater transformation of these impulses. This is why Freud sees Leonardo's scientific interests as regressive. Leonardo's scientific research represents a claim to independence from the authority of the father (and God), because he is using judgement and observation rather than the teachings of the church. It also reflects the absence of his father in early childhood, and a reliance on nature as a nurturing mother.[7] Freud claims that Leonardo was an unbeliever and this is reflected in his work. (*S.E.* XI: 122-23). Furthermore, his obsession with the problem of flight represents the wish for sexual activity and performance. Sadly, according to Freud, Leonardo was frustrated in both these ambitions although his other achievements were remarkable. At this point, the concept of sublimation undergoes a subtle change – repression has a detrimental effect on the nature or character of sublimation, rather than simply on the amount. Leonardo's repressed sex life coloured his way of working, and explains the indecisiveness, delay and lack of satisfaction Leonardo experienced in relation to painting.

In general, Freud finds the details of Leonardo's sexual life reflected both in his typical methods of working and in the details of his paintings and drawings. The artist's choice of medium reveals much about their sexual preferences. For example, in turning to the visual arts of painting and sculpture, Leonardo is following the scopophilic instinct of his childhood (*S.E.* XI: 132). With regard to content, the artist's secret impulses are expressed in their works, but of course they are greatly changed and need to be interpreted (*S.E.* XI: 107). In Leonardo's paintings, Freud finds expression of the unhappiness of his sexual life, and his longing for the blissful union between himself and his mother he experienced in his early life (*S.E.* XI: 118). Both the *Mona Lisa* and the painting *Madonna and Child with St Anne* represent such a return to infancy, with the bliss of that period reflected in the faces of the women. Furthermore, Freud argues that Leonardo is a narcissistic homosexual, as he is identifying with his mother and loving little boys as she loved him, so in loving boys he is loving himself (*S.E.* XI: 100). Particular artistic creations provide an outlet for sexual desire by depicting desired sexual objects – laughing women and beautiful boys in Leonardo's case.

This description of Leonardo's life and work does not account for all the questions we might like answered about the nature of sublimation and creativity. Freud cannot explain exactly why Leonardo had a tendency toward instinctual repressions, nor his great capacity for sublimating instincts, and only suggests that we should look to biology to explain the founding of character (*S.E.* XI: 136). The capacity for sublimation might depend in part on the severity of the repression of the researches, the paucity of information about sexuality, or the kind of relations the child has with its parents. People's levels of creativity may differ in that repression may not be extreme, and different consequences may follow from repression (*S.E.* XI: 135).

Freud notes that critics may complain that the form of Leonardo's creativity is made dependent on a few chance events (his close early life with his mother and subsequent shift to his father's house), yet again this is not necessarily to its detriment.[8] Given that every life, to a great extent, is governed by chance events – whether it be in our relation to our parents or in other respects – it is hard to see how Freud could avoid that aspect of his explanation. Knowing that a process of sublimation goes on does not tells us precisely how it is supposed to occur. Furthermore, positing the existence of a process of sublimation cannot explain the origins of talent, although it can give an explanation of the forms and limitations of it. As Freud says, only Leonardo (psychoanalytically speaking) could have painted the *Mona Lisa* and the *Madonna and Child with St Anne*. This claim has more substance if we consider the striking composition of the painting in the depiction of Mary sitting on Anne's lap.[9] Yet any understanding of an artist's work has to be connected with considerations of artistic practice and social context, which Freud does not provide. Subsequent writing about Leonardo's work has gone some way toward providing that detail.

We should not really expect psychoanalysis or any other theory to explain the exact workings of sublimation or the origin of talent; we can only describe the conditions which make it more likely that sublimation can take place and talent will be able to flourish. Clearly the conditions must be right for the flowering of creativity: the individual must have the energy, the talent in execution and ideally society and intimates will provide support and encouragement. These points are particularly relevant to a consideration of Freud's views on women and sublimation.

5 Women and sublimation

In Freud's work, the connection between women and sublimation is a fraught one: his claim in his paper 'Femininity' that women have a lesser ability to sublimate than men (and consequently a lesser capacity for all kinds of productive achievement) is well known. It occurs in the context of a discussion of the differing psychosexual development of boys and girls. The most significant point to note here is that the Oedipus and castration complexes occur in reverse order in the two sexes. He claims that for little girls, the sight of a boy's penis causes penis envy and leads to the female version of the Oedipus complex: attraction to their father and regarding their mother as a rival. Because this complex follows after the castration complex (the recognition of their castrated state), their Oedipus complex is not overcome – it has a tendency to remain unresolved. So the girl's attachment to the father tends to continue much longer than the boy's corresponding attachment to the mother.

More importantly, a number of consequences are thought to follow from the fact that a girl imagines a castration that has actually been carried out, rather than merely threatened, as boys imagine it. Because there is no threat of castration, girls fail to internalize the authority of their father, and consequently fail to fully develop a super-ego and a capacity for sublimation. It is as if there is no motivation for sub-limation, as there is no fear of the father. Furthermore, shame at their 'inferior' genitals causes repression rather than sublimation of women's sexuality. On the other hand, Freud argues here that women's desires to have an intellectual profession are often a sublimation of penis envy (*S.E.* XXII: 125).[10] He claims, however, that desires for achievement (to the limited extent that they can be satisfied), can only be satisfied through having a child, preferably a son who will appease their mother's ambition. Freud's claim that women have a lesser capacity than men for sublimating instincts is based not just on differing psychosexual development but also on his belief that women have a lower libido than men. And even though he admits that the capacity for sublimation is subject to great individual variation, women's libidos seem to Freud to be fixed at thirty – it does not seem possible for women to alter the paths of the libido through sublimation (*S.E.* XXII: 134). This is not the place to go into all the problems with the notion of penis envy which underlie these particular views about women and sublimation. In my judgement, the idea has been thoroughly discredited as simply a reflection of Freud's account of male development and as having little basis in experience.[11] This means that the account of psychosexual development needs to be reworked to account for females' autonomous development and sexuality. Such a reworking need not necessarily affect important Freudian theses concerning the existence of infantile sexuality, the structure of the mind, and the workings of the unconscious. The challenge is to Freud's claims of the primacy of the penis in the psychosexual development of women and the inevitability of women's creative limitations.

If this was all Freud had to say on the subject of women and sublimation, there would be little point in pursuing the connection between sublimation and the creativity of women. But he also offers a more plausible and interesting explanation of differences in the capacities of men and women to sublimate in an earlier paper, '"Civilized" Sexual Morality and Modern Nervous Illness'. There he argues that it is the repression of women's childhood sexual researches which makes creativity difficult in later life. The argument goes like this. All behaviour in human beings is modelled on a sexual pattern which emerges from sexual research in childhood. Women's intellectual development is stunted by harsh repression of their sexual curiosity in childhood and this repression is continued into later life, where women are expected to only gain sexual satisfaction within marriage – if then. This repression is the cause of women's lesser capacity to sublimate as it inhibits thought and uses up valuable energy which might otherwise be available for sublimation: 'they are scared away from *any* form of thinking and knowledge loses its value for them' (*S.E.* IX: 199). It is a consequence of this view that women need fuller expression of their libido in order to be great artists and researchers. Thus, openness about sexuality in childhood, breaking down the double standard that allows men but not women to seek sexual satisfaction outside marriage, and removing sexual repression are the keys to enhanced achievement for women because the removal of excessive sexual repression enables sublimation.

Clearly, this explanation for differences between men and women in capacity for sublimation is far more plausible than the one given in 'Femininity' because it does not rest on the notion of penis envy and because it can be tied to actual social circumstances. Nevertheless, it needs more investigation. One problem with accepting sexual repression as an explanation for the way women's abilities to succeed in a variety of fields was limited in the past (what Freud called 'the undoubted intellectual inferiority of so many women' [*S.E.* IX: 199]) is that there were so many other kinds of repression going on. Most of women's attempts to participate in fields outside home and marriage were discouraged. Freud thinks that all other explanations reduce to a sexual one because we find a correspondence between the form of neuroses and sexual origins (*S.E.* IX: 186). A useful way to think about this question is to consider that sexual repression is both symptomatic of and reinforcing of a wide range of other repressions of women, such as educational, political and artistic. Clarifying the relationship between love and creativity will go some way towards describing the conditions which make it possible for the capacity to sublimate to develop in both sexes.

6 Love and creativity

If erotic love is a form of sublimated sexuality, then does the expression of love prevent sublimation into creative activities? Or does creativity via sublimation need a stable loving relationship in which to flourish? From the discussion of Leonardo, it seems that Freud thinks that at least some sexual outlets are necessary for sublimation to work well, and not to regress back into a less creative state where either inhibition or brooding is likely. In one sense, sublimation is a favourable outcome for the individual because inhibition and neurosis are avoided. On the other hand, if sexuality is severely repressed and one's capacity for sublimation is not great, it may mean the loss of a happy love and sex life. A repressed sex life can mean that creativity itself cannot reach its potential. As happened to Leonardo, 'the almost total repression of a real sexual life does not provide the most favourable conditions for the exercise of sublimated sexual trends' (*S.E.* IX: 133). When sublimation is accompanied by severe repression, activities fail and there is hesitation and delay in producing work. Freud exclaims in '"Civilized" Sexual Morality' that 'An abstinent artist is hardly conceivable' (*S.E.* IX: 197)![12] This view is at odds with his claim that evidence for Leonardo's sublimation can be found in his lack of sexuality in adulthood. What this inconsistency suggests is that a mechanistic account of sexuality, in which a discrete measure of sexuality moves from one place to another, does not adequately account for the complexities of sexuality or variations in individual experience. Creativity and a minimal sex life are not necessarily paired.

In the case of artists (at least), a real sexual life can provide ideal conditions for great creativity. Contrary to common mythology about sublimation, which takes it that if sexuality is expressed, then it is lost to creative purposes, the expression of sexuality works to provide the conditions for the highest forms of sublimation. This understanding also shows that the mechanistic model of sublimation by itself is misleading, because on that model, sublimation would necessitate a limited sex life or a gargantuan libido. Remember the distinction between the component of the sexual instinct which is available for sublimation and that which is not. If this is combined with Freud's view that a satisfying sex life makes sublimation more successful, then it suggests that if both sexes lead more satisfying sex lives then much more energy would be available for sublimation and creativity could reach its potential. Otherwise, sexuality is repressed and that repression pervades all activities, making them obsessive and compulsive, rather than sublimations. The existence of such a capacity in both sexes is more consonant with our experience, particularly now that many of the former sexual (as well as other) repressions of women have been lifted. Perhaps surprisingly and contrary to what is frequently thought to be the case, Freud's view is that the expression of sexuality actually enables sublimation, or more sexuality in a different form. He holds that sexual abstinence only leads to weakness and conformity.[13]

This establishes that sexual satisfaction is important to sublimation. But what about love? It is often thought that Freud makes a radical separation between sex and love. Yet in 'On the Universal Tendency to Debasement in the Sphere of Love', Freud argues that while love and sex are separated for most people in varying degrees, nevertheless 'There are only a very few educated people in whom the two currents of affection and sensuality have become properly fused' (*S.E.* XI: 185). His point that it is only an educated few who achieve this fusion of sex and love suggests that there is a connection between it and the capacity for sublimation and also that such a fusion is a goal we should aspire to – an ideal. Presumably, what Freud means by education is encouragement to research of all kinds, rather than a specific type of education. In connection with creative artists and research, the view that sexuality and love are tied together is also rendered more plausible in Freud's view. If we take the connection between sublimation and research seriously, it is just those who have the greatest capacity for sublimation who also have the greatest capacity for intertwining sex and love. In that case, it is a satisfying love and sex life that provide the ideal conditions for the development of creativity. The play between love and creativity is not a zero-sum game. Conversely, those with the greatest capacity for sublimation may have potentially the greatest basis for satisfying relationships.

Freud's discussion of Leonardo suggests that true creativity will occur within the context of a satisfying relationship. Taken together with his early views about the excessive repression of women, it is clear that such creativity is potentially open to both men and women. This view has a great many implications, particularly in the area of aesthetics, where some of the traditional myths about creative genius need to be dispelled and more realistic ideas investigated. Freud personally held the view that women had a lesser capacity than men to sublimate, and he states this even in his '"Civilized" Sexual Morality' paper. (*S.E.* IX: 192). But as I noted earlier, Freud's judgement on this point does not rest on any sound basis. In contemporary life we are now in a good position to judge that Freud's view of women is false, based on the actual achievements of women in art, science, and philosophy, for example. Think of Georgia O'Keefe, Frida Kahlo, Barbara McClintok, Jean Rhys and Simone de Beauvoir, to name a few. Of course, there were many talented women both prior to and during Freud's lifetime who he was well aware of, such as Marie Curie and his friend Lou Andreas-Salomé. His view was that there were fewer talented women than men partly because what may have appeared to be a lack of talent in many cases was a result of sexual suppression. By noting that sexual repression is connected to a series of other repressions, we have a clearer understanding of the apparent deficiency. Perhaps it is also the case that more than a few individuals (of either sex) have a great capacity for sublimation.

The repression of female sexuality has been lifted (to a great degree) together with other forms of repression. At the same time as women were excluded from the most desirable activities and professions, the activities which women could engage in were not regarded as socially valuable so in Freud's terms would not count as sublimations. Take, for example, housework. It is clearly socially useful, but has not been recognized as valuable and was often not even recognized as work. Housework can be understood as a sublimation just like other work (provided it is not compulsive). This example suggests an important modification to the definition of sublimation – sublimation must be characterized as emerging in those activities which are genuinely socially valuable, rather than those which are perceived as such at any given time. As with so much of Freud's work, for example in his discussion of women's psychosexual development, what appears to be a descriptive claim is revealed on closer examination to be a normative or prescriptive one. Yet, given the importance of connecting sublimation with an understanding of society, this is probably appropriate .

As well as being beneficial to the individual, sublimation is also beneficial, indeed necessary, for society, because it makes people useful citizens. This aspect of sublimation has made some critics of Freud suspicious of sublimation as a process which brings about conformity and socially useful art.[14] Yet making sexuality 'socially useful' does not necessitate that art and research which is boring and supports the status quo must be produced. Rather, it means that the aspects of sexuality which might be both destructive of civilization (in a very general sense) and destructive of the individual are made better use of. Yet nothing about that claim means that avant-garde art or challenging research cannot be produced under the aegis of sublimation.[15]

It is possible to conceive creativity in a new way, a way that recognizes the importance of human interaction and intimacy. Myths about relationships making creativity impossible have either been based on destructive, unstable relationships or on women's relationships to men who dominated them (and sometimes vice versa) and required all their attention and energy. A related claim about the necessary equation of creativity and self-obsession has been a convenient fiction for the self-obsessed. Many men have thought that a talented partner would only be a drain on their genius – take, for example, Georg Lukács who wrote to the woman he loved, a painter: 'What I wish to accomplish only an unattached man can accomplish'.[16] Many women artists have lived alone, which may once have been necessary due to the demands of marriage and childbirth, but is less applicable now. It has often been thought that only one member of a couple can be successful, with the other providing the nurturing the great person needs – taking care of any children and personal needs. Yet societal changes have shown that these considerations reflect cultural stereotypes, rather than an intrinsic difficulty with combining love and creativity. Furthermore, barriers to a good, loving relationship pointed out by Freud, such as fear of conception and the inadequacy of contraception, are also less relevant. The problem he describes in *Civilization and its Discontents* – that women become frustrated with men who withdraw their sexuality into sublimation – can now be overcome to a great extent, because women have a greater stake in civilization, because sublimation is not the exclusive province of men, and because sublimation and sexual expression can now exist together, due to social conditions in at least some places.

Moreover, the concept of creativity itself should be extended. Creativity should not be understood as something which is exclusively associated with art, considering other forms of valuable activity as essentially non-creative. Creativity can emerge in almost any area of intellectual work, and artistic work can be non-creative: repetitive, boring, unoriginal. Freud may well have believed this, but his focus on art as the pinnacle of creative achievement and on only great artists seems to imply otherwise.

7 The couple as creative

If we think that women have a capacity for sublimation equal to that of men, a number of interesting possibilities emerge. One is that there will be many more women artists and researchers, which we already know. The other is that women and men will be able to work together in ways they have very rarely been able to before, when most women's sexuality and curiosity was suppressed. Luce Irigaray's suggestion that the heterosexual couple is particularly creative is relevant here. She thinks that sexual difference creates the ideal conditions for a productive relationship (1993: 5). With different views about the abilities of women and men, the theory of sublimation can be transformed to understand the relation of love between a man and a woman as a source of creativity. While Irigaray's claim that the heterosexual couple is the *most* creative couple doesn't seem justified, it is worth exploring.[17] The idea of the heterosexual couple as particularly creative is valuable as an inversion of the Platonic view (presented in the *Symposium*) that the male homosexual couple is the most creative, as well as Freud's view of homosexuals as specially creative and artists as narcissistic.

Furthermore, a view of the couple as creative presents a challenge to traditional views of women as helpmates or muses to the exclusively creative male, the 'genius'.[18] While Freud did not think there was such a thing as creative femininity, a use of his ideas about sublimation does not have to posit a specific form of creativity in order to accept that women create. While, most obviously, the heterosexual couple can produce a child, it is suggestive to think of the creative powers of a woman and a man working together in a non-oppressive relationship. Such a relationship is rare enough in history to suggest unexperienced possibilities. This century has witnessed the growth of such creative couples, and released from the sexism and obsessive individualism which has often pervaded discussion of such couples, it is potentially a new way of understanding how to be creative.

This interest in partnership is not intended to downgrade the achievements of individuals, but to note the potential of creative couples. Simone de Beauvoir and Jean-Paul Sartre are one such couple. The work that each was able to produce as individuals in the context of their relationship is certainly greater than either would have been able to produce alone, and it is more fruitful to consider the ways their being together was a creative force, rather than focusing on the vexed question of who came up with particular ideas first. Any theory of sublimation should be realistic enough to take into account this aspect of human existence, rather than maintaining an exclusive focus on individuals. The implications of Freud's theory of sublimation need to be traced through the ways creativity develops within sexual partnerships.

The partnership of Frida Kahlo (1907-1954) and Diego Rivera (1886-1957) is an interesting example of creative interaction, where both partners are very success-ful in their chosen genres: small, intimate paintings in Kahlo's case and large public murals in Rivera's case. We can see their influence on each other in the specific details of their work – their use of each other as subjects and their political commitment, for example, which could only develop in the way it did in the context of their relationship. One could say that the relationship itself is an artistic resource, both in the general sense of providing the conditions for sublimation and in the specific sense of providing subject matter. The two shared symbols and political beliefs, yet these emerged in their paintings in very different ways. Rivera placed Kahlo in tableaux; Kahlo painted Rivera as husband, lover and child. Both fit Freud's model of artists being far from abstinent, both having numerous sexual partners apart from each other, yet both playing a central role for each other in their lives and imaginations. Two people who spend a lifetime working together and loving each other shape each others' psyches and the products of their sublimation. Both depict birth, death, political subjects and Mexican history in their work.

Perhaps even more important than this creative partnership is Kahlo's success as an artist in her own right. Her legacy is a coherent, significant and influential body of work. Writing about a modern painter such as Kahlo presents particular problems for analysis, for few can fail to have become aware of Freud's theories and they often refer in a self-conscious way in their paintings to psychoanalytic ideas and interpretations.[19] Instead of having to search Kahlo's paintings for clues to her sex life, as Freud did with Leonardo, we are presented with pictures of Rivera and other lovers of both sexes. Instead of needing to connect a detail of the painting with a surmise about parental relationships (like the Mona Lisa's smile and Leonardo's fantasy about his mother), Kahlo paints a picture of her family tree (*My Grandparents, My Parents and I*, 1936) and even one of her own birth (*My Birth*, 1932). And instead of trying to find a life-story in classical scenes, we can see Kahlo's life story in self-portraits and paintings of people, places and events.

Moreover, in Kahlo's own self-ascriptions, she does the analysing for us. She makes the connections between earlier and later events in her life. She calls Rivera her second accident, with reference with to a horrific bus accident she was involved in as a teenager which debilitated her for life. She and her paintings tell of her anguish at being unable to have a child. What is there left for a psychoanalytic reading to do? The realism and accessibility of her work makes interpretation seem obvious. When she paints a wedding picture of herself and Rivera (*Frida and Diego Rivera*, 1931, San Francisco Museum of Modern Art, San Francisco) surely it is just a portrait of him as artist and her as wife? Or we could easily read the painting as a representation of Rivera as a protective father-figure and she as a diminutive daughter. But perhaps we should remember what Freud said about the psycho-analyst looking at the details which others might neglect (*S.E.* XIII: 222). Although Rivera is holding brushes and palette and is so large as to dwarf the Kahlo figure, she does not thereby become insignificant or even diminished. Rivera is almost ludicrously large, especially his feet when compared to Kahlo's, and he seems to float in the air, which makes him a comical rather than statuesque artist. The tilt of her head towards him can be understood as almost mocking rather than diffident.[20] In the ribbon commenting on the scene, her name comes first. Although on one level the wedding portrait is a representation of a fantasy of blissful love, these details reveal ambivalence in feelings as well as some humour in the nature of the depiction. A conception of her as an artist issues from her work despite her attempts to mythologize herself as just the wife of Rivera. A reading of such a painting does not have to follow the obvious and literal interpretation, so there is still plenty of material for a more complex psychoanalytic reading.

Furthermore, a Freudian reading of art does not entail an exclusive focus on biographical scenes in art. An aspect of Kahlo's works is her depiction of her own birth, a miscarriage and her numerous operations. These are often interpreted as indicative of her desperation to have a child and her incredible suffering. Yet they can also be understood as a fascination with the workings of nature, the human body and human development. We can deduce that she, like Leonardo, had an intense curiosity about nature. Also, Kahlo's work cannot be understood without an acknowledgement of her fierce pride in being a Mexican, an aspect of identity which interacts with more personal influences in art. This is reflected in the materials, subject matter and style she used, which modified the popular Mexican ex-votos or retablos. These are scenes depicting survival of an illness or accident which are painted as an expression of thanks to God, usually on tin.

Kahlo's paintings suggest a complication in the understanding of sublimation, as they demonstrate that it is not only pleasure which becomes transformed in an artist's work. The pain of her life – the repercussions of her accident, her difficulties with Rivera and her miscarriage – is transmuted into a reflection on the nature of this pain and its role in human existence. However, this expression of pain in art does not contradict Freud's views. Sexuality can be connected with pain and frustration just as it can with other aspects of life.[21] Freud would have made a further connection between Kahlo's two accidents and an earlier trauma – her contraction of polio at the age of six, which permanently damaged her right leg. Her experience of the bus accident would have been shaped by the earlier experience and this close relation to pain and its aftermath is depicted in her work.

Like Leonardo, Kahlo often worked slowly and had long periods where she produced little, suggesting that the workings of sublimation were not ideal in her case either. (Her *oeuvre* of 143 paintings is today considered small, which is interesting if we compare it to Leonardo's 15 surviving paintings.) Still, the relative level of sublimation is not the only influence on artistic production. An understanding of cultural, historical and social context are needed to extend the Freudian analysis of art beyond an exclusive focus on psychosexual development. Such a comprehensive approach to the relation between sublimation, love and creativity can make best use of Freud's insights for a philosophical understanding of art and culture. Freud begins the project of understanding the significance of biographical elements in artists' work. Other important uses of Freud's work include the understanding of spectators' responses to work in terms of identification and the interpretation of the depiction of characters in literature through readings of *their* dreams and neuroses.[22] Putting these insights together with a rich appreciation of artistic resources can lead to a comprehensive, though ever-developing body of theory and criticism.

8 Conclusion

Only Freud's early work in '"Civilized" Sexual Morality and Modern Nervous Illness' gives a plausible account of the relation between sexuality and creativity. It is the repression of women's sexuality and curiosity which has hindered their achievements in the past. While sublimation cannot be understood in its details, this is precisely because it is not the mechanical process of shifting something from one place to another that it is often thought to be. Rather, sublimation is the transformation of sexual impulses into contributions to the development of civilization. The character of our sexual experience colours other aspects of our lives, including the forms our creativity takes. We can see that women have a great capacity for sublimation and creativity, and that love and creativity can and should exist side by side. The notion of sublimation cannot explain the origin of talent and creativity, so in that sense psychoanalysis must 'lay down its arms before the problem of the creative artist'. But it can suggest ways in which the conditions for the flourishing of creativity can themselves be created, and thus we should continue to develop and use the theory of sublimation, as well as trying to create the conditions for its flourishing.

Notes

1 It is important to keep in mind Freud's distinction between aim and object in relation to sexuality. The aim is what we wish to do with the object. See *'Three Essays on the Theory of Sexuality'* (*S.E.* VII: 136). Abel (1989: 74) argues that given sublimation still aims at pleasure, it should be considered sexual, so the distinction should be between 'genital (or closely allied) aims and non-genital ones'. This does not seem entirely satisfactory because it would seem to include many of the perversions as sublimations. A common suggestion is that the proviso that the result of sublimation be 'socially useful' should be added. Laplanche and Pontalis (1974: 432) note that Freud later admitted in *New Introductory Lectures in Psychoanalysis* (*S.E.* XXII) that changes come about in the objects as well.

2 In Freud's earlier work, there is a distinction between the sexual instincts and the 'ego' instincts which are self-preservative or life and ego-enhancing, later replaced by the distinction between life and death instincts.

3 Joel Whitebook notes this in an excellent chapter on sublimation (1995: 227).

4 Although the biographical elements in the essay are important, I disagree with Richard Wollheim's claim that 'the connection with art is *almost* exhausted by the fact that the subject of the biography happens to be one of the greatest, as well as one of the strangest, artists in history' (1973: 205). As we shall see, this essay gives an insightful account of the connection between biographical details and the composition, subjects and working methods of the artist. It also suggests a way at least to begin thinking about how to interpret particular works of art.

5 A further factor in this outcome is that his father was absent much of the time in his early years, before Leonardo was taken from his mother's home to live with his father and stepmother.

6 There are good reasons for thinking that there are important connections between the Freudian view of sublimation and Plato's view of the ascension towards love of beauty in the *Symposium*. Indeed, Freud may well have deliberately pursued this connection. Plato, through Diotima in that dialogue, argued that we have to move through stages from love of beauty in human beings to love of beauty, truth, wisdom in themselves. Freud's views are interestingly parallel in that he believes that artistry or love of beauty is higher than science, which is higher than sexuality. See Price (1990: 247-70), for a comparison of their views on these issues.

7 See Garrard (1995) for a fascinating discussion of Leonardo's representation of women as creative.

8 Bernard Williams's discussion of Gauguin is another good, though very different, example of the enormous effects of chance events in an artist's life on the development of their talent (1981: 20-39).

9 Freud's claim that Leonardo's depiction of Anne and Mary as the same age even though they are mother and daughter means that they represent his mother and stepmother has been disputed on the grounds that it was quite common for figures a generation apart to be depicted as the same age, or even, as in Michelangelo's *Pietà*, for example, for Jesus

to look older than Mary. See Bramly (1992: 320). However, this historical point does not by itself affect Freud's view.

10 This is interestingly different from his claims about sublimation in general, or rather, sublimation in men, as we shall see. For men, sublimation is always of sexuality, perhaps of a perverted sort, rather than an emotional state like penis envy.

11 Many thinkers, both feminist and non-feminist, psychoanalytic and non-psychoanalytic, have criticized Freud's notion of penis envy. See, for example, Horney (1967), Jones (1948: 485-95), de Beauvoir (1983 [1949]), Millet (1971) and Irigaray (1985 [1974]).

12 However, Freud thinks that *savants* may well be celibate.

13 Whitebook argues that it is in relation to the non-climactic pleasures and pleasurable tensions of sublimations that Freud is pushed to abandon the 'constancy' theory of sexuality, as well as the 'release of tension' theory of pleasure (1995: 253-4).

14 Whitebook (1995: 261), notes that Adorno is lead to reject the idea of sublimation because he equates it with social conformism.

15 There is a complication concerning Freud's later separation of sexuality into Eros and the death drive. While the idea of the energy of sublimation as a general life-force is appealing, along with Whitebook's suggestion that such a drive can be understood as always directed to higher things without limit, there seems a destructive aspect to creation itself. The death drive is united with Eros in outward aggression, but in sublimation this unity is defused and some of the death drive is released (see Sulloway [1979: 411] and Freud ([*S.E.* XIX]). Probably the best way to think about this question in relation to sublimation is that the sexual instinct has both creative and destructive elements which are transformed in sublimation. Also, one has to think of different pleasures as differing qualitatively and not define it as the release of tension.

16 Quoted in Agnes Heller's essay 'Georg Lukács and Irma Seidler' (1983: 33).

17 See the interview with Irigaray (1998: 19) where she makes her view very clear: 'if I decided to stop at homosexuality, I would never know the following stages'.

18 See Battersby (1989: 157). She believes that for the notion of genius to be useful for feminists, a genius must be thought of as a person whose work crosses boundaries between old and new and whose work endures in worth and influence.

19 Kahlo would have been familiar with Freud's work. She was connected with the surrealists for some time and one of her paintings, *Moses* (1945) was a direct response to a reading of Freud's *Moses and Monotheism* (Zamora 1990: 102). Late in life she underwent psychoanalysis (118).

20 Lowe also notes that this painting marks a significant development in Kahlo's stylistic independence (1991: 45).

21 Freud noted in *The Ego and the Id* (*S.E.* XIX: 25–6), that we gain an understanding of our body through pain. He also thought that imaginary recreations of painful emotions could be sexually exciting (*S.E.* VII: 204). Thus, pain, like tension, is not necessarily something that must be eliminated from life and art. See note 15 on the creative and destructive aspects of sexuality.

22 See Mulvey (1975: 6-18) and Cavell (1996) for the development of the notion of identification in relation to cinema, and Freud (*S.E.* IX) for his interpretation of dreams in literature.

References

Abel, Donald. C. (1989) *Freud on Instinct and Morality*, New York: State University of New York Press.

Battersby, Christine (1989) *Gender and Genius: Towards a Feminist Aesthetics*, Bloomington: Indiana University Press.

Beauvoir, Simone de (1983 [1949]) *The Second Sex*, trans. H.M. Parshley, Harmondsworth: Penguin.

Bramly, Serge (1992) *Leonardo: The Artist and the Man*, Trans. Siân Reynolds, London: Michael Joseph.

Cavell, Stanley (1996) *The Cavell Reader*, ed. Stephen Mulhall, Oxford: Blackwell.

Freud, Sigmund (1905d) *Three Essays on the Theory of Sexuality*, in J. Strachey (ed.), *Standard Edition*, London: Hogarth Press, *S.E.* VII.

—— (1907a) 'Delusions and Dreams in Jensen's *Gradiva*, *S.E.* IX.

—— (1908d) '"Civilized" Sexual Morality and Modern Nervous Illness', *S.E.* IX.

—— (1908e) 'Creative Writers and Daydreaming', *S.E.* IX.

—— (1910c) *Leonardo da Vinci and a Memory of his Childhood*, *S.E.* XI.

—— (1912d) 'On the Universal Tendency to Debasement in the Sphere of Love', *S.E.* XI.

—— (1914b) 'The Moses of Michelangelo', *S.E.* XIII.

—— (1923b) *The Ego and the Id*, *S.E.* XIX.

—— (1928b) 'Dostoevsky and Parricide', *S.E.* XXI.

—— (1933a) *New Introductory Lectures on Psychoanalysis*, *S.E.* XXII.

Garrard, Mary D. (1995) 'Leonardo da Vinci and Creative Female Nature', in Peggy Zeglin Brand and Carolyn Korsmeyer (eds), *Feminism and Tradition in Aesthetics*, Pennsylvania: Pennsylvania University Press.

Heller, Agnes (ed.) (1983) *Lukács Revalued*, Oxford: Basil Blackwell.

Horney, Karen (1967) *Feminine Psychology*, London: Routledge and Kegan Paul.

Irigaray, Luce (1985 [1974]) *Speculum of the Other Woman*, trans. Gillian C. Gill, Ithaca, NY: Cornell University Press.

—— (1988) 'Interview', *Times Literary Supplement*, 18 September.

—— (1993) *An Ethics of Sexual Difference*, trans. Carolyn Burke and Gillian C. Gill, Ithaca, New York: Cornell University Press.

Jones, Ernest (1948) *Papers on Psychoanalysis*, London: Ballière, Tindall and Cox.

Kofman, Sarah (1988) *The Childhood of Art: An Interpretation of Freud's Aesthetics*, New York: Columbia University Press.

Laplanche, J. and J.-B. Pontalis (1974) *The Language of Psychoanalysis*, trans. Donald Nicholson-Smith, New York: Norton.

Lowe, Sarah M. (1991) *Frida Kahlo*, New York: Universe Publishing.

Millet, Kate (1971) *Sexual Politics*, London: Rupert Hart-Davis.

Mulvey, Laura (1975) 'Visual Pleasure and Narrative Cinema', *Screen*, 16: 6-18.

Price, A. W. (1990) 'Plato and Freud', in Christopher Gill (ed.), *The Person and the Human Mind: Issues in Ancient and Modern Philosophy*, Oxford: Clarendon Press.

Sulloway, Frank (1979) *Freud, Biologist of the Mind: Beyond the Psychoanalytic Legend*, New York: Basic Books.

Whitebook, Joel (1995) *Perversion and Utopia: A Study in Psychoanalysis and Critical Theory*, Cambridge, MA: MIT.

Williams, Bernard (1981) 'Moral Luck', *Moral Luck: Philosophical Papers 1973-1980*, Cambridge: Cambridge University Press.

Wollheim, Richard (1973) 'Freud and the Understanding of Art', in *On Art and the Mind: Essays and Lectures*, London: Allen Lane.

Zamora, Martha (1990) *Frida Kahlo: The Brush of Anguish*, San Francisco: Chronicle Books.

14

FREUD AND THE RULE OF LAW

From *Totem and Taboo* to psychoanalytic jurisprudence

José Brunner

Introduction

Despite the psychoanalytic discussions of the law that have been published by a number of Lacanian writers in recent years (e.g. Caudill 1997; Goodrich and Carlson 1998), it still may seem somewhat outlandish to invoke Freud's name in relation to the rule of law. By providing a detailed picture of the complex and provocative perspective on the origins and logic of the rule of law that Freud's writings offer, this essay aims to show that contrary to appearances, it is not so strange to have recourse to them in this context.

Traditionally, legal theorists speak of the rule of law as an impersonal body of rules, norms and prohibitions ordering social life, articulating and formalizing community standards of justice, fairness and moderation. The rule of law is endowed with an aura of transcendence, giving it authority over legislators and judges, denying the latter the status of creators, and relegating them instead to the role of interpreters. Often a capitalized Rule of Law is opposed to a 'rule of men', under which one has to be afraid of arbitrary uses of power by individuals in positions of authority, such as legislators, police, leader figures and judges (Sharone 1994: 330). It is the law's transcendent status, beyond the 'rule of men', which is supposed to provide it with the capacity to safeguard the rights and liberties of all and impose duties in an equitable manner. As Richard Epstein puts it: 'To attack the Rule of Law is to risk condemning ourselves to the arbitrary power of other individuals, who may be bound by nothing more than their own endless capacity of self-interest and personal gratification' (quoted in Sharone 1994: 331). Epstein's statement points to a broader cultural meaning of the rule of law ideal that always accompanies its narrower, legal uses. It indicates that the rule of law can also be taken to mean the rule of reason, in contrast to the unbridled and hence dangerous rule of passion, which in the last instance is bound to lead to coercion and oppression.

As long as reason is conceived as an independent and powerful force in the mind, and perhaps also in society, the representation of its struggle against the passions is fairly straightforward. However, things become more complicated when reason is not seen as an autonomous player and when it is assumed that reason always remains, and should remain, a slave to the passions, as David Hume postulated in his famous dictum. In such visions reason appears as incapable of being the cause of law on its own. Instead, the origin of the rule of law is located in an interplay of passions. As Hume pointed out, under such circumstances the restraint that legislation imposes on the passions cannot be 'contrary to these passions; for if so, it cou'd never be enter'd into, nor maintain'd; but it is only contrary to their heedless and impetuous movement' (Hume 1964 [1740]: 489). Hume also mentioned that, ironically, the presence of law may sometimes have the effect of increasing passions rather than harnessing them; for 'we naturally desire what is forbid, and take a pleasure in performing actions, merely because they are unlawful' (Hume 1964 [1740]: 421).

While Hume thought that humans would learn self-restraint by experience, Rousseau assumed that control over unruly passions could only be established by the intervention of a charismatic leader, who would teach the people the principles of a disinterested, higher form of legislation. In his chapter 'On Law' in *The Social Contract*, Rousseau explained that just civil law – i.e. the rule of law – has to be composed of principles ordained by the whole people for the whole people. They have to be abstract and cannot refer to any particular object or represent a particular will (Rousseau 1968 [1762]: 81). However, Rousseau did not believe that 'a blind multitude, which often does not know what it wants' could discover the principles of universalistic legislation. Therefore he assumed that there was a need for a 'lawgiver', towering above the common people and capable of understanding 'the passions of men without feeling any of them'. For Rousseau, the rule of law can arise only in a 'superior intelligence' characterized by the absence of passion. However, though such a rule of law is the product of pure reason, it has to mobilize the passions to gain authority. As he explains, reason cannot establish itself by its own merits. The law has to rely on deceit, a fictional origin in God's will and irrational fears of punishment, 'thus compelling by divine authority persons who cannot be moved by human prudence' (Rousseau 1968 [1762]: 84).

Freud's genealogy of the rule of law in *Totem and Taboo* and *Moses and Monotheism* belongs to this tradition of thinking, which regards the rule of reason and the law as inevitably dependent upon the passions. Moreover, like Hume, Rousseau and other modern thinkers before him, Freud addresses the rule of law only in the broader sense of the term, in which it is portrayed as arising from desire and yet pitched against it. He never expresses himself on more narrow legal issues (cf. Sharone 1994: 369). Thus, when he mentions the rule of law (*Recht* or *Rechtsordnung* in the original German) in *Civilization and its Discontents*, he clearly uses the term in its cultural meaning:

> Human life in common is only made possible when a majority comes
> together which is stronger than any separate individual and which remains

united against any separate individuals. The power of this community is then set up as 'right [Recht]' in opposition to the power of the individual, which is condemned as 'brute force'. The essence of it lies in the fact that the members of the community restrict themselves in their possibilities of satisfaction, whereas the individual knew no such restrictions. The first requisite of civilization, therefore, is that of justice – that is, the assurance that a law [Rechtsordnung] once made will not be broken in favour of an individual. This implies nothing as to the ethical value of such a law. The further course of cultural development seems to tend towards making the law [Recht] no longer an expression of the will of a small community . . . The final outcome should be a rule of law [Recht] to which all . . . have contributed by a sacrifice of their instincts [Triebopfer], and which leaves no one . . . at the mercy of brute force.

(Freud 1930: 95)

It is the argument of this essay that, nevertheless, Freud's vision of the rule of law may be worthwhile pondering by legal scholars. It can heighten awareness of its unconscious dimensions and point to a variety of ways in which the law functions as part of culture or civilization, rather than as a system with its own rules.

The first two parts of the essay seek to reconstruct Freud's notion of the rule of law as a dialectical or paradoxical civilizatory force, restraining the passions even though they drive it. These two parts retrace Freud's genealogy of the law's prehistoric origins and unconscious dynamics, which can be found in *Totem and Taboo* and, in summary form, in *Moses and Monotheism*. Then, the third section critically assesses the problems and limitations of some of the uses legal scholars made of Freud's genealogy. Finally, the essay returns to the intellectual context of Freud's conception of the rule of law, concluding with the claim that a Freudian perspective implies, in fact, that legal studies should be conceived as cultural studies.

Dialectics of desire

As has been mentioned, Freud develops his genealogy of the rule of law in *Totem and Taboo* and restates it in *Moses and Monotheism*. Among many other themes, these texts contain a myth of origins that serves Freud to explain the emergence of impersonal and commonly accepted rules of conduct governing society and keeping its fabric more or less intact. In the early period of humanity with which *Totem and Taboo* deals, strong males are said to have taken females as permanent sexual partners in order to ensure that their sexual needs will be satisfied on a regular basis. According to Freud women agreed to provide men with sexual satisfaction in order to guarantee their own safety as well as that of their children; they do not seem to have had any sexual desires of their own. Primordial women are supposed to have traded sex for their lives as well as the lives of their children. Freud argues that primal patriarchs jealously kept to themselves as many women as they could obtain and support, and oppressed their children by means of physical force. They deprived their sons of all sexual satisfaction and punished opposition with death, expulsion or castration. As Freud recapitulates in *Moses and Monotheism*, '[t]he strong male was lord and father of the entire horde and unrestricted in his power' (Freud 1939: 81; cf. 1912–13: 141).

By imposing a pleasure-denying law on his sons but exempting himself from it, thus being both inside and outside the law at the same time, the primal father constituted himself as a primal sovereign; for while the sons were totally excluded from sexual satisfaction, the law remained confined to them. According to Freud, the primal father's ability to make the law autocratically and impose it on his sons originated not so much in his superior physical strength than in his exclusive possession of females, which frustrated the sons and made them emotionally dependent on their father. Thus, the hypothetical prehistoric legal order of the primal horde established a composite relationship of prohibition, obedience and punishment between the law and those affected by it. Those who abode by the father's command saved their lives. Disregard was punished with castration or death. The primal father lived a life of pleasure in excess of the law. However, in the long run his excessive pleasure, combined with the excessive sexual repression that the primal law imposed upon the sons, brought about his violent death.

According to Freud, the intolerable demand for sexual abstinence prompted the sons to escape. Removing themselves from their father's control and regrouping into a community of outlaws living beyond – that is, in excess of – his law, the sons created what Freud describes as the first egalitarian social order in history. Liberating themselves from their emotional dependence on their father by homosexual satisfaction, they got ready for what *Totem and Taboo* depicts as the first collective action in history: patricide for the sake of incest (Freud 1912–13: 144). As we see, Freud's tale presents human sexuality from the very beginning as a polymorphous, variable desire with no fixed object. Outside the realm of the father's law, homosexual satisfaction can lead to liberation as well as heterosexual pleasure, especially since the father had outlawed both of them.

Ultimately, however, the sons returned to kill their father and have sex with their mother. Freud fails to explain why young tribal males, who were no longer sexually frustrated, should have been ready to kill for an older female, even if she was their mother. Of course, at the time he promoted the Oedipus complex as the shibboleth of psychoanalysis. However, since he does not specify any reason for the primordial sons' desire for their mother, the only logic that can be found in the story itself is one in which the father's monopolization of the mother and his prohibition of her turns her into such an immensely desirable sexual object. According to this reading, Freud's myth presents the law as sparking off or creating desire, or at least injecting it with force; for rather than as a natural given, incestuous desire is made to appear as the result of the particular socio-legal constellation of the primal horde.

In sum, Freud's story pitches various forms of desires and excess against each other. In the first place there is the father's law, deriving from too much sexual desire, allowing him too much pleasure, while leading to too much frustration in the sons, ultimately bringing about the violent destruction of the legal order. Then, there is the sons' attempt at satisfaction outside – i.e. in excess of – the scope of the father's law, their overflowing aggression, also driven by sexual desire, leading to yet another form of excess: an incestuous and cannibalistic murder.

According to Freud, only the aftermath of transgression and destruction allowed the sons to reflect upon the consequences of their act and realize the impossible nature of their incestuous desire and their deed. They understood that although each of them would have liked to replace the father, none of them could take his place, since such an attempt would lead to a war of all against all and to a complete collapse of all social organization. Thus the sons decided to renounce the satisfaction of all excessive desires and impose on themselves a law that preserved the fundamental prohibitions characteristic of the primal horde, with all the inevitable consequences for both desire and the law. *Moses and Monotheism* provides a succinct summary:

> The first form of social organization came about with a *renunciation of instincts*, a recognition of mutual *obligations*, the introduction of definite *institutions*, pronounced inviolable (holy) – that is to say, the beginnings of morality and justice. Each individual renounced his ideal of acquiring his father's position for himself and of possessing his mother and sisters. Thus the *taboo on incest* and the injunction to *exogamy* came about.
> (Freud 1939: 82; original emphasis)

A prohibition on murder, too, was imposed at this stage, and thus the nucleus of humankind's first rule of law was complete, if one is to believe Freud. It was both constituted and threatened by desire, as well as preserving it, albeit within limits, allowing no excessive satisfaction and tolerating no exception or exclusion from its norms.

As is the case in other areas of his thinking, the logic of Freud's genealogy is based on the principle of *Nachträglichkeit*, that is, a combination of delay, belatedness and hindsight. The rule of law comes on to the scene of history – or rather, catapults humankind from prehistory into history – not in order to prevent or ban an act as a crime before its occurrence, but because a deed has been carried out, which retrospectively comes to be regarded as a crime. In other words, for Freud the aim of the rule of law is to prohibit the act that lies at its origin.

The taboo on incest and the prohibition of murder can be seen as forming the foundation of the rule of law, since from the very beginning they were presented and accepted as holy, that is, as impersonal, transcendent rules of conduct. However, for the rule of law to become effective, a significant change in the social distribution of power had to take place. As Freud stresses in *Civilization and its Discontents*:

> Human life in common is only made possible when a majority comes together which is stronger than any separate individual and which remains united against all separate individuals . . . This replacement of the power of the individual by the power of a community constitutes the decisive step of civilization. The essence of it lies in the fact that the members of

the community restrict themselves in their possibilities of satisfaction, whereas the individual knew no such restrictions.

(Freud 1930: 95)

At first, it appears that the self-imposed renunciation of desire under the rule of law does provide a happy trade-off. The excessive desire of one (male) is given up for the safety and some pleasure of all (males); for although the rule of law always demands a certain degree of renunciation, it also always offers some legitimate avenues to sexual satisfaction. The sons' entry into the domain of the law also safeguards their pleasure.

Dialectics of guilt

So far, this reconstruction has made Freud's account of the origins of the rule of law appear as a narrative in which a 'rule of men' – or rather, of one man, the father – gives way to the rule of law, equality succeeds autocracy, and renunciation replaces excess. This is too good to be true. It is guilt that is still missing from the picture. Freud makes collective reason and its public manifestation, the rule of law, enter the history as supplements of a sense of guilt. As he explains in *Totem and Taboo*, when the murderous brothers were depleted of their aggression, they recalled that their father's presence had not only been punitive, but also protective, and they missed his sheltering force. Thus they started to feel remorse over their deed, which they now regarded as a crime. Freud's argument appears to be that patricide turned into a crime for the sons when they realized that the father's absence not only benefited them, but also harmed them. With time their remorse turned into guilt and to allay the latter they resurrected their father symbolically in the form of a totem, i.e. as an animal deity to whom they attributed the superhuman, protective powers they now wished their dead father had possessed. This father-substitute was turned into the object of their communal worship and subservience, and the clan's ancestor. By becoming a totem, the dead father was immortalized, thus the deed undone and the concomitant guilt relieved.

Of course, Freud assumes that the primordial brothers were not consciously aware of the unconscious layer of meaning that he attributes to the totem. However, as is evident, in the Freudian version of the social contract story the sons not only bound themselves to one another by rational agreement; they also concluded an unconscious, posthumous 'covenant with their father' (Freud 1912–13: 144).

Not only in *Totem and Taboo*, but throughout Freud's writings on culture, history and society, his argument is that humans could not transform themselves into a self-governing community under the rule of law without belatedly submitting to a father substitute – first the totem and then God. The lesson is that what on a conscious, manifest level may appear to be a rational contract among equals, is on an unconscious level a pact of delayed or belated – that is, *nachträgliche* – submission to the father. In this sense, then, the rule of law is not so much an antithesis replacing the father's rule, as the latter's masked and transformed continuation.

However, while the father's law was an expression of his desire, the sons' law was a consequence of their guilt; therefore it demanded the renunciation of the very same incestuous desires that previously had been prohibited by the father's law. Moreover, it used the means associated with the father's rule – violence – to require compliance with its prohibitions. Thus, in Freud's story the rule of law became implicated in that which it outlawed; for Freud presents the rule of law as maintained by the two forces it claimed to supersede: violence and submission to authority. Addressing this point in his famous letter to Albert Einstein, he states: 'right [*Recht*] is the might of a community. It is still violence, ready to be directed against any individual who resists it; it works by the same methods and follows the same purposes. The only real difference lies in the fact that what prevails is no longer the violence of an individual but that of a community' (Freud 1933: 205). The rule of law not only originated in violence against an autocratic regime; in order to prevent the latter's recurrence it deploys the very same violent means that safeguarded the father's despotic regime, the difference being only that violence is deployed for the sake of the community. As Freud emphasizes: 'The community must be maintained permanently, must be organized, must draw up regulations to anticipate the risk of rebellion and must institute authorities to see that those regulations – the laws – are respected and to superintend the execution of *legal acts of violence* [*rechtmässige Gewaltakte*]' (Freud 1933: 205, original emphasis).

To sum up, although the rule of law replaces external obedience by self-restraint, for Freud the most fundamental legal relation always is one of prohibition and punishment. His genealogy offers no simple and clear-cut opposition between the rule of law and the father's violent despotism, the former always also conceals a collective form of the latter. Nevertheless, Freud does regard obedience to a self-imposed law as constitutive of the transition from savage beast to moral subject. Since only acceptance of the rule of law turns the brothers from murderous brutes into self-restraining individuals who can form a civilized society, we see that for Freud it is guilt that makes law, and law that makes the moral subject – and not the other way round. As Costas Douzinas puts it: 'we do not repress desire because we have conscience, we have conscience because we repress desire' (Douzinas 1995: 1330).

Freud depicts the rule of law as an *Aufhebung* of that which it forbids, that is, as unconsciously maintaining in the act of negation that which is consciously negated. The rule of law not only abolishes violence in its original form, but also preserves it at the same time, while elevating it from being dangerous excess to the status of legal procedure, thus serving society. A similar dialectic is at work in the relationship between the father's autocratic law and the sons' rule of law. While the latter abolishes the father's sexual prohibitions in their original, autocratic form, it also preserves them by raising them to the higher level of a self-imposed ban on incest that is part of a universally accepted norm.

At the time of *Totem and Taboo* Freud still had no term for the mind's agency that allows humans the internalization of moral and legal principles, and their mental perpetuation after the primal father's demise. Later, of course, he came to use the term 'super-ego' for it, opening up a whole realm of discourse on what he describes as the mind's '"critical agency", performing functions of self-assessment and self-punishment, as well as providing moral ideals and judgments' (Freud 1930: 136). Freud depicts the mind as a whole in analogy to a modern state, conceptualizing the super-ego akin to law-enforcing agencies in the outside world and comparing its role to that of a 'garrison' set up in a 'conquered city' (Freud 1930: 124; cf. Brunner 1995: 45–88 for a detailed elaboration of Freud's mind–state analogy).

Freud's portrayal of the super-ego's origins in the child's mind retraces the argument of *Totem and Taboo*. Again, he presents autonomy and morality as the result of belated submission to the father. Obviously, civilized sons no longer kill their fathers. Instead, Freud explains, 'the boy deals with his father by identifying with him' (Freud 1923: 31). In the wake of the Oedipus complex, the son is said to accept the father's role as sole possessor of the mother and the concomitant prohibition on incestuous desire. From then on all desire that appears to undermine paternal authority and transgress its prohibitions is rigorously suppressed by the super-ego, and all aggression that is directed against the father is turned against the son himself. 'By means of identification [the son] takes the unattackable authority into himself. The authority now turns into his super-ego and enters into possession of all the aggressiveness which a child would have liked to exert against it' (Freud 1930: 129).

Freud's account of the origins of the super-ego provides a second genealogy of the rule of law, in which the real, living father is transposed into a disembodied psychological agency policing the mind. This account is constructed as an individual, ontogenetic parallel to his philogenetic tale concerning the transformation of the dead primal father into an immortal and superhuman entity governing the fate of humans from a metaphysical realm. In both cases such a father substitute is presented as the necessary catalyst in a developmental process in which an externally imposed law is replaced by a self-imposed rule of law. In Freud's words: '[a]s the child was once under compulsion to obey its parents, so the ego submits to the categorical imperative of its super-ego' (Freud 1923: 48).

However, contrary to the public nature of the rule of law in the outside world, much of the super-ego's intrapsychic law-enforcement and adjudication activities remain unconscious, that is, inaccessible to the subject whose mind is regulated by them. The super-ego enforces not only consciously accepted moral and legal principles, as are articulated in civil and criminal law and moral codes, but also additional, hidden laws, whose unwitting violation may give rise to feelings of guilt, worthlessness and depression. Indeed, Freud's eloquent description of the mental dynamics underlying melancholia or, as we would call it today, depression – in which the super-ego crushes the ego with guilt – portrays it like a judge in a Kafkaesque trial. In such cases, he writes, the super-ego 'becomes over-severe, abuses . . . humiliates . . . threatens . . . as though it had spent the whole interval in collecting accusations and had only been waiting for its present access to strength in order to bring them up and make a condemnatory judgment on their basis' (Freud 1923: 61).

In Freud's discourse, not only depression is marked by such an unforgiving attitude. In his view, 'even ordinary normal morality has a harshly restraining, cruelly prohibiting quality' (Freud 1923: 54). As he also stresses in *The Ego and the Id*, the stricter the super-ego is, the more unyielding it is toward those who break its rules, however minor and insignificant they may be; and the less ready it is to allow open expressions of aggression, the more it stores of it for self-punishment. As he explains, the most moralistic and law-abiding people may be precisely the ones who feel most guilty and punish themselves most violently and excessively for slight transgressions of rules that others may ignore with complacency. Again, we note that in Freud's discourse the law – or, in this case, the mind's adjudicating and law-enforcing agency – has a tendency to excess that is fuelled by feelings of guilt.

As long as such feelings are conscious, Freud regards them as relatively unproblematic; they are, he says, simply 'the expression of a condemnation of the ego by its critical agency' (Freud 1923: 51). Neuroses stem from unconscious guilt that is said not only to make people ill, but also to constitute a most serious obstacle for their treatment, leading to what Freud calls a 'negative therapeutic reaction' preventing patients 'to give up the punishment of suffering' (Freud 1923: 49). Evidently, the mind's internal judge may become sadistic and enjoy the pain it inflicts on the ego.

In fact, *The Ego and the Id*, which introduces the super-ego as a psychic agency, associates it not only with conscience and lawful obedience, but also with crime, self-humiliation, violence and death. Thus, this essay can be read as a catalogue of the many forms of excess in which the super-ego is implicated, listing its various pathological results: obsessional neurosis, hysteria, melancholia, and suicide. Freud even raises the possibility that the guilt instilled by an excessively severe super-ego may make criminals out of moralists: 'In many criminals, especially youthful ones, it is possible to detect a very powerful sense of guilt, which existed before the crime, and is therefore not its result but its motive. It is as if it was a relief to be able to fasten this unconscious sense of guilt on to something real and immediate' (Freud 1923: 52). Perhaps this category of criminals, driven to transgress the rule of law in the *external* world by the unbearable force of an excestringent and oppressive *internal* rule of law, may be regarded as the ultimate perversion to which the law's hidden dialectic of guilt and excess can lead.

Dialectic of jurisprudence

Freud's work had only a negligible impact on contemporary legal thinking, and in recent years most contributions that may be regarded as psychoanalytic rely on Lacan (cf. Goldstein 1968; Ehrenzweig 1971; Schoenfeld 1973; Sheleff 1986; Kaplan and Rinella 1988; Caudill 1991; Goodrich 1995; Caudill 1997; Goodrich 1997; Legendre and Goodrich 1997; Goodrich and Carlson 1998). Moreover, as will be shown below, the few legal scholars who did deploy Freudian categories in an attempt to demystify the rule of law ideal in jurisprudence, divested Freud's approach of its tragic element.

Published in 1930 – the year in which Freud published *Civilization and its Discontents* – Jerome Frank's *Law and the Modern Mind* is an early but classic example of the jurisprudential application of Freud. Frank argues that contrary to the claims of legal scholars and lawmakers, the law is unstable, vague and tentative. Moreover, Frank holds this to be a good thing, since the fluidity of human relationships cannot be embedded in a rigid legal grid (Frank 1949 [1930]: 6). However, he asks, if instability and uncertainty are both necessary and desirable features of the law, why do judges, lawyers, lay people and legal theorists share in the pretence of a stable and transcendent rule of law?

Relying not only on Freud but also on Piaget, he traces the irrational wish for legal transcendence, such as is attributed to the rule of law, to an early wish for paternal omnipotence. For him, the rule of law serves society as a substitute father akin to the way Freud portrayed the function of the totem and God. Rather than referring to the myth of the primal horde, however, Frank adopts Freud's scheme of early childhood development, which posits that the first days and months of infancy are characterized by an illusion of omnipotence. When the child comes to realize that dependence rather than omnipotence characterizes his or her early life, this illusion is projected upon parental figures, especially the father, who is imagined as an all-powerful protector providing security. Thus, Frank argues, people 'seek unrealizable certainty in law . . . because . . . they have not yet relinquished the childish need for an authoritative father and unconsciously have tried to find in the law a substitute for those attributes of firmness, sureness, certainty and infallibility ascribed in childhood to the father' (Frank 1949 [1930]: 21, see also 203).

Frank's rhetoric is polemical and critical; presenting itself as a new form of jurisprudence, it aims to relieve legal discourse and legal practitioners of a heavy and unnecessary burden. Like Freud, he states that he wishes to foster humanity's growth into a more rational adulthood, characterized by the 'modern mind' he refers to in the title of his book. Such a mind is supposed to be equipped with a mature view of society and the knowledge that men rule the law, that it is made and remade by appointed officials who decide on what is right and wrong, and does not emerge from the community. As Frank puts it, 'we must face the fact that we are ruled by judges, not abstract law. If that is tyranny or despotism, make the most of it' (Frank 1949 [1930], 136n; cf. Chase 1979: 46–50).

As we see, Frank's attack on the rule-of-law notion is directed against a specific legal doctrine that he regards as childish and illusionary, not against the rule of reason over desire and wishful fantasies. On the contrary, Frank's opposition to the rule of law in the legal sense of the term is animated by his quest to further the rule of law in the wider, cultural sense of the term. Frank is optimistic that humanity will soon grow out of the need for myths and into maturity. He assumes that ultimately both the legal system and the rule of reason may exist without dangers of excess and without being embedded in an unconscious quest for omnipotent father-figures. However, from a Freudian perspective one is bound to wonder whether, if judges were socially and legally accepted as the makers and changers of the law – rather than as its interpreters and adjudicators – would it not be them, rather than the rule of law, who became objects of fantasies of omnipotence? The projection of omnipotence upon judges and, not the least, their own fantasies of omnipotence that are enhanced by approaches such as Frank's, may be no less infantile and have no less undesirable social effects than the myth of a transcendent rule of law (Schoenfeld 1988). It seems thus that while Frank's argument against the rule of law in the narrower sense of the word is guided by psychoanalytic insights into the dialectics of desire, he does not subject the alternative he suggests to psychoanalytic reflection. His text exhibits none of the scepticism that marks so much of Freud's work in relation to the rule of reason in culture and society. For Frank, the rule of law illusion is one that can be diagnosed and removed without loss.

Recently, Robin West has summoned Freud in defence of the doctrine of the rule of law. Surprisingly enough, she argues that Freud's work can be used to establish a better defence of this ideal than that provided by American liberal legal theorists such as Laurence Tribe, Owen Fiss, Ronald Dworkin and Charles Fried (West 1986: 818). For West, Freud's method is preferable since it is naturalistic in the sense of relying on assumptions concerning human nature and history. She acknowledges that the legal liberals, whose position Freud's work is said to support, are bound to reject his approach as fallacious. According to West, legal liberals cannot suffer a naturalistic line of argument because of their methodological commitment to a strict fact–value distinction, which allows them only to produce arguments for the rule of law that rely on 'intuitively grasped and noncontingent moral truths' (West 1986: 820).

West's argument in favour of Freud is directed against transcendence in legal theory. She supports Freud's position against that of the legal liberals because it is presented as rooted in a factual, historical account. But although she states that 'Freud's analysis is grounded upon facts about our history and nature, while the liberal response is grounded on intuitively grasped moral truths' (West 1986: 844), in the concluding pages of her article she doubles back from this uncritical endorsement, admitting that Freud's assumptions 'about our nature and history may well be false', and that recent scholarship has thrown 'considerable doubt on both the empirical and the historical assumptions of Freud's theory of law' (West 1986: 881). Moreover, she concedes: 'If Freud's account of our nature is wrong, his defense of legal liberal commitments fails' (West 1986: 844). Thus, in West's own terms, Freud leaves us with a failed defence of the rule of law that, nonetheless, is praised for being superior to intuitionist arguments because of its coherence and its grounding in purportedly factual claims.

Clearly, Freud's mythical tale of the origins of civilization is rather a problematic source for anybody seeking to base arguments for the rule of law on facts of human nature and history. In addition, much of West's argument is vitiated by her failure to distinguish Freud's broader concern with the origins of the rule of law in the dialectics of sexuality and aggression, from the narrower, jurisprudential engagement of American legal theorists with constitutionalism and the role of the judiciary. Freud's argument concerning the necessity of a rule of law as a condition of civilization does not necessarily lead to a defence of the rule of law in the legal sense, which is designed to limit the role of judges and legislators in order to prevent possible undemocratic ramifications of a 'rule of men'. On the contrary, Freud's portrayal of modern society exhibits a striking blindness to the dangers emanating from authority figures. Somehow he seems to have forgotten that – in his own terms – they are heirs to a killing and castrating primal patriarch. Instead he regards them as necessary for social cohesion and the control of 'the masses' whose unrestrained passion he fears. While Freud was an old-style liberal, he was by no means a democrat. In his eyes, the control of the masses necessitates powerful father-figures inspiring the former to renounce desire; for in his view, '[i]t is only through the individuals who can set an example and whom crowds recognize as their leaders [*Führer*] that they can be induced to perform the work and undergo the renunciations on which the existence of civilization depends . . . it therefore seems necessary that they shall be independent of the crowd by having means to power [*Machtmittel*] at their disposal' (Freud 1927: 8; see also Freud 1930: 115–16, Freud 1933: 212; Brunner 1995: 166–170). Freud argues that throughout history breakthroughs to higher and more rational cultural stages have been initiated and achieved by outstanding individuals who managed to mesmerize the masses. The biblical Moses, a lawmaker inventing a new code and thus acting as 'an outstanding father-figure' to the ancient Hebrews, provides Freud with the paradigmatic example of a leader moving history forward by his will (Freud 1939: 89).

It is difficult to reconcile such a historical vision with the rule of law ideal in American legal liberalism. Moreover, West seems reluctant to accept that as part of his naturalism, Freud also denies that reason – and therefore law – can ever become fully autonomous from sexuality and aggression. In fact, it appears that driven by her quest to pair Freud with American legal liberals, she underplays this fact. Although she quotes extensively from Freud's texts and arguments concerning the rule of law, she omits from them all instances in which Freud points to the intricate rootedness of law in desire and violence. For instance, she provides a lengthy quote from Freud's letter to Einstein, which has been quoted earlier in this essay as well. However, West leaves out all sentences that refer to the violence immanent in the law, covering the gaps in her quotation by innocent dots. Similarly, her quotation also omits Freud's reference to 'legal acts of violence' (cf. West 1986: 830; Freud 1933: 205).

More than six decades after the publication of Frank's *Law and the Modern Mind*, Ofer Sharone also has recourse to Freud in order to make a stand against what he sees as the deceptions inherent in the rule of law ideal. Following Frank in viewing the rule of law as an abstract father-substitute, he, too, claims that social progress requires the 'exposition and eradication of the rule of law illusion' (Sharone 1994: 329). He agrees with Frank that the rule of law imposes a detrimental rigidity on the work of judges. But in contrast to Frank, Sharone develops his argument by presenting the rule of law analogous to the way in which Freud portrayed religion in *Future of an Illusion*, arguing that the protection offered by the rule of law is equally an illusion. Freud had argued that the decline of religion would enable science to find ways to improve society. Similarly Sharone contends that '[t]he demystification of the rule of law would . . . allow judges and lawyers to be bold and to experiment in finding ways to optimally reconcile the needs of men and of society' (Sharone 1994: 359). Moreover, he argues that a more activist image of the judiciary will lead to an exposure of the subjective nature of judicial review, making people aware of the power invested in it, thus fostering increased democratic involvement in political decision-making (Sharone 1994: 361).

Like Frank, Sharone suggests to get rid of the rule of law illusion, since this can be done without loss or danger. Since his argument relies on the analogy between Freud's view of religion as a childish illusion and the rule of law, it draws on the optimistic and combative *Future of an Illusion*, rather than on the much more sombre *Civilization and its Discontents*. Thus, like Frank and West before him, Sharone replaces the tragic sentiment of Freud's vision with hopefulness, arguing that Freud's approach 'provides a powerful critique of the rule of law [in the narrow sense of the term] and an optimistic turn toward a society without illusions' (Sharone 1994: 358).

Unlike West, Sharone is aware that the jurisprudential notion of the rule of law he deals with is not the one Freud refers to in *Civilization and its Discontents*. Acknowledging that Freud's idea of the rule of law has nothing to do with 'the law's independence from the leader nor the law's aim to protect society from its leader', he points out that for Freud the rule of law has to do with the renunciation of desire, which can be achieved only by submission to father-figures (Sharone 1994: 369, n. 82). Nevertheless, the parallel between law and religion on which he builds his position, leads him to ignore the tragic element in Freud's vision of the rule of law, which sees the latter as ineluctably embedded in the dynamics of guilt and desire. For Freud the rule of law is not a collective neurotic symptom one can get rid of like religion, but an inevitable part of civilization, whose contradictions have to be suffered and tolerated by all, since the only alternative is social collapse and a war of all against all. Plainly, by constricting Freud's genealogy within the boundaries of legal discourse, legal theorists become blind to the cultural implications of Freud's stance; by 'legalizing' Freud, they abandon the terrain of cultural critique.

Conclusion

As we have seen, Freud's genealogy of the rule of law – in the wider sense of the term – is both dialectical and critical, grounding the law in desire and guilt, and inserting it in a logic of excess. In the first place, Freud claims that the rule of law arises when desire becomes so excessive that it turns against itself, causing suffering rather than pleasure. Thus the law restrains desire for its own sake as well as in the service of survival. In the second place, since the rule of law is driven by guilt and contains the very desire it seeks to constrain, Freud argues that the law, too, is marked by a tendency toward excess.

The aim of this genealogy is to unravel a high-minded moral and legal concept in order to uncover its origins in forgotten violent passions and struggles that are said to have shaped them and to govern much of their effects. Freud seeks to provoke and disturb by the construction or reconstruction of a past that may throw light on that which has been hidden in official histories of the rule of law in order to be forgotten. His aim is to show that neither the constitutive origins nor the actual workings and effects of the law are subsumed under its declared purpose. He supposes that original conflicts and the forces involved in them can never be entirely nullified. The protagonists of this dialectic are preserved in the unconscious depth of the rule of law, which contains dangerous tendencies toward excess, driven by guilt and desire. Its dark corners are inhabited by a surreptitious tendency to submit to father substitutes and a secret complicity with that which the law forbids. They are populated by hidden but ubiquitous elements of violence and sadistic components.

Friedrich Nietzsche stands out as an intellectual ancestor of Freud's conception of the rule of law. In *On the Genealogy of Morals* Nietzsche endeavours to show that the law originated in *ressentiment*, that is, in a negative passion, hostile to life's overflowing impulses, not unlike the excessive, unconscious guilt to which Freud refers (Nietzsche 1972 [1887]). Nietzsche builds his genealogy upon the assumption of a hypothetical original state of society ruled by 'masters', i.e. humans who were not bothered about what others did and how they did it. Sufficient to themselves because of their surplus passion, they were completely egocentric, affirmed their own deeds as 'good' and dismissed what hindered them as 'bad'. In other words, they behaved not unlike the primal father in Freud's story.

For Nietzsche, the moralizing rule of law that banned acts of the masters as evil was the result of a revolt of 'slaves' who lacked the energetic surplus of the masters, but managed to remove the latter from their superior position, just as the sons did in Freud's tale. Although Nietzsche does not use the term rule of law in *On the Genealogy of Morals*, he traces the origins of the law to slavish concern for what others do and feel, and to the resentful negation of everything that is different from the way the weak are capable of acting and feeling. Thus, he portrays the rule of law as a weapon of those who failed to experience the power of overflowing passion and, out of resentment, sought to exclude such passion by condemning them as evil.

Freud's outlook also shares much with that of the cultural and literary critic Walter Benjamin. Benjamin, a contemporary of Freud whose historical vision was strongly influenced by Nietzsche, published an essay in 1921, which recently has received much attention by philosophers and legal scholars. Like Freud, Benjamin drew attention both to the presence of violence or force at the foundation of the rule of law and to their law-preserving exercise later on (Benjamin 1921; see also Derrida 1990; LaCapra 1995).

Four decades after Freud's death, Michel Foucault developed a tragic and explicitly Nietzschean perspective on the law that seems somewhat like an exaggerated version of Freud's view. According to Foucault, 'the law is a calculated and relentless pleasure, delight in the promised blood, which permits the perpetual instigation of new dominations and the staging of meticulously repeated scenes of violence'. Thus, for Foucault '[h]umanity does not gradually progress from combat to combat until it arrives at universal reciprocity, where the rule of law finally replaces warfare; humanity installs each of its violences in a system of rules and thus proceeds from domination to domination' (Foucault 1977: 151; see also Hunt 1993; Leonard 1995).

However, as we have seen, the critical edge of this vision of the rule of law, which Freud shares with Nietzsche and other twentieth-century Nietzschean thinkers, is absent from the psychoanalytic legal discourse on the rule of law. The latter recasts Freud's tragic myth in an optimistic mould. Reading Frank, West and Sharone, one is led to the conclusion that much is lost and perhaps not all that much is gained by limiting Freud's conception of the rule of law to jurisprudence. After all, Freud offers no sustained analysis of the legal system and cannot recommend a methodology or prescribe a procedure for legal thinking. But although there is no fruitful 'hard' Freudian contribution to debates on the rule of law in terms of theoretical system building or methodology, his work may offer a 'soft' input, that is, a sensibility to the hidden, unconscious dimensions of the rule of law, on which he has focused. However, Freud's vision of the rule of law can serve critical legal thinking only if the law is seen as part of culture rather than as a self-enclosed system; i.e. only insofar as legal studies are conceived as a form of cultural studies. And, to conclude on the same note on which this essay began, one has to acknowledge that whatever else their shortcomings may be, this is one point in which Lacan and the thinkers inspired by him are right on target (but a comprehensive discussion of Lacan, Lacanians and the rule of law will have to await another occasion).

Acknowledgements

I am grateful to the Cegla Institute for Comparative and Private International Law of Tel Aviv University for the financial support I received for this project. Thanks also go to Daniel Strassberg, who was involved in an earlier formulation of the essay; to my colleagues at the Buchman Faculty of Law for the opportunity to present my argument at the faculty seminar; to Moran Svoraee, who collected some of the material I used and commented on an earlier draft; and last but not least to Arnona Zahavi for her patient and incisive reading of successive versions of this essay.

References

Benjamin, W. (1921) 'Zur Kritik der Gewalt', *Archiv für Sozialwissenschaften und Sozialpolitik*, 47: 809–32.

Brunner, J. (1995) *Freud and the Politics of Psychoanalysis*, Oxford: Blackwell.

Caudill, D. S. (1991) 'Freud and critical legal studies: contours of a radical socio-legal psychoanalysis', *Indiana Law Journal*, 66: 651–97.

—— (1997) *Lacan and the Subject of Law: Toward a Psychoanalytic Critical Legal Theory*, Atlantic Highlands: Humanities Press.

Chase, A. (1979) 'Jerome Frank and American psychoanalytic jurisprudence', *International Journal of Law and Psychiatry*, 2: 29–54.

Derrida, J. (1990) 'Force of law: the "mystical foundation of authority"', *Cardozo Law Review*, 11: 919–1045.

Douzinas, C. (1995) 'Law's birth and Antigone's death: on ontological and psychoanalytical ethics', *Cardozo Law Review*, 16: 1325–62.

Ehrenzweig, A. (1971) *Psychoanalytic Jurisprudence: On Ethics, Aesthetics, and Law*, Leiden: Dordrecht.

Foucault, M. (1977) 'Nietzsche, Genealogy, History', in D.F. Bouchard (ed.), *Language, Counter-Memory, Practice: Selected Essays and Interviews*, Itahaca: Cornell University Press.

Frank, J. (1949 [1930]) *Law and the Modern Mind*, London: Stevens and Sons.

Freud, S. (1912–13) *Totem and Taboo*, in J. Strachey (ed.), *The Standard Edition of the Complete Psychological Works of Sigmund Freud*, London: Hogarth Press, 1953–1974 (*S.E.*) vol. 13: 18–51.

—— (1923) *The Ego and the Id*, *S.E.*, vol. 19: 12–59.

—— (1927) *The Future of an Illusion*, *S.E.*, vol. 21: 5–56.

—— (1930) *Civilization and its Discontents*, *S.E.*, vol. 21: 64–145.

—— (1933) 'Why war?', *S.E.*, vol. 22: 203–9.

—— (1939) *Moses and Monotheism*, *S.E.*, vol. 23: 7–137.

Goldstein, J. (1968) 'Psychoanalysis and jurisprudence: on the relevance of psychoanalytic therapy to law', *Psychoanalytic Study of the Child*, 23: 459–79.

Goodrich, P. (1995) *Oedipus Lex: Psychoanalysis, History, Law*, Berkeley: University of California Press.

—— (1997) 'Maladies of the legal soul: psychoanalysis and interpretation in law', *Washington and Lee Law Review*, 54: 1035–74.

Goodrich, P. and Carlson, D. (1998) *Law and the Postmodern Mind: Essays on Psychoanalysis and Jurisprudence*, Ann Arbor: University of Michigan Press.

Hume, D. (1964 [1740]) *A Treatise on Human Nature*, L.A. Selby-Bigge (ed.), Oxford: Clarendon Press.

Hunt, A. (1993) *Explorations in Law and Society: Toward a Constitutive Theory of Law*, New York and London: Routledge.

Kaplan, L. V. and Rinella, V. (1988) 'Jurisprudence and the appropriation of the psychoanalytic: a study in ideology and form', *International Journal of Law and Psychiatry*, 11: 215–48

LaCapra, D. (1995) 'Violence, justice and the force of law', *Cardozo Law Review*, 11: 1065–78.

Legendre, P. and Goodrich, P. (1997) *Law and the Unconscious: A Legendre Reader*, New York: St. Martin's Press.

Leonard, J. (1995) 'Foucault and (the Ideology of) Genealogical Legal Theory', in J. Leonard (ed.), *Legal Studies as Cultural Studies: A Reader in (Post)Modern Critical Theory*, Albany: State University of New York Press.

Nietzsche, F. (1972 [1887]) *Zur Genealogie der Moral*, Oxford: Blackwell.

Rousseau, J.-J. (1968 [1762]) *The Social Contract*, Penguin: Harmondsworth.

Schoenfeld, C.G (1973) *Psychoanalysis and the Law*, Springfield, IL: Charles C. Thomas.

—— (1988) 'Omnipotence and the law: a psychoanalytically oriented analysis', *Journal of Psychiatry and Law*, 16: 421–58.

Sharone, Ofer (1994) 'Freud and the rule of law', *Journal of Psychiatry and Law*, 22: 329–78.

Sheleff, L. S. (1986) 'The illusions of law – psychoanalysis and jurisprudence in historical perspective', *International Journal of Law and Psychiatry*, 9: 143–58.

West, R. (1986). 'Law, rights and other totemic illusions: legal liberalism and Freud's theory of the rule of law', *University of Pennsylvania Law Review*, 134: 817–82.

15

THE JOKE, THE 'AS IF' AND
THE STATEMENT

Edmond Wright

Freud's *Jokes and their Relation to the Unconscious* (1976 [1905]) has had a fragmented history. Within psychoanalysis itself it was seen as an early application of the insights of his dream theory to a by-way of human behaviour, in which the unconscious adopts techniques against the censor similar to those that are operative within the dream. In his essay 'Humour' (1985 [1927]) Freud himself later added an addendum on humour *per se* which related it to his id–ego–super-ego topology, thereby extending the context of relevance to the operations of the super-ego as an 'heir to the parental agency', but he did not widen the generality of his explanation further.

From within other disciplines his Joke theory took its place among older theories of humour. Psychologists have set it down as one of the 'Relief' theories, typified by that of Herbert Spencer, in which the arousal induced by some threat is allowed a convulsive escape in laughter when the stimulus proves incongruously false, allowing us to 'descend' from 'great to small', that is, from fear to safety (Spencer 1891, II). Anthropologists have connected his notion of a covert temporary relief from inhibition with practices of 'permitted disrespect' found in early societies; such practices tend to enter behaviour where there are ambivalences that create points of tension, as between generations or between kin bound by custom (Radcliffe-Brown 1952). Linguists have noted how close Freud is to Incongruity theories, in which two rival 'scripts' are unexpectedly brought together by some ambiguous 'trigger', and single out his insistence that the more alien the two 'circles of ideas', the greater the pleasure the joke delivers (Attardo 1994: 56; Freud 1976 [1905]: 168). This feature has also been of interest in cognitive theories about which Freud comments that they are characterized by a stress on a movement from 'bewilderment to illumination' (ibid.: 42). This relating of humour to the applicability of concepts is traceable back to Schopenhauer who saw humour as attending the mismatches between concept and action:

> It occurs just as often, however, that the incongruity between a single real
> object and the concept under which, from one point of view it has rightly

been assumed, is suddenly felt. Now the more correct the subsumption of such objects under a concept may be from one point of view and the greater and more glaring their incongruity with it from another point of view, the greater is the ludicrous effect which is produced by this contrast.

(Schopenhauer 1957, II: 252)

A recent statement on the same lines is that of Jonathan Miller's which takes Freud's as a 'Relief' theory and relates it to the humorous as being 'a sabbatical let-out that lets us redesign categories and concepts' (Miller 1988: 12). What is noteworthy is his insistence that, despite our immediate prejudice against seeing humour as meriting serious study, in studying it 'we may be undertaking the most serious thing we do in our lives' (ibid.: 13). What is hoped will be made clear later is that this prejudice against the correction of existing concepts by 'jokers' and 'jesters' has a traceable source in a practical need for the time being to take those existing concepts for granted.

Nowhere in the later developments of these theories, however, has there been a consideration of whether Freudian psychoanalysis might have an input to the theory of humour beyond the connections noted above. One conspicuous exception is Jerry Aline Flieger's discussion of the relation of Freud's comic theory to the postmodern text (Flieger 1991), in which she demonstrates how psychoanalytic theory can formulate a critique of high-rationalist theory that does not descend into relativism. Although she does not refer to cognitive theories, the measure of overlap is marked. The present essay adopts a similar strategy in extending the psychoanalytic perspective by making reference to current investigations of humour in sociology, linguistics and psycholinguistics. The further aim is to show that psychoanalytic theory in its Lacanian form can prove cogent enough to place the cognitive theory itself in a wider epistemological frame. The aim of this argument is to show how social adherence to a universal acceptance of concepts is consonant with their correction from a particular standpoint.

1 Freud's theory

One of the witticisms that Freud himself cites as example is the Italian '*Traduttore – Traditore!*' ('To translate [is] to betray!'). With this he shows how a slight alteration can produce the shift taking us from one from one context to another, and then he adds a comment on the 'similarity':

> The similarity, amounting almost to identity, of the two words represents most impressively the necessity which forces a translator into crimes against his original.

(Freud 1976 [1905]: 67)

This notion that the shift is associated with a 'crime' is unsurprising in the context since throughout the book Freud views the joke – when not 'innocent' play – as an attempt to evade the censor, to enjoy a temporary challenge to authority, to collude with another in a momentary escape from internal and external repression. The very meaning of the Italian epigram is itself a comment on the Joke from Freud's point of view for any Joker's 'translation' is intended 'to betray' some strict rule that he finds irksome. This is for Freud the 'tendentious' joke, where 'tendentious' means not merely *with a hidden purpose*, but distinctly *biased*, the colluding participants illicitly enjoying the breaking of a rule while being protected from criticism by the ambiguity on which the joke is trading. The 'scrutiny of criticism' is rendered ineffectual by it, so that the Joker and his/her Hearer can enjoy the pleasure of their brief rebellion in safety, immune from repercussions. Freud sees a strong parallel here with the defeat of the censor in dreams, and by using the same mechanisms (condensation, displacement and indirect representation – i.e. by symbol or analogy). The result is an 'economy of psychic expenditure', the pain of repression now assuaged with unwanted energy required for repression escaping in the fits of laughter. Even the 'innocent' joke, which appears to rely solely upon the pleasure derived from the play of words, is not wholly non-tendentious in Freud's view, his reason being that there is pleasure in escaping the rules of language themselves: all jokes thus set themselves up 'against an inhibiting and restricting power' (ibid.: 183).

Throughout his book Freud thus tends to see the Joke as a safety-valve, offering an occasional relief from the repressive demands of internal and external authorities. At the very beginning he considered theories that suggested that the joke might involve a 'playful judgement' characterized by a 'comic contrast', but regarded these as 'scarcely intelligible' because they consider jokes out of their real context, so that they fail in coherence, merely producing something corresponding to a series of anecdotes about the Joke rather than its full-length 'biography' (ibid.: 45). As regards the claim of those cognitive theories which find 'sense in nonsense' (e.g. Lipps 1898: 87), he considers his own explanation as sufficient, because it takes the 'sense' as providing the excuse that 'prevents the pleasure [in the play on words] being done away with by criticism' (ibid.: 180–1). In the case of the Comic, the joke resides in the unavailing performance of an external victim, who characteristically is expending too much effort in a situation where we think ourselves superior in knowledge and therefore in our economy, which gives us the illusion of being on the side of authority (a point to be returned to later).

In his later paper 'Humour' (Freud 1985 [1927]) he continues to see laughter as a psychic defence, a palliative to the inexorable pressure on the unconscious. Humour, possessing 'a greater dignity' than jokes or the comic, is attributed to the capacity of the ego to refuse to suffer, which amounts to a 'triumph of the Pleasure Principle against the unkindness of real circumstances' (ibid.: 429). The ego identifies with the father, sees its sufferings in a wider context from the perspective of a benign super-ego. While Freud admits that it is unusual for the super-ego to refrain from exercising its customary severity, he insists that, to the degree the ego can see itself as child consoled by amusement, so it is enabled to bear the frustrations of life, which, in his view, would be one convincing general reason for the wider significance of humour.

Freud's reflections on jokes and humour thus exhibit a somewhat conservative tendency. The translation in a joke is inevitably an act of treachery that we are lucky to get away with, the authorities being as bemused by the ambiguity as the censor is by the tropings of the dream. It matches his strict opposition of the Pleasure Principle to the Reality Principle, as if notions of 'reality' could not be invested with desire, as if they were given obstacles that could only be accepted for what they were with the aid of the illusory play of the joke and the resigned shrug of humour. Flieger makes the comment that Freud is more concerned with the veiling that the joking process performs than any unveiling that might come from it (Flieger 1991: 59). Freud, indeed, regards reason as one of the enemies of the joking process: 'Reason, critical judgement, suppression – these are the forces against which [the joke] fights in succession' (1976 [1905]: 189), where one can see Freud's conservative bias at its plainest in that he is unable to see the joke as a critical judgement, *on the side of reason*. A later Freudian, Edmund Bergler, is equally conservative, taking the satisfaction of laughter to reside in the temporary debunking of the feared super-ego, achieved through the creation of a substitute victim that betrays the psychic masochism that the ego itself suffers. The escape remains momentary, a kind of quick fix that soon returns the ego to its erstwhile subjection (Bergler 1956: x–xii).

Nevertheless, Freud is surely right inasmuch as there is an economizing of psychic expenditure, that in some way authority passes on from the existing ethical and political authorities to new ones as a result of the transformation: the question is whether authority must necessarily return to them, for the investigation of humour raises the whole question of what authority is, how it is constituted, and how it relates to the linguistic process.

2 The linguists

The recent progress in the linguistic investigation of humour has been remarkable, providing an increase in sophistication that shows the linguists as not in the least prejudiced against the subject for its supposed triviality. The most prominent American theoretician, Victor Raskin, after giving a comprehensive survey of the theories of humour, including Freud's, presents a strictly linguistic theory, confined solely to verbal humour. He regards his theory as compatible with existing theories, which in his view achieve only a partial success. He divides those theories into three groups: (1) Repression theories, Freud's in particular; (2) Incongruity theories, which have a cognitive-perceptual basis; and (3) Disparagement theories, which function as a social-behavioural type of explanation (Raskin 1985: 30). His threefold classification is useful here in preparing the ground for the forthcoming argument.[1]

Incongruity theory might be said to have begun with Kant, for whom 'Laughter is an affection arising from a strained expectation being suddenly reduced to nothing' (Kant 1957 [1790]: 199). He instances accounts of grief, which normally would arouse some measure of concern in us, but when we hear the following story the seriousness is banished and we 'laugh and enjoy' (at least those in the eighteenth century for whom people in trade were still a courtly object of fun):

A merchant was returning from India with all his wealth in merchandise. A great storm blew up in which the only hope for the vessel lay in casting all the cargo overboard. On seeing his whole wealth cast into the sea, the merchant's wig turned quite grey with grief.

(Ibid.: 200)

Kant does not analyse the link between the two incongruous fields as later theorists in this tradition were to do. Jerry Suls, from psychology, insists that there has to be this 'resolution' of the incongruity for the humour to be present and gives as proof the effect of certain substitutions in the following joke:

'Doctor, come at once! Our baby has swallowed (a) a fountain-pen (b) a rubber-band.'
'I'll come right over. What are you doing in the meantime?'
'(c) Using a pencil.' (d) 'We don't know what to do.'

(Suls 1983: 45)

(a) and (c) together produce the joke since they contain both the incongruity and the resolution. (b) and (c) produce an incongruity but no resolution. (a) and (d), (b) and (d) have no incongruity to be resolved (Suls 1983: 45). Here (c) functions as the 'punchline', common to all jokes, the element that effects the transition from one context to the other. Here it changes the meaning of 'What are you doing in the meantime?' (the 'trigger' of the joke) from *doing something to help the baby*, a threatening interpretation, established in the context of the call to the doctor, to *doing for a writing implement*, which has harmless connotations, established by the phrase 'Using a pencil'. All jokes without exception have at least these five elements:

 (i)   the *ambiguous trigger* over which the interpretations play;
 (ii) a *clue to a first context of interpretation*;
 (iii) the *first meaning* resulting from this first clue;
 (iv) a *clue to a second context of interpretation*; and
 (v)   the *second meaning* resulting from this second clue.

The punchline can be either the Second Clue or the Trigger. In the joke above it was the Second Clue; in the following joke it is the Trigger: 'What did the big telephone say to the little telephone?' – 'You're too young to be *engaged*' – with Telephones as one context and One's-Age-as-relevant-to-Marriage being the other (Ahlberg and Ahlberg 1982: 27; my italics). The qualification 'at least' was added to the number five of the constitutive elements because there can be more than two incongrous fields: in this joke from the Fool in *King Lear* it is possible to elicit six with resulting multiple polysemy in the word 'asses', each new field producing another meaning from the ambiguous element (here pronounceable as both, to use the symbols of the International Phonetic Alphabet, /æsiz/ and /ɑː siz/, for whoever acts the Fool can fudge between them):

298

LEAR: . . . Be my horses ready?
FOOL: Thy asses are gone about them.

One can detect and justify all the following meanings for it in the context of the play: *donkeys*, *fools*, *servants*, *bottoms* (and hence, by metaphor *disregarded persons*), and *animals* (with connotations of the human/animal imagery and its significance throughout the play).

Disparagement theories begin with Plato who in the *Philebus* (48b–e) traces comedy to the clownishness of ignorance, particularly the absence of self-knowledge. Hobbes saw the cause of laughter either in some self-applauding act or in the perception of 'some deformed thing in another' which enables one to triumph over him (Hobbes 1962 [1651]: 93). This is is in accord with the view of Henri Bergson, who saw the ridiculous in anything mechanical or automatic in someone's behaviour so that they are acting unthinkingly to their own disadvantage, with the sense that we are superior in knowledge in thus escaping their fate (Bergson 1956 [1900]: 70–4).

To return to the linguists: Salvatore Attardo, in the wake of Raskin, sees Freud as joining a Relief theory to an Incongruity theory, and credits him with careful analysis of types of jokes, though without producing a theory general enough to account for the structure of verbal humour (Attardo 1994: 53–6). Raskin and Attardo believe that generality is to be obtained if the joke can be analysed as being heard by speaker/hearers possessed of an idealized Chomskyean competence.[2] The aim in this 'General Theory of Verbal Humour' is to screen out all that might distort a scientific assessment of what constitutes a joke and what does not. The incongruous fields are reduced to two 'scripts' that are 'opposite' and yet 'overlap'. A script is defined as an organized set of information which the participants have internalized, a semantic network which may be either generally known or private to a small group. 'Oppositeness' is defined ostensively: Raskin lists three classes of opposition: actual/non-actual, normal/abnormal, possible/impossible, and specifies examples (e.g. life/death, obscene/not obscene, money/no money). The communication of competent speakers in all cases varies between '*bona fide*' and 'non-*bona fide*', the former governed by H. P. Grice's 'Cooperative Principle' (Grice 1975) (trustworthy statements) and the latter untrustworthy ('lying, play-acting, joke-telling'). It is of course admitted that in ordinary language there is a constant to-ing-and-fro-ing between the two, but it is taken for granted that the competent speaker can readily distinguish them, but the two never combine.

The 'General Verbal Theory of Humour' is thus an Incongruity theory dependent upon regarding language from the point of view of *la langue* (Saussure's idealization of the language as agreed by all participants, as fixed in a timeless or 'synchronic' perfection). Clearly it appears to do what it claims to set out to do, namely, given the 'oppositeness' of scripts and given the 'overlap' or 'trigger' that permits the shift from the one to the other, all verbal jokes can be analysed in this way and declared funny or not. The later additions to the theory (Attardo 1994: 221–26) endeavour to bring in pragmatic, situational and narrative considerations:

299

all needful 'knowledge resources' are in play, the target of the joke is clear, the clues, if any, in the situation are plain, the story of the joke is well performed, and the 'logical mechanism' of the trigger functions adequately. With these caveats and with the premises about competence and 'oppositeness' in place, it would seem that no verbal joke can escape the scientific definition which Attardo says a linguist should be in search of. If the objection is made that the funniness of the joke seems to be unassessed, the answer is that that is dependent upon the degree of 'oppositeness' between the two scripts in any particular case.

Several objections that spring to mind (for example, to say that to leave assessment of funniness to an unexamined premiss is to leave out a key feature of any joke) can easily be dismissed by the proponents of this theory by pointing to their original intention, which was to produce a *verbal* theory of humour that would work given speaker/hearers of ideal competence. Anyone who complains about the omission of pragmatic and situational elements will be referred to the addenda to the theory just mentioned. Raskin and Attardo's case seems watertight as a theory operative upon *la langue*, language taken as a synchronic logically complete whole, made up of the complex of 'scripts' possessed by competent users of a language. If one produces a joke in which one of the elements involved is nonsensical, then the answer will be that the nonsensical element falls under a 'sense/nonsense' opposition.[3]

However, there is a further objection which is not so readily turned aside, concerning their reliance on the division of *bona fide* from non-*bona fide* communication. As was mentioned above they make appeal to Grice's 'Cooperative Principle' to underpin this distinction. Grice argues that normal communication cannot take place unless the participants to a dialogue operate upon certain assumptions that define common purposes tacitly understood. He summed them up in four categories or maxims (with some 'sub-maxims'). These were as follows:

1. *The Category of Quantity*: 'Make your contribution as informative as is required (for the current purposes of the exchange)' and possibly 'Do not make your contribution more informative than is required'.

2. *The Category of Quality*: 'Try to make your contribution one that is true', with two more specific maxims: 'Do not say what you believe to be false' and 'Do not say that for which you lack adequate evidence'.

3. *The Category of Relation*: 'Be relevant'. [Grice admits that 'foci of relevance' may be difficult to fix in any particular case].

4. *The Category of Manner*: 'Be perspicuous', which includes as sub-maxims. (i) 'Avoid obscurity of expression'; (ii) 'Avoid ambiguity'; (iii) 'Be brief (avoid unnecessary prolixity)'; (iv) 'Be orderly'.

(Grice 1975: 67)

With these maxims being observed, the communication is guaranteed to be *bona fide*, and it is obvious that 'lying, play-acting and joke-telling' are ruled out, as is fiction in general. The sub-maxim alone 'Avoid ambiguity' prevents the trigger of the joke being used at all. If a psychoanalyst or literary theorist were to protest that unconscious elements of meaning cannot be ruled out, the answer would be that in the scientific analysis of communication we are not centrally concerned either with neurotic invasions of speech or with poetic or narrative elaborations of it – rather with what constitutes 'normal' utterance, which obviously, they believe, must be our main topic in the investigation of language.[4]

3 The idealization of reciprocity

None of this appears to be immediately questionable. There is no doubt that normal communication could not proceed unless all parties made Grice's assumptions. After all, when we hear something we can hardly believe, we often respond with 'You must be joking!' However, before Grice produced his Cooperative Principle, three other analyses had been made of the cooperation that goes on in communication, coming from linguistics, sociology and psycholinguistics. Alan Gardiner insists that 'without a give-and-take between speech and language, linguistic theory is an impossibility', a view that rules out an overly secure reliance on the synchronic view of language (Gardiner 1932: 174). His main contention about communication, which also predates Grice's analysis of meaning (Grice 1957), is that 'the thing meant by any utterance is whatever the Speaker has intended to be understood from it by the listener' (Gardiner 1932: 82), but he adds that the intention as conceived of by the speaker can never be identical with how that intention is conceived by the Hearer. Speaker and Hearer inevitably have different angles of intentional perspective and consider different aspects of the situation relevant, but, as long as a sufficient evidence of an overlap in their understanding remains salient to them, the 'postulate' that they are referring to 'the same thing' will serve. Gardiner even asks 'Was the thing seen by Mary really the same thing that James had meant?' and regrets that he has resolutely 'to turn his back on this metaphysical question' since he is concerned with the 'common-sense assumptions' that are being made by the speaker and hearer (Gardiner 1932: 80).

Alfred Schutz addressed the same question from the sociologist's point of view, taking up the very notion of *assumption*. He argues that, when something is assumed by two people in communication, it is 'merely unquestioned until further notice, sufficiently determined for the purpose actually in hand at the time' and this is no guarantee that something on the periphery of attention, perhaps noticed by one participant and not by another, emerged into common awareness. It might even contradict the understanding of the other, and neither know since nothing in their common practice at the time revealed it (Schutz 1970: 61).[5] Schutz refines his concept of the common understanding that makes up *la langue* by his notion of the 'idealizing of reciprocity', of 'a congruency of our system of relevances', such that 'I take it for granted – and assume my fellowman does the same – that if I change places with him so that his "here" becomes mine, I shall be at the same distance from things and see them with the same typicality that he actually does' (Schutz 1962, I: 11–13).[6]

The phrase 'take for granted' is a slippery one, because its reassurance depends solely upon trust, evidenced by the fact that it contains the phrase *take for* which we use when we accept an illusion or a surrogate for the real thing ('It was so misty I *took* him *for* his brother.'). There is then the implication that our 'granting' is only *pro tempore*, and it needs stressing here that 'to grant' is *to allow, to permit*, because we believe that there is nothing in the agreement which could run against our desires or cause us suffering. The rational agreement underpinning *la langue*, its timeless logical idealization, is thus only a viable one that depends on a mutual trust that cannot rule out actual differences of intention, of existing differing desires that, not being at the conscious level of mutual identification, are therefore *unconscious*.

The psycholinguist Ragnar Rommetveit complains of the 'Platonic cast of modern linguistics' that treats meaning only from the point of view of *la langue*, noting that experiments in concept attainment have shown convincingly that people know more than they are able to put into words (Rommetveit 1978: 16). The question then is, if their concepts remain different however much they use words to make them converge, how it can be that they communicate at all? The answer is like the answer to a riddle: that, in order to achieve at least the *partial* coordination of their words they have to act as if they have achieved a *perfect* coordination (Rommetveit 1978: 31; see also 1974: 22–52). The ability to construct a 'thing' together out of the ever-changing continuum of the real lies in their very habit of acting *as if one thing is in front of them*, even though each sees his or her own 'thing'. This superimposition of perspectives will not come apart until action with that part of the real shows up a so-far-concealed difference. Any 'object', any 'self' is held in *viable* place as a mutual hypothesis that remains always open to modification when subjective differences emerge.[7] The fact that we should be tempted to use the phrase 'to all intents and purposes' in saying that 'there is *one* thing in front of us' betrays the reliance of this 'as if' upon an impossibility, since no one can list all the intents and purposes of those involved in the mutual definition; it is only the 'taking for granted' all over again. The flux, the real, over which the hoped-for coordinations move, remains stubbornly *existent* all the time: what proves continually in need of repair is *objectivity*, that human system for the coordination of action in and with unpredictable existence. Existence and objectivity are not to be equated, except in the practical Idealization.

A number of things now become clear. First, that Grice's 'Cooperative Principle', on which the American linguists rely, is no more than the Schutzian principle without the latter's awareness that this very idealization is what creates *la langue*, the 'normal', in the first place. Second, that Raskin's use of the term *bona fide* betrays the fact that 'normal' speech depends upon the habitual *faith* of participants that their differing perspectives converge on a putatively 'common' referent. Though there is a real *Continuum of Reference*, there are no actual *referents* that are precisely the same for everyone: the taking for granted that there are discrete separable entities is what enables us to maintain viable holds on ever-changing portions of it. The *bona fide* versus non-*bona fide* distinction in all its forms –

fact/fiction, serious/comic, etc – is one *within* the Schutzian idealization on which we mutually rely. It is indeed of the structure of the Joke: we each have a separate referent from everyone else, but *take* it *for* a common one since nothing in our actions with it to date has proved it otherwise. Here Lacan's epigram is apposite: '*riddle*: it is through you that I communicate' (Lacan 1977a: 122). Every statement thus hopefully moves from an illusory superimposition of Speaker's and Hearer's understandings to a new adjustment of them, in which the Hearer's moves closer to that of the Speaker's. The Hearer's language suffers a change from its supposed synchronic state in moving diachronically to a new one: the *traduzione* ('translation') is felt as a *tradimento* ('treachery') since the Speaker disobeyed the rules agreed so far – 'forced into crimes against the original' (Freud 1976 [1905]: 67). But this is just what the Joke enacts, so Statement, Joke, Metaphor, Metonymy, Tragic Irony, Story, all evidence the Joke's pattern of conceptual shift upon the real.[8] Many of the researches into humour have made the mistake of considering it as a linguistic feature distinct from all others, that it could have no relation, for example, to tragedy. But 'the comic is composed of just such elements . . . as are found in many a tragic situation' (Sedgewick 1967: 26).[9] So, to go back to Jonathan Miller, the 're-designing of concepts' is a serious matter, and we do it by behaving as if we are in perfect agreement in order to discover where we are not: this is the way we perform a universal acceptance in order that there can be correction from a particular standpoint. The fact that comedy and tragedy are an actual outcome of this process provides the proof that, valuable as this system has been to human beings, indeed, constitutive of their very humanity, it cannot guarantee an inevitable progress, since human judgements often involve concepts that are structural parts of a self and are not readily to be 'corrected'. At the end of Molière's 'comedy' *Le Misanthrope*, Alceste, even though all understandings are now out in the open, will not accept the comic correction, even at the price of losing his love:

ALCESTE: Trahi de toutes parts, accablé d'injustices,
Je vais sortir d'un gouffre où triomphent les vices.

[Betrayed on every hand, weighed down with wrongs,
I must flee from the abyss in which the vices dwell in triumph.]

In Kant's example of a joke, the shift from a threatening interpretation (real human grief causing someone's hair to turn white) is transferred (via the likeness of real hair to a wig on someone's head) into a (for Kant) comically nonsensical interpretation (the merchant's wig turning grey). This provides the relief that emerges in laughter, with the further subtlety that the merchant's 'grief' would be as inappropriate in the moral field as the nonsense is in the logical. In the following interchange in *King Lear*, precisely the same transfer goes on between two scripts by means of a trigger. In this scene the mad Lear is imagining himself as a judge holding a trial with his daughters as the accused, the 'daughters' being two wooden stools in the hut where they are sheltering from the storm:

FOOL:	Come hither, mistress. Is your name Goneril?
LEAR:	She cannot deny it.
FOOL:	Cry you mercy, I took you for a joint-stool.
LEAR:	And here's another, whose *warpt* looks proclaim
	What store her heart is made on.

(II.6.49–53)

There is more than one ambiguity here, but we will examine only the word 'warpt'. Lear is using the word 'warpt' metaphorically of 'Regan's' face to express the distortion of her evil, in particular her filial ingratitude, but in this circumstance it literally applies to the second stool (that is standing for Regan), which no doubt has warped legs. Lear has made the stool into a visible metaphor. Though we may be tempted towards amusement, the context is such that the shift on the 'trigger' *warpt* refuses to leave the 'threatening' script of Lear's tragic predicament for the harmless 'stool' one; the result instead is that the power of the tragedy is increased. Yet this tragic interchange has exactly the same five structural elements as Suls's joke example (the baby swallowing the fountain-pen), namely, the trigger, the two clues, the two resultant meanings.

The Incongruity theories had thus grasped one essential about the Joke, that there has to be an *affective* distance between the two 'languages', because one is adaptive, delivering what we desire, avoiding what we fear, the other not. The Disparagement theories had grasped the fact that the Speaker successful in communication is putatively superior in his ability to improve another's concept; whoever is operating with a maladaptive concept is defeating him- or herself, and will appear therefore not to be behaving with conscious purpose but like a machine (characterized by its ultimately not being able to change its own programming). But it is a cognitive theory that best explains the Joke because the structure of each joke matches that of all cognitive advance, as Schopenhauer had suggested. It explains the resultant 'economy' that Freud was in search of, for the new concept, we believe, will work for all of us more efficiently with the Flux than before. Such advance can obviously occur with a single mind: someone can burst out with laughter at the joy of a new discovery, a riddle that finds its punchline.[10]

4 Lacan

There is a special difficulty in admitting to the Idealization of Reciprocity, in accepting that the way we understand any concept in the language might not be the same as that of another's. If in order to get a partial understanding we have to behave to each other as if we have already reached a perfect one, it becomes easy to imagine that the common agreement enshrines our *own* perspective, that our personal 'referent', apparently confirmed in communication with our fellows, is exactly the same as everyone else's. Those nearest to the established order will claim that any deviance from 'law', 'rule', or 'word-meaning' can only be a subjective distortion, a 'self-deception': *mutatis mutandis*, those at the periphery of power will accuse the authorities of 'pretence' and 'hypocrisy'. The favoured interpretation, whether on the right or on the left, will accrue to itself an aura of 'objectivity', when that is precisely what the 'as if' maintains.[11] It is insidiously easy to move from the faith that we are in perfect agreement, the faith that is necessary to effect the initial act of rough coordination, to the narcissistically consoling view that the other necessarily perceives exactly as we do. But what proves comic or tragic is a subject's endeavour to hold to the self-defeating interpretation in defiance of the clearest clues to a second one.[12]

Lacan warns against such narcissistic rigidifying of the Symbolic (his term for the order of language that constructs us as speaking subjects and draws us together), calling it a 'formal stagnation':

> Now this formal stagnation is akin to the most general structure of human knowledge: that which constitutes the ego and its objects with attributes of permanence, identity and substantiality, in short, with entities or 'things' that are very different from the *Gestalten* that experience enables us to isolate in the shifting field, stretched in accordance with the lines of animal desire.
>
> (Lacan 1977a: 17)

Lacan is thus here in line with Schutz, Rommetveit and the genetic epistemologists (see note 7), in that he sees our selection of what we together call 'objects' as taking place from an ever-changing continuum, those 'objects' being rather hopeful and merely viable coordinations of our separate and subtly differing *Gestalten*, the percepts that each of us have. This 'serious mode' can be used 'to control and dominate' even though it is not 'a neutral medium for making sense of the world' (Mulkay 1988: 220). And among those who do so control and dominate there are some who are able to manipulate the social drama cynically, well aware of the mismatch between their apparent 'authority' and its performance (Sloterdijk 1987).

In his *Seminar on 'The Purloined Letter'* (Lacan 1972), Lacan uses Poe's story as a model for the effects of transfer of the authority of the Symbolic. The character in the story who imagines that she/he is in the position of Hobbesian 'superiority', in control of the symbol, in possession of the Phallus, is subverted by another whose perspective transforms its meaning. The trigger is significantly a letter that can be taken to be either something negligible or something of high importance. For example, the Minister is able to exchange a substitute letter for the Queen's own compromising one in full view of her while she is unable to do anything about it. The minister in turn, who hid the Queen's letter in full view in his letter-rack, has the same trick played on him, for the detective Dupin manages to distract his attention sufficiently to exchange his own substitute for the Queen's. In each case someone who considered themselves to be invulnerable proves helpless in an ambiguous situation. Flieger identifies the comic pattern in each exchange: someone who imagined themselves secure was by that very complacency exposed to subversion; they become the butt of the joke when the authority they thought they possessed is stolen through a transformation of what had been supposedly objectified (Flieger 1991: 111–13). The whole becomes an allegory of what happens to the metaphorical 'letter', the Statement at the core of the Symbolic, in that it remains open to subversion from the detective/trickster. He is successful because he detects the traumatic incongruity between the Symbolic and the Real (the brute materiality on which the Symbolic 'works'). But that is what all speakers who manage to communicate their adjustment of another's concept are able to do.

Lacan's Real can be linked with the Continuum of Reference that has emerged in the epistemological inquiry above, distinct from the 'things' and 'selves' which our mutual hypotheses endeavour to render secure. His Real 'laughably casts down throws of its dice' which can upset the most embedded of Imaginary identifications, emerging in puns, errors and 'misapprehensions' (Lacan 1988: 220; 1977a: 122). His declaration that 'the paths of truth are in essence the paths of error' (Lacan 1988: 263) would be rejected as postmodern paradox by those mired in the 'formal stagnation', but it makes sense when the structure of the Statement is made clear. Speakers and Hearers cleave to the 'Laws of Thought' ('X is X'; 'X is either B or not-B'; 'X is not not-X') in order to hold the Idealization of Reciprocity in place, but, if those laws were applied from the beginning to the end of the uttered Statement, no concept could ever be adjusted, with words frozen to an impossible single meaning in a timeless inanition.

To illustrate: a statement in an actual situation might go 'Those trees have been cut down' – this really amounts to the Speaker saying 'You know those trees that we have just been talking about and that we both know about in exactly the same way' and Hearer replying 'Yes' – 'Well', says the Speaker, 'we don't know about them in the same way, for they have been cut down.' Take the Hearer to be miserable because the trees were Lawson's Cypresses that have been blocking out the light in her house for years, and her concept of the trees moves, as in a joke, from being invested with misery to joy. In psychoanalytic terms, the pain of castration that attends upon the laws of the Symbolic will have been to a degree eased, as two subjects bring their desires and expectations closer into line. But for that communication to have been made, Speaker and Hearer did have to entertain in a fictive manner the hypothesis that there was *one* set of trees that was *identical for both of them*, even in this case when the speaker knew that the trees had virtually ceased to exist. This is the logical subject that the logical predicate, the correction of the concept, will change.[13] It was fictive because, although they knew that there was hopefully a sufficient overlap in their understandings to get a mutual grip on that portion of the Real 'the trees', they did not coincide perfectly in those understandings and the predicate helped towards a closer superimposition. This 'sliding-away' (*glissement*) from that performed security of reference 'conceals what is the true secret of the ludic, namely the most radical diversity constituted by repetition in itself' (Lacan 1977b: 61).

So there is a sense in which the struggle between Freud's Reality Principle and Pleasure Principle informs every joke, every statement, every story, but a re-reading is possible – and here I, as Speaker, am endeavouring to adjust your conceptualization of these two principles. 'Reality', if taken to be the objectivities such as received opinion presents them, as *la langue* has declared, is now seen to be no more than the structure that the Idealization of Reciprocity has constructed for us and history has delivered to date. To take that 'reality' to be a given obstacle against which 'pleasure' must vainly struggle is to remain within the Idealization, dealing as it does with hypothesized distinctions of 'fact'/'fiction', 'sense'/ 'nonsense', 'rational'/'irrational', 'objective'/'subjective' in order to keep the *as if* in place. This 'reality' is a fictively maintained selection from the undoubted Real; it has to be so fictively maintained so that speakers and hearers can go on adjusting the selections, and that includes those selections that we have constructed of our selves. The 'Pleasure Principle' is at once the motivation of the whole Symbolic edifice and the cause of its continual adjustment. *Jouissance*, as Lacan would call the source of all drive, is not to be viewed as in opposition to the 'Reality Principle', but as the drive behind the fictions of logical coordination that are supposed to serve it. What has been called cool objectivity, impartial logic, derives its calmness from the fact that desires are there running in that apparent agreement, that fictive agreement necessary as the first step in every statement, its logical subject: however, this agreement is deceptive and fortunately so, for otherwise no one would have cause to speak, since to speak is to produce the logical predicate that hopefully corrects the alignment of word to world, Symbolic to Real. It is the old concept that is then proved to be 'tendentious', to be an antiquated rule that needed to evolve. In humour the ego can identify with the father, not as in a consolation as Freud thought, but as one who can be a maker of law in its own right, overcoming not bearing the frustration it feels. The 'economy of psychic expenditure' can often be, not merely a brief escape for the repressed individual, but beneficial to the community.

Notes

1 For up-to-date surveys of the field see Durant and Miller, 1988; Dziemidok 1993; Gutwirth 1993; Hutcheon 1994; Palmer 1994. For thorough accounts of the past theory see Piddington 1933; Bergler 1956.

2 Chomsky (1965: 27) distinguishes *competence*, a speaker's knowledge of the language on the level of *la langue*, the idealized agreement that establishes understanding across persons, from his or her *performance*, the actual use in concrete situations, corresponding to Saussure's *la parole*.

3 To give an illustration: the psychologist B. F. Skinner asked his subjects to read rapidly and repeatedly this nonsense sequence, 'bell-lie-mud-dum'; it was some time before they found that they were saying *I'm a dumb-bell* (Skinner, 1957: 282). One can generalize jokes of this kind so that the 'nonsensical' element is not even uttered by a human being: some children were found laughing because the door to their classroom actually made a noise when opened that sounded exactly like an odd voice saying 'Creak!' The response would no doubt be that this is not strictly a *verbal* joke, but, though one can concede this to the linguists, it still points up the fact that as a general theory of humour as such theirs is hardly satisfactory. To hedge themselves inside *la langue* is to ignore the very problem of the relation not only of *la langue* to *la parole*, but of language to the world.

4 Attardo even produces a series of counter-maxims that allow a joke to be told: for the Quantity category – 'Give exactly as much information as is necessary for the joke'; Quality – 'Say only what is compatible with the world of the joke'; Relation – 'Say only what is relevant to the joke'; and Manner – 'Tell the joke efficiently' (Attardo 1994: 205; Raskin, 1985, 103). These then define the type of non-*bona fide* communication that enables a joke to be told. With a good joke and a good joke-teller indications in the context and 'co-text' help us to switch confidently from *bona fide* to non-*bona fide*. What this rules out, unfortunately, is the Hearer perceiving something funny in the joke that the Speaker did not.

5 Gardiner makes the same point that actual contradictions may be concealed in the interchange between speaker and hearer (Gardiner 1932: 80). The sociologist Aaron V. Cicourel points to the 'open horizon of unexplored content' that exists between Speaker and Hearer, and argues that the communication can only function on what he calls the 'Et Cetera Principle', which states that the Speaker assumes that the Hearer will fill in for him- or herself the unstated but intended meanings, which obviously allows for unnoticed slippage between the two understandings (Cicourel 1971: 148). This recalls the insistence of the philosopher C. I. Lewis that 'common reality' is a social achievement projected by agents each with *differing* subjective access to the world (Lewis 1956 [1929]: 111). Lewis's view now finds support among those philosophers, psychologists and neurophysiologists who argue for radically private sense-experience (Lowe 1981; Brown 1987; Ramachandran and Smythies 1996; Edelman 1992; Gregory 1993; Alroy 1995; Wright 1990, 1996), for if sensing is wholly confined to the brain, all agents are achieving coordination only through an indirect channel, and therefore cannot have any supposedly 'direct' contact with external 'objects'.

6 Michael Mulkay, and Melvin Pollner to whom he refers, follow Schutz in stressing the 'unitary realm' of common presuppositions that constitutes the everyday world: 'we *take for granted* that we are dealing with objective phenomena which exist independently of our actions and discourse and which are experienced in much the same way by other human beings' (Mulkay 1988: 22–3; Pollner 1987; my italics).

7 Those who take their lead from Jean Piaget's 'genetic epistemology' come to the same conclusion, that objects are constructed from the flux of experience and are only viable 'until further notice' (von Glasersfeld, 1985: 99; see also Furth 1987: 162–71; Rescher 1992: 187–90; Hooker 1995: 310–41).

8 Add to any metaphor a Second Clue that restores a context indicative of a related literal meaning and you are likely to produce a pun. For example: The metaphor in this pair of sentences works perfectly well – 'He was in a state of great anxiety: his nerves were on the rack'; but in this pair the Joke pattern has emerged – 'He got into the railway carriage in a state of great anxiety; his nerves were on the rack.'

9 Marcel Gutwirth quotes Helen Bacon as making the same claim: 'Both comedy and tragedy center around man's relation to error. The unacknowledged error is the cause of misplaced complacency which is comic; the acknowledgement of error, with its shattering of complacency and illusion, is in essence a recognition scene, which is the heart of tragedy' (Bacon 1959: 430; Gutwirth 1993: 183). Attardo does note that the pattern of humorous stories bears a relation to that of the Joke (Attardo 1994: 254–70); what he does not go on to argue but could have done was that *all* stories, including tragic ones, have the same pattern.

10 In the same way there can be anguish at the tragic realization, the *anagnorisis*: the handkerchief that proved Desdemona's faithlessness becomes the proof of her loyalty when Emilia's 'punchline' is uttered, the 'second clue' that gives her the right to call Othello 'fool'. What bears out the psychoanalytic insight is that affect always attends the transformation of concept, or the resistance to it.

11 Wittgenstein's protests about a 'private language' (Wittgenstein 1967 [1953]: 92e–94e)

have been thought by the conservatively minded to contribute to a healthy rejection of relativism. What he did not recognize was that, while there cannot be a private language, there can certainly be a *private understanding* of a word in a *public language* which might be a better understanding than that enshrined in the received opinion. He did consider reform of a language possible, but never explained how it could come about (ibid.: 51e).

12 As when Emma in Jane Austen's novel takes all the clues to Mr Elton being in love with her as being evidence of his being in love with Harriet. What will prove tragic is when the shift to a new interpretation produces suffering in the outcome, as when Pip in Dickens's *Great Expectations* resolutely takes all the clues that his benefactor is a criminal as mere oddities typical of the legal milieu in which Mr Jagger moves.

13 The logical subject and predicate are not necessarily the grammatical subject and predicate. The item of new information that is the logical predicate changes according to what it is that the Hearer does not know. This is easy to see: try discovering the logical predicate for the sentence 'The cat is on the mat' when the Hearer has asked (1) 'Where is the cat?'; (2) 'What is on the mat?'; and even (3) 'Which cat is on the mat?' (here the answer requires a special stress on and pronunciation of the word 'The').

References

Ahlberg, Janet and Ahlberg, Allan (1982) *The Ha Ha Bonk Book*, Harmondsworth: Puffin Books.

Alroy, Daniel (1995) 'Inner light', *Synthese*, 104: 147–60.

Attardo, Salvatore (1994) *Linguistic Theories of Humor*, Berlin and New York: Mouton de Gruyter.

Bacon, Helen (1959) 'Socrates crowned', *Virginia Quarterly*, 35: 415–30.

Bergler, Edmund (1956) *Laughter and the Sense of Humor*, New York: Intercontinental Medical Book Corporation.

Bergson, Henri (1956 [1900]) 'Laughter', in Wylie Sypher (ed.), *Comedy*, Garden City, NY: Doubleday, pp. 59–190.

Brown, Harold I. (1987) *Observation and Objectivity*, New York: Oxford University Press.

Chomsky, Noam (1965) *Aspects of the Theory of Syntax*, Cambridge, MA: MIT Press.

Cicourel, Aaron V. (1971) 'The Acquisition of Social Structure', in Jack D. Douglas (ed.), *Understanding Everyday Life*, London: Routledge and Kegan Paul, pp. 136–68.

Durant, John and Miller, Jonathan (eds) (1988) *Laughing Matters: A Serious Look at Humour*, Harlow: Longman.

Dziemidok, Bohdan (1993) *The Comical: A Philosophical Analysis*, Dordrecht: Kluwer Publications.

Edelman, Gerald M. (1992) *Bright Air, Brilliant Fire*, London: Allen Lane, Penguin Press.

Flieger, Jerry Aline (1991) *The Purloined Punch Line: Freud's Comic Theory and the Postmodern Text*, Baltimore and London: The Johns Hopkins University Press.

Freud, Sigmund (1976 [1905]) *Jokes and their Relation to the Unconscious*, The Penguin Freud Library, vol. 6, Harmondsworth: Penguin Books.

—— (1985 [1927]): 'Humour', in *Art and Literature: Jensen's 'Gradiva', Leonardo da Vinci and Other Works*, The Penguin Freud Library, vol. 14, Harmondsworth: Penguin Books, pp. 425–33.

Furth, Hans (1987) *Knowledge as Desire: An Essay on Freud and Piaget*, New York and Guildford: Columbia University Press.

Gardiner, Sir Alan (1932) *The Theory of Speech and Language*, Oxford: Clarendon Press.

Glasersfeld, Ernst von (1985) 'Reconstructing the concept of knowledge', *Archives de Psychologie*, 53: 91–101.

Gregory, Richard L. (1993) 'Hypothesis and Illusion: Explorations in Perception and Science', in Edmond Wright (ed.), *New Representationalisms: Essays in the Philosophy of Perception*, Aldershot: Avebury, pp. 232–62.

Grice, H. P. (1957) 'Meaning', *Philosophical Review*, 66: 377–88.

—— (1975) 'Logic and Conversation', in Donald Davidson and Gilbert Harman (eds), *Logic and Grammar*, Encino, CA: Dickenson Pub. Co., pp. 64–75.

Gutwirth, Marcel (1993) *Laughing Matter: An Essay on the Comic*, Ithaca, NJ and London: Cornell University Press.

Hobbes, Thomas (1962 [1651]) *Leviathan*, ed. John Plamenatz, London: Collins.

Hooker, Clifford A. (1995) *Reason, Regulation and Realism: Toward a Regulatory Systems Theory of Evolutionary Epistemology*, Albany, NY: State University of New York Press.

Hutcheon, Linda (1994) *Irony's Edge: The Theory and Politics of Irony*, London and New York: Routledge.

Kant, Immanuel (1957 [1790]) *The Critique of Judgement*, trans. James Creed Meredith, Oxford; Clarendon Press.

Lacan, Jacques (1972) 'Seminar on "The Purloined Letter"', Yale French Studies, 48: 39–72.

—— (1977a) *Écrits: A Selection*, trans. Alan Sheridan, London: Tavistock Publications.

—— (1977b) *The Four Fundamental Concepts of Psycho-Analysis*, ed. Jacques-Alain Miller, trans. Alan Sheridan, London: Hogarth Press and the Institute of Psycho-Analysis.

—— (1988) *The Seminar of Jacques Lacan, Book II: The Ego in Freud's Theory and the Technique of Psychoanalysis, 1954–1955*, trans. Sylvana Tomaselli, Cambridge: Cambridge University Press.

Lewis, Clarence Irving (1956 [1929]) *Mind and the World-Order: Outline of a Theory of Knowledge*, New York: Dover Publications.

Lipps, T. (1898) *Komik und Humor*, Hamburg and Leipzig.

Lowe, E. J. (1981) 'Indirect perception and sense-data', *American Philosophical Quarterly*, 31: 330–42.

Miller, Jonathan (1988) 'Jokes and Joking: A Serious Laughing Matter', in John Durant and Jonathan Miller (eds), *Laughing Matters: A Serious Look at Humour*, Harlow: Longman, pp. 5–16.

Mulkay, Michael (1988) *On Humour: Its Nature and its Place in Society*, Cambridge: Polity Press.

Palmer, Jerry (1994) *Taking Humour Seriously*, London and New York: Routledge.

Piddington, Ralph (1933) *The Psychology of Laughter: A Study in Social Adaptation*, London: Figurehead.

Pollner, Melvin (1987) *Mundane Reason: Reality in Everyday and Sociological Discourse*, Cambridge: Cambridge University Press.

Radcliffe-Brown, J. (1952) *Structure and Function in Primitive Society*, London: Cohen and West.

Ramachandran, V. S. and Smythies, J. R. (1996) 'An empirical refutation of the Direct Realist Theory of Perception', *Inquiry*, 40: 437–8.

Raskin, Victor (1985) *Semantic Mechanisms of Humor*, Dordrecht: D. Reidel.

Rescher, Nicholas (1992) *A System of Pragmatic Idealism, Vol. I: Human Knowledge in an Idealistic Perspective*, Princeton, NJ: Princeton University Press.

Rommetveit, Ragnar (1974) *On Message Structure: A Framework for the Study of Language and Communication*, London: John Wiley and Sons.

—— (1978) 'On Negative Rationalism in Scholarly Studies of Verbal Communication and Dynamic Residuals in the Construction of Human Intersubjectivity', in Michael Brenner, P. Marsh and Marilyn Brenner (eds), *The Social Contexts of Method*, London: Croom Helm, pp. 16–32.

Schopenhauer, Artur (1957 [1819]) *The World as Will and Idea*, 2 vols, London: Routledge and Kegan Paul.

Schutz, Alfred (1962) *Collected Papers, Vol. I: The Problem of Social Reality*, The Hague: Martinus Nijhoff.

—— (1970) *Reflections on the Problem of Relevance*, New Haven and London: Yale University Press.

Sedgewick, G. G. (1967) *Of Irony: Especially in Drama*, Toronto: University of Toronto Press.

Skinner, B. F. (1957) *Verbal Behavior*, New York: Appleton-Century-Crofts.

Sloterdijk, Peter (1987) *The Critique of Cynical Reason*, London: Verso.

Spencer, Herbert (1891) 'The Physiology of Laughter', in *Essays Scientific, Political and Speculative*, 2 vols, New York: Appleton Century, Vol. II, pp. 452–66.

Suls, Jerry (1983) 'Cognitive Processes in Humor Appreciation', in P. E. McGhee and J. H. Goldstein (eds), *Handbook of Humor Research, Vol. I: Basic Issues*, New York: Springer Verlag.

Wittgenstein, Ludwig (1967) *Philosophical Investigations*, Oxford: Basil Blackwell.

Wright, Edmond (1985) 'A defence of Sellars', *Philosophy and Phenomenological Research*, 56: 1: 73–90.

—— (1990) 'New Representationalism', *Journal for the Theory of Social Behaviour*, 20: 1: 65–92.

—— (1996) 'What it isn't like', *American Philosophical Quarterly*, 33(1): 23–42.

311

AUTHOR INDEX

SUBJECT INDEX

316